Agrarian Crossings

AMERICA IN THE WORLD

SERIES EDITORS
SVEN BECKERT AND JEREMI SURI

A list of titles in this series appears at the back of the book.

Agrarian Crossings

Reformers and the Remaking of the US
and Mexican Countryside

Tore C. Olsson

PRINCETON UNIVERSITY PRESS

PRINCETON AND OXFORD

Published by Princeton University Press,
41 William Street, Princeton, New Jersey 08540
In the United Kingdom: Princeton University Press,
6 Oxford Street, Woodstock, Oxfordshire OX20 1TR

press.princeton.edu

Jacket photograph courtesy of the Rockefeller Archive Center

Portions of chapters 2 and 3 were previously published as Tore C. Olsson, "Sharecroppers and
Campesinos: The American South, Mexico, and the Transnational Politics of Land Reform
in the Radical 1930s," *Journal of Southern History* 81, no. 3 (August 2015): 607–46.

Library of Congress Cataloging-in-Publication Data

Names: Olsson, Tore C., author.
Title: Agrarian crossings : reformers and the remaking of the US and Mexican countryside /
Tore C. Olsson.
Other titles: America in the world.
Description: Princeton : Princeton University Press, [2017] | Series: America in the world |
Includes bibliographical references and index.
Identifiers: LCCN 2016047513 | ISBN 9780691165202 (hardcover : alk. paper)
Subjects: LCSH: Land use, Rural—Southern States—History—20th century. | Land use,
Rural—Mexico—History—20th century. | Land reform—Southern States—History—20th
century. | Land reform—Mexico—History—20th century. | Agriculture and state—Southern
States—History—20th century. | Agriculture and state—Mexico—History—20th century.
Classification: LCC HD207 .O47 2017 | DDC 333.760975—dc23
LC record available at https://lccn.loc.gov/2016047513

British Library Cataloging-in-Publication Data is available

This book has been composed in Sabon NEXT Lt Pro

Printed on acid-free paper. ∞

Printed in the United States of America

1 3 5 7 9 10 8 6 4 2

To Kelli, Juniper, and my parents

CONTENTS

List of Illustrations   *ix*

Acknowledgments   *xi*

INTRODUCTION   1

CHAPTER ONE
Parallel Agrarian Societies
The US South and Mexico, 1870s–1920s   12

CHAPTER TWO
Sharecroppers and Campesinos
Mexican Revolutionary Agrarianism in the Rural New Deal   40

CHAPTER THREE
Haciendas and Plantations
Finding the Agrarian New Deal in Cardenista Mexico   73

CHAPTER FOUR
Rockefeller Rural Development
From the US Cotton Belt to Mexico   98

CHAPTER FIVE
Green Revolutions
US Regionalism and the Mexican Agricultural Program   129

CHAPTER SIX
Transplanting "El Tenesí"
New Deal Hydraulic Development in Postwar Mexico   159

EPILOGUE   191

Notes   *201*

Archives and Manuscript Collections Consulted   *265*

Index   *269*

ILLUSTRATIONS

FIGURE 1.1. Emiliano Zapata, Mexican agrarian revolutionary.   22

FIGURE 1.2. Thomas E. Watson, agrarian populist from Georgia.   23

FIGURE 2.1. Frank Tannenbaum researching his dissertation in rural
Mexico, 1920s.   48

FIGURE 2.2. Crowds welcoming Henry A. Wallace to Ciudad Victoria,
Tamaulipas, November 1940.   68

FIGURE 2.3. Henry A. Wallace meets with farmers in Tamazunchale,
San Luis Potosí, November 1940.   69

FIGURE 3.1. 1941 Roberto Montenegro painting of Henry A. Wallace
and Centeotl, the Aztec god of maize.   84

FIGURE 3.2. Henry A. Wallace receiving Roberto Montenegro's painting
from the Sociedad Agronómica Mexicana, Washington, DC,
October 1941.   85

FIGURE 3.3. Josephus Daniels and his wife, Addie, in charro costumes,
Mexico City, 1937.   92

FIGURE 4.1. General Education Board corn demonstration in Mississippi,
late 1900s or early 1910s.   107

FIGURE 4.2. South Carolina General Education Board corn demonstrator
sits by his record-breaking harvest of 1910.   108

FIGURE 4.3. John A. Ferrell of the Rockefeller Foundation's International
Health Board.   114

FIGURE 4.4. Henry A. Wallace, Josephus Daniels, and their wives, Ilo and
Addie, respectively, in Mexico City, December 1940.   121

FIGURE 5.1. Jalisco farmers receiving iron plows under the Plan de
Movilización Agrícola, 1943.   137

FIGURE 5.2. Lázaro Cárdenas, Henry A. Wallace, and Marte R. Gómez
touring the Rockefeller crop test plots at Chapingo,
September 1946.   145

FIGURE 5.3. President Miguel Alemán inspecting seed to be distributed
by the Comisión del Maíz, 1947.   148

FIGURE 6.1. Engineers Armando Bravo and José Yépez at Fort Loudoun
Dam, Lenoir City, Tennessee, in August 1942.   171

FIGURE 6.2. President Miguel Alemán standing beside Chickamauga
Dam, Chattanooga, Tennessee, May 6, 1947.   176

FIGURE 6.3. President Miguel Alemán with a family of former
sharecroppers in Muscle Shoals, Alabama, May 6, 1947.   177

FIGURE 6.4. Front page of Mexico City's *Novedades*, May 7, 1947.   178

FIGURE 6.5. Cuauhtémoc Cárdenas and Lázaro Cárdenas with
Tennessee Valley Authority chair Herbert Vogel in
Knoxville, Tennessee, February 3, 1959.   186

FIGURE 6.6. Lázaro Cárdenas crossing Fort Loudoun Dam, Lenoir City,
Tennessee, February 3, 1959.   187

ACKNOWLEDGMENTS

LIKE THE cooperative farming communities that Mexican and US reformers idealized during the 1930s, this book has been the product of many hands pitching in. I am deeply beholden to the generosity of countless people who gave their time and energy, over more than a decade, to help me complete this project. Though these words on paper will hardly settle my outstanding debts, I hope they serve as a beginning.

First off, I would never have had the time and resources to write this book if not for the assistance of several institutions. Perhaps my greatest debt lies with the Social Science Research Council, whose International Dissertation Research Fellowship launched this project and sustained me while I dug into US and Mexican archives for nine straight months. Then, a national fellowship from the University of Virginia's Miller Center for Public Affairs gave me time to digest what I had found and complete my dissertation. In more recent years, the University of Tennessee's Humanities Center provided me invaluable writing time as a resident scholar, while a National Endowment for the Humanities fellowship in 2016 allowed me to complete the final manuscript. Small grants from the Society for Historians of American Foreign Relations, Rockefeller Archive Center, University of Tennessee, New Orleans Gulf South Center at Tulane University, and University of Georgia's history department as well as Latin American and Caribbean Studies Institute helped finance shorter research trips, too.

This book can trace its intellectual roots to my graduate career at the University of Georgia, and the extraordinarily brilliant and exceptionally generous community in Athens that shared its wisdom with me. Foremost, Shane Hamilton shepherded this project from a confused hodgepodge of ideas to a finished dissertation, and then into a final manuscript. Shane's steadfast commitment to me and my work has been nothing short of astounding. That I was his first doctoral student is particularly mind-boggling, and I will never understand where he learned the sage-like patience, devotion, and mentorship he showed me over so many years. Pamela Voekel single-handedly instilled in me a fascination with Mexican history, and lent support and enthusiasm at every turn of the journey. Jim Cobb taught me the ins and outs of US southern history, and trained me to think like a historian. Bethany Moreton schooled me in transnational history, pushing me to pursue a multilingual, multinational project despite my initial reluctance. Paul Sutter introduced me to environmental history, and the early seeds of this book grew out of his America and the World research seminar. John Inscoe, Stephen Mihm, and Reinaldo Román each played foundational roles in my growth as a scholar. Yet I probably learned as much from graduate colleagues as from my faculty mentors, and special thanks and love are due to Derek Bentley, Rachel Bunker, Jessie Fly, Darren Grem, Dave Himmelfarb, Tim Johnson, Keri Leigh Merritt, Chris Manganiello, Jason Manthorne, Kathi Nehls, Tom Okie, Lesley-Anne Reed Beadles, Blake Scott, and Levi Van Sant for their inspiration, support, and laughs along the way.

In navigating the fields of US, Mexican, political, rural, agricultural, environmental, and transnational history, I've had the good fortune of being welcomed into these communities by generous scholars. My deepest thanks and gratitude go out to those who devoted countless hours to carefully reading my work and commenting on it. Chad Black, Chris Boyer, Sterling Evans, Luke Harlow, Amelia Kiddle, Dan Klingensmith, Prakash Kumar, Tom Rogers, Julie Weise, and Mikael Wolfe each read substantial portions of the manuscript and provided incredibly useful feedback. Greg Downs, Daniel Immerwahr, Ann Jefferson, Jeff Norrell, and Sarah Phillips should in all fairness have their names on this book's cover alongside mine, as each read the entire manuscript and played the most essential role in molding it into what it is today. Lengthy conversations and exchanges with Venus Bivar, Pete Daniel, Mona Domosh, David Ekbladh, Bart Elmore, Liz Fitting, Jim Giesen, Randal Hall, Mark Hersey, Susan Levine, Tim Lorek, Stephen Macekura, April Merlaux, Marcela Mijares Lara, David Nally, Adrienne Petty, Jeffrey Pilcher, Dan Rood, Gabe Rosenberg, Sigrid Schmalzer, Micol Seigel, Kendra Smith-Howard, John Soluri, Gabriela Soto Laveaga, Christy Thornton, and Andrew Zimmerman greatly helped me clarify my work's argument and significance. I am also deeply thankful to Cuauhtémoc Cárdenas for speaking with me at length about his father and hydraulic development across national borders.

A handful of scholars deserve special recognition for the extraordinary role they played in making this book possible. First is Sarah Phillips, who agreed to serve as my "dream mentor" at the Miller Center, and then stayed on as both booster and valued critic. Chris Boyer has been my indispensable tutor in modern Mexican agrarian and environmental history as well as a dedicated champion of my work for years. Sterling Evans was my earliest and most devoted ally in thinking about agriculture across national borders, and I deeply value his feedback and friendship. Amelia Kiddle arranged my interview with Cuauhtémoc Cárdenas, and I am forever indebted to her for it. Brian Balogh's crucial help was hardly contained to my year at the Miller Center. And lastly, Greg Downs went above and beyond in offering me the pointed criticism my work needed, and the book is much improved for it.

Thanks and acknowledgments are also due to my Mexico City research compatriots, particularly María Balandrán-Castillo, Derek Bentley, Jennifer Boles, Brian Freeman, Vanessa Freije, Devi Mays, Diana Schwartz, and Larisa Veloz. From you all, I probably learned more about Mexican history, culture, politics, food, and *pulque* than from all the books I ever read. I also owe enormous thanks to Herzonia Yáñez as my host in the DF and an invaluable guide to the city.

Every historian knows that their research success is in large part determined by the archivist assisting them, and I was incredibly lucky to work with some of the finest and most dedicated archivists out there. Foremost was Tom Rosenbaum of the Rockefeller Archive Center, whose unparalleled knowledge of his archive's many collections made possible my close exploration of Rockefeller philanthropy in agriculture over several decades. Tom and his colleague Nancy Adgent undertook countless wild-goose chases on my behalf, and this book would have been impossible without their help. At the US National Archives in College Park, Maryland, Joe Schwartz played an instrumental role in helping me locate obscure but pivotal US Department of Agriculture and Farm Security Administration documents. Arlene Royer and Patricia Ezzell served as invaluable guides to the records of the Tennessee Valley Authority at the National Archives in Atlanta and the authority's Knoxville library, respectively. In Mexico, at the Archivo Histórico de la Secretaría de Relaciones Exteriores, Jorge Fuentes Hernández generously aided me. Silvia Gómez García at the Colegio de Michoacán's library graciously helped me navigate the papers of agricultural economist Ramón Fernández y Fernández, and was essential in locating several of the book's key images. At the Archivo General de la Nación, I owe particular thanks to Angélica Pérez Nava in the photography division. Lastly, I'd like to thank Marte Gómez Leal and his wife, who opened their Mexico City home to me for a whole week to browse Marte R. Gómez's private papers collection.

In completing this book, I was also fortunate to work with several talented research assistants. Tracy Goode dug deeply into the Mexico City archives I had neglected, and discovered crucial evidence of US and Mexican entanglements. Amada Beatriz Beltran and Sheila Ann Dean gathered critical documents at the Bancroft Library and Cornell University, respectively. At the University of Tennessee, Alicia Maskley served me ably as a digital research assistant, while Andrea Perales and Leonor Lundy provided valuable transcription and translation assistance. Special thanks are also due to Tom Heffernan and Joan Murray at the University of Tennessee's Humanities Center, whose generous support made possible my timely completion of the manuscript.

At Princeton University Press, an expert team of editors guided me, and showed me unwavering support and patience. The press's reputation for excellence and professionalism is well deserved. I'm particularly thankful to Eric Crahan, who provided vital feedback and oversaw every element of the manuscript's path from rough draft to finished product. I am likewise grateful to Brigitta van Rheinberg for her early interest in and commitment to the project, and Sven Beckert and Jeremi Suri for their wise suggestions and welcoming my book to their fantastic series. My production editor, Natalie Baan, and my copyeditor, Cindy Milstein, expertly orchestrated the manuscript's metamorphosis from a digital mess to a beautiful bound volume. I'm also especially indebted to Princeton University Press's two anonymous referees, whose insights dramatically improved the final product.

The University of Tennessee has been a wonderful place to call home for the past four years. I'm astoundingly lucky to have a set of colleagues as smart, warm, and giving as mine in the history department. This book has particularly benefited from discussions with Chad Black, Monica Black, Kristen Block, Dan Feller, Ernie Freeberg, Luke Harlow, Bob Hutton, Chris Magra, Jeff Norrell, Denise Phillips, Julie Reed, Lynn Sacco, Charles Sanft, Brandon Winford, and Shellen Wu. I have also learned much from my intellectual community in Latin American and Caribbean studies, especially Rudy Alcocer, Jacky Avila, Enrique Chacón, Dawn Duke, and De Ann Pendry.

My academic colleagues and collaborators have been the source of much inspiration, but theirs can hardly match the unconditional support and love offered by my family. My parents, Carl Hugo and Margareth, raised me with the values that guide my life: respect, humility, open-mindedness, intellectual curiosity, and optimism. When they transplanted our family from Sweden to the United States in 1990, they likely didn't expect their eldest son to become a historian of the Americas. Their sacrifices for my success are immeasurable, *och jag kan inte tacka er nog*. My brother and sister, Ragnar and Ingrid, are my closest confidants, closest friends, and an eternal source of encouragement. My adopted US family, Russell and Bip Guinn, have embraced me since the day we met, in spite of my oddities and eccentricities.

Lastly, I want to thank the ones who matter the most, and I could easily fill the rest of this book's pages doing so. I met Kelli Guinn-Olsson during my first semester of graduate school, and I shudder to think of the madness she endured because of it. In the eleven years since, she became my partner in everything: my sounding board, my counselor, my inspiration, my proofreader, my booster, and the bedrock of my existence. Kelli, you hold in your hands the physical embodiment of your decade of support and love; it's yours as much as mine. The book's completion also marks a new beginning for us, as our beautiful, delightful, and perfect daughter, Juniper Astrid, was born during the rush to finish it. Though she likely won't remember those first years, Juniper's little footprints are all over the book's pages. She has endowed our lives with new meaning and indescribable love, and to watch her grow up is the greatest reward I can imagine.

Agrarian Crossings

INTRODUCTION

BORDERS MATTER. Borders regulate the flow of people, the movement of commodities and capital, and the exchange of ideas. Borders separate citizens from aliens, the familiar from the foreign, and those belonging from those unwanted. And perhaps no border in recent history is more iconic in its power of partition than the line bisecting the United States and Mexico. In the century and a half since it was mapped onto desert and water, the US-Mexico border has become a powerful visual representation of the strikingly unequal relationship between the two nations it anchors. The border has estranged families from their kin, dividing the communities that straddle its boundary; it has claimed the lives of thousands who sought to cross its arid waste without legal consent. The border has served as a lightning rod for US nativists in moments of national anxiety, and its razor wire security fences grimly allude to enduring hierarchies of race and class. As one writer unforgettably observed a generation ago, the US-Mexico border is an "open wound" where "the Third World grates against the first and bleeds."[1]

Yet the work that borders do is not only cultural, material, and political—it is also intellectual. The thin line winding through the deserts of Alta and Baja California, and along the Rio Grande/Bravo, also demarcates to many scholars where "American" history ends and "Latin American" history begins. In the same pernicious manner that the geopolitical border divides human beings, that intellectual border has segregated a common past. It has split historians of North America into two camps, each with different theoretical traditions and vocabulary, rarely engaging with the other. This intellectual border blinds scholars on either side into thinking that aside from the manifestations of inequality that bind the two nations together—immigration, imperial interventions, free trade agreements, and television assembly plants—the national historical trajectories of the United States and Mexico are fundamentally distinct. Excepting the "borderlands" historiographical tradition—and even that school has largely confined its conclusions to the immediate US and Mexican border states—scholars continue to frame the two nations within a neat disciplinary dichotomy. Such divisions reassure us that those hoping to understand phenomena as diverse as state building, popular social movements, economic transformations, and policy making in either nation would benefit little by transcending the intellectual border's well-policed perimeter.

H. L. Mitchell would surely have disagreed. In summer 1939, he left the
United States to seek inspiration and guidance in La Laguna, a vast cotton
district spanning the northern Mexican states of Coahuila and Durango.
Mitchell was hardly a stranger to the white fiber that stretched across La
Laguna's horizon, or its discontents; he headed the Southern Tenant Farmers' Union (STFU), a multiracial organization of cotton tenants and sharecroppers founded in Arkansas in 1934 that counted tens of thousands of
members throughout that decade. He journeyed to Mexico that summer to
witness a political experiment he had long been following. Three years earlier, La Laguna gained international renown when a strike by landless cotton laborers brought populist president Lázaro Cárdenas (1934–40) to the
region in hopes of brokering a compromise. Invoking the legacy of the
agrarian revolution of 1910–17, Cárdenas shocked the nation and world by
expropriating hundreds of thousands of Mexico's most productive, irrigated
acres, and then deeding them to tillers of the soil. Wide-eyed STFU organizers north of the border could hardly contain their excitement. One described La Laguna as "one of the most thrilling spots in the world to anyone
who wants to see a new world built on release from slavery."[2] Mitchell, on
touring the region in 1939, eagerly agreed. *Lagunera* cotton pickers were
once "exploited and without hope as were Arkansas sharecroppers," but now
stood ready to reap the fruits of their labor. The sojourn pushed Mitchell
to wonder whether his union too "should consider a legislative program of
expropriating our absentee landlords."[3]

If Mitchell rejected the belief that national borders mark the bounds of
political possibility, so too did Ramón Fernández y Fernández. An agricultural economist whose political education coincided with the violent drama
of the Mexican Revolution, Fernández devoted his professional career to the
pursuit of agrarian social justice. As secretary of the Liga de Agrónomos
Socialistas (League of Socialist Agronomists) and statistician for the influential agrarian census of 1930, Fernández stood at the vanguard of Mexico's
land reform campaign of that decade. Yet his marriage of social science and
revolutionary politics also led him to the US countryside. Long enchanted
with President Franklin D. Roosevelt's New Deal and its assault on rural
poverty in the United States, in 1942 Fernández volunteered to participate
in a yearlong "in-service training program" with the US Department of Agriculture (USDA).[4] Of that department's many divisions, he decided his time
would be best spent working with the Farm Security Administration (FSA),
arguably the New Deal's most socially reformist agency, which particularly
targeted the stark inequalities of the southern Cotton Belt. That year and
the next, Fernández followed his FSA hosts around the region, studying
agricultural cooperatives in Georgia and Mississippi before settling down in
eastern Arkansas for an intensive study of what his US hosts deemed "credit
problems more nearly related to those in his own country."[5] Fernández re-

turned to Mexico seduced by the FSA's "revolutionary faith," his "natural impulse ... to push a campaign to have our own Farm Security."[6]

What persuaded Fernández and Mitchell to think outside the national containers that became so naturalized and pervasive during the twentieth century? As this book demonstrates, they lived in an era of dramatic social and political convergence between the two nations, where dialogue and exchange regarding rural matters was frequent and lively. In the generation between the Great Depression and the advent of the Cold War, government and civil society in the United States and Mexico waged unprecedented campaigns to remake their countrysides in the name of agrarian justice and agricultural productivity. The following chapters reveal the rarely acknowledged entanglement of those campaigns. The book reconsiders several key historical moments—the Mexican Revolution and its crescendo under Cárdenas, the New Deal's contradictory agrarian program, and campaigns to promote scientific agriculture in the so-called Third World—and unshackles them from the separate national frameworks to which they are frequently bound. In doing so, I hope to reveal that the rural histories of the United States and Mexico share far more than is often imagined.

Agrarian Crossings advances two primary arguments, both of which take aim at artificial but widely accepted geographic dichotomies mapped onto the US-Mexico border. I will elucidate each separately in this introduction. First, I argue that the disciplinary distinction between "American" and "Latin American" history has obscured the confluence and interaction between US and Mexican state-led rural reform along with its attendant social upheaval during the radical 1930s. In 1933 in the United States and 1934 in Mexico, two state governors known for their political experimentation— Roosevelt and Cárdenas—rode a current of rural and industrial unrest into the presidency. Each promised to shatter the political stasis and economic stagnation that had mired the 1920s, pledging voters in the countryside a "New Deal" and "Six-Year Plan" to right rural wrongs. Though each began that campaign tentatively, by 1935 both diagnosed agrarian inequality as a vital problem, and poured astounding resources and political capital into its resolution.[7]

In the years that followed, agents of the state fanned out across each nation's landscape, seeking to transform farming, rural culture, and country people's relationship with the land. They engineered projects to resettle vast multitudes in order to improve agricultural efficiency and defuse political dissent; they constructed massive dams to harness waterpower to an ambitious program of economic development. They planned model rural communities, serviced by new federal programs in credit, technical assistance, and education. They attempted to conserve endangered forests, water, and topsoil. And perhaps most important, they sought to reverse deep-seated patterns of uneven land tenure by subdividing latifundia—large estates, from the Latin *latus* plus *fundus*—and deeding small plots to the landless and dispossessed. On this last point Cárdenas was ever more aggressive, pioneering the most successful land reform program ever undertaken in the Western Hemisphere, encompassing nearly fifty million acres. The New Deal's effort to remake land tenure was comparatively timid, cautious, and largely symbolic, but it nevertheless marked a watershed in US history; it was the first time since Reconstruction's hollow promise of "forty acres and a mule" that the federal government seriously considered land redistribution. And in each nation, the frenzy of reform and pervasive rhetoric of change could hardly be contained by the walls of government, encouraging and emboldening civil society to demand ever-greater promises from their leadership.

Yet the US and Mexican agrarian campaigns of the "long" 1930s, stretching from roughly 1933 to 1943, not only ran parallel; they frequently intersected. Indeed, this book is not a comparative history but rather a history of comparisons, a study of interactions and exchanges.[8] As politicians, bureaucrats, agronomists, economists, tenant farmer unions, and peasant leagues waged a multifaceted war on their varying diagnoses of rural injustice, they looked across the border to learn from their counterparts' successes and failures. New Deal policy makers seeking to dismantle the long reign of plantation agriculture within their borders drafted programs inspired by Mexico's revolutionary land reform. Nearly every key leader of the USDA, perhaps the most aggressively reformist bureau in 1930s' Washington, DC, visited Mexico during the Roosevelt years, captivated by its agrarian ferment. The highest rungs of Mexico's political leadership, including Cárdenas himself, traveled to tour the works of the Tennessee Valley Authority (TVA), hoping to replicate its formula of hydraulic agrarian transformation. And countless activists not on the federal payroll, such as H. L. Mitchell, likewise looked across the border for insight and encouragement. None of these pilgrims glibly equated the New Deal and Cardenismo, nor should we as students of history; most recognized that the latter was far more radical and revolutionary than the former. It was precisely because of this ideological imbalance that the majority of the decade's intellectual traffic flowed from south to north.

Mexico was not the only nation from which the New Deal borrowed. The Roosevelt administration's reform agenda was forged in the global crucible of the Great Depression, where common hardships invited common solutions. As important recent scholarship has revealed, key legislation in nearly every field of New Deal intervention both resembled and reflected examples from across the globe. The Civilian Conservation Corps surprisingly paralleled Nazi Germany's voluntary labor service, though New Dealers were wary to eschew its militarism; the Public Works Administration's housing program openly imitated similar efforts in Great Britain. The National Recovery Administration's famed "blue eagle" logo, as one contemporary critic argued, "was plainly an American adaptation of [Benito Mussolini's] Italian corporate state in its mechanics." But among this global bricolage of influence, Mexico stood out. As one of the few non-Western, nonindustrialized nations to impart its footprint on US policy, it deserves special attention.[9]

Curiously too, not every region of the United States shared equally in the agrarian dialogue with Mexico. As Mitchell and Fernández's pilgrimages suggest, it was the US southern Cotton Belt that produced the most emissaries and greatest interest in Mexico's rural transformation. Indeed, at its heart this book is a work of southern history, although it seeks to emancipate that region from the straitjacket of national history by charting the US South's rarely acknowledged relationship with its own southern neighbor.[10] To many readers, this may be surprising, as the plantation South is rarely included in what many scholars term the US-Mexico "borderlands," a geographic container that traditionally encompasses northern Mexico and the southwestern United States.[11] Likewise, few historians have imagined the early twentieth-century US South as globally connected in *any* sense, swallowing whole contemporary characterizations of the region's "miasmatic jungles" and "cesspool[s] of Baptists" as entirely distinct from the United States and the world beyond.[12] Recent studies, though, are forcing a revision of such assumptions.[13] After all, on the eve of the Great Depression, the southern Cotton Belt looked far more like Mexico, Cuba, or Brazil than it did Massachusetts or Iowa. If compared to its northern US neighbors, the South's one-party politics, racial hierarchy, plantation agriculture, concentrated land tenure, and pervasive rural poverty may have seemed an aberration. Yet should the South have looked south, such characteristics would hardly appear exceptional at all.

Therefore, is it perhaps appropriate to consider the US South as the northernmost reach of the Latin American and Caribbean world? Scholars of the seventeenth through nineteenth centuries would hardly object, as studies of slavery, emancipation, and the black diaspora have long connected the plantation colony of the South with those of Cuba, Brazil, Haiti, and Mexico.[14] But after the demise of Reconstruction in the late nineteenth century, those transregional perspectives disappear almost entirely from scholarship, and their absence suggests that the South withdrew from these earlier networks.[15] This book challenges such an assumption, revealing that even in the wake of slavery, it was the persistence of the plantation and its social organization that linked Louisiana and Mississippi to Mexico and beyond. If US northeastern social reformers in the first third of the twentieth century adopted Western European experiments with welfare capitalism, social security, and urban planning—as Daniel Rodgers's *Atlantic Crossings* demonstrated—the lessons of Berlin and London meant little to agrarian reformers concerned with the plantation society of the US South.[16] Instead, their gaze turned toward the Caribbean basin, where they exchanged ideas with a diverse group of Latin American actors that approached rural inequality in dramatically different ways.

* * *

Yet the border between the United States and Mexico not only separates "American" from "Latin American" history. It also marks where Global North meets Global South, or as was once popular, where the First World meets the Third World. This book's second major argument concerns that planetary dichotomy, and how it has warped scholarly understandings of a vast campaign that would remake countless human societies during the twentieth century: development. "Development" is a word heavy with historical baggage, not unlike "civilization" in the nineteenth century. To its millions of faithful, it encapsulated a belief that human societies evolve similarly and can be charted linearly, and that assistance from "developed" societies to "developing" ones can speed the latter's progress. Given its complete absence from global discourse at the dawn of the twentieth century and ubiquity sixty years later, one may well wonder: From where did this crusade arise?

In the prevailing scholarly account—whose faults we will consider shortly—development was a child of the 1940s. It grew up with the slow sunset of European colonialism and the geopolitical polarization of the escalating Cold War. It came of age when intellectuals and policy makers in the United States grew increasingly anxious that the Soviet Union held a distinct advantage in its appeal to the hundreds of millions of Asians, Africans, and Latin Americans then emerging from colonial or neocolonial subjugation. To forestall the global advance of Communism, US strategists presented development aid as their alternative to the nascent Third World, suggesting that technical expertise from First World societies might produce economic growth far more rapidly than any five-year plan drafted in Moscow. In this telling, President Harry Truman's 1949 "Point Four" speech announced the arrival of the development era, while social scientist Walt Rostow's 1960 formulation of modernization theory in *The Stages of Economic Growth: A Non-Communist Manifesto* marked its zenith.[17]

Of the Cold War era's myriad development projects, none has been more widely celebrated or fiercely critiqued than the concerted effort to teach US scientific agriculture to Latin American, Asian, and African farmers in pursuit of boosting global food production. None, too, was more transformative of land and life. Concerned that material want might provide fertile ground for Communist insurgency, US policy makers and their partners in philanthropy hoped to meet a geopolitical need—containing Soviet expansion—under humanitarian cover: they would feed a hungry world. Armed with recent advances in plant breeding, pest control, and synthetic fertility, US agronomists and engineers approached the global countryside with a swaggering confidence. At the campaign's climax in 1968, US policy maker William Gaud conferred on it an enduring name; in contrast to the Soviets' "violent Red Revolution," theirs was a "green revolution" that lifted all boats, a war on hunger beyond the narrow politics of left and right. Whether Gaud's optimism was warranted has been hotly debated, though the persistence, if not exacerbation, of hunger into the twenty-first century has unquestionably dulled the luster of the green revolution. What is certain is that the campaign forever remade the human and ecological fabric of our planet. Its expansion of grain production enabled the meteoric rise of world population, unimaginable just decades earlier. Its uprooting of millions of "inefficient" peasant cultivators played a pivotal role in the rapid urbanization of our planet, made strikingly clear in 2008 when city dwellers outnumbered rural people for the first time in human history. Indeed, future scholars may well look back at these twin transformations as the twentieth century's most important legacy, outweighing wars both hot and cold.[18]

Mexico has long played a leading role in the history of the green revolution, and has been ubiquitously designated as the "birthplace" of that global campaign. It was there in 1943 that the Rockefeller Foundation, a US philanthropic powerhouse, undertook an initially modest program of agricultural technical assistance, in partnership with the Mexican agriculture secretariat and headquartered not far outside Mexico City. On fields expropriated in the agrarian revolution, Rockefeller scientists and their Mexican collaborators sought to increase the yields of the nation's staple food crops, primarily corn and beans. Over several years, they experimented with seed collection, plant breeding, disease control, and the application of fertilizers and pesticides. Declaring a revolution in productivity by the early 1950s, the foundation sought to make its Mexican Agricultural Program (MAP) a blueprint for replication elsewhere. In 1950, it expanded to Colombia; by 1957, the foundation was operating in India, and then in the Philippines by 1962. Looking back at this path of global proliferation, scholars have long studied the MAP, seeking seeds of what would later bear fruit elsewhere in Latin America but particularly in Asia and Africa. Unsurprisingly, many have found in Mexico a microcosm of the mature green revolution: a campaign driven by Cold War geopolitics, obsessively focused on hunger, dismissive of indigenous knowledge, and neglectful of the poorest farmers. In this telling, Mexico's green revolution was evocative of the stark divide between the First World and Third World—an idealistic but dangerously shortsighted Cold War development scheme hatched by the former for application in the latter.[19]

This book presents a fundamentally different understanding of the green revolution's origins and motivation. When in 1943 the Rockefeller Foundation intervened in Mexico's countryside, its officers drew on a deep well of prior experience in rural development *within* the United States. Rockefeller philanthropy could trace its birth to the first years of the twentieth century, when the oil tycoon John D. Rockefeller and his reform-minded son diagnosed the poverty and "backwardness" of the US South as a national disgrace. Their first undertaking, the ambiguously named General Education Board (GEB), established in 1903, devoted itself explicitly to regional shortcomings. Between 1906 and 1914, the board waged a sweeping effort to transform the practice of southern agriculture, believing that the adoption of scientific cultivation techniques might unravel the bonds of debt and dependence that submerged so many millions of black and white farmers in marginal poverty. The board's leadership targeted two crops, cotton and corn, and sought to dramatically raise their yields, confident that a revolution in productivity would grant common farmers a higher standard of living as well as greater independence from merchants and other creditors.

The Rockefellers' southern crusade was a contradictory campaign, divided as to the root cause of inequality, and one that could claim little enduring success. But it was precisely this model that inspired foundation planners to attempt its replication in Mexico, as that nation's problems were "similar to that which confronted the South following the war between the states," in the words of one Rockefeller administrator in 1941.[20] Such comparisons provided the framework and structure of the MAP, and were hardly a secret to its participants. Even the Mexican agriculture minister partnering with the foundation was well aware of the philanthropies' prior efforts to "improve the conditions of life of the rural population of the Southern States of the American Union."[21]

Why, then, have the regional US roots of the green revolution been so long neglected? Just as was true for studies of 1930s' agrarian reform, the history of agricultural transformation in Mexico has been skewed by artificial geographic dichotomies and the conventional wisdom that the green revolution was a phenomenon of the Third World, not the First World. Yet when we acknowledge that the US South served as the domestic laboratory for Mexico's green revolution, the entire "development" project suddenly appears in a new light. It no longer seems to be the natural product of post-1945 geopolitics, but is born instead of far earlier efforts to address the enduring existence of an impoverished agrarian periphery within the core of the industrial United States. Such a prehistory reveals the similarities rather than the differences apparent in the rural transformations of the First World and Third World. And it deeply problematizes any characterization of development as a neat project of "Americanization"—for what good can such a concept serve if it does not recognize the profound importance of regional distinctions within that patchwork nation?

This book therefore probes the rarely acknowledged link between two geographic containers, the US South and Global South, that newly fashionable term that recently replaced the Cold War relic of "Third World." In many ways, this is hardly a novel pursuit. As early as 1953, historian C. Vann Woodward argued that with its troubled past of poverty, military defeat, and underdevelopment, the US South was not exceptional, as many northerners viewed it, but rather representative of the normative global human experience.[22] Yet despite Woodward's observation, few US historians have begun to explore these linkages in a global context. Southern history, which shares equally with points south as with points north, too often remains submerged within a national narrative. In Mexico, the stark borders separating it today from its northern neighbor, both physical and imagined, have also precluded an open conversation about historic commonalities and shared lives.

* * *

The following chapters explore the entangled history of agrarian politics and agricultural development in Mexico and the United States in rough chronological order. The first chapter sets the stage for the dialogues and exchanges of the 1930s and 1940s with a comparative analysis of social, political, and economic change in the US southern and Mexican countryside between the 1870s and 1920s. Where prior scholars have largely seen difference—if they have looked at all—I argue that the two shared strikingly similar historical trajectories. During the late nineteenth century, each region was violently thrust into the web of global commerce as railroads, investment capital, bankers, and merchants came to reorder the business of agriculture. While large-scale landholding was hardly unknown on either side of the border, in those decades export-oriented plantations and haciendas further tightened their grasps on the rural landscape. Paying the price were formerly independent smallholders, who were unwillingly pulled into the plantation complex as wage laborers, tenants, and sharecroppers. Simmering resentment among those dispossessed would boil over in two dramatic agrarian revolts: the Mexican Revolution and US Populist movement. Each insurgency challenged the rural status quo, but in each case the most radical visionaries were vanquished politically or militarily. Yet in defeat, the rebels forced their rivals to grudgingly adopt their demands for social and economic justice—demands that would later animate future generations, most notably during the Depression era.

The second and third chapters are complementary, with each detailing how during the "long" 1930s, US as well as Mexican rural reformers inside and outside government revived earlier campaigns to address inequality in the countryside. In doing so, they frequently looked to each other for inspiration, support, and importable strategies. The second chapter considers the south–north intellectual exchange of that decade. It demonstrates how a host of US liberal reformers within what I call the "agrarian" New Deal—those concerned with poverty, inequality, and environmental decline—eagerly observed Mexican political experimentation and sought to incorporate its insights in their own policy making. It traces the pilgrimages undertaken by a diverse group of agrarian critics, from the chief of the USDA to socialist organizers well outside the New Deal, and how their travels to Mexico forced a rethinking of US political possibilities. In each of these exchanges, it was either US southerners or those interested in the South who paid closest attention to Mexico. The third chapter, meanwhile, reverses the intellectual flow to examine how New Deal politics shaped the agrarian program spearheaded by Cárdenas and opened possibilities for its success. On the one hand, it explores how Mexican bureaucrats drew on the rural rehabilitation projects of the Roosevelt administration. On the other, it shows that New Deal sympathies among US diplomats stationed in Mexico facilitated Cárdenas's expropriation of millions of acres of US-owned land—land that the embassy was formally tasked to protect. Had Cardenismo not coincided with the agrarian New Deal, it would likely have had a far different outcome.

Chapters 4 and 5 turn away from US and Mexican state policy, and toward the rural development campaign that ultimately became known as the green revolution. The fourth chapter begins by considering the Rockefeller philanthropies' first exercise in agricultural extension and education, waged between 1906 and 1914 in the US Cotton Belt. As a blueprint for future undertakings, it was decidedly ambiguous in its vision for a renewed countryside. Yet during the turbulent decade of the 1930s, US southern veterans of the first Rockefeller campaign revived its unfulfilled promises as a potential solution for Mexico's agricultural dilemmas during the Cárdenas years. The heart of the chapter, therefore, analyzes the transregional comparisons that inspired the Rockefeller Foundation to embark on its influential MAP in 1943. Chapter 5 then narrates the pivotal first decade of that program. Surprisingly, the early years of the Rockefeller experiment in Mexico diverged sharply from the developmental model of the mature 1960s' green revolution. Instead of focusing obsessively on hunger, it emphasized living standards and economic mobility; instead of partnering with wealthy, commercial landlords and neglecting the rural majority, the MAP of the 1940s explicitly sought to reach smallholders who had recently received land in the Cárdenas era redistribution campaigns. The chapter demonstrates that it was precisely the lessons and memories of the US South that motivated such sympathies for the rural poor. But by the early 1950s, as growing conservatism in Mexico and the escalating Cold War narrowed the spectrum of political possibility, Rockefeller planners disavowed the regionally informed experimentation of earlier years, to the great detriment of millions of farmers worldwide.

Chapter 6 explores the last great exchange of the US-Mexican agrarian dialogue: the Mexican government's enthusiastic embrace of the TVA's hydraulic development program after World War II. More than any other New

Deal agency, it was the TVA's monumental effort to harness waterpower for social and environmental transformation that most deeply impacted the Mexican countryside. When in 1947 Miguel Alemán made the first Mexican presidential tour of the United States since the revolution's outbreak in 1910, northern Alabama and eastern Tennessee were foremost on his trip agenda. His pilgrimage would engender extensive discussion among Mexican policy makers about the similarities between the southern US and their own tropical south, coming to a climax in the several river valley commissions that Alemán established in 1947 to replicate the TVA's ambiguous success in coastal southern Mexico. Yet because of its late incidence, long after the political passions of the 1930s had cooled, this last agrarian exchange would be a far more conservative affair that tended to exacerbate rural inequality rather than erase it.

By the 1950s, the agrarian crossings of the previous generation were rapidly coming to an end. In both the United States and Mexico, an increasingly restrictive political atmosphere ensured that elites were able to subdue once-vigorous debates about rural inequality and the human impact of agricultural change. Questions of productivity and efficiency, rather than landlessness and poverty, were the watchwords of the decades that followed. The book's epilogue addresses the shared rural transformations of the twentieth century's latter half. Where country people had once contested their marginalization through political mobilization and alliances with state reformers, in the Cold War era they more often abandoned their small plots, seeking elusive possibilities in urban slums or as wageworkers in the agribusiness sector. As they left their farms, the plantation complex they had long struggled against achieved its nearly total hegemony, but with pesticides and machines replacing sharecroppers and campesinos. In unexpected ways, the US and Mexican countryside during the Cold War saw new convergences.

When H. L. Mitchell of the STFU returned to his union's Memphis headquarters in 1939, after several weeks in La Laguna's cotton belt, he was firmly convinced that poor US and Mexican farmers sought exactly the same thing: "to see the land and all its resources owned by the people who earn their living by the sweat of their brow." Indeed, the visit reaffirmed for him that "we are all members of the same human family no matter what color we are or what language we speak."[23] Few historians today would disagree with such a hopeful conclusion. Yet when we segregate the past into nationally bounded containers, we risk perpetuating such distinctions. I hope that the following pages suggest an alternate path.

Chapter One

PARALLEL AGRARIAN SOCIETIES
The US South and Mexico, 1870s–1920s

In the last days of 1890, thousands of outraged farmers gathered in a small city, far from the halls of power, to protest their chronic exclusion from the fruits of land and labor. Those gathering were a diverse lot, yet they made their pilgrimage united in the belief that an unholy alliance of bankers, landlords, and railroad executives sought to pauperize tillers of the soil. In the past generation, these farmers had bitterly seen the erosion of their political and economic independence by the steady expansion of plantation agriculture, with many unwillingly pulled into the orbit of that system as tenants and sharecroppers. Most were bound up in the cultivation of a single cash crop that promised them abundance but rarely delivered on it, instead binding them to merchants and markets far beyond their control and understanding. In 1890, they decided that enough was enough. The grievances of the displaced and dispossessed crystallized that week in a list of "Demands" devoted to "the poor of our land." Its authors sought to restrain the financial institutions that sacrificed farm autonomy to the barons of industry; they insisted on government action to reclaim and redistribute "all lands now held by aliens," "foreign syndicates," railroads, and "other corporations in excess of such as is used and needed by them." Much publicized, their demands resonated widely and swelled the tide of their historic rural revolt.[1]

Some twenty years later, in 1911, another group of agrarian rebels gathered with similar purpose. Congregating around their leader, a quiet but charismatic village councillor, dozens of marginalized farmers ranging from wageworkers to sharecroppers to small landholders put forth a prescription for rural justice. They presented a litany of angry objections not unlike those voiced two decades earlier. They, too, had seen commercial landowners dispossess formerly independent country people, claiming their land and binding them to staple-crop plantations as day laborers and tenants. They also had seen the ascent of the railroad agent and country merchant threaten the autonomy of the common farmer. As "lands, timber, and water are monopolized in a few hands," the gathered protesters desperately confronted "the horrors of poverty without being able to improve their social condition." At their meeting, the rebels distilled their grievances into a formal "Plan" for change that demanded the immediate restoration of "that real estate of which [small cultivators] have been despoiled by the bad faith of our oppressors." On the plan's proclamation, word of it spread across the countryside like wildfire, calling countless thousands to its cause.[2]

The 1890 meeting took place within the United States—in Ocala, Florida, where the southern Farmers' Alliance convened to formalize its political platform; the 1911 gathering was held in Mexico, where in Ayala, Morelos State, Emiliano Zapata and his followers protested the government's indifference to the dispossessed farmer. Their manifestos for change, the Ocala Demands and the Plan de Ayala, would prove foundational to two sweeping rural social movements: the US Populist revolt and the Mexican Revolution, respectively. Yet despite their parallels and proximity in time and space, the juxtaposition of Ocala and Ayala will be surprising and unexpected to many scholars. Segregated by the intellectual border dividing "American" from "Latin American" history, these two rural insurgencies are rarely placed in conversation. US southern populism is commonly remembered as a contradictory political movement, ultimately co-opted and destroyed; the Mexican Revolution is recalled as a bloody social uprising fueled by peasant discontent. Turn-of-the-century agrarian revolt in the United States and Mexico, most scholars therefore assume, has little common ground.

This chapter argues otherwise. The rural societies that gave birth to the Ocala and Ayala demands—the US cotton South and the diverse plantation zones of Mexico—underwent parallel social, political, and economic transformations between the 1870s and 1920s. Though in Mexico the violence and dislocation of those transformations was far magnified, a common trajectory underlay both. After the mid-nineteenth century's chaos of war and instability, a muscular political elite came to power in each region with seductive promises of stability and growth. Together they sought to rationalize and order a chaotic and diverse countryside to produce export crops for global consumers, adopting the latifundium—large estate—as the basic unit of production.[3] Their reordering of the countryside was both sweeping and rapid, but it largely benefited landlords while eroding the last semblances of independence and self-sufficiency among the rural majority. In response to the assault on their autonomy, country people revolted against the new order, putting forth their own vision for a stable and equitable rural society. Those rebels who led the most pointed attacks on the status quo were defeated politically and militarily. Yet in unanticipated ways, their smothered cry for change would live on and animate future generations of agrarian reformers later in the twentieth century.

Therefore, key moments in US and Mexican history—the "New South" era, the Porfiriato, the US Populist revolt, the Mexican Revolution, and their respective aftermath—might well be understood in common context.

Historians of each nation have long pondered similar questions about the expansion of the plantation, enclosure movements, popular revolt, and land reform, but few have reached across the intellectual aisle to consider kindred elements within both. To do so decisively undermines narratives of US exceptionalism, as in the late nineteenth and early twentieth centuries the history of the cotton South converged far more neatly with that of the Caribbean basin than with the rest of the United States. In some ways, this is hardly a novel conclusion, as scholars of race, slavery, and emancipation have for generations employed comparative or transnational perspectives to understand the US South.[4] Yet few such studies have looked beyond Reconstruction, and because of their emphasis on communities of the black diaspora, those scholars often excluded Mexico with its well-concealed heritage of African slavery.[5] If historians were to look at race beyond the white/black binary, though, and expand their analysis to agrarian class relations in rural spaces, they would likely realize that Mexico provides as compelling a counterpoint to the US South as does Cuba, Haiti, or Brazil.

This book, at its heart, is an examination of the United States' and Mexico's intersecting and interactive agrarian histories. This chapter, which emphasizes parallel but largely *separate* transformations, thus is by definition an outlier. As a whole, it does not consider the ways that comparison informed the deeds and rhetoric of historical actors themselves. In fewer words, I do not argue that the Plan de Ayala was born from the Ocala Demands. Comparison here is our method rather than our subject; instead of a transnational history, it is a comparative one, with all the disadvantages that such an approach brings.[6] But the rewards of such a comparison outweigh the risks, as the overlooked parallels between US and Mexican agrarian history and historiography in the turn-of-the-century period deserve examination. Narrating the shared history of dispossession, revolt, and its aftermath also sets the stage for the chapters following, revealing how and why rural reformers in each region came to discover and speak to one another in the 1930s and 1940s.

DISPOSSESSION

The middle decades of the nineteenth century brought utter chaos to both the US South and Mexico. While neither region could boast of a tranquil past, the years from 1846 to 1876 in Mexico and 1861 to 1877 in the South were each exceptional in their social disruptions and bloodletting. Each region underwent military invasion. In Mexico, the 1840s brought war with the United States and the loss of more than half its national territory. The 1860s ushered in a French imperial intervention, and a vicious struggle between liberals and conservatives that ultimately expelled the French but left

Mexico devastated. In the US South, the Civil War of 1861 to 1865 toppled the institution of chattel slavery that had provided the region's economic and social foundation. Like Mexico, the Confederate states weathered a northern invasion and occupation, and the war destroyed much of the region's agricultural and industrial base. When the South and Mexico emerged from the martial turmoil of the mid-nineteenth century, their cities and countrysides lay in ruin.

Yet as the smoke of the battlefield began to clear, the questions raised by the US Civil War and Mexican political struggle of the 1860s lingered and demanded resolution. What fate awaited the millions once enslaved in the plantation South, and how would their quest for independence and freedom converge with demands for economic revival and stability? The Reconstruction experiment following the war's end proposed one solution, but white southern resistance raised questions as to its permanence. Likewise, if Mexican liberals had triumphed over a monarchist elite, what would the seductive words of "democracy" and "progress" mean to the vast rural masses of the nation? Such dilemmas invited few easy answers.[7]

Over the next generation, a new—or at least reinvented—political ruling class in the US South and Mexico took the reins of power, seeking to guide their divided, war-torn lands toward a vision of social and economic progress that was startlingly alike. Indeed, two historical epochs that scholars rarely juxtapose—the "New South" period between 1877 and the century's end, and the rule of Porfirio Díaz from 1876 to 1911—share much in their guiding ideologies, processes, and consequences. Both were decidedly exclusive of the rural majority, and under each, the system of commercial, large-scale, export-oriented agriculture flowered and grew to unprecedented dominance.

After decades of turmoil in Mexico and the US South, the first step toward stabilization came in the arena of governance and rule, and their political transitions occurred strikingly close to one another. In 1876, General Díaz overthrew former ally Sebastián Lerdo de Tejada to take his place in the presidential palace. Born to a Mixtec Indian family in Oaxaca, near Mexico's southern Pacific coast, Díaz came to prominence fighting in support of the nationalist liberal Benito Juárez during the 1850s and 1860s. Díaz justified his coup d'état against Lerdo by insisting that his rival had betrayed the liberal ideologies of effective suffrage and opposition to reelection that they had earlier fought for. On taking office, however, Díaz cast aside the slogans that had energized his coup. After surrendering the presidency to a puppet leader in 1880, Díaz returned in 1884 and remained in the presidential seat until evicted from it in 1911. As a ruler, Díaz was hardly a rigid ideologue, freely mixing political philosophies in search of social stability and economic growth. The long years of his rule, known in Mexico as the Porfiriato, were motivated by the twin goals of "order" and "progress," as Díaz repeatedly emphasized. It was not a wholly unfair characterization of his regime. Of order there would be plenty, but it was enforced at the end of a rifle bayonet; likewise, Porfirian "progress" was a narrow and exclusive concept intimately wound up with elite yearnings to emulate US and European society.[8]

At nearly the same moment Díaz stabilized and harnessed the Mexican state, the campaign to reinstate home rule in the US South through the Democratic Party reached its climax. The bedrock of Republican political control established during Reconstruction had been steadily eroding since the early 1870s, due in large part to white vigilante violence, and became alarmingly visible in 1874 when Democrats gained a majority in the House of Representatives. But it was only in 1877, just months after Díaz's coup, that the Democratic "redemption" of the South achieved its consummation. It was then that the US Army declared it would no longer prop up Republican state governments, thereby signaling a symbolic retreat from the past decade's efforts to remake the region's society and political economy. Across Dixie, a triumphant Democratic elite loudly proclaimed that a "New South" had been born from the ashes of the old—a South that nursed no regional grudges, but openly embraced northern industry and capital; a South not of black political participation and mobility, as the Reconstruction era had witnessed, but rather subservience and stability. Above all, the New South leadership imagined a diversified and commercial southern economy, liberated by the end of slavery, yet firmly preserving the class and caste hierarchies that had structured antebellum society.[9]

Once in power, Díaz and the New South Democrats subscribed to rather analogous programs of agrarian transformation. Both gazed out on patchwork landscapes starkly divided between commercial plantations and a peasant-yeoman agriculture rooted primarily in security and subsistence, and both strove to expand the former at the expense of the latter. In the US Cotton Belt, the New South leadership primarily sought to guarantee the availability of cheap black labor in plantation districts—a goal often accomplished through extralegal violence and intimidation. But they simultaneously worried about the large white yeoman class that existed on the outskirts of the cotton economy, clinging to its small plots despite the deprivations and debts incurred by the war. In the eyes of the planter elite, yeomen farmers offered the freedpeople a dangerous alternative, and indeed many former slaves sought to emulate the yeomanry's landed independence.[10]

In Mexico, Díaz and his allies confronted a kaleidoscopic diversity of rural life, as Mexico was and indeed remains a nation of stark regional contrasts. The arid and mountainous north, sparsely populated and with far fewer indigenous people, then bore little resemblance to the temperate and densely settled center-south, anchored by Mexico City and with long traditions of native agriculture and land use. The coastal tropics and Yucatán Peninsula, in turn, diverged from both north and center. Even within the central-southern core that Díaz knew best, the countryside of 1876 was one of contrasts within contrasts. Vast cash crop haciendas coexisted alongside Indian and mestizo (mixed race) pueblos, or autonomous rural villages, where hunting, fishing, and agriculture on communally held lands served local rather than national needs. Such island communities, unmoved by the dreams and desires of urban elites, were ubiquitous in the central plateau, but could be found in nearly every region of Mexico. Like the New South Democrats, Díaz hoped to thrust this peasantry into capitalist and national-ist modernity, disdaining their marginal economies as obstacles to growth and centralization.[11]

Both regimes began their effort to undermine noncapitalist agriculture by closing loopholes that had allowed country people to subsist beyond the market economy. In both the US South and Mexico, this amounted to an all-out war on the commons. As soon as the Civil War had ended and Afri-can American freedpeople struggled to flee the plantation, elite white south-erners grew concerned that access to communal lands would provide the former slaves with enough land, food, and fuel to subsist beyond the cash crop economy. To guarantee their access to cheap and pliable labor, states across the former Confederacy passed fencing and stock laws during the 1860s and 1870s to privatize formerly public lands as well as restrict unau-thorized hunting, fishing, and foraging on them, with considerable success. To the freedpeople, this closed an important path to independence. Yet it was not only African Americans who were affected by such enclosures. The privatization of the open range also presented a fundamental threat to the economic autonomy of the white yeomen, whose reliance on public lands was essential to their livelihoods.[12]

In Mexico, the war on the rural commons was even more dramatic. For centuries after the Spanish conquest, the landed elite and indigenous pueb-los had negotiated an unspoken agreement wherein landlords rarely fretted about peasant use of communal lands as long as labor was regularly sup-plied to the hacienda for the planting and harvesting of cash crops. Across the Mexican countryside, such common space most often manifested itself in the ejido—derived from the Latin *exitus*, or "exit"—which was an ambig-uous legal category encompassing forest, pastureland, or fields belonging to pueblos, and reserved for their communal use. Beginning in the 1850s, though, liberals inspired by laissez-faire economic doctrine waged war on these informal agrarian economies. Díaz continued those campaigns with even greater vigor, believing that only private landownership would stimu-late Mexico's agricultural growth. During his rule, a legion of land survey-ors crisscrossed rural Mexico, signing over ejidos with murky colonial era legal titles to commercial landowners. Yet land privatization was not solely the product of state intervention. In coastal Veracruz, where export vanilla production boomed in the late nineteenth century, prosperous indigenous cultivators took the lead in carving up village plots for individual use. All in all, during Díaz's three decades in power, more than 127 million acres of communal, idle, or unoccupied lands, representing over half of Mexico's arable farmland, fell into private hands.[13]

Hoping to open up newly privatized lands to intensive use, US southern and Mexican elites courted external capital. In the former Confederacy, enterprising northern businesspeople had already arrived in large numbers following the end of the Civil War, and New South Democrats smiled on these newcomers. Under the watch of the new political elite, New York-, Boston-, and London-based financiers invested heavily in the postbellum southern economy. Bankers, merchants, and investors from across the United States and Europe siphoned untold sums into new plantations, cotton mills, logging and forestry operations, and mining towns. The influx of capital fueled a burst of rapid industrialization and economic expansion that delighted the New South boosters who had wooed outside investors. But as with other extractive enclave economies around the world, little wealth remained behind as cotton, cloth, coal, and timber flowed out from the region. As one historian concluded memorably, Dixie under New South Democrat rule provided "juleps for the few and pellagra for the crew."[14]

The penetration of external capital in Porfirian Mexico was both more extensive and perceptible, and it was primarily US and British investors who footed the bill for the construction of new plantations, mills, oil wells, railroads, and mines. Díaz and his advisers collaborated closely with these foreign economic interests, often seeking to play Britons, Frenchmen, and US nationals off each other to cut the best deal for Mexico. But despite efforts to balance extranational capital with local investment, by the turn of the century much of Mexico's natural wealth was the property of foreigners. The size and scale of foreign-owned agricultural estates varied enormously. On the extreme end were gigantic holdings like US journalism magnate William Randolph Hearst's 1.2 million acre hacienda Babícora in the northern state of Chihuahua. More representative, however, was the comparatively modest estate of San Pedro Coxtocán, owned by Texan widow Rosalie Evans in the Puebla-Tlaxcala Valley of central Mexico, where she oversaw a wheat plantation staffed with local day laborers. As was true in the US South, the lion's share of the wealth generated by these extractive enterprises flowed outward beyond Mexico's borders, rarely shared by those whose sweat and blood had produced it. "Mexico," went a popular lament of the era, was "mother of foreigners and stepmother of Mexicans."[15]

Porfirian and New South elites together worshipped at the altar of "progress," and no technology was more symbolic of that persuasion than the railroad. In both the US and Mexico, the connective power of the railroad track forcefully thrust agrarian communities into the capitalist world system, binding local harvests to speculative markets and distant consumers.

Yeomen and peasants who had previously lived on the periphery of cash economies learned that the shrill whistle of the locomotive often brought a spike in land prices, new commercial pressures, and the eclipse of mutualist social relations. The US southern rail network, shattered by the Civil War, grew rapidly in the years following, and by 1890, nine out of ten southerners lived in counties intersected by railroad track. Mexico's rail expansion was equally explosive, with more than twenty thousand kilometers of track laid during the Díaz era. While the advent of rail transport and travel was not inherently disadvantageous to small-scale farmers—in the US South especially, railroads provided greater mobility along with a new fluid arena for the interaction of whites and blacks—their management and operation was heavily tilted toward the landlord elite. Discriminatory rate policies and exclusive political networks frequently ensured that the railroad was the handmaiden of the bank and plantation rather than the common farmer.[16]

Once the revolutions of privatization, commercialization, and globalization had uprooted the US and Mexican yeoman and peasant, the bonds of debt and credit ensnared them in the plantation's web. In the US South, wartime devastation and the postwar scarcity of cash and capital forced countless white yeomen to sell their lands and return, with swallowed pride, as renters. The former slaves, with nothing but their freedom and all other means of subsistence forcibly closed to them, grudgingly joined the former yeomen as tenants in the expanding plantation archipelago. Both would be expected to raise cotton, a crop despised by the freedpeople because of its link to slavery and one unfamiliar to many yeomen, whose agriculture had been far more diversified in the antebellum era. Even so, the emerging system of tenancy was not inherently exploitative; indeed, to the freedpeople it was a much-preferred alternative over wage labor. But it would become increasingly so because of the uneven relationship between debtors and creditors. Tenants—and especially sharecroppers, renters of the lowest class who supplied nothing but their labor—had to rely on furnishing merchants for food, clothing, agricultural implements, and supplies. Often illiterate and unschooled in accounting or contract law, and thus highly susceptible to chicanery, such tenants often found it impossible to turn red ink black at season's end. Exorbitant interest rates only worsened affairs. Debt carried over into the next year, keeping renters in a state of semibondage.[17]

A similar pattern grew visible across Porfirian Mexico, where peasants-turned-peons and resident laborers were forced to feed and clothe themselves through the *tienda de raya*, the hacienda's on-site commissary. Especially in the central-southern regions most dominated by cash crop production, such as the sugar plantations of Morelos, the tobacco fields of Oaxaca's Valle Nacional, or the henequen zones of peninsular Yucatán, debt proved to be a powerful tool in extracting labor from resident populations and restricting their mobility. As in the United States, widespread illiteracy invited contractual and mathematical manipulation on the part of hacienda managers. Though the rigidity of debt peonage in southern Mexico was far more pronounced than in the southern United States, where the practice of moving to exchange landlords was common at season's end, the parallels between the *tienda de raya* and the furnishing merchant are nevertheless striking.[18]

The final ingredient that accelerated rural dispossession and the ascent of *latifundismo* in the New South and Porfirian Mexico was the invidious racial hierarchy permeating each society. Both were built on a pigmentocratic caste system that relegated African Americans in the US South and indigenous Mexicans to the lowest rungs of work, citizenship, and land tenure. At first glance, notable differences abounded. The color line in the United States was rigidly policed in the spheres of sex and public space; in Mexico, intermarriage had long been tolerated, and a doctrine of "whitening" taught Indians that an adoption of elite cultural mores and intermixture with Spanish blood held the key to social advancement. Likewise, the realm of political possibility in each place was starkly distinct. In the US Cotton Belt, the Reconstruction experiment had made black men full citizens, although white resistance truncated the scope of suffrage and citizenship after 1877. Mexico had scant experience with effective multiracial democracy, but military service allowed for astounding social ascent: both presidents Díaz and Juárez had strong indigenous roots, inconceivable among the nineteenth-century US political elite. Yet despite these contrasts, each society's racial ideology performed similar work in the rapidly changing countryside. Elites disparaged southern blacks and native Mexicans as lazy, indolent, incapable of self-government, uncaring of material progress, and productive workers only by coercion. In both places, racial rhetoric served to defuse alliances among the dispossessed, alienating the former yeoman from the former slave, and the mestizo sharecropper from the Indian peon.[19]

Thus, in the decades following 1876 in Mexico and 1877 in the US South, a potent cocktail of agrarian ferment—the closing of the commons, the commercialization of agriculture by the penetration of rail and external capital, and the deepening indebtedness of common farmers—fundamentally reordered land and life on both sides of the border. That common era witnessed the rapid expansion of the cash crop plantation, which dedicated soil and society to distant export markets, and funneled its proceeds to a small landholding minority. Those elites were eager to boast of the rapid pace of regional and national progress as well as its enduring stability. As Atlanta journalist Henry Grady, the New South's most renowned champion, confidently declared in 1886, his reborn region was "thrilling with the consciousness of growing power and prosperity," "the light of a grander day ... falling fair on her face."[20]

Yet such sunny pronouncements could not dispel the long shadows of inequality and deprivation that stretched across the landscape. Whether in Mississippi or Michoacán, Tennessee or Tabasco, the rural masses saw few tangible benefits in the economic miracle heralded by boosters in Atlanta or Mexico City. John Kenneth Turner, a US muckraking journalist visiting southern Mexico in 1908, quickly recognized this on seeing the "pitiful misery" of Yucatecan debt peons, who were regularly "beaten," "half starved," and "worked almost to death." He was hardly exaggerating; in 1910, agricultural real wages were a quarter of what they were a century earlier, and life expectancy across the nation was a pitiful thirty years.[21] Though the depths of desperation in the US Cotton Belt were not as extreme, it was impossible at century's close to deny the suffering of the "peons of the South," as one observer termed the rural poor in 1893, and their "thralldom of the crop lien."[22] "Each year the plunge is deeper, each year the burden is heavier," wrote another observer of US southern farm debt in 1894, and the result was "deep wrinkles," "wan faces," and "abject poverty."[23]

By the 1890s in the US South and the 1900s in Mexico, the dispossession and beggaring of yeomen, freedpeople, pueblos, and peasants had created a potential powder keg of social discontent. Especially for those among the rural poor who could distantly remember an earlier era of relative independence and stability, the stark disparities of the plantation were especially galling. The spark to ignite that keg was not long in coming, and marginalized rural people in both the United States and Mexico would mobilize vast rebellions to overturn the institutions that kept them in debt and poverty.

Revolt

At first glance, Tom Watson and Emiliano Zapata appear to have inhabited impossibly distant worlds. The former was a white country lawyer from rural Georgia, born in 1856; the latter a mestizo horse trainer and small landowner, twenty-three years Watson's junior, from central Mexico. The political vocabulary and cultural milieu of one would undoubtedly have been foreign to the other. Yet unpredictably, in the heady decades surrounding the turn of the twentieth century, both young men would champion daring revolts of country people against the entrenched powers that dispossessed and impoverished them. Though Watson and Zapata were themselves of moderate means, both had seen their humbler neighbors steadily lose hold of their land, independence, and dignity in previous years. Channeling such miseries into their political crusade, both demanded justice for the tiller of the soil. In 1911, Zapata promised to fight for the "immense majority of Mexican pueblos and citizens [who] are owners of no more than

Figure 1.1. Emiliano Zapata, Mexican agrarian revolutionary. Courtesy of Art Resource.

the land they walk on"; Watson in 1888 raised "the Standard of Revolt" on behalf of the "powerless–oppressed–shackled."[24]

The grassroots social movements that Watson and Zapata led—agrarian populism in the 1880–90s' US South, and agrarian revolution in 1910s' Mexico, respectively—diverged in undeniable ways. The former was largely non-violent, often more reformist than radical, perishing with a whimper in the climactic election of 1896. The latter was forced to pursue change with the

Figure 1.2. Thomas E. Watson, agrarian populist from Georgia. Courtesy of Watson-Brown Foundation.

bullet rather than ballot and exploded into a decade-long civil war that claimed upward of a million lives, fundamentally altering the course of Mexican history. Despite these obvious contrasts, striking commonalities lay submerged below. At heart, each rebellion sought to address the inequalities of a countryside in the grip of global capitalism, and each was characterized by a wildly diverse array of political visions that were ultimately more contradictory than cohesive. Although each revolt's most radical leaders would be defeated at the ballot box or on the battlefield, their vision for a transformed countryside would guide subsequent reformers.

Scholarship on the origins, processes, and consequences of agrarian unrest in the United States and Mexico has long been segregated by intellectual dichotomies. Curiously, though, each national historiographical trajectory closely mirrors the other. The first generation of scholars to examine US populism and the Mexican Revolution understood those movements as singular rather than plural: that there was "a" Mexican Revolution or "a" Populist movement to isolate and describe. These early historians sympathized with each movement's most radical and visionary protagonists, agreeing that both were idealistic and progressive campaigns toward democratization and economic justice.[25] Following them, a less optimistic generation of revisionists claimed that each rebellion was ultimately conservative in nature, representing little more than an antimodern backlash in the United States or a minor, insignificant face-lift among the capitalist leadership of Mexico. Such scholars, however, did not question the monolithic, singular nature of the revolts.[26] A postrevisionist generation had a doubly difficult task: to both rehabilitate the radical and emancipatory visions of each revolt while also struggling to digest the vast outpouring of state-level and regional studies that threatened the broad, national conclusions that earlier historians had drawn. Ultimately, scholars of the Mexican Revolution were more successful in accomplishing both tasks at once.[27]

Before US and Mexican farmers rose in revolt, early voices of dissent began to dispel Porfirian and New South illusions of rural stability and prosperity. In Mexico, Andrés Molina Enríquez's 1909 book *Los grandes problemas nacionales* (The great national problems) best encapsulated the agrarian discontent of the late Porfiriato. Serving as a country lawyer in the central state of México during the 1890s, Molina witnessed wheat and maguey cactus haciendas swallow the region's most productive lands, seeing firsthand the ubiquitous transfer of communal plots to private interests. Though he held a romantic and rather simplistic understanding of the dynamics of the indigenous pueblo, Molina grew convinced that the dispossession of village lands and ejidos was a fundamental injustice, and that the ascent of the hacienda crippled the productive capacities of the countryside. His widely read 1909 volume expounded on the betrayal of the small pueblo cultivator and the immediate need for land redistribution. Mexico's uneven land tenure, Molina argued passionately, was the defining feature of both the colonial and postcolonial era, and was the nation's primary obstacle to social justice and stability.[28]

In the United States, early resistance to the New South plantation elite registered first on the peripheries of the Cotton Belt. In northeastern Texas, white farmers began to organize cooperative institutions, such as the Farmers' Alliance, founded 1878, to foster autonomy from furnishing merchants and the crop lien system. Yet because its constituents were not deeply enmeshed in the plantation regime, the early Farmers' Alliance was largely moderate and reformist. More than anything, its members wanted freer access to credit, more transparency in negotiation with railroads, and greater cooperation among farmers so as to avoid gluts at harvest time. But as the alliance pushed eastward into the Cotton Belt during the late 1880s, its initially moderate demands entered a social landscape far different from where they were first forged. In regions where landownership and wealth were more extremely concentrated than in central Texas, rhetorical attacks on planters, bankers, railroads, and merchants were potentially explosive. In the Deep South, alliance campaigns more explicitly adopted the vocabulary of class war; one Georgia chapter sought to rally "the peasantry of America." Cotton Belt firebrands like Georgia's Watson charged alliance rhetoric with a frenzied urgency born of the deep divisions of the plantation system. Watson stridently damned the holders of the purse strings of the southern economy and the external forces that dispossessed former yeomen; the uprising of the farmers was "not a revolt," he claimed, "it is a revolution."[29]

In the heart of Dixie, some alliance members cautiously extended the promise of class-based cooperation to African Americans. "The crushing burdens which now oppress both races in the South," Watson proclaimed in 1892, must force a recognition that "each should help the other in the work of repealing bad laws and enacting good ones." In the racially polarized history of the postbellum South, such overtures marked a watershed. Yet they were also exceptional, and often deeply resisted by the white rank and file. In stark contrast to Watson's tentative outreach, other white alliance members imposed a rigid racial boundary that consigned black recruits to a separate Colored Farmers' Alliance, stymieing true biracial cooperation. Likewise, despite the fiery rhetoric of class antagonism, those drawn to the southern alliance were usually not the most marginal farmers, but those who either owned some land or had fresh memories of a former independence beyond the plantation. The farmers deepest submerged within the plantation complex—especially African American freedpeople and the poorest whites—occupied too precarious of a position to fully engage the potential of organization. Notwithstanding its contradictions, the alliance's momentum barreled forward. By 1890, the Farmers' Alliance claimed more than eight hundred thousand members across the cotton South.[30]

In Mexico, too, it would take an initially moderate protest to uncork more radical discontent. In 1910, when an eighty-year-old Díaz announced his plans to seek reelection once again, a host of reformers inflamed by critics like Molina targeted the presidential succession as a window of opportunity. Francisco Madero, a young and idealistic landowner from the northern state of Coahuila, rose to prominence as Díaz's primary opponent. After Díaz briefly imprisoned Madero during the election and declared himself the victor, Madero and his allies led an insurrection against the dictator that November. With promises of democratization and political opening, Madero rallied enough support among middle-class Mexicans to overthrow and exile

Díaz in a few short months. On the dictator's departure, Madero's supporters were euphoric; it seemed they had fomented an overnight revolution,
with little bloodshed.[31]

As Madero's rhetoric of liberal democracy filtered down to rural people
who had suffered the most in the Díaz years, however, it sparked the fuse of
an entirely different insurgency. The most notable example came in the
central-southern state of Morelos, where Madero's revolt provided the impetus for thousands of disfranchised and dispossessed country people to
address local grievances over land. Leading the Morelos revolt was Zapata,
who epitomized the demands of the dispossessed campesino. He came from
a lower-middling background, a horse trainer and trader as opposed to a
day laborer or peon. Rather than the most marginal and dependent of the
rural poor, Zapata had some education and semblance of autonomy from
the plantation complex. The sugar districts of Morelos, likewise, exemplified
the regions that were most hospitable to rural revolt. Where planter power
was most absolute and the working poor most degraded, such as in the
henequen plantations of Yucatán, agrarian revolt was far slower in manifest-
ing, just has it had been among the poorest southern sharecroppers. But in
Morelos, where rural people had recently lost land and independence, or
felt the threat of an encroaching plantation elite, the potential gains of open
resistance outweighed the many risks.[32]

Hopeful that Madero would support the Morelos peasants' demand for
land, Zapata rose in revolt in 1911 to support the northerner's cause against
Díaz. But when Madero assumed the presidency, and ignored questions of
land titles and agrarian reform, Zapata refused to demobilize his troops.
When it became abundantly clear that Madero's revolution was meant for
the urban middle classes and not defrauded campesinos, Zapata broke his
alliance with Madero and vowed that his revolt would continue until the
government addressed demands for land. It was not long before a host
of other social factions equally unhappy with Madero's compromises and
moderation—such as northerner Pascual Orozco from the border state of
Chihuahua—joined in rebellion. As the contagion of revolt spread outward
from Morelos, it was becoming plainly apparent that Madero's uprising
had not brought an end to Mexico's revolution. Instead, during the coming
years the countryside deteriorated into a vicious civil war as a host of regional leaders battled each other to fill the vacuum left by Díaz.[33]

Zapata's unwavering emphasis on land rights was immortalized in his November 1911 Plan de Ayala, written in cooperation with campesino allies in
a village of the same name in Morelos. The plan provided the founding
document of Mexican *agrarismo*—technically "agrarianism," but more closely
meaning the campaign for land redistribution that would define Mexican
politics for decades to come. Repudiating Díaz, Madero, and the "landlords
... and bosses who enslave us," the plan mandated that any lands unlawfully

defrauded from rural communities during the Porfiriato be immediately restored and "maintain[ed] at any cost with arms in hand." Additionally, Zapata demanded that one-third of the lands held by "powerful proprietors" be expropriated so that "citizens of Mexico may obtain ejidos, colonies, and foundations for pueblos." The plan was simultaneously radical and conservative. On the one hand, it threatened private property law in its call for immediate land redistribution, which the US Populists were careful to tiptoe around. Yet the Plan de Ayala did not call for an immediate abolition of the hacienda, seeking instead to reestablish a balance between large- and small-scale landholding. And in looking to the pre-Porfirian ejido as key to future stability in the countryside, Zapata and his allies betrayed their strident conservatism—in their eyes, it was not them but rather the railroad and plantation that were truly revolutionary.[34]

If the Plan de Ayala epitomized rural revolt in plantation Mexico, in the US South the agrarian insurgency of the late nineteenth century claimed a similar founding document in 1890, put to paper when the southern Farmers' Alliance and Colored Farmers' Alliance convened that December in Ocala, Florida. The meeting's resolutions, known as the Ocala Demands, clearly reflected the alliance's radicalization since its early Texas beginnings. Its authors demanded the abolition of national banks, often the perpetrators of the crop lien system that ensnared farmers and reduced their status to tenants and croppers. Ocala's Clause Four obliged "the passage of laws prohibiting alien ownership of land." But even more illustrative of the alliance's critique of the plantation complex was its demand that land held by railroads and corporations "in excess of such as is actually used and needed by them be reclaimed by the government and held for actual settlers only," although how this was to be enforced was left unspoken. Considered side by side, the Ocala Demands and Plan de Ayala shared deep commonalities, though the former was notably silent about infringements of private property and was thus far more conservative.[35]

While the authors of the Ayala and Ocala demands intended them to mark a beginning rather than an end, both documents would come to represent the high-water mark of radicalism, followed only by a receding tide. In Mexico and the US South, the years following 1911 and 1890, respectively, brought a series of political and military defeats, disillusionment, and co-optation for those who sought an immediate shake-up in the political economy of the countryside. Unable to overcome the tooth-and-nail resistance of the landed elite or heal the internal divisions cleaving their own ranks, agrarian rebels in the United States and Mexico saw their core demands largely unfulfilled during their lifetimes.

In the US Cotton Belt, rural insurgents confronted not only the steadfast opposition of organized capital but also the vexing dilemma of formal political engagement. In the early years of the alliance movement, its leadership chose to eschew the political binary of Republican and Democrat, and the Ocala platform reflected that decision. But as membership grew rapidly and hopeful organizers came to imagine sweeping political change on a national level, the temptations of formal politics became too great to ignore. The dilemma of party affiliation fueled a bitter internal debate, dividing the alliance and playing a significant role in its downfall. When a third party—the People's Party, or the Populists, as they became known—emerged in 1892, the Farmers' Alliance was already hemorrhaging membership. The Populists were divided over what to emphasize in their national platform, but a vocal minority was successful in making the main plank of the party the unlimited coinage of silver, which promised to expand the money supply and credit, and ultimately farmers' access to it. When party leaders on the national stage came to stress this demand over others, they lost many of their earlier supporters. The Democratic Party, too, co-opted several of the Populists' more moderate resolutions, further fracturing their coalition.[36]

Likewise, the deep-seated culture of individualism and bootstrap self-help commonly espoused by southern farmers precluded the sorts of cooperative, class-based alliances that Zapata championed in Mexico. Private property, sacrosanct to the agrarian ethos of much of the United States, would not be violated even in the regions most bitterly divided. Similarly, that the most marginal farmers were largely nonparticipants in the southern agrarian revolt would limit its attack on the social and economic bonds of the plantation. But perhaps the greatest stumbling block of all to the political agenda proposed at Ocala and beyond was white racism and the exclusion of African American farmers. Despite the tentative rhetoric of leaders like Watson, most southern white participants in the Farmers' Alliance and People's Party were distrustful of their black neighbors, seeing them as both economic and political threats. Therefore, when southern Democratic opponents employed race-baiting tactics to divide the agrarian rebels, racial fault lines broke open easily.[37]

Zapata and his *agrarista* allies faced even greater obstacles in Mexico. In the turmoil of revolt, landowners frequently organized troops of hired guns to resist rebel encroachment on their holdings, including one group in Veracruz that—in a frightening moment of cosmopolitanism—dubbed itself a "Klux clan."[38] The Zapatistas' unflinching dedication to land redistribution also placed them at odds with the military leadership that emerged triumphant in the political civil war of 1914–16 and sought to harness the social upheaval to a new revolutionary state. Such leaders, particularly Venustiano Carranza of Coahuila and Álvaro Obregón of Sonora, were large landowners from Mexico's north, reluctant to pursue sweeping agrarian restructuring. While more committed to social reform than Madero had been, their primary goal lay in forging a modern, urban, and secular nation rather than appeasing the peasantry. In their eyes, Zapata and the northern rebel Francisco "Pancho" Villa posed the gravest threat to Mexico's political and economic stability. Thus, during the latter years of the 1910s, the nascent revolutionary leadership did its best to marginalize both these opponents. Zapata continued to mount resistance from the mountains of Morelos, but in April 1919, Carranza's troops lured him into negotiations and shot him dead. Villa was first bribed into political withdrawal and then assassinated in 1923 on presidential order.[39]

Yet despite military defeat and betrayal, the Zapatista vision for a transformed countryside struck a deep chord among Mexico's rural masses, and the slogan of "land and liberty" echoed far beyond Morelos. Even as the new revolutionary leadership tried persistently to bury agrarista demands, it was unable to do so. In late 1916, when Carranza and his allies convened in the central state of Querétaro to write a revolutionary constitution, the "First Chief" showed little interest in implementing sweeping social reforms, deliberately excluding supporters of Zapata and Villa from the drafting process. But Carranza's allies worried that peace and stability in Mexico would be impossible if the yearnings of the rural dispossessed went ignored. Over the course of several weeks in Querétaro, the constitutional delegates largely scrapped Carranza's reformist, liberal suggestions and drafted a strikingly radical document. The blueprint of the Mexican state that emerged in early 1917 was one that was more aggressive on questions of social and economic justice than perhaps any other in the Western Hemisphere—certainly in the United States. In various articles, the Constitution of 1917 granted labor the right to organize and bargain collectively; indigenous people were recognized as key contributors to the nation's past and present; the Catholic Church was severely restricted in its role as educator and landlord; and the state was given the duty of ensuring economic balance by regulating and limiting monopolies.[40]

To the agraristas, though, one clause eclipsed all others: Article 27, which addressed concerns of land tenure. Penned in large part by Molina, the original critic of land disentailment during the Díaz years, Article 27 presented both a diagnosis and cure for Mexico's agrarian discontent. Conjuring a romantic vision of a pre-Porfirian countryside of contented pueblos subsisting on communal lands, the Constitution's authors argued that the abuse of property rights in the late nineteenth century had shattered the prospects of rural social peace. As a corrective, Article 27 mandated that all land and subsoil wealth in Mexico was ultimately the property of the state rather than private individuals, and that the government had the power to transfer that ownership should it be in the public good. As a blueprint for the future practice of land reform, the Constitution's drafters revived the ejido, that hazy legal category for communal lands managed by rural villages since the colonial period. But if the definition of the prerevolutionary ejido had been extremely fluid—more frequently designating grazing, hunting, and foraging lands as opposed to cultivated fields—Molina and his allies sought to reinvent this earlier concept for a new era. The new revolutionary ejido was to be an inalienable, state-deeded land grant to be worked either cooperatively or individually. Rather than the equivalent of private property, an ejido could not be mortgaged or sold by its lessees. It was to be primarily agricultural, and its occupants, dubbed *ejidatarios*, would benefit from state mentorship and credit. Whether the ejido constituted a means or an end was the subject of great debate in revolutionary circles. To Molina, it was solely intended as a temporary transition to small-scale, private individual ownership not dissimilar from the yeoman ideal of the United States. Others, however, drawing on the communalist indigenous cultures of central Mexico, saw the ejido as a permanent institution that would serve as the basis for cooperative cultivation.[41]

The Constitution's invocation of the ejido was intentionally vague, in large part because many of its drafters never expected it to represent anything other than words on paper. Carranza was perhaps the foremost skeptic of land reform, viewing Article 27 as an unwanted but necessary compromise in pursuit of social stability. Promises of ejidos, he hoped, would pacify a dangerously mobilized peasantry. His presidential successors of the 1920s, Álvaro Obregón and Plutarco Elías Calles, did not depart significantly from this basic conclusion. Thus, for a decade and a half, the nascent Mexican revolutionary state paid lip service to Article 27, but was not prepared to realize its mandate with any hurry. Immediately following the Constitution's ratification, expropriation and *ejidal* grants were rare, and only conducted as political theater to suppress wider protest. But words on paper can bear greater weight than anticipated, especially when given constitutional backing. After the financial crash of 1929, the forgotten promises of 1917 would haunt the leadership that had earlier swept them under the rug. Thus, even in military defeat, Mexico's agrarian rebellion had forced the inclusion of its agenda into the most important political document of the postrevolutionary regime.

In the United States, too, the Populist revolt's political demise sowed seeds that would later, unexpectedly, bear fruit. Across the country, rural insurgency shifted the bounds of political possibility, instilling in the public a belief that government had a fundamental duty to ensure the stability and independence of the small farmer. In the following generation, many of the Populist Party's reformist demands for federal oversight of unfettered capitalism and regulation of banks and railroads would be enacted into law. But in the depths of the Cotton Belt, where dispossession was most rampant and inequality sharpest, and where the Farmers' Alliance and Populist challenge had most aggressively threatened the foundations of class hierarchy, the defeats of the 1890s suggested less optimism for future change. Indeed, not long after populism's death rattle, New South Democrats took rapid measures to tighten the political system so as to prevent future challenges from below. Poll taxes and literacy tests, instituted across the South during the late 1890s and early 1900s, brought an end to the political fluidity and unpredictability of an earlier era. The physical and legal separation of blacks and whites was also formalized in Jim Crow segregation law during the last years of the century to permanently prevent the sorts of biracial alliances elites had feared during the Populist era. Barred from political participation and split by racial prejudice, poor rural southerners sank deeper into poverty and dependence. Rates of tenancy climbed upward in the new century, leaping from 38.5 percent in 1890 to 49.6 percent in 1910, and the declining price of cotton exacerbated rural suffering.[42]

When the flame of agrarian revolt was extinguished in Mexico and the US South, the latifundia system continued to dominate the rural landscape. To many observers, it appeared that neither insurgency had undone the status quo. The specters of landlessness and deprivation stalked the land, barely diminished. Yet through the compromises that mobilized country people had extracted from a begrudging elite—most visibly in Mexico and to a lesser degree in the South—the rhetoric and parameters of rural politics in the next generation were permanently altered. The aftermath of revolt produced both convergence and divergence between the US and Mexican countryside, setting the stage for their ultimate collision with the revival of rural reform in the era of Franklin D. Roosevelt and Lázaro Cárdenas.

Aftermath

To the countless thousands who swelled the ranks of agrarian revolt in Mexico and the US South, their defeats were sharply felt. The betrayal and murder of Zapata, memorialized in song and verse, galvanized the agrarista cause and convinced many of the treason of the new revolutionary state. Likewise, the stinging defeat of the Populist-Democratic presidential ticket in 1896 shook the foundations of the US agrarian movement, persuading many of its participants of the folly of direct political action. But if the uncontrollable fire of revolt had been snuffed out, the embers of rural discontent glowed fiercely, demanding action lest they flare up again. Therefore, in the decades following each uprising's denouement, the political mainstream tentatively adopted a surprising share of the rebels' rhetoric and attempted to address the most grievous injustices that had earlier incited social upheaval. Many of those solutions addressed the symptoms rather than underlying causes of rural unrest. Yet in sustaining the debate on agrarian poverty and inequality into a new era—even if in a refigured, depoliticized guise—those who subdued the revolts of the fin de siècle era would inadvertently facilitate their revival in the turbulent decade of the Great Depression.

In 1920, President Carranza, who had both orchestrated the assassination of Zapata and the stabilization of Mexico's political bloodletting, was himself overthrown and murdered by his rivals in the last successful coup d'état of the Mexican Revolution. On his death, the leadership of the new revolutionary state came into the hands of what historians frequently term the "Sonoran dynasty." During the decade and a half between 1920 and 1934, politicians from the northwestern state of Sonora occupied the presidency for eleven of those years. Two leaders in particular—Obregón (1920–24) and Calles (1924–28)—came to dominate national politics. While the two differed in background and political style, they shared a similar vision for Mexico's future. The Sonorans formalized and consolidated the Partido Nacional Revolucionario (National Revolutionary Party, or PNR), which would remain in power under various names for more than seventy years. Obregón and Calles were undoubtedly more radical than Madero, and they pioneered the expansion of rural schools to instill a nationalistic modernity among country people, waged a dramatic war against the Catholic Church and popular religiosity, and supported cultural industries that championed Mexico's indigenous past.[43]

On the question of land, however, Obregón and Calles were hardly fervent agraristas. Far more familiar and comfortable with the individualist, commercial, rural culture of Mexico's arid northwest, the Sonorans cast a leery eye toward central Mexico's indigenous traditions of communalism and cooperation. Both were deeply skeptical that the ejido—in whatever form—might represent a path toward a more prosperous rural Mexico. The problems of the countryside, they believed, would not be solved by carving up haciendas to create subsistence-oriented plots but instead by the cooperation of skilled agronomists and efficient producers to augment production, bringing down food prices and fueling economic growth through foreign exports. Yet because of the smoldering state of quasi-revolt that continued to mark the nation's agrarista hotbeds, the Sonorans could not safely ignore their demands for change. Calles, for example, formally inaugurated his 1924 presidential campaign in Cuautla, Morelos, where exactly five years earlier Zapata had been murdered by Carranza's troops. But homage to agrarista martyrs was one thing; aggressive expropriation of productive plantations was another. Though Calles accelerated the glacial pace of Obregón's redistribution campaign, deeding nearly eight million acres to rural villages as well as founding federal agencies to provide credit and irrigation to small farmers, much of this land was marginal. The Sonoran dynasty's land reform, predictably, was more symbolic than real, undertaken to preserve social peace rather than remake the political economy of the countryside.[44]

As the Mexican political climate cooled during the 1920s, the public face of agrarismo likewise shifted. In a handful of states, the fiery campesino radicals of the revolution's bloodiest years persisted in leading the push for land redistribution. More often, though, educated professionals—school-teachers, engineers, surveyors, and particularly agronomists—supplanted these revolutionaries. Indeed, the fields of agronomy and hydraulic engineering grew dramatically following the revolution's violent phase, attracting idealistic middle-class youths who hoped to marry the pursuit of rural social justice and a professional career. Graduates of Mexico City's National School of Agriculture and National Autonomous University of Mexico frequently staffed the nascent bureaucracies tasked with administering agrarian reform, such as the Comisión Nacional Agraria (National Agrarian Commission, founded 1917). Armed with the surveyor's tripod and agronomist's textbook, these new converts to agrarismo typically served as the vanguard in implementing the state's constitutional mandate for rural redistribution. But if many were unflinchingly committed to the agrarian project, few were campesinos themselves, and many harbored romantic and often condescending attitudes toward the country people they were tasked to uplift.[45]

The co-optation—if not hijacking—of the insurgent agrarian agenda was even more pronounced in the United States, where the rhetoric, tone, and leadership of the debate over rural life and agriculture swerved dramatically after 1896. In the wake of the Populist defeat, public attention to rural decline and discontent hardly disappeared. Indeed, early twentieth-century commentary on the "crisis" in the US countryside was ubiquitous. But if the agrarian rebels of the 1880s and 1890s rooted that crisis in dispossession, debt, and monopoly power, reformers contemplating the dilemmas of rural life in the new century drew markedly different conclusions. These newcomers to the debate were largely urban, middle-class, and captivated by progressive visions of positivist social reform. None was more influential than the so-called Country Life movement of the century's first two decades. Like the Populists, Country Lifers fretted about the uneven relationship between urban consumers and rural producers, but they wrung their hands not about rural exploitation. Instead, they worried the countryside was unsuccessful in keeping pace with urban modernity, and that farmers were a drag on the nation's growth and progress. These intellectuals feared that if rural life failed to offer opportunities for profit, then country people would flee for the slums of cities, exacerbating urban social problems. Such reformers hoped to reinvent rural life to make it more attractive, though they rarely paused to consider rural people's opinion in the process.[46]

Recasting and largely depoliticizing the Populist agenda, Country Life progressives had far more success translating their bloodless vision of rural reform into law. During the first decade and a half of the twentieth century, an avalanche of legislation expanded federal assistance to the agricultural sector. Antitrust law regulated the machinations of railroads and the largest corporations, vastly expanded land grant colleges sought to provide rural people affordable education, and a graduated income tax secured the funds to pay for these expensive programs. The US Department of Agriculture grew dramatically under progressive stewardship, particularly through the Cooperative Extension Service, a massive program that commissioned an agent to each of the nation's thousands of counties to communicate innovations in agricultural science to practicing farmers. These legislative accomplishments were proof that the Populists' heirs had not entirely ignored their predecessors. The farmers who benefited most from Progressive era programs, however, were often those of moderate means, reformists rather than radicals, such as the Kansas wheat farmer and California fruit grower. The millions without land and most deeply submerged in the plantation complex, especially in the cotton South, could tally few advantages in the early twentieth century's rural reform.[47]

Indeed, the regional peculiarities of southern Progressivism ensured that the post-Populist fever of reform would leave poor black and white farmers out in the cold. The Democratic architects of regional reform in the 1900s and 1910s—demagogic figures like South Carolina's Ben Tillman and Mississippi's James Vardaman—concerned themselves with social stability far more than they did social justice, preferring to silence agrarian critics rather than confront their grievances. Segregation and disfranchisement, which promised to pacify the tumultuous political arena of the late nineteenth century, were thus promoted as rational, modern, and enlightened measures. Likewise, in their agricultural policy, southern Progressives carefully avoided questions of land and lending, and devoted themselves single-mindedly to boosting efficiency and production. Farm advocates outside government did little better in pursuing redress for the growing majority of tenants and sharecroppers. The Farmers' Union, organized in 1902, could count hundreds of thousands of members across the southern states by the end of that decade, but its agenda was limited to concerns such as supply control and marketing, which promised little to those lacking land and capital.[48]

With the Cotton Belt's poorest farmers abandoned by the region's political establishment and civil society, it would be left to reformers outside the South to intervene on their behalf. In fact, the dawn of the new century coincided with a massive expansion of northern philanthropic interest in poor southerners, inspired by the growing chasm that yawned between the industrial metropolis and the South's benighted countryside. During the 1900s and 1910s, titans of northern industry funneled astounding sums toward projects of regional uplift, diagnosing the hopeless deprivation of the South's rural majority as a national disgrace. Julius Rosenwald of the Sears and Roebuck retail empire oversaw the construction of thousands of rural schools, particularly in black-majority counties. Oil magnate John D. Rockefeller and his General Education Board embarked on a vast campaign to transform the practice of southern agriculture, which—as chapter 4 will demonstrate in detail—would later have a profound impact on Mexico in the 1940s. But if northern philanthropists drew inspiration from populism's critique of rural poverty and dispossession, the solutions they advanced were consciously apolitical and unsurprisingly ineffectual. Extremely cautious of white southern resentments of external intervention, northern philanthropy avoided an open confrontation of economic and racial hierarchies.[49]

Nevertheless, northern philanthropy did empower an enormously influential black southern campaign to emancipate the poor farmer from debt and dependency. Embittered by the orgy of violence and race-baiting that marked the demise of populism's tenuous biracialism, many black southern leaders in the new century abandoned the prospect of a class-based politics and looked inward for salvation. Pioneering the quest for black economic autonomy and independence in the Cotton Belt was Booker T. Washington, born a slave in Alabama and the mastermind behind the renowned Tuskegee Institute of his home state. Convinced that an open political confrontation with organized white supremacy would be disastrous, Washington prescribed persistence, hard work, and industrial training as the path toward economic and ultimately political equality for African Americans. With steady support from northern donors, Washington built a rural model community at Tuskegee for black farmers to emulate, while his lieutenant and agronomist George Washington Carver taught sharecroppers the agroecological practices that would reduce their dependence on landlords and merchants. The Tuskegee vision for black rural progress was far more emancipatory than many scholars have acknowledged, but it confronted impossible obstacles. The downwardly mobile price of cotton, the South's cash-poor economy and resultant webs of debt, and unwavering white opposition conspired to blunt Washington's hopes for a transformed countryside.[50]

Therefore, the plight of the black southern farmer after populism's failure was perhaps unparalleled in its bleakness. Often termed the "nadir" of African American history, the early twentieth century saw a crescendo in lynching, tenancy, and disfranchisement. And though they did not face the constant threat of extralegal violence, landless white farmers fared little better in this era. With their political voice silenced, small farmers of either race could do little more than observe their continuing dispossession by King Cotton's ever-growing plantation empire. No observer better recorded the stark deprivation in the rural South than the young New York journalist Frank Tannenbaum, who in 1923 toured the Cotton Belt and penned a scathing indictment of regional ills. "The beautiful sunny South is afflicted by a plague, a white plague," denounced Tannenbaum—"cotton." Cotton "is not only king; it is tyrant," dictating that the farmer in its grasp "does not own the soil he tills," "does not work for himself," and "is 'run' by the local merchant." Yet the globe-trotting Tannenbaum—who will make several appearances in future chapters—understood the US countryside in light of another he knew well. "In Mexico," he warned in the same essay, "Morelos and Yucatan, the two single crop areas, had the greatest slavery and the most bitter revolution and are now the most radical." Should the hacendados of the US South not consider the powder keg they unknowingly sat on, implied the writer, they might face a similar explosion. It was not long before Tannenbaum's warning came to have the ring of prophecy.[51]

***

In the late 1870s, both the US South and Mexico emerged from chaotic periods of war and social turmoil, shepherded by a new political elite that championed stability and economic growth above all. In the generation that followed, that leadership waged an aggressive campaign to rationalize the countryside in hopes of incorporating rural people and their landscapes within the web of global capitalism. They were strikingly successful in doing so, and under their stewardship, the export-oriented plantation and hacienda blossomed. But if bankers, planters, boosters, and bureaucrats benefited from the new economic regime, those profits were hardly shared by the rural majority, which instead saw the last vestiges of its independence and autonomy washed away.

In response, dispossessed country people rose in revolt against both regimes. In the United States, the Farmers' Alliance and then Populist Party challenged the New South Democratic elite and their alliance with foreign capital, bankers, and the railroad. Yet in choosing formal political avenues over violent revolt, they were ultimately unable to dethrone those opponents during the 1880s and 1890s. In Mexico, a diverse group of rebels—rural and urban, middle and lower class, northern, central, and southern—joined together to expel their aging dictator, Díaz, in 1910. But when those diverse forces could not agree on what would replace Díaz, the revolt deteriorated into a long and astonishingly violent civil war. When the smoke cleared, the faction that most closely represented the marginalized farmer—Zapata's agraristas—had been militarily defeated. Still, by the force of their lingering popular support, they were able to force their agrarian vision into the revolutionary Constitution of 1917.

While neither rural revolt reversed the social and economic transformations earlier instigated by their elite adversaries, each insurgency significantly shifted the tone and content of agrarian politics in the years following 1896 and 1917. In Mexico, stark memories of social upheaval and the lasting popular appeal of land reform ensured that when the Sonoran presidents of the 1920s began to institutionalize the revolution, they grudgingly adopted agrarista rhetoric and paid lip service to martyred heroes like Zapata, even while actively marginalizing their political agenda. Demands for rural social justice, even if voiced by a newer generation, thus endured long after the demise of the Zapatistas. In the United States, Populist agrarian rebels were successful in publicizing the uneven relationship between town and country, but in their defeat they lost the political momentum to force their agenda on the debate that followed. Those who would carry the torch of rural reform—middle-class progressives such as those of the Country Life movement—interpreted the crisis in the countryside quite differently from their predecessors, and their legislative successes targeted only the upwardly mobile landowner. In the cotton South, where the deprivations of the plantation system were sharpest, and where agrarian revolt had posed its most radical challenge, there was little cause for celebration. Poor blacks and whites lost their political voice in the frenzy of disfranchisement following populism's demise, and the wedge of legally encoded racial segregation drove them further apart. While Progressive demagogues of the new century were eager to defend the small (white) farmer, they rarely questioned the economic matrix that perpetuated their consignment to tenancy, debt, and dispossession.

During the conservative interregnum of the 1920s, poor country people in the US South and Mexico confronted political and economic stagnation. Global commodity prices steadily slid downward following the spikes of World War I, truncating the possibilities of rural economic mobility and exacerbating annual cycles of debt. Mexican campesinos throughout the decade heard again and again how the new revolutionary state was their most loyal champion, yet they gazed out on a rural landscape that was hardly less unequal than it had been in 1900. The meager land redistribution of the decade's early years dwindled to nearly nothing by its close, and in 1930 political strongman Calles publicly declared that the Mexican land reform program was a failure and "the agrarian problem has reached its end."[52] In the United States, probusiness Republicans in the White House likewise refused to acknowledge their own agrarian problem, despite a prolonged depression that sapped the US countryside during the entire decade. In the Deep South, that crisis was most pronounced. Regardless of global competition, sagging prices, and the ecological disruptions of the boll weevil insect, King Cotton's grasp on the region only tightened, and its despised retainers—peonage, bankruptcy, and soil erosion—extended their reach. But with few political outlets after disfranchisement and few leaders to look to, poor rural southerners could offer little resistance except with their feet, as did the hundreds of thousands who began to stream out of the region following World War I.[53]

Throughout the 1920s, the leadership of Mexico and the US South neglected the simmering discontent in their countryside, calculating that rural people either lacked the momentum or capacity to contest their exploitation. The 1929 market crash along with the economic disaster it heralded abruptly awakened the political elite from this contented reverie. Few sharecroppers or peons, admittedly, paid much attention to the New York stock market crash that October. But within just a few short years, the global Great

Depression would stretch and snap the minimal safety nets that had suspended poor rural people during the previous decade. As already-low crop prices and agricultural incomes spiraled downward in the early 1930s, a growing number of country people came to believe that capitalism had utterly failed. Large landlords, with their wealth dependent on global commodity markets, saw their power and influence wane during the crisis years. The orthodox economic doctrines that had guided policy making during the 1920s likewise crumbled in step with the financial sector.[54]

On both shores of the Gulf of Mexico, this deepening economic crisis encouraged and emboldened agrarian radicals silenced during the stalemate of the 1920s. Indeed, the Depression dramatically expanded the bounds of the politically possible, opening avenues of opportunity unimaginable just years earlier. In Mexico, village agraristas long frustrated with indifferent or openly hostile governors and local caciques—strongmen—escalated their demands that the neglected promises of the Constitution of 1917 be realized. Unauthorized peasant invasions and occupations of hacienda land saw a sharp uptick in the early decade. And the revolutionary ruling party, having openly dismissed the agrarian reform program just years earlier, now scrambled to respond to the social upheaval, announcing a newly aggressive Agrarian Code in the early Depression. In the US Cotton Belt, where protest had been almost entirely absent during the 1920s, the advent of radical agrarianism in the early 1930s was far sparser than in Mexico, but equally terrifying to the landed elite. The Communist Party made surprisingly deep inroads into Alabama in the early years of the decade, organizing primarily black farmers into the Share Croppers' Union, which could count several thousand members in its heyday. And in 1934 in eastern Arkansas, the Southern Tenant Farmers' Union presented perhaps the boldest challenge to the rural status quo, inviting black and white landless farmers to join in striking for better wages and land of their own.[55]

But perhaps most important, the social ferment accompanying the global economic crisis paved the road to power for two populist leaders whose presidencies would fundamentally transform each nation's political landscape for generations to come: Lázaro Cárdenas in Mexico and Franklin D. Roosevelt in the United States. Both had been governors in the early years of the Depression—Cárdenas in west-central Michoacán, from 1928 to 1932, and Roosevelt in New York, from 1929 to 1932—and in their home states had experimented with unorthodox solutions to the crisis. Though they came from astoundingly distinct walks of life—Cárdenas was born to humble parents and ascended in politics through his military service in the revolution, while Roosevelt was the scion of New York's aristocracy—both nurtured deep sympathies for the dispossessed and destitute country people who made up much of their nations. Having joined the struggle to oust Díaz at age fourteen, Cárdenas came of age in the revolutionary violence of the 1910s, and eagerly imbibed the agraristas' demand for "land and liberty." Roosevelt, despite the comforts of his upbringing, was crippled by polio in his thirties and over time learned to sympathize with the downtrodden "forgotten man." His illness also drew him to the rejuvenating baths of Warm Springs, in west-central Georgia, where in his frequent automobile excursions of the 1920s, the New Yorker personally witnessed the marginal lives of the southern tenant and sharecropper—a reckoning that would long guide his years in the White House.[56]

Both Cárdenas and Roosevelt ran unprecedented whistle-stop campaigns, crisscrossing their nations and promising hopeful crowds a new era for the industrial worker and suffering farmer. Roosevelt came to speak of a "New Deal," and Cárdenas talked about a "Six-Year Plan" that pledged a revival of social revolution. Yet when each took office—Roosevelt in March 1933, and Cárdenas in December 1934—they took only tenuous steps in fulfilling their pledge of aid to the rural poor. In his first year as president, Cárdenas tiptoed carefully around the long shadow of Calles, the former president who had handpicked each of his successors since 1928 and hoped to continue his rule in all but name. A significant overhaul of the state's agrarian policy, therefore, would have to wait until Cárdenas could break free of Calles's grip. Roosevelt, too, began his administration reluctant to address landlessness and rural poverty. The New Deal's first measure to aid farmers, a crop reduction and commodity price support plan called the Agricultural Adjustment Administration, was explicitly aimed at middling and well-to-do farmers particularly in the Midwest, and did few favors for the cotton tenant and sharecropper.

But by 1935, when Cárdenas exiled Calles and declared his political independence, and as Roosevelt grew more steadfast in his experimentation and commitment to attacking rural poverty, the reformist visions of the Mexican and US governments dovetailed in striking and unexpected ways. Bucking decades of neglect and denial, the Six-Year Plan and New Deal—alongside a civil society hungry for change—reached back to the long-deferred vision of the agrarian rebels who preceded them. It was at this moment that parallel histories swerved together and collided, intersecting and intertwining. It was then that defenders of the sharecropper and campesino, having long struggled in solitude, discovered their counterpart across the border. It was then that the distinctions between Mexican and US history began to blur and recede. The next two chapters recover the fundamental significance of this exchange.

Chapter Two

SHARECROPPERS AND CAMPESINOS
Mexican Revolutionary Agrarianism in the Rural New Deal

THE MEXICAN embassy on Washington, DC's Pennsylvania Avenue was unusually busy in winter 1934–35. Telegraphs chattered and telephones rang, typewriters rhythmically punctuated the din, and clerks and attachés rushed—even more frantically than usual—through the halls on their business. Some of this bedlam was to be expected with the recent regime change in Mexico City and its bureaucratic reshuffling, as President Lázaro Cárdenas took office in December 1934. But consular officials that winter also found themselves devoting unexpected time to a new task: answering the growing number of curious queries by US citizens about what the Cárdenas government was planning in Mexico. In the political ferment that marked the United States during the radical 1930s, Mexico's revolution was rapidly capturing the spotlight. Pablo Campos Ortiz, an embassy clerk responsible for distributing publications, felt particularly burdened by the attention newly lavished on his office. In January 1935, he wrote urgently to the Mexico City headquarters of the Partido Nacional Revolucionario (National Revolutionary Party, PNR), beseeching the party to immediately send a new printing of the Plan Sexenal—the Six-Year Plan, a declaration of goals for the Cárdenas administration—"with the object of meeting the requests being made." And in case the Plan Sexenal was translated into English, Campos urged that the shipment should be doubled.[1]

The sudden US interest in Mexico's program of revolutionary reform was hardly accidental, but rather born from the convergences of an exceptional decade. In the first half of the 1930s, the US and Mexican governments both unveiled bold plans for reconstructing their national political economy, with a primary emphasis on righting rural wrongs. Cárdenas, campaigning for the presidency during spring and summer 1934, vowed a fulfillment of the Mexican Revolution's long-postponed promise of "land and liberty." In the six years that followed, he oversaw the most sweeping agrarian reform campaign in the history of the Western Hemisphere, ultimately redistributing nearly fifty million acres of land previously held in large estates. In the

United States, President Franklin D. Roosevelt and his ambitious wing of reformers in the US Department of Agriculture (USDA) proposed a similarly unprecedented effort to rescue the rural United States from depression and poverty. While ultimately never as radical as Cardenismo and indeed quite conservative in its initial years, by decade's end, the agrarian New Deal challenged the status quo in a manner surprisingly comparable to the Mexican effort.

Despite the contrasting motives and outcomes of those two campaigns for rural reform, they were frequently in conversation, and this dialogue had profound impacts on each. Rather than discrete political movements that can be understood in solely national terms, the Mexican and US agrarian reform movements of the long 1930s—from about 1933 to 1943—were closely interwoven. That entanglement broadened their respective visions of rural social justice and economic democracy. It gave birth to one of the New Deal's most aggressively redistributionist agencies—the Farm Security Administration (FSA)—and inspired Washington's highest echelon of rural policy makers to undertake pilgrimages to Mexico. This chapter will examine the decade's political traffic from south to north, and how Mexican revolutionary agrarianism radicalized the rural vision of the New Deal; the following chapter will chart the flow in the opposite direction.

To look beyond national boundaries in the study of the 1930s forces a rethinking of US-Mexican relations and the radical potential of the rural New Deal. While scholars have agreed that the economic crash of 1929 ushered in a global spike in nationalism, only recently have they begun to acknowledge how truly cosmopolitan programs of national reform could be.[2] Roosevelt's New Deal and Cárdenas's Plan Sexenal did indeed turn inward to stress domestic problems, but they never lost sight of the global connections that linked activist governments in an era of economic crisis. Internationalist nationalisms may seem an oxymoron to some, but such a concept made sense to actors of the time. Likewise, for those who study the uneven relationship between the United States and Mexico, the 1930s deserve special emphasis as a moment when traditional patterns of influence and intellectual transfer were upset. Where Mexico had previously served the United States predominantly as a supplier of low-cost labor and raw materials (as it would function again later), the 1930s represented a significant departure. In those years the flow of political strategies, rather than farmhands and tomatoes, marked the south-north transfer between the two neighbors. Though many remember the decade primarily for the mass deportations of Mexican and Mexican American workers in the Herbert Hoover years, such bitter exchanges did not mark its entirety.[3]

The 1930s were hardly the first moment that US reformers looked to Mexico for inspiration, or the only time that Mexican domestic politics reverberated north of the border. In the middle of the nineteenth century, Mexico had served as a beacon for runaway slaves and abolitionists.[4] The revolution of 1910–17 captivated countless US radicals desiring sweeping social change at home, from anarchists to Mexican Americans and African Americans.[5] Then, during the 1920s, US social scientists, suffragists, labor unionists, journalists, and art collectors entered Mexico in unprecedented numbers to revel in the social ferment and cultural release following the revolution's violent phase.[6] Likewise, during the radical 1930s, agrarian issues did not monopolize the current of south-north influences. Spurred by Roosevelt's highly publicized "Good Neighbor" policy, US interest in Mexico surged during that tumultuous decade.[7] Artists and writers skeptical of urban industrial modernity during the Great Depression embraced romantic visions of a supposedly precapitalist Mexico. US educators paid close attention to revolutionary literacy programs, anthropologists and bureaucrats concerned with Native American assimilation studied Mexico's official revival of *indigenismo*, while a nascent state-funded tourism industry attracted hundreds of thousands of US visitors to behold Mexico's natural and cultural wonders.[8] These simultaneous exchanges, alongside dialogues preceding the 1930s, provide important context and precedent for the agrarian crossings of that decade. Yet none of those transnational networks, whether prior or coinciding, enlisted participants of as high political profile or made as concrete an impact on US policy making as the agrarian dialogue of the 1930s. Though born from kindred instincts, the dialogue on agriculture and rural life far overshadowed others in its prominence, intensity, and consequence.

US rural reformers' interest in Mexican *agrarismo*, the revolutionary movement to subdivide large estates, was most dramatically manifested in the plantation belt of the South, which the New Deal diagnosed as "the Nation's No. 1 economic problem" and made its primary target.[9] Indeed, it was particularly those people concerned with regional southern poverty who best understood the bonds between their countryside and Mexico's. In their eyes, Mexico and the US South shared a plantation, or latifundia, heritage, as each suffered from a common legacy of highly concentrated land tenure, social and racial stratification, and environmental decline. But if it seemed self-evident to US observers of the 1930s that they could learn from Mexico's countryside, agrarian historians have been far slower to rediscover the era's transnational exchanges. The major scholarly works on the rural New Deal adopt strictly national frameworks, and if they look to external influence, their main emphasis has been on western Europe and the Soviet Union.[10] Likewise, historians of US-Mexico relations in the period have underscored diplomats' formal negotiations rather than examining nonstate actors or how the domestic politics of each nation influenced those of its neighbor.[11] There are encouraging signs, however, that scholars are beginning to think beyond the nation in their analysis of rural reform in this critical era. A handful of essays have explored, in comparative terms, how

Mexican and US approaches toward ending rural poverty in the 1930s shared common goals but differed in their prescriptions, although those essays do not reveal how each campaign influenced the other.[12] Likewise, recent work in US history has stressed the global consequences of the New Deal by tracing how rural experts took their agenda into the nascent Third World after they were marginalized at home.[13] Still, none of these works have highlighted the transnational crucible in which the programs themselves were originally forged.

The New Deal was an unusually contradictory political affair, renowned for its conflicting visions and inconsistency in social and economic policy. In turn, not every element of the rural New Deal looked toward Mexico, nor were Mexican observers eager to borrow from every rural New Deal program. Instead, it is helpful to consider the New Deal's policies for the countryside as dichotomous. On one side was the "agricultural" New Deal, which had its origins in Roosevelt's first hundred days, and sought primarily to boost commodity prices and farm incomes among larger, commercially oriented cultivators. The agricultural New Deal's primary accomplishment was the price-control crop subsidy program of the Agricultural Adjustment Administration (AAA). Such measures were among the most long-lived ones of the New Deal, but they by no means represented its entirety. Indeed, as reformist bureaucrats discovered the millions ignored or injured by these earlier programs, they responded with a sweeping effort to address the suffering of a rapidly growing rural underclass—one most visible in the US South. This was the "agrarian" New Deal: a host of often-dissonant programs that targeted culture, environment, poverty, land tenure, and the fostering of rural democracy. It was the leadership of these agencies—the Subsistence Homesteads Division, Resettlement Administration, FSA, Bureau of Agricultural Economics, and early Tennessee Valley Authority, among others—that displayed the greatest curiosity toward Mexico. Likewise, it was the agrarian, not agricultural, New Deal that most captured the Mexican imagination.[14]

Bridging the political worlds of Cárdenas and Roosevelt, this chapter explores the decade's south-north exchanges. First, it examines how a cadre of left-leaning US reformers, led by the peripatetic academic Frank Tannenbaum, attempted in 1934 and 1935 to translate the blueprint of Mexican agrarian reform into political action for the US South. That campaign ultimately played an essential role in the founding of the FSA, one of the most ambitious federal agencies of the New Deal. While much of the New Deal's rural policy was quite conservative and aimed toward placating commercial farmers, scholars since the 1930s have nevertheless struggled to make sense of how openly redistributive agencies like the FSA, which represented the US government's only land reform program of the twentieth century, were forged in the same New Deal political environment and managed to thrive for several years. While the FSA was a contradictory agency born from diverse impulses of both national and transnational origin, its forgotten Mexican roots provide a missing piece of the puzzle in charting its successes and failures.

Second, the chapter looks at the myriad Mexican pilgrimages undertaken by a host of influential US rural reformers during the Cárdenas era. Perhaps no group outside Washington, DC, was more renowned—or feared—for its agrarian radicalism than the multiracial Southern Tenant Farmers' Union (STFU), whose political legacy has been closely studied. Few scholars, however, have studied its cosmopolitanism. In 1939, the union organized and led a workshop in Mexico's northern cotton zone of La Laguna, the site of Cárdenas's most dramatic expropriation campaign, to inform its membership of the political possibilities it suggested. Yet interest in Mexican agrarismo was not only confined to the radical sphere; in the more staid halls of New Deal bureaucracy, it had even wider impact. The chapter's last pages examine the Mexican journeys of three influential USDA policy makers: Rexford Tugwell, M. L. Wilson, and Henry A. Wallace. Their wide-eyed observations of Mexico's agrarian experiment would ultimately reshape how they understood the New Deal's promises at home and abroad.

Agrarismo and the FSA

The capitalist regimes that ruled Mexico and the US South in the late nineteenth century pulled formerly independent rural people into the plantation nexus. In Mexico, the Porfirian state and its capitalist allies evicted villagers and peasants from subsistence-oriented plots, and converted them into peons and wage laborers on cash crop haciendas. In the South, the bonds of debt and credit chained white yeomen and African American freedpeople to cotton plantations as tenants and sharecroppers. While the Mexican Revolution shook the foundations of the agrarian status quo and suggested alternative solutions, US southern populism achieved no such victory. Therefore, in the early twentieth century, the numbers of landless farmers only grew as rapid fluctuations in cotton prices forced repeated cycles of bankruptcy and dispossession. The constant threat of vigilante violence perpetuated African American landlessness and dependence, but most white farmers did not enjoy much greater economic mobility or autonomy. By 1930, more than 55 percent of US southern farmers both black and white were working someone else's land, as compared with 38.5 percent in 1890.[15]

For much of the early twentieth century, though, southern sharecropping and tenancy reflected the Mexican rural maxim of *duro pero seguro*—hard but certain. Communal networks of assistance served rural families as a loose

social safety net. While deeply paternalist, the region's landowners cultivated a sense of noblesse oblige that endowed them with the duty of social
responsibility for those who worked their land. These uneven moral economies between landowners and tenants, policed by the constant threat of
white violence toward blacks who rocked the boat, lent southern rural life
an uneasy equilibrium in the early twentieth century. But that balance was
not long lasting. The increasing availability of northern industrial jobs beginning in World War I inaugurated a prolonged rural out-migration. With
the flight of hundreds of thousands of African Americans from the region,
the foundations of the southern cotton plantation economy felt the first
tremors of change.[16]

Yet if the northbound Great Migration of black southerners was the first
blow to the plantation's permanence, any sense of rural equilibrium in the
region was forever lost during the first few years of the New Deal. As soon
as Roosevelt took office in 1933, there was a vast clamor among farmers that
the president address plummeting crop prices and farm incomes. That outcry came from rather diverse sources. Radical groups such as the STFU demanded assistance for landless farmers and opportunities for purchasing
plots of their own, but more politically prominent midwestern grain and
livestock farmers simply wanted government aid in raising crop prices. Roosevelt initially favored this latter group, and the agricultural legislation of
1933 reflected this alliance.

The New Deal's first attempt to address the declining price of farm commodities was the AAA. Since the mid-1920s, agricultural economists in the
United States had pushed for production limits to combat the falling prices
of food and fiber, but they had achieved little success under that decade's
Republican administrations. Roosevelt proved far more receptive, inaugu-
rating the AAA in his first hundred days. The program was based on a simple idea: if farmers took a portion of their land out of production, supply
would decline, and prices would naturally rise. The AAA thus asked farmers
to reduce their acreage of key crops by about one-third and then compen-
sated them for their lost profits. Though the AAA marked a vast expansion
of state power in the agricultural sector, it was hardly a program of social
leveling; as such, it lay at the heart of the agricultural New Deal, not the
later agrarian New Deal. The program was intended as a stopgap mechanism to raise rural incomes for commercial farmers, and in the Midwest it
was popular and quite successful.[17]

In the US South, however, the program had vast and unanticipated consequences. Control of the cotton section of the AAA, both federally and
locally, lay squarely with southern planters and their allies. These administrators worried little when they discovered that landowners were pocketing
federal payments and evicting the tenants whose land was retired. Indeed,
southern planters saw the AAA as a long-awaited opportunity to erode the

hated compromise of sharecropping, and the expulsion of landless families grew rampant during 1933 and 1934. For countless black and white tenants, therefore, the coming of the AAA was nearly apocalyptic. Some packed up and left the region for points north and west, while others organized and joined radical organizations such as the STFU. Within months, thousands of black and white farmers were roaming the South, set adrift from the plantation economy. It appeared as if the fabric of southern rural society was quickly unraveling.[18]

As evictions escalated, the plight of the uprooted sharecropper began to attract attention, and one group that took particular notice of the chaos wrought by the AAA in the Cotton Belt was the Julius Rosenwald Fund of Chicago. Founded by the Sears and Roebuck chief executive of the same name in 1917, the Rosenwald Fund had spent an enormous amount of money after the war on improving the welfare of black southerners through the building of thousands of so-called Rosenwald schools—simple, one-room buildings devoted to African American education. After hosting a number of conferences in fall 1933 about the havoc that the AAA was wreaking on black southerners, Rosenwald Fund president Edwin Embree allied with Will Alexander of the Atlanta-based Commission on Interracial Cooperation to draft a "long-term program of rehabilitation of the rural Negro."[19] In early 1934, they successfully secured a $50,000 grant from the Rockefeller Foundation to "set in motion or strengthen movements that may be expected to have some effect" on the crisis in US southern agriculture.[20]

Both Embree and Alexander were members of a growing interracial network of liberals who challenged the status quo in southern race relations, politics, and economics. Like their allies Clark Foreman, Charles S. Johnson, Howard W. Odum, and others, they were inspired by Roosevelt's rhetorical commitment to economic democracy and sought to use the crisis of the Depression to push for a change in the "solid South" of the 1930s. Reformist rather than radical, well educated, and strongly linked to the academic world, they were nevertheless an instrumental group in pressuring the often-reluctant New Deal administration toward black rights. Embree was a well-to-do white midwesterner who had first entered philanthropy during World War I. Interestingly, when Embree joined the Rosenwald Fund in 1928, he immediately planned a study of Mexican revolutionary schools to be used as an example for US southern rural education. Alexander was a southern-born white theologian who had taken leadership of the Commission on Interracial Cooperation on its founding in 1919. From the group's headquarters in Atlanta, Alexander pushed for antilynching laws, an end to the all-white Democratic primary election, and the overturning of Jim Crow segregation.[21]

In early 1934, Embree and Alexander began to strategize about how best to reduce the escalating eviction of southern tenants and sharecroppers. At

first glance, their task seemed insurmountable. Desperately seeking guidance, Alexander reached out to his elderly mentor George Foster Peabody.
Peabody was a crucial hub in the 1930s' southern liberal network. Born in
Columbus, Georgia, in 1852, he moved to New York City after the Civil War,
and made millions investing in Mexican banking and railroads during the
Díaz years. By the outbreak of the Mexican Revolution, Peabody had withdrawn from business and entered the world of US southern philanthropy,
notably as treasurer of John D. Rockefeller's General Education Board, but
also as an independent donor to black institutions such as the Hampton
and Tuskegee Institutes. During the 1910s and 1920s, he was a gentle, internal voice of criticism for the region, genuinely interested in the welfare of
blacks and poor whites, but always a gradualist in his solutions. Peabody
also had a unique back door to the White House: during the 1920s, he had
convinced the young polio sufferer Franklin D. Roosevelt of the curative
effects of the hot springs in southwest Georgia, and would remain a close
informal adviser to the New Yorker throughout his life.[22]

After a long discussion with Alexander at Peabody's Warm Springs, Georgia, winter home in March 1934, Peabody decided that the best way to arrive at an action program for the rural South was to organize a conference
of leading reformers on "the very desperate conditions resulting in that section from the wide-spread influence of the economic debacle of these past
years."[23] He offered to host such a conference, planned for summer 1934,
at his scenic summer estate located on upstate New York's Lake George.
Alongside Embree, Alexander, and a slew of academic sociologists, Peabody
invited the presidents of major universities in the South for a weeklong retreat. Then, possibly as an afterthought, Peabody also decided to invite Frank
Tannenbaum, then a young scholar of Mexico, and whose presence at the
conference would prove instrumental.[24]

Born to a Jewish family in Austria in 1893, Tannenbaum along with his
parents emigrated to rural Massachusetts at the turn of the century and ultimately settled in New York City by 1906. During the next decade, Tannenbaum became enmeshed in the labor struggle and grew to be a close confi-
dant of famed anarchist Emma Goldman. After he enlisted in the US Army
during World War I and was stationed in South Carolina, Tannenbaum grew
fascinated with the US South, viewing it as a feudalistic society that seemed
entirely at odds with the urban and industrial world he knew in New York.
His horror at the social and economic dilemmas of the South moved him
in 1924 to write *Darker Phases of the South*, a Menckenesque exposé of cotton
monoculture, the Ku Klux Klan, and textile mill towns. It was during his
research for that book that he met Peabody, a sympathetic critic of the region's social problems. Yet Tannenbaum's interest in the US South was soon
eclipsed by a passion for Mexico, a country that he first visited in 1922. That
same year, he applied for a graduate scholarship at Massachusetts' Amherst

Figure 2.1. Frank Tannenbaum researching his dissertation in rural Mexico, 1920s. Frank Tannenbaum Papers, box 57, folder 3. Courtesy of Columbia University.

College to do a comparative study of the US South and Mexico—two regions he believed shared the common problems of hierarchical societies and uneven land tenure. It is unclear whether Amherst decided to fund Tannenbaum; he later enrolled in the Robert S. Brookings Institution in Washington, DC, in 1924 to begin graduate work.[25]

At Brookings, Tannenbaum undertook a broad education in history, political economy, and sociology. He ultimately chose to write his doctoral thesis on the Mexican Revolution, with a focus on land reform. His research took him on mule back across rural Mexico in the mid-1920s, into state, federal, and regional archives, and into close acquaintance with political elites in the revolutionary state. Throughout the writing and editing process, Tannenbaum sent chapters of the dissertation to his friend Peabody, who shared his interest in Mexico. Published in 1929 as *The Mexican Agrarian Revolution*, Tannenbaum's dissertation was the first scholarly examination of the revolt against Díaz. Beneath the myriad charts and tables that filled the book lay a rather simple thesis: the Mexican Revolution was a struggle of oppressed peasants for social justice; it was "democratic and popular"; and it "has freed approximately one-half of the rural population from serfdom." The access of the rural poor to land, Tannenbaum insisted, was the fundamental demand of the revolution and a requisite for social peace in Mexico.[26]

Therefore, when Tannenbaum joined Embree, Alexander, and the other southern liberals at Peabody's Lake George conference in July 1934, he brought a distinctly Mexican perspective on agrarian politics. Over several days, the dozen or so reformers discussed the deepening crisis of the rural US South and proposed possible courses of action. Of the many distinguished guests, Embree and Alexander were most taken by Tannenbaum. Embree had long been fascinated with the Mexican Revolution, especially after spending three weeks in Mexico during 1928.[27] Alexander, too, grew captivated by Tannenbaum's knowledge of "another kind of agrarian problem that wasn't altogether foreign to this one here in the South." It was not long before the two told Tannenbaum that "we'd like to hire you to go South in your own way. If you've looked at Mexico, land reform, and rural poverty ... we want you to go ... with your background of experience in looking at that sort of thing in other countries, and tell us what you see."[28] They offered Tannenbaum $500 to tour the cotton South, and then interpret his observations "dramatically and strikingly" in a short volume meant for a popular audience. Second and most important, they asked him to write a policy proposal that they hoped to present before the USDA. Tannenbaum wholeheartedly accepted.[29]

That winter, Tannenbaum crisscrossed the Southeast in his automobile. Beginning in Washington, DC, he drove to Nashville and then on to the Mississippi Delta, southeastern Arkansas, Memphis, and finally Atlanta, investigating public schools, plantations, and universities along the way. When Tannenbaum met with Alexander in Atlanta, his last stop after two weeks on the road, Alexander remembered that the young researcher was stunned by what he had seen. The old tenancy system has "collapsed," Tannenbaum declared. "It calls for long-time heroic treatment.... You've got to do something about it, and this New Deal's got to do something about it."[30]

In diagnosing a solution to the southern rural crisis, Tannenbaum predictably drew on his prior experiences with Mexican agrarismo. Particularly, he looked toward the Constitution of 1917, which provided the revolutionary mandate for a national program of agrarian reform. Article 27, concerning land tenure, granted the government power to expropriate private land and deed it to villagers in the form of ejidos, state-owned plots to be worked either individually or cooperatively, but not leased or sold to others. Ejidatarios—those cultivating the land reform plots—would also benefit from government loans, irrigation, and agricultural education. Article 27 was the fruit of the radical Zapatista wing of the Mexican Revolution, and as a blueprint for rural social justice, it was unparalleled in the history of the Western Hemisphere. Having seen the Constitution cautiously applied in Mexico during the 1920s, Tannenbaum had a deeply romantic understanding of it. In his doctoral thesis, he described Article 27 as "one of the great political documents that has appeared in the last two decades."[31]

It was thus no surprise that echoes of Article 27 resonated in Tannenbaum's proposal to the southern liberals. Writing to Alexander in late 1934, Tannenbaum argued that to counter the "unexpected flood [that] has carried away the narrow foothold [southern tenants] had managed to achieve," reformers must pursue an initially modest program of land reform. Starting in one model county, they would "settle [about] three hundred families in a community with perhaps a half acre of land about each house," and then supply them with "pasture, forest and tillable land." "Agricultural lands," he recommended, "might be turned over to the community" or "given to each family individually." Equally essential to the settlement would be a small school serving as "a community centre where all activities of the community and all public functions could take place."[32] To settle any doubts as to where Tannenbaum's inspiration came from, he simultaneously invited Embree to travel with him in Mexico. While Embree found the invitation "alluring," it is uncertain whether he went to Mexico that year.[33]

Having convinced his southern allies of the necessity of agrarian reform, in December 1934 Tannenbaum distilled his vision into a formal proposal to present to the Roosevelt government. Titled "A Program to Develop a New System of Rural Land Tenure," the twelve-page document suggested a profound shift in how the US state should govern its countryside. To combat the "abnormal and unsocial aspects of the system of land tenure" in the South, the federal government would create an independent agency dedicated to land reform. Endowed with $300 million per year, that agency would purchase land held by insurance companies and federal land banks in addition to acreage "held by private landlords, particularly lands where the landlord function is not [serving] an adequately social purpose." When such land was distributed to worthy tenants, it would "insure reasonable stability of occupancy of those farmers who are willing to work and save." Perhaps most powerful, however, was Tannenbaum's declaration on the first page of the proposal: "Most civilized nations of the world have long since developed far-reaching measures for the amelioration of conditions of land tenure. Recently, our neighbor to the south has converted its peons into peasant proprietors. We have done nothing in the United States."[34]

Alexander and Embree decided that with his base at Washington's Brookings Institution, Tannenbaum was the best candidate to collaborate with the USDA and push Congress for legislation. Increasing his salary, they hired Tannenbaum for an additional eight months for "conferences with government officials," which would begin a long relationship between the young scholar and the agrarian New Deal.[35] Just before Christmas 1934, Tannenbaum had his first meeting with Paul H. Appleby, the assistant to Secretary of Agriculture Henry A. Wallace, and then with Chester C. Davis, the administrator of the AAA, to discuss Tannenbaum's "proposal for a comprehensive land distribution program." Tannenbaum claimed that both men were enthusiastic about his program, though it is rather unlikely that Davis, as a staunch conservative, would have approved of Tannenbaum's vision had he known the full extent of it.[36] Nevertheless, both men encouraged

Tannenbaum to prepare a shorter, simplified draft of his proposal for circulation in the department. Tannenbaum did so within a few days, slightly moderating his proposal. Likely anticipating charges of radicalism, he cut any direct references to Mexico or plans to purchase private lands, but kept intact all else. In order to secure "the conversion of the tenant and sharecropper, and those recently set afloat, into an independent small landowning agriculturalist," they would be sold federal land that had formerly been held by insurance companies and the government land banks. As in Mexico's Article 27, Tannenbaum's implicit model, that land could not be resold, mortgaged, or placed under lien "to any person other than the Federal corporation set up to carry out this program."[37]

With the pressure building, Embree joined Tannenbaum in Washington, DC, and on January 8, 1935, they met with Secretary Wallace and his staff for the first time. The USDA chief suggested that Embree and Tannenbaum adopt a Senate sponsor to present their proposal as a bill in Congress, and on the afternoon of January 9, Tannenbaum met with Senator John H. Bankhead Jr. of Alabama. Bankhead was a moderate Democrat who had been active in his support for New Deal legislation, but was also a firm opponent of antilynching bills and other civil rights measures. Yet Bankhead was coming to realize that by the 1930s, most sharecroppers and tenants were white, rather than black, which to the senator justified class-based action versus the usual race-baiting.[38] When approached by Tannenbaum in early January, Bankhead was surprisingly receptive. Tannenbaum, Alexander, Embree, and the black sociologist Charles S. Johnson of Fisk University wrote the blueprint for Bankhead's bill in the next week, titled "Rehomesteading on Small Farms," which retained Tannenbaum's framework for land reform based on government distribution of underutilized land.[39] On February 11, Bankhead introduced Senate Bill S.1800, the Farm Tenant Homes Act, to create a federal agency under the control of the USDA to purchase and resell land. The bill mirrored the recommendations of Tannenbaum's team and sought to promote "a democratic system of land tenure ... in accordance with the example of many other civilized countries."[40]

With the tenancy bill before Congress, Tannenbaum proved to be an unusually adept political negotiator. In addition to his constant meetings with the USDA leadership through winter and spring 1935, Tannenbaum entered the public sphere as a proponent of the bill he had played such a decisive role in writing.[41] In a letter to the editor of the *New Republic*, Tannenbaum boldly asserted that the Bankhead bill would "make possible the break-up of the plantation system in the South."[42] He also started assembling a personal network of supporters for the bill. From his close relations with the New York labor movement twenty years earlier, Tannenbaum earned the bill supporters in the American Federation of Labor.[43] Yet acknowledging contemporary US perceptions of revolutionary Mexico as radical or chaotic, he eschewed any direct references to that nation as a source of inspiration. When Tannenbaum publicly employed global comparisons, he relied on the safer examples of Denmark and Ireland, but such references were purely a political ploy. He had little interest in or knowledge of western Europe, and was most fascinated with the Mexican case.[44]

With Tannenbaum preoccupied with the logistics of passing the Bankhead bill, Embree, Alexander, and Johnson decided themselves to write the short volume that Tannenbaum had originally undertaken. Working from an outline prepared by Tannenbaum, the three reformers digested the current crisis in the US South and the possible solutions to it. Their study, published in 1935 as *The Collapse of Cotton Tenancy*, was a watershed account that detailed the damage done by the AAA in the Cotton Belt. Their solution lay with Tannenbaum and Bankhead's bill: "The pressing needs of the millions of tenants" can only be met by a "general wide-scale distribution of lands ... conducted in unified and carefully directed types of communities." Like Tannenbaum, the authors cast the crisis in global terms. In the book's last paragraph, Johnson, Embree, and Alexander declared, "Most civilized nations of the world long ago faced the problem of tenancy.... Denmark systematically abolished tenancy completely, Ireland and Germany and Mexico have made drastic reforms." In contrast to the safer comparisons with western Europe, Mexico certainly stood out as a non-Western revolutionary nation.[45]

In Washington, DC, and beyond, the book made a tremendous splash. Johnson gave a copy to Eleanor Roosevelt, who placed the book on her husband's bedside table and insisted he read it. The president was so moved by the slender volume that he told Secretary of Agriculture Wallace, "Those fellows wrote the best book that has been written on Southern Agriculture." Selling thousands of copies and stimulating a lively debate, *Collapse of Cotton Tenancy* generated the very publicity that Alexander had hoped for at the outset of the project.[46] Combined with Tannenbaum's political successes in Washington, the book's prominence gave a major boost to the Bankhead bill, which passed the Senate on June 24, 1935.[47] To the Rosenwald team, the bill's passage was a milestone. Embree immediately congratulated Tannenbaum on his "brilliant leadership" and their "great victory."[48] Euphoric with their success, Tannenbaum boasted that the bill was "assured of passage, especially if we can keep it alive in the White House."[49]

Yet in spite of his sympathetic rhetoric, President Roosevelt was not yet committed to taking political risks for poor white and black tenants—a constituency that had little political clout in Washington. The president's attention to rural affairs at the time was dominated by his recent creation of the Resettlement Administration, an independent agency that was the brainchild of his agricultural adviser, Rexford Tugwell. The Bankhead bill, therefore, with little support from above and plenty of opposition from conservatives, was not even raised for debate in the House before Congress adjourned on August 26.[50] As a conciliatory gesture, Tugwell asked Alexander to join him as the second in command of the nascent Resettlement Administration. Alexander and Tannenbaum agreed that while they waited for direct action on their bill, Tugwell's agency would serve as a temporary medium for achieving the same results. Alexander pleaded for Tannenbaum to join him in the Resettlement Administration: "I don't know just how I will get along without you," he wrote to the young scholar.[51] Yet Tannenbaum was uncertain whether he wanted to compromise by joining a government agency other than the one he hoped to create himself. Having received a fellowship from the Guggenheim Foundation, he decided instead to return to Mexico that summer for an extended trip.[52]

Throughout 1936, from their different vantage points, the team of reformers continued to work for the rescue of the Bankhead bill, which remained buried in the Agriculture Committee of the House of Representatives. From within the Resettlement Administration, Alexander chafed under Tugwell's vision for the US countryside, which was far less sympathetic toward small-scale agriculture.[53] Tannenbaum, who by 1936 had begun teaching at Columbia University, nevertheless assured Alexander that "[you can] count on me for the Bankhead Bill for every bit of usefulness in me."[54] But Tannenbaum grew frustrated with the lack of support from Roosevelt, Bankhead, and Representative J. Marvin Jones of Texas, who was responsible for the bill's future in the House. In an unusually angry letter to Bankhead in February 1936, Tannenbaum fumed that if the Roosevelt administration did not work toward the passage of their bill, the president would be "faced with the charge that the New Deal had neglected to do anything for those who are least among us."[55]

To Tannenbaum, the United States' failure to address the injustices of land tenure seemed especially galling when contrasted with Mexico, which was in 1936 undergoing a radical renaissance. Lázaro Cárdenas had won the presidency in 1934 with his humble charisma and promises to fulfill the long-postponed social reforms of the 1917 Constitution. After declaring his independence from party bosses in 1935, Cárdenas invested all his political capital into realizing that pledge. The next three years were a whirlwind of legislative action, without precedent in Mexican history. The president expanded the rights of organized labor in ways that paralleled Roosevelt's Wagner Act of 1935; the revolutionary state vastly enlarged its rural education and school-building program. But most pivotal was the federal expropriation of nearly fifty million acres of land for use by cooperative ejidos, including some of the most productive irrigated acres in the nation. To accompany land grants, the president unveiled plans for a vast federal infrastructure to support ejido cultivators' future harvests. Though Cárdenas's motives were not purely altruistic, as he primarily wanted to consolidate one-party power and defuse more radical alternatives, his season of reform marked a milestone in Mexico's revolutionary project. By the last years of the decade, Cárdenas had attained political immortality among many humble Mexicans.[56]

Although Tannenbaum could hardly have predicted it in early 1936, the New Deal too was on the cusp of a major political reorientation. That fall, Roosevelt moved dramatically leftward in his rhetoric to counter political opponents like Huey Long and Father Charles Coughlin, and his reinvention was only accelerated by the presidential election of that November. After achieving one of the largest electoral landslides in US history, Roosevelt interpreted his popularity as a mandate on the New Deal and boldly pushed to expand its reach. Projects that had earlier been postponed or neglected because of their political sensitivity now returned to the table.[57] At the USDA, the renaissance of November 1936 was keenly felt. Shortly after the election, Secretary of Agriculture Wallace declared that the USDA was entering a "newer phase of agricultural development," which would target "that growing part of our farm population which during the past has been submerged in poverty."[58] Farm tenancy and land reform, controversial topics that had been marginalized in earlier years, were now granted high priority.

Beyond Washington, the intellectual and political climate for agrarian reform also grew far more hospitable. If Tannenbaum, Embree, Alexander, and Bankhead had begun their crusade against tenancy in 1934 as voices in the wilderness, by 1937 they had been joined by a wide chorus demanding similar action. The unionization drives of the STFU, along with their much-publicized violent repression, had earned the cause new allies. Likewise, pressure from publicly engaged intellectuals fostered a broader critique of the South's rural status quo. During the mid-1930s, a cadre of influential sociologists and geographers, mostly anchored at the University of North Carolina, penned scathing indictments of the plantation system such as Rupert B. Vance's *How the Other Half Is Housed* (1936), Arthur F. Raper's *Preface to Peasantry* (1936), Charles S. Johnson's *Shadow of the Plantation* (1934), and Howard Odum's especially influential *Southern Regions of the United States* (1936). Read and cited widely, these books placed tenancy and its ills at the center of regional and national discourse.[59]

Encouraged by the supportive political and intellectual climate of the day, President Roosevelt himself began to assist in the popular swell toward action on the farm tenancy problem. First, he oversaw the transfer of Tugwell's independent and increasingly unpopular Resettlement Administration to the USDA, where it would be under Wallace's oversight. When Tugwell resigned, Roosevelt made Will Alexander chief of the Resettlement Administration.[60] Then, in November 1936, he formed the President's Committee on Farm Tenancy and ordered its members to submit a report by February 1, 1937, on a "long-term program of action to alleviate the shortcomings of our farm tenancy system."[61] New Deal scholar Jess Gilbert has characterized that report as "one of the most radical official documents ever issued by the U.S. Government."[62] The report blended statistical data on the dramatic rise of tenancy and evictions with an emotional plea for federal action. Like the earlier *Collapse of Cotton Tenancy*, the committee's conclusions included an extended discussion of how other nations had approached rural inequality. Alongside references to programs in western Europe was an analysis of "recent land reforms in Mexico," detailing the revolutionary state's formalization of land redistribution through Article 27 of its constitution.[63]

To Tannenbaum and his allies, who had been promoting agrarian reform for years, this sudden federal commitment was exhilarating. Sending Tannenbaum a copy of the president's committee report in early March 1937, Alexander cheered, "The prospects for a real program are better than they have been at any time."[64] He was not wrong. With a boost from new Washington allies, the Bankhead-Jones Farm Tenant Act of 1937 passed the House of Representatives on June 29 by a wide margin. On July 22, President Roosevelt signed the bill, creating the FSA, which absorbed the Resettlement Administration but kept Alexander as its chief.[65] While the final act structuring the FSA was more moderate than the original proposal that Tannenbaum had presented to the USDA in early 1935, it retained a great deal. The law authorized the FSA to purchase land held by private banks, insurance companies, and federal land banks, and resell it at low cost with modest interest rates to tenants who qualified. As Tannenbaum had hoped, access to land was accompanied by federal guidance on how and what to plant, with the aim of ending the cycle of soil exploitation that had characterized tenant farming.[66]

Alexander, Embree, Johnson, and Tannenbaum were understandably elated when hearing news of the bill's passage. "In this legislation we have gone a long way," exulted Alexander to Tannenbaum. "The germ of it I think started in your mind, and when I found that it finally passed I wished that you were here so that we might have a drink and discuss the next war." Their satisfaction in seeing the bill passed, however, was somewhat dampened by the many compromises that had been required to make it palatable to a wider political audience. "The bill is not all that I think we should have," Alexander admitted to Tannenbaum, but it was still more than they expected "when we wrote the original memorandum in my house in Atlanta."[67]

In Mexico, where inspiration for the bill had originated, curious journalists and bureaucrats observed the US government's tentative steps toward land reform. Two days after Roosevelt created the FSA, Mexico City newspaper *El Nacional* printed an article titled "The Situation of the North American Campesino." After providing a brief sketch of "the lands of cotton, where tenancy has become a social cancer in the past decades," the article pointed readers to the recent efforts of the US federal government to overcome this "hopeless situation."[68] Yet other Mexican observers, especially those within the Cardenista government, saw the US federal reorientation toward agrarian issues as an empty gesture. The Mexican ambassador in Washington, Francisco Castillo Nájera, privately observed that the New Deal's rural reform program only sought "to augment the ranks of the rural petit bourgeoisie." While acknowledging that "this is the first time that a president of the United States has interested himself concretely in this aspect of the US agrarian situation," Castillo Nájera pessimistically noted that there was no reference in the president's committee report of January 1937 to "any form of agricultural collectivization."[69]

Within the United States, too, many who had been involved in the struggle for tenant legislation and rural reform were equally disappointed. In their eyes, the program was too small and too timid. Tugwell, the architect of the Resettlement Administration and still a close adviser to Roosevelt despite a temporary exit from public affairs, also viewed the creation of the FSA as more of a compromise than a victory. "It really is too bad that the tenant bill as it passed allowed nothing for communal and cooperative activities," he wrote to Roosevelt in the immediate aftermath of Bankhead-Jones's passage. Yet Tugwell's judgment was in direct relation to another program that he was intently following. "I shall have to go to Mexico if I am to see the aims of the Resettlement Administration carried out," he proclaimed in the same letter. "Do you see what Cárdenas does to the big farmers [who] object to the confiscation of their estates?"[70]

In comparison with the agrarian campaign then being intensified in Mexico by Cárdenas, the FSA, as Tugwell and Castillo Nájera correctly observed, was strikingly unambitious. Yet in the context of US politics, it nevertheless marked a dramatic departure. The FSA represented both a rhetorical and a real attack on rural poverty in the United States, particularly in the US South. Under the leadership of Alexander and then C. B. Baldwin, the FSA converted thousands of tenants and sharecroppers into small landowners, and endowed them with credit and basic technologies. Unlike the AAA, the FSA also offered its promises to black southerners, though it was decidedly slow in their fulfillment. Numerous scholars in the last generation have rediscovered these achievements and celebrate the FSA as representing a much more radical New Deal. Jess Gilbert has described the "radical reformist" impulses of the FSA, while Clifford Kuhn has demonstrated how the FSA's actions in one Georgia county "challenged local racial etiquette," and brought poor farmers "real, concrete improvement in their diet and standard of living."[71]

Equally captivating, between 1937 and 1943, when the FSA achieved its greatest successes, its leadership continued to keep a close eye on Mexico's agrarian experiment. In 1942, the agency commissioned a consultant to visit ejido farms in northern Mexico, "where similar enterprises [to the FSA] are being carried on for the benefits of farmers of low income."[72] FSA chief Baldwin—Alexander's successor—himself visited Mexico in spring 1942, where he toured several cooperative agricultural settlements. While he critically observed—with some racially inflected disdain—that "the Indians have apparently been turned loose without adequate credit or guidance," he did believe that "we could also learn much from their experience with ejidos."[73]

Nonetheless, the FSA departed from both the Mexican effort and what its drafters had originally hoped for. Tannenbaum and his allies had begun their crusade against tenancy by seeking to grant land to those who tilled the soil, parroting proponents of agrarismo in Mexico. By the time the FSA was having its greatest impact, however, during the early 1940s, the original emphasis on land and independence had been shunted to the side. Likewise, there is growing proof that the FSA was far less successful than some of its recent scholarly champions suggest. As one historian has demonstrated, most of the agency's resources went toward supervised credit programs, which fostered dependence as much as independence and largely benefited white tenants. In another's telling, the FSA was far less concerned with land or credit, but was instead motivated by a paternalist attempt to remake "cultures of poverty" in the rural United States, wherein planners saw structural and economic limitations as secondary to cultural obstacles. Even more damning is evidence that the FSA frequently evicted black tenants to create all-white client enclaves. Similarly, only a few thousand family farms benefited from the FSA's credit and land programs—a drop in the bucket considering the millions that needed assistance most. Following these bleak interpretations, it is easy to conclude that the FSA did little to challenge the status quo.[74]

Yet if that was entirely true, it is difficult to explain the vicious opposition of the US southern planter class to the FSA. Oscar Johnston of the National Cotton Council was not alone in his fiery condemnation of the FSA as a "giant bureaucracy" in pursuit of "a philosophy of state land socialism."[75] Indeed, Johnston and his allies fought tooth and nail to neutralize and dismantle the agency, which they ultimately succeeded in doing by 1943. Federal rhetoric, as it turns out, matters. But if the FSA failed to establish a secure and contented peasantry in the Cotton Belt, it did have other far-reaching effects. It played a significant role in convincing poor white and black southerners that the party of Roosevelt was their ally, aiding in the construction of a political coalition that defined much of the twentieth century. The FSA's empty promises of economic democracy and racial cooperation, while unfulfilled in its lifetime, were recalled and renewed during Lyndon B. Johnson's Great Society. There is also growing evidence that the African American families that received land from FSA programs would later become vanguards in the push for black civil rights during the 1950s and

1960s.[76] As long as these dilemmas are unresolved, historians will return to the heady days of the FSA and its quixotic challenge to the plantation complex. And without looking toward Mexico, it would be impossible to understand its origins and ideology.

Still, it was not only New Deal bureaucrats who looked to Mexico for inspiration. Groups beyond the halls of government and reformers with more radical aspirations for agrarian change likewise followed political currents south of the border. Next, I examine how such observations impacted one especially influential advocate for rural social justice.

THE STFU IN LA LAGUNA

Not long before Tannenbaum made his automobile trip across the cotton South, black and white landless farmers in Tyronza, Arkansas, convened to form the STFU in summer 1934. Furious at planters and complicit bureaucrats over their exclusion from federal aid, Arkansas tenants and sharecroppers united to fight for a fair share of New Deal relief and "Land for the Landless," their unifying slogan. Two white men who had long been active within the Socialist Party of America, H. L. Mitchell and Howard Kester, rose to the leadership of the organization, although their radical beliefs did not always reflect its rank and file. Over the course of the next few years, the STFU built a formidable reputation across the cotton South as it organized strikes to raise wages for cotton pickers. Its leadership also garnered national publicity when planters mercilessly attempted to crush their union with brute force. To many sympathetic observers, the biracial union presented an unprecedented challenge to the South's agrarian power structure. In reality, however, its problems were manifold. Even beyond the external challenges posed by its powerful enemies, internal racial prejudice and ineffective organization fractured the STFU, and many of its early victories were often more symbolic than real.[77]

Nevertheless, the public support generated by the union likely pushed the White House to reconsider rural issues after the election of 1936. But ironically, among the STFU leadership, Roosevelt's reelection was no cause for celebration, as many had supported the Socialist Party candidate Norman Thomas. Especially dismayed was Clarence Senior, a longtime STFU collaborator who had served as Thomas's campaign manager that year. Senior was a young white Missourian, and saw in the 1930s a tangible opportunity for political revolution in the United States. Roosevelt's landslide reelection, coupled with a string of recent setbacks for the STFU, left Senior bitter. He wrote to union head Mitchell a month after the 1936 election to express his frustration. "I am going to Mexico," he told Mitchell, "at least for a couple of months, because I need a real change of climate."[78] Like Tannenbaum a decade earlier, Senior saw in Mexico the opportunity to witness social reforms impossible in the United States.

Mitchell, who had long been following Mexico's evolving experiment with agrarian reform, eagerly embraced Senior's planned trip. He particularly encouraged him to visit the northern cotton-growing region of La Laguna, where "some 1,500,000 acres of cotton lands have been taken over by the Cárdenas government and turned over to the cotton workers." Spanning the states of Coahuila and Durango, La Laguna was probably the most important national showcase of Cárdenas's agrarian experiment. In September 1936, not long before Senior contemplated his trip, a successful strike by cotton pickers had brought the president into the region to defuse a potentially bloody confrontation. Cárdenas's unprecedented response would shock Mexico's landed elite. Whereas much of the land redistributed prior to 1936 was of little economic value, in La Laguna the president decisively expropriated thousands of acres of the most valuable irrigated cropland in Mexico. Cárdenas further broke precedent by announcing that La Laguna's cotton lands would be farmed collectively rather than by individual ejidatarios. The STFU's leadership, predictably, grew captivated with the region's progress. "We would greatly appreciate it if you could get facts, etc. about this program," wrote Mitchell to Senior, "and let us have a first hand report."[79]

Mitchell's encouragement fueled Senior's enthusiasm. "From what I can see so far [the Mexican land reform program] looks more like the Bankhead bill than anything else," he told Mitchell, tying Tannenbaum's legislation—then before consideration in the House of Representatives—to Cárdenas's experiment. Indeed, like Tannenbaum, Senior and Mitchell viewed what was happening in Mexico as a potential vehicle for advancing their own political interests in the US South. Therefore, Senior gladly accepted Mitchell's invitation to travel as a representative of the STFU in La Laguna. He suggested that if he found the project as fascinating as he expected, he would write and publish "a comparison of [US] sharecropper conditions with the conditions of the cotton workers in the Laguna region."[80] Mitchell agreed. "Surely a story about the cotton workers of Mexico contrasted with our people ought to be timely," Mitchell told Senior, writing his contacts in La Laguna to inform them of Senior's upcoming voyage.[81]

In spring 1939, Senior arrived by rail in Torreón, Coahuila, the Laguna region's largest urban center, three hundred miles from the Texas border. Beyond his railcar window, he would have seen vast cotton plantations stretching between the Nazas and Aguanaval Rivers—streams that fed an intricate system of irrigation canals that brought life to the dry valley. La Laguna had been the site of extensive capital investment since the late nineteenth century, when foreign and Mexican investors sought to build a cotton kingdom not unlike that of the Gulf South. One US company had even tried to import a large African American labor force during the 1890s, but a smallpox outbreak sent survivors fleeing back to Alabama. In the early years of the revolution, the region's large landowners had successfully dodged threats of land redistribution. But with the ascent of Cárdenas and the militarization of the region's cotton pickers, La Laguna's hacendados faced a serious challenge, climaxing in the 1936 subdivision of the zone's plantations and distribution to resident laborers. Accompanying land grants was a vast, government-directed plan of cooperative and collective cultivation, along with inexpensive loans through the National Bank of Ejidal Credit. Yet rather than bolstering subsistence farming, Cárdenas envisioned La Laguna's land redistribution as a stepping-stone to commercial production by united smallholders—creating "haciendas without hacendados," as the contemporary saying went.[82]

Senior, predictably, was astounded when he arrived in La Laguna. He quickly became a fixture in Torreón, spending his days in conversation with government agents and workers, touring the region's cotton farms, and visiting schools. His weeks there turned into months, as he bounced back and forth between La Laguna and a new apartment in Mexico City. La Laguna "is one of the most thrilling spots in the world to anyone who wants to see a new world built on release from slavery," he gushed to STFU organizer J. R. Butler. "Most of the problems are just about the same thing one runs into in the South."[83] Senior even felt compelled to write to Cárdenas about the solidarity that La Laguna inspired. "Here [in the United States] we are fighting arm in arm for the resolution of agrarian problems very similar to those in Mexico," he told the Mexican president in summer 1938. "Our 'sharecroppers' are your *peones acasillados* [resident wage laborers]."[84] While simplifying questions of class identity between the two regions, Senior saw deep commonalities in their rural struggles.

Above all, Senior wanted his US southern colleagues to see La Laguna with their own eyes. Therefore, in spring 1939, he invited dozens of activists concerned with the plight of the southern sharecropper to a conference in Mexico's premier cotton district. "We might utilize the current interest in southern affairs and in Mexico," proposed Senior, "to secure some consideration of our approach to the solution of human problems connected with a cotton economy." As he envisioned it, over the course of a week, US visitors would tour La Laguna and ponder "what has been done in the cotton collective farm region in the light of problems of the south and the New Deal's attempts to solve them." His first invitees were Mitchell and the leadership of the STFU, but Senior also approached southern academics, farm leaders, and even the administrative staff of the FSA. With the cooperation of Mexico's National Bank of Ejidal Credit, Senior planned sessions for the first week of July 1939. The conference was titled, with intentional irony, Forty Acres and a Mule: Cooperative-Collective Farming.[85]

Particularly keen to attend was STFU chief Mitchell. In June 1939, along with Farish Betton, the African American vice president of the union, Mitchell traveled from Memphis to Torreón by rail. Arriving, they found themselves in a land that "reminds one of the rich fertile lowland along the Mississippi River. Cotton grows just as high as in Eastern Arkansas." Absentee landlords in La Laguna, they noted, once held land there "just as they own the cotton plantations of Eastern Arkansas," and the tillers of its soil were once "exploited and without hope as were Arkansas sharecroppers." During the first five days of July, alongside Senior and two dozen other attendees, Mitchell and Betton toured ejido farms, met with workers, and inspected fields of cotton. They heard speeches on the history of the revolution and importance of the Mexican Constitution's Article 27. On the last day, they helped lay the cornerstone of a new schoolhouse at the ejido San Tomás, joining with the crowd for a rendition of the "Corrido del Agrarista," or "Song of the Agrarian."[86] Mexican officials in Torreón regarded the US visitors with respectful curiosity. One regional PNR operative—believing mistakenly that the "Union of Campesino Sharecroppers of the South" were representatives of the US government—translated the union's report and sent it to Cárdenas, arguing that the visit revealed "the interest which the US government has always had in following, step by step, the revolutionary movement in this region."[87]

Deeply moved by the experience, Mitchell and Betton reflected on the meaning of their visit on the way back to Memphis. "The government of the United States," both agreed, "has not been as responsive to the plight of the sharecroppers as the Mexican government in its handling of the Mexican peasant problems." Likewise, "the Farm Security Administration in the United States might well take some lessons from the National [Ejidal] Credit Bank in Mexico." While Mitchell and Betton did "not believe that we can work out our own problems just as the Mexican farmers are doing," the land reform project suggested to them possible avenues in crafting policy for the future. They, too, "should consider a legislative program of expropriating our absentee landlords by taxation on large individual holdings.... When our Union is built strong enough to do this then we, who have plenty of rich, fertile land and no deserts to contend with, can show the Mexican farmers something."[88]

Their union, though, would never be "built strong enough" to make that demonstration possible. Increasingly seeing their political power eroded by a sense that the New Deal was addressing rural inequality, the STFU would never regain its former position of national influence. In the red-baiting that followed World War II, conservatives erased the STFU from national memory. Yet Senior remained in Mexico for several years, and would host three more La Laguna conferences during the summers of 1940, 1941, and

1942. The year after Mitchell and Betton came to Torreón, Senior published a book on the region titled *Democracy Comes to a Cotton Kingdom: The Story of Mexico's La Laguna*, in which he boldly claimed that La Laguna's success "will not only hold aloft a torch for the millions of landless peasants in all the Latin American countries, but will also shed light on the sharecropper and tenant problem of the United States."[89]

The success of La Laguna's experiment was questionable, however. While the region continued to produce cotton wealth for some time, and served as a prominent showcase for the possibilities of marrying irrigation and mechanization to socially conscious land use planning, its recipe for success was ultimately unsustainable. Historian Mikael Wolfe has demonstrated that the Mexican state's decision to hitch rural social justice to dam building and cheap irrigation in La Laguna was a shortsighted solution to far deeper economic and environmental problems. Redistributing water, state planners found, was even more difficult than redistributing land, and natural ecosystems did not respond predictably to state visions of control. Indeed, the dams completed during the 1940s upset the fragile ecology that had made the region productive. As excessive irrigation from the water table rapidly increased soil salinity, the ejidatarios of La Laguna, like millions of others across Mexico in the 1950s and 1960s, abandoned their once-promising plots.[90]

While it displayed a striking moment of pan-American leftist solidarity, the STFU's engagement with La Laguna in 1939 thus would not significantly impact policy in either nation. Yet Mitchell, Betton, and Senior were only a handful of the agrarian intellectuals who traveled to Mexico in the late 1930s and early 1940s. Other US nationals who crossed the border were far better placed within the New Deal political machine, and such voyages would reshape their thinking on agricultural and agrarian reform.

NEW DEAL BUREAUCRATS IN CÁRDENAS'S MEXICO

When Roosevelt entered the White House in 1933, he brought with him a diverse group of advisers that would become the intellectual architects of the New Deal. These "Brain Trusters"—people like Frances Perkins, Adolf Berle, Harry Hopkins, and Harold Ickes, along with dozens of other lesser-known bureaucrats—represented a dramatically different approach to policy making than previous administrations. Critical of unbridled laissez-faire economics, they sought to merge state regulation with the principles of social and economic science in forging a more equitable and balanced capitalism.[91]

Within the USDA, the social planning impulse was especially strong. Administrators like Henry A. Wallace, Rexford Tugwell, and M. L. Wilson each embodied the Brain Trust's instincts toward scientific rationalization of the messy realities of agriculture and farm life, though they were not mere technocrats. While this liberal wing of the USDA differed in the degrees to which it romanticized the social benefits of rural living and small-scale farming, nearly all the Brain Trusters shared a commitment to reconstructing the US farm economy along more equitable lines. The ideologies of these agrarian intellectuals have been well studied, but few works have examined their persistent internationalism.[92] During the Roosevelt years, many of the USDA's policy architects looked to foreign experiments in rural reform, frequently traveling abroad to witness those results in person. Their geographic imagination and curiosity was wide, and took them across the world, but particularly notable was their fascination with Mexico, the primary non-European source of inspiration.

The USDA's first pilgrim to Mexico was Tugwell, a Columbia University economist who served as undersecretary of agriculture between 1933 and 1935, and then administrator of the Resettlement Administration from 1935 to 1936. Tugwell had earned renown by the early 1930s as a prominent critic of unbridled capitalism and proponent of state intervention in the agricultural sector.[93] Just a few months after being granted control of the Resettlement Administration, Tugwell announced that he would travel to Mexico City accompanied by a team of USDA scientists with the nominal purpose of observing control of the Mexican fruit fly and pink cotton bollworm.[94] Given Tugwell's reputation as a political firebrand and his lack of any training in entomology, the trip's announcement raised eyebrows. When notified of the visit, US ambassador to Mexico Josephus Daniels prodded Tugwell for the true purpose behind his trip, as "no man in public office in the United States can come here unless some particular motive is attributed to him."[95] The Mexican ambassador to Washington, DC, Francisco Castillo Nájera, was similarly aware of the political purposes underlying Tugwell's trip. "I suspect he means to take advantage of his journey to consider the agrarian question," Castillo Nájera wrote the week before Tugwell's visit.[96]

Ambassadors Daniels and Castillo Nájera were, of course, correct. Tugwell was "looking forward to this as a period of rest as well as valuable education," he admitted to Daniels before leaving.[97] In his two weeks spent in Mexico City, Tugwell met with leading figures in the revolutionary ruling party and joined them on inspections of rural communities outside Mexico City. Tugwell clearly delighted in "talk[ing] at length about the common aims" of rural reform in both nations.[98] "I wish you could have seen him last night," Daniels wrote to Agriculture Secretary Wallace, "exchanging views with General [Saturnino] Cedillo, the Minister of Agriculture, and Mr. [Emilio] Portes Gil, President of the Partido Nacional Revolucionario.... They got along famously through an interpreter, and I think they came to the conclusion that much of our New Deal and the Mexican Six-Year Plan have much in common."[99]

Tugwell's 1935 Mexican visit fostered a strong interest in that nation's land reform experiment, and he would continue to advocate for attention to Mexican models during his time in the USDA and beyond. As Cárdenas intensified land redistribution in 1936 and 1937, Tugwell pushed his New Deal colleagues to turn their gaze southward. "I have been much impressed with the way in which Cárdenas has tackled the agrarian problem in Mexico," he wrote USDA chief Wallace in August 1937, and "I think we should keep a close watch on this process for the lessons we may learn."[100] That same month, he mailed a PNR newsletter on land reform in the state of Yucatán to President Roosevelt as a suggestion for planning the strategic approach of the newly created FSA.[101] But perhaps most important in Tugwell's observations of Mexico was his later tenure as the last appointed colonial governor of Puerto Rico—a post he held from 1941 to 1946. In San Juan, Tugwell broke dramatically with his colonial predecessors, engineering a transition to independent government and free elections. He also pioneered a land reform and agricultural diversification program in Puerto Rico that borrowed both from the rural New Deal and Mexico's efforts. Therefore, Tugwell's education in the 1930s would echo across the Caribbean basin in later years.[102]

Tugwell was but one of many in the USDA's leadership who kept a steady eye on Mexico. In December 1938, M. L. Wilson undertook his journey south of the border. Trained in agricultural economics at the University of Wisconsin, Wilson was a prominent advocate of cooperative farming and became one of the New Deal's foremost champions of economic democracy in the countryside. During the 1930s Wilson served as assistant secretary of agriculture, undersecretary of agriculture, and chief of the Subsistence Homesteads Division of the Interior Department, a "back-to-the-land" program for unemployed urbanites.[103] He had also been Tannenbaum's primary USDA ally when drafting the Bankhead tenant bill. Wilson planned his trip to Mexico in preparation for the second Inter-American Conference on Agriculture, and his official mission was to "improv[e] and expan[d] the facilities for the interchange between the interested persons of both countries."[104] Arriving in Mexico City, Wilson met President Cárdenas and his agricultural staff in a public ceremony that demonstrated to the US visitors "Mexico's attempt to establish a collective cultivation of the land," as one Mexican newspaper described the event.[105] Over the course of several days, Wilson and Mexican secretary of agriculture José Parrés discussed the future of Mexican agriculture, weighing the ejido model against that of larger, private farmers.[106]

Perhaps even more so than Tugwell, Wilson was captivated by Mexico and its agrarian revolution. "I am anxious to go back again and make a longer trip," he wrote to a USDA colleague shortly thereafter.[107] To another friend, Wilson remarked, "I realize more than I ever did before what a wonderful country and civilization Mexico has, ... and how [we who] live in the United States should understand it [and] the recent social and economic movements that are taking place."[108] Rather than mere romantic musings, however, such observations moved Wilson to forge a formal bond between the USDA and its Mexican counterpart. On returning to Washington, DC, Wilson proposed a continuing exchange where "policy-forming people in the [US] Department of Agriculture ... spend ... a week or ten days [in Mexico] primarily for studying their history, their culture, and their agriculture." Such US visitors would "endeavor to understand Mexico and help Mexico express herself rather than assume that we must force our ideology and our ideas and institutions upon them."[109] He had no trouble convincing an already-sympathetic Secretary of Agriculture Wallace, and together they lobbied for resources to begin a formal program of US-Mexican agrarian exchange. However, conservative State Department officials were reluctant to begin any such partnership before Cárdenas was out of office.[110]

Ultimately, Wilson had little success in coordinating a formal cooperative exchange with Mexico. Yet he would continue to actively pursue agrarian reform in the United States, and it is likely that his Mexican observations served as an inspiration. Between 1939 and 1942, Wilson led an unprecedented effort within the USDA to realize the New Deal's commitment to a just and equitable countryside, launching an aggressive campaign of land use planning, adult education, and participatory agricultural research. Sociologist Jess Gilbert recently judged Wilson's crusade of those years as "second to none in its promise of transforming rural America into a more egalitarian society, turning it toward a wider distribution of power and resources for common people."[111] During these years, Wilson continued to keep a close eye on Mexico; in 1942, he and Frank Tannenbaum attempted—unsuccessfully—to bring former president Cárdenas to the United States for a tour of New Deal projects.[112] After growing conservatism at home marginalized USDA activists like Wilson, he would join other New Dealers who took their agrarian ideology abroad in the years after World War II. In the late 1940s, Wilson left the United States to work on similar projects in India and Pakistan during the "development" era. The lessons he learned from rural poverty in the 1930s would inspire his firm belief that scientific planning combined with balanced social politics could uplift the most "backward" societies.[113]

The most significant USDA pilgrimage to Mexico, however, came in the last days of the Cárdenas era when Henry A. Wallace, US secretary of agriculture from 1933 to 1940, traveled to central Mexico in December 1940. Wallace is an enigmatic figure, largely forgotten to US popular memory, but in his life are wound up the great contradictions of the twentieth century's rural transformations. Born in Iowa in 1888, Wallace was the scion of a family of agricultural leaders. His grandfather had founded the popular *Wallaces'*

Farmer newspaper, and his father, Henry C. Wallace, had been US secretary of agriculture during the early 1920s. As an introverted young man, Henry A. devoted his time and passion to corn breeding, and in 1926 founded the Hi-Bred Corn Company, the first commercial seed company to develop and sell hybridized corn seed. Rather than a mere pawn of agribusiness, though, Wallace believed that new technologies and increased production could save the small-scale agriculture that he championed, not destroy it.[114]

When Wallace joined Roosevelt's cabinet in 1933, he was initially cautious about the political ideologues that surrounded him, especially Tugwell. He had, after all, come from a Republican family and had voted Republican for most of his life. The initial conservatism of the AAA reflected this. When political conflict flared in 1935 over the fate of sharecroppers within the AAA, pitting the USDA's urban liberals against its southern conservatives, Wallace chose to avoid a confrontation with entrenched interests and fired the younger leftist contingent. But instead of marking the end of Wallace's reformism, the 1935 "purge" was merely a brief nadir. In the later years of the New Deal, Wallace underwent a political reawakening as he confronted rural poverty of a sort far different from the Iowa countryside of his childhood. Wallace's transformative journeys through the plantation South, which he made during 1936 and 1937 with Tugwell as a guide, played a decisive role in that radicalization. His stewardship of activist agencies like the FSA testified to his conversion. By his last years as secretary of agriculture, Wallace had developed a deep sensitivity to the social impacts of technological transformations; he wrote in summer 1940 that agricultural development should be "putting people first and machines and land second and third."[115]

Wallace had also, for many years, cultivated a deep interest in Latin America. That curiosity grew initially from his fascination with corn, a plant native to Mexico, and the indigenous peoples who had domesticated it. But Mexico's revolutionary agrarian program also piqued Wallace's interest, and in 1937 Wallace suggested that the newly formed FSA study "what they are doing in Mexico" before embarking on a US program.[116] During the last years of the 1930s, these early interests blossomed into a near obsession with all things Hispanophone. In 1939, Wallace organized a regular Spanish-language luncheon for USDA staff to discuss Latin American issues, and within a year he spoke slow but confident Spanish.[117]

Wallace's 1940 visit to Mexico grew from a moment of political transition in both nations. By late 1938, Cárdenas initiated a slow but steady retreat from his most socially activist policies. Land redistribution, after peaking in 1938, began to slow down in the last two years of his presidency. Knowing that his presidency had made many enemies, Cárdenas started to favor stabilization and moderation. That became especially clear when the revolutionary ruling party convened in early 1940 to choose its candidate for the

July election. In a surprise to many, Cárdenas snubbed his predicted successor, the radical Francisco Múgica, in favor of a less-known, middle-of-the-road candidate: Manuel Ávila Camacho, Cárdenas's defense minister. Conservatives, however, were still not satisfied. Juan Andreu Almazán, a northerner who enjoyed broad support among businesspeople and the middle classes, challenged Ávila Camacho as an opposition candidate. When in July Ávila Camacho claimed victory in an undoubtedly undemocratic election, Almazán contested the ruling and promised armed revolt if the government did not recognize his rightful claim by the presidential inauguration on December 1, 1940.[118]

As Mexico's political elite leaned rightward in 1940, the United States leaned toward the left. With his eyes on the developing European war, Roosevelt declared an unprecedented third candidacy for office. The Democrats rallied behind Roosevelt, but conflict erupted in July 1940 when party leaders convened in Chicago to choose Roosevelt's vice presidential candidate. Roosevelt's health was already showing signs of deterioration, and Democratic leaders recognized the importance of the position. Southern conservatives were adamant about placing an ally of theirs on the ticket, as they had grown increasingly at odds with the New Deal's left turn in recent years. But Roosevelt and his allies, bitter toward the southern wing's obstruction of the New Deal, pushed through the nomination of Wallace, the New Deal's secretary of agriculture and one of the chief architects of its agrarian program. The choice, representing the socially activist New Deal at high tide, predictably infuriated conservative Democrats.[119]

After stepping down as secretary of agriculture in September 1940 to campaign with Roosevelt for their November election—which they won by a wide margin—Wallace awaited the January 1941 inauguration. In the meantime, though, he had three months to spend however he liked. With little vacillation Wallace chose to fulfill his long-held dream of Latin American travel. But when Wallace notified Roosevelt of his plans, the president decided to kill two birds with one stone. Concerned about political insecurity in Mexico surrounding the presidential succession, Roosevelt notified an exuberant Wallace that he would be representing the United States at Ávila Camacho's December 1940 inauguration in Mexico City. Wallace's presence, Roosevelt hoped, would signal US support for Cárdenas's party and its candidate as well as making gestures toward pan-American unity. It would be the first visit to Mexico of a major US official since the outbreak of the revolution in 1910. The US press heralded the trip as a historic display of leftist solidarity: Mexico's revolutionary government, wrote the *Washington Post*, had the "fortunate coincidence" of welcoming Wallace, "America's apostle of social experimentation."[120]

Instead of flying or traveling in a large diplomatic caravan, Wallace chose to drive his own car from Washington, DC, to Mexico City, so as to get a

Figure 2.2. Crowds welcoming Henry A. Wallace to Ciudad Victoria, Tamaulipas, November 1940. Courtesy of Getty Images.

better sense of the Mexican countryside. At the border, Ávila Camacho's soon-to-be agriculture secretary—and former Zapatista—Marte R. Gómez joined Wallace, serving as his tour guide. As they drove southward, the two men stopped frequently to speak with farmers, visit ejidal schools, and inspect cornfields, often to the great frustration of schedule-minded State Department coordinators. Gómez insisted that the vice president elect visit El Mante, a showcase collective sugar ejido in Tamaulipas, which deeply impressed Wallace.[121] The December 1 inauguration in Mexico City's National Palace brought together a diverse crowd that epitomized the US-Mexican agrarian exchange of the past decade. Wallace and US ambassador Josephus Daniels discussed farm policy with Cárdenas, Ávila Camacho, and Gómez. Other formal invitees from the US government included Marvin Jones, the Texas representative who had earlier sponsored the Bankhead bill in the House.[122] Also joining them at the National Palace was the ubiquitous Tannenbaum, who had been invited to the inauguration by Cárdenas and was by then an intimate friend of the president.[123] After Ávila Camacho's inaugural address, the US and Mexican guests walked over to the Palacio de Bellas Artes to watch Tomás Escobedo's play "El canción del ejido" (The song of the ejido), which mythologized land redistribution as the crowning achievement of the Mexican Revolution.[124]

Figure 2.3. Henry A. Wallace meets with farmers in Tamazunchale, San Luis Potosí, November 1940. Courtesy of Getty Images.

Following the inauguration, Wallace remained in Mexico for more than a month, trekking across the central states of Michoacán, Jalisco, and Puebla on a personal vacation with his wife. During those weeks, Wallace grew fundamentally convinced that those grappling with rural and agrarian reform in the United States must learn from Mexico's progress. On returning home, he decided to write a series of columns about the visit in *Wallaces' Farmer*, his first since 1933. To thousands of readers, Wallace introduced a country where "for a long time, 98% of the people who worked the land had none of their own." But the recent agrarian experiment had reversed that, and Wallace described how Cárdenas "had broken up the haciendas or big estates and put them under the control of the campesinos or small farmers." Those efforts somewhat paralleled the New Deal, he believed, as the ejidos were "a little bit like self-subsistence farm projects." Yet Wallace was perhaps most impressed by the "hundreds of ejidal schools [that] have been constructed during the last six years," which "will probably do more than any other single thing to determine the productivity of the agriculture and the quality of life in Mexico fifty years hence."[125]

But if Wallace was firmly convinced that more people in the United States needed to learn about Mexico's agrarian reform, he also believed that the New Deal could teach Mexico much in return. Writing to US secretary of state Cordell Hull, Wallace insisted that for "eighty percent of the Mexican people, ... one of the greatest needs is a hard headed, soft hearted [Farm] Security Administration" to provide affordable credit to farmers. Wallace was convinced that "production under the ejidal system would eventually be greater than under the hacienda system," but in 1940, "the average ejidatario produces with his present technology less than the average share cropper in the South." US technical assistance, Wallace believed, might be the key to solving this dilemma. "One of the great foundations in the United States," he told Hull, "could render a great service by setting up a rather small experiment station designed both to discover and demonstrate more efficient methods of growing corn and beans."[126] As chapter 4 will illustrate, this is exactly what the Rockefeller Foundation would undertake in 1943.

Wallace's 1940 journey to Mexico showcased a rising liberal lodestar whose prominence would only grow in the years that followed. While he would not return to the USDA as an agrarian policy maker, as vice president Wallace became the most prominent advocate of an egalitarian US relationship with Latin America as well as a critic of cultural and economic imperialism in the Western Hemisphere. The Second World War, he famously declared, was being fought not to usher in an "American century" but rather a "century of the common man"—a message he repeated frequently during an unprecedented five-week diplomatic tour of Central and South America in 1943. For a US official, Wallace commanded a respect and admiration in Latin America unmatched in the middle of the century. Ultimately, his commitment to economic democracy and global peace would alienate him from the Democratic Party, which he broke with in 1948 to run for president on a platform opposing the escalating Cold War. Yet in charting Wallace's topsy-turvy career, it is crucial to acknowledge the importance of the 1940 voyage to Mexico—his "first love" in Latin America, as he often claimed—which served as a bridge between his domestic and internationalist liberalism.[127]

Tugwell, Wilson, and Wallace—while the most prominent—were not the US government's only pilgrims to Mexico during the heady days of the New Deal. Less renowned bureaucrats in the USDA and other agrarian bureaus, such as Mordecai Ezekiel, Claude Wickard, Paul Appleby, Norman Littell, Hugh Bennett, and John Collier, along with many others, also engaged in such political tourism to Mexico during the Roosevelt years.[128] A decade earlier or a decade later, such journeys would have been exceedingly rare. But at the crossroads of the New Deal and the Plan Sexenal, the parameters of political possibility seemed wider than ever before.

***

The 1930s were a decade when Mexico captured the US imagination in unprecedented ways. At a moment of national crisis and self-doubt, many in the United States looked southward in search of a perceived authenticity and alternatives to industrial modernity. In the decade of the Depression, Mexican folk artists, musicians, and painters found vast new audiences in the so-called Colossus of the North. Diego Rivera and José Clemente Orozco, muralists whose work evoked the radical promises of the Mexican Revolution, would put some of their most influential works to the brush in Detroit, Michigan, and Hanover, New Hampshire. During that turbulent decade the United States fawned over the "enormous vogue of things Mexican," in the words of the *New York Times* in 1933.[129]

Far less known than the decade's cultural exchanges was the south-north traffic in agrarian political strategies. As the US and Mexican governments each inaugurated extraordinary experiments to remake the social, political, and economic fabric of their countrysides, a growing number of hopeful reformers in the United States looked beyond their nation's borders in search of blueprints and inspiration. The comparisons that they made, alongside the journeys they undertook, would profoundly reshape campaigns for rural social justice both within the US government and beyond it. And no part of the United States would be more shaken by that transborder exchange than the cotton South, for in the eyes of cosmopolitan reformers, that region most closely paralleled the rural dilemmas of Mexico and would most benefit from its solutions.

US agrarian pilgrims experienced varying levels of success in translating political projects across national boundaries. The leadership of the STFU, perhaps the most renowned champion of the disfranchised sharecropper, turned toward Mexico in hopes of reinvigorating its campaign, but was unable to incorporate its lessons as the union declined in influence. Yet among the ranks of the New Deal bureaucracy, the gaze toward Mexico would carry greater weight. In Roosevelt's USDA, a cadre of agrarian liberals struggled to reverse that department's emphasis on aiding wealthier, commercial farmers. In looking for inspirations abroad, these liberals turned to the rhetoric and action of Mexican revolutionary *agrarismo*, which after 1934 was undergoing a renaissance of its own. Forgotten by historians, this engagement with the Mexican Revolution played a crucial role in the rural New Deal's radicalization. Many of the USDA's leading policy makers traveled to Mexico during the decade, gauging their own work by what they observed south of the border. But the most tangible fruit of the agrarian exchange was the FSA, widely considered the most aggressively reformist agency of the rural New Deal—and conceived from Tannenbaum's juxtaposition of the US South and revolutionary Mexico.

That the US-Mexico dialogue on rural reform lasted less than a decade may be proof to some that it was an ephemeral moment, a lost window of opportunity that was ultimately shuttered by growing conservatism in both nations. It is difficult to deny that US and Mexican politicians of the 1940s and 1950s turned their backs on both the FSA and the ejido system. In 1946, the same year that the FSA was gutted and renamed the Farmers Home Administration, incoming Mexican president Miguel Alemán signaled a clear departure from the agrarian policies of his predecessors and began to roll back Cárdenas's successes in land reform.

But because of its timing, at the dawn of US postwar expansion into the nascent Third World, the conversation between Mexican and US agrarians had global echoes. Even though the rural New Dealers who staffed agencies like the FSA were increasingly marginalized in US politics by the mid-1940s, in the postwar decades they fanned out across the planet as the shock troops of "development," employees of institutions such as the Food and Agriculture Organization of the United Nations and the US Agency for International Development. Recent scholarship has demonstrated that even as the rural New Deal's most socially conscious and redistributive rural programs perished at home in the wake of World War II and the Red Scare, they lived on abroad. As bright-eyed, idealistic agrarian planners left behind Arkansas, Alabama, and Georgia for the countrysides of Africa, Asia, and Latin America during the Cold War, they doubtless imagined themselves as proud torchbearers of 1930s' US liberalism, exporting the New Deal to new lands. While it is unlikely that many of them realized the models they bore with them were themselves imports, historians can surely recognize the irony.[130]

The conversation between Roosevelt's United States and Cardenista Mexico, however, was characterized by dialogue rather than monologue. Each side spoke *and* listened. Mexican reformers, emboldened by political changes at home and curious about the Roosevelt administration's evolving program of rural reform, eagerly took note of its reach and accomplishments. More often than not such observers looked specifically to the US South, where the stakes for reform were the highest. The following chapter, therefore, will examine the ways that the New Deal's rural social reforms took root in Mexican soil.

Chapter Three

HACIENDAS AND PLANTATIONS
Finding the Agrarian New Deal in Cardenista Mexico

The Rio Grande is not wide and good things of each country
manage to get across the border.

—*US ambassador to Mexico Josephus Daniels, 1937*

By summer 1938, the reformist visions of the agrarian New Deal and Mexico's Plan Sexenal were converging in dramatic ways. Franklin Roosevelt's US Department of Agriculture (USDA) was then entering its most aggressive stage of rural social engineering, while Lázaro Cárdenas could look back at the expropriation and subdivision of millions of acres of land. Not surprisingly, comparisons between the leaders and politics of the two nations grew increasingly frequent in this era. Perhaps no observer better recognized their common struggle than Adolfo Ruiz Cortines, a federal deputy in Mexico City and a rising star in Cárdenas's ruling party who would later become the nation's president in the 1950s. In an *El Universal* editorial in July 1938, Ruiz Cortines assumed that "almost no [Mexican] is unaware that in the United States, a paladin of social justice has tenaciously confronted the gigantic hydra of plutocracy that controls everything there with the merciless dollar sign." But if "Roosevelt has deserved the world's admiration for his great political achievements," Ruiz Cortines insisted that "in our country there also exists another paladin of distributive social justice." That champion was energized by a similar "purpose of social transformation," and he had "forge[d] a strong national identity that we never have had." President Cárdenas, therefore, should be considered "the author of the New Deal in Mexico."[1]

That Ruiz Cortines should measure Cárdenas's accomplishments by reference to US politics—to a Mexican audience, no less—suggests the extent to which extranational comparisons influenced Mexico's reform atmosphere during the radical 1930s. This chapter, like the last, will explore such comparisons and the transfer of political models, particularly for the countryside, across the US-Mexico border. But if previous pages examined the ways that Mexico's agrarian revolution impacted the New Deal's rural campaign, this chapter will analyze traffic on the other side of the highway of political exchange. It will look at how the architects of Cárdenas's land reform closely followed Roosevelt's experimentation in the US countryside, with an emphasis on the cotton South. While Cárdenas is widely considered one of modern Mexico's premier nationalists in his aggressive resistance to the domination of foreign capital, his government's borrowing from the rural New Deal confounds such simple characterizations.

Over the past few generations, there has been vigorous debate and disagreement over the motivations, reach, and consequences of the Cárdenas presidency and especially its agrarian program. Scholars have drawn wildly diverse conclusions about the political transformations of the 1930s, with characterizations of Cardenista reforms ranging from the redemption of the revolution's populist dream to a co-optation and betrayal by corporatist bureaucrats.[2] Yet if scholarship on this contentious era remains divided, nearly all accounts agree that Cárdenas was a nationalist with an agenda restricted to the nation-state. It is only recently that students of the period have begun to acknowledge the global crucible in which Cardenista political reform was forged, through examinations of international Marxist networks, how the Mexican state grappled with world economic depression, and how Mexico sought to broadcast its reforms as a model to other Latin American nations.[3] In specifically considering land reform, though— arguably Cárdenas's most consequential campaign—little is known about the extranational influences that shaped Mexico's agrarian redistribution in the 1930s.[4]

Why has Cárdenas's agrarian program been viewed for so long within a strictly Mexican context? Much of that instinct stems from the land reform's direct linkage to the popular demands of the 1910–17 revolution—demands that were rooted in local conflicts and born from the domestic transformations of Porfirio Díaz's dictatorship. As historian Alan Knight claimed in a recent meditation on Mexico during the global 1930s, the Cardenista agrarian project was "clearly revolutionary and thus peculiar to Mexico."[5] Indeed, Cárdenas himself frequently espoused his reform agenda as a response to Mexico's exceptional revolutionary moment, unique within Latin America and indeed the world. Yet to understand the Cardenista agrarian project solely in terms of expropriation and redistribution conceals the multistage complexity of that campaign. Highly conscious of Mexico's food and fiber needs, Cárdenas did believe that a *reparto de tierras*—distribution of lands—was essential to forging a contented and productive Mexican countryside. But as he saw it, land alone was insufficient; it was to be immediately followed by conservation, irrigation, land use planning, cooperative credit structures, and increasingly scientific cultivation. These programs defined the last years of

Cárdenas's presidency—and those of his successor, Manuel Ávila Camacho—and have been the focus of several recent studies.[6] It was precisely in this latter stage of the agrarian project that Cardenismo was its most cosmopolitan; it was here that Mexican planners sought the experience and suggestions of the United States' agrarian New Deal, with unexpected consequences.

US intellectual and technological models for transforming agriculture and rural life had impacted Mexico long before the 1930s. Social scientists like Robert Redfield, Ruth Benedict, John Dewey, and Franz Boas had exercised a profound influence on Mexican theorizing of indigeneity, rural education, and the future of the peasantry during the 1910s and 1920s.[7] Likewise, politicians and technicians had eagerly borrowed from US agricultural science since the Porfiriato, when Mexican agronomy turned from its traditional French roots toward an admiration of the "modernized" agriculture promoted by the USDA.[8] Nevertheless, these earlier observations were almost exclusively apolitical and technical, engaged with increasing agricultural production and little else. But as the agrarian New Deal launched a wide-scale assault on the cultural, social, and political problems of the US countryside, the volume and tone of the earlier exchange with Mexico would shift dramatically. Acknowledging that a socially conscious leftism inspired the 1930s' USDA, wide swaths of reformers in Mexico—many of whom were sworn nationalists otherwise—capitalized on the political convergence of US and Mexican agrarian experimentation.

Seeking to illustrate the unacknowledged footprints of the rural New Deal on 1930s' agrarismo, this chapter follows two intersecting avenues of exchange. First, it explores how the architects of Mexico's land reform—popular peasant organizations, politicians and bureaucrats, and agronomists and engineers—sought guidance and inspiration in the New Deal's evolving program of rural social transformation. This exchange was at once formal and informal, practical and symbolic. It manifested itself in countless Mexican bureaucratic requests for New Deal publications, circulars, and bulletins, but also in the direct solicitation of US personnel to staff key Cardenista projects. It surfaced in rituals of admiration for the New Deal's progressive leadership and agraristas' political pilgrimages to USDA laboratories of social transformation, located primarily in the US South.

Second, I consider the New Dealer in Mexico whose sympathies and solidarity contributed most significantly to the success of the Cardenista program: the US ambassador to Mexico from 1933 to 1942, Josephus Daniels. Daniels was a paradoxical figure: a North Carolina agrarian populist and simultaneously a renowned white supremacist; a vocal opponent of US imperialism yet the one who had overseen the occupation of Veracruz in 1914 as secretary of the US Navy. Charged with defending US property rights in Mexico during Cárdenas's expropriation campaign, Daniels wielded astounding power over the future of agrarian reform. With a telegram or phone call,

Daniels could have disrupted the path of agrarismo and indeed Mexico's national sovereignty by inviting US military intervention, as had been so common in previous decades when US capital felt the heat of Latin American nationalism. Yet Daniels's steadfast allegiance to the rural New Deal, heightened by his southern regionalism as well as discomfort with tenancy and landlessness in North Carolina, informed an alternate response. The ambassador ultimately proved to be an unexpected champion of land reform and the Mexican campesino, opening avenues of political possibility that Cárdenas was quick to capitalize on. That unspoken compromise was essential to the success of the most transformative land redistribution campaign in the Western Hemisphere.

Agrarismo Looks North

On October 6, 1936, the Liga Nacional Campesina, or National Peasant League, convened in Mexico City to draft a resolution of praise and "warmest congratulations" to a "great statesman." Its meeting came in a year when President Cárdenas had dramatically escalated his agrarian campaign, but the league did not gather to praise its Mexican patron. Its letter was addressed instead to US president Roosevelt and "his 'New Deal,' which has resulted in such great benefit to the proletarian organizations in our Sister Nation." Perhaps responding to Roosevelt's newly aggressive rhetoric on rural poverty, the league expressed its hope that "the millions of votes of our brothers of this class in the United States will result in [his] re-election."[9] When the league handed its resolution to US ambassador Daniels for delivery to Roosevelt, Daniels marveled at "how these people keep up with what is going on in the world and feel that they are a part of all movements to the enlargement of the prosperity of the long forgotten man."[10] Yet rather than a rarity, such border-crossing political allegiances and exchanges would become common during the coinciding years of the New Deal and the Plan Sexenal.

Though the trails of north-south exchange on agricultural and agrarian issues were blazed long before the rise of either Roosevelt or Cárdenas, the realization among Mexican reformers that a seismic shift had occurred in the US government's approach to rural affairs was widespread during the mid-1930s. As the conservative Agricultural Adjustment Administration (AAA) gave way to the Farm Security Administration (FSA) and a reenergized Bureau of Agricultural Economics (BAE), more and more Mexican observers took note of the changing political tides in the United States. Pedro de Alba, a Mexican representative at the Pan American Union in Washington, DC, told Mexican agriculture chief José Parrés in 1938 that the USDA was conducting both a "social and scientific task," and was "one of the departments most in sympathy with Mexico's advances."[11] Mexican ambassador to the United States Francisco Castillo Nájera concluded that "there is a unanimity in the [Roosevelt] cabinet toward a left-wing orientation toward agriculture," emphasizing that "both of the chiefs of the USDA [Henry A. Wallace and M. L. Wilson] are liberals."[12] Not surprisingly, domestic policy makers in Mexico responded quickly to such news. Fernando Foglio Miramontes, Cárdenas's subsecretary of agriculture, wrote to Wilson in 1939 to confess that he took "much interest in the progressive movement of your country in agriculture."[13]

Acknowledging the newly sympathetic climate in Washington, DC, and the dynamic reorientation of US agrarian policy, Cardenista policy makers began studying the New Deal's rural program for elements that might be adapted to their nation. This interest gave rise to a flurry of Mexican requests for publications and literature, particularly in the later Cárdenas years when state planners pondered how credit, housing, irrigation, and agricultural science might bolster recent ejidal grantees. The Instituto Mexicano de Estudios Agrícolas (Mexican Institute for Agricultural Studies) therefore requested information on Alabama senator John Bankhead's "Farmers' Home Act" in summer 1935, while the Confederación Nacional Campesina (National Peasant Confederation)—the newly founded state organization meant to represent rural interests—wrote to the BAE in early 1939 to request "technical, economic, and social information concerning the agricultural population of the United States."[14] But the agency perhaps most alluring to Mexican observers was the FSA, the most aggressively reformist organism of the USDA. Cárdenas himself admitted to being well aware of that agency's "similar experiments for the low-income farmers in the U.S."[15] He was hardly alone: in 1937, the Mexican embassy wrote the FSA leadership to request information on "the building of houses for families of modest income"; in 1941, consular officials sought publications from the agency on "helping needy farm families to become self-supporting."[16]

The top leadership of Cárdenas's ruling party also evidenced an intimate knowledge of the New Deal's rural agenda. In 1937, the party leadership published an unusual propaganda pamphlet aimed at US readers titled *The New Deal and the Six Year Plan*. Written—in English—by Gilberto Flores Muñoz, the party's secretary-general who would later serve as agriculture chief in the 1950s, the volume sought to win US liberal support for Mexico's reform agenda with frequent references to "common social ideals for human betterment." Yet it also revealed Flores Muñoz's close familiarity with Roosevelt's agrarian project. The secretary-general was well aware of "the conditions of poverty among workers in the industrial north and even more especially among farmers in the southern states," highlighting "virtual peonage among the labouring masses in the eastern part of the State of Arkansas." Thankfully, argued Flores Muñoz, these abject social problems had motivated the USDA to "carry ... on an intense campaign to raise the standard of living in that area." Underscoring rural electrification, housing programs, and cultural campaigns that "inculcate[d] a higher sense of social realities," Flores Muñoz concluded that the US government had already achieved substantial success. The New Deal, in his judgment, "has rescued the farmers of the United States from the ruin into which they were violently being submerged."[17]

Yet Cardenista paeans to the New Deal were not merely rhetorical; they were also practical, as when the revolutionary ruling party brought US planners and social scientists to Mexico for a direct application of their knowledge. Perhaps the most surprising example of this occurred at ground zero of the decade's land reform campaign: in the cotton region of La Laguna. As the previous chapter described, in 1936 President Cárdenas intervened in a heated struggle between militarized cotton workers and landlords in La Laguna, the wealthy cotton belt spanning the northern states of Coahuila and Durango. In October of that year, Cárdenas struck fear into landlords across Mexico by expropriating millions of acres of irrigated cotton land from major estates—a far cry from the marginal, rocky plots usually reserved for ejidatarios—and then turning them over to newly organized worker cooperatives. Paying much of the price were absentee foreign owners, such as the US- and British-owned Tlahualilo Land Company, one of the largest landlords in the region.[18]

Economic nationalism had played a fundamental role in La Laguna's land reform. Yet paradoxically, in the midst of this nationalist atmosphere, Cardenista planners decided that New Deal economics and social science would be essential in bolstering the newly established system of cooperative cotton agriculture. Immediately after the division of the cotton haciendas, the Cárdenas government drafted measures for endowing La Laguna's ejidatarios with irrigation, credit, and technical assistance to ensure their survival and productivity. In seeking that goal, the Cárdenas administration looked northward. Just weeks after the dramatic expropriation of land in October 1936, Mexican minister of finance (*secretario de hacienda*) Eduardo Suárez contacted the US embassy in Mexico City indicating that he was "very anxious" to acquire "a first-class expert on agricultural cooperative credit and a first-class expert on agricultural credit economics" to work in La Laguna.[19] He particularly hoped that those experts "could be secured from the Department of Agriculture of the United States," likely aware of that bureau's political inclinations and sympathies for the Mexican agrarian reform.[20]

New Deal officials were eager to meet the Cárdenas government's request. Ambassador Daniels, a firm supporter of both the agrarista movement and US rural reform—as will be explored later—saw La Laguna's experiment as "akin to our re-settlement projects."[21] He wrote to convince USDA chief Wallace to "let two good men go down for this service," noting that they in turn would "learn much" and become "experts in your Department about Mexican agriculture."[22] Secretary Wallace, too, was enthusiastic and suggested several candidates, but added that departmental regulations did not permit the USDA to pay for its employees working abroad; therefore, the Mexican government would be responsible for the specialists' salaries.[23] Despite this setback, Suárez remained committed to the hire. In Mexico City, he interviewed one USDA candidate in March 1937, and then traveled to Washington, DC, in April to interview another, and also meet with the Resettlement Administration's director for rural resettlement to discuss the possibilities of an exchange.[24] Financial pressures forced Suárez to hesitate in making the hire, though. In the midst of a late-decade recession and massive internal pressures to pay for recently expropriated properties, the not-insignificant $25 a day that the Resettlement Administration's top candidates demanded was difficult to justify. Summer 1937 passed with Suárez's request unfulfilled.[25]

Efforts to partner the agrarian New Deal with the *lagunera* cotton experiment, however, received an invigorating push in fall 1937 when USDA agricultural economist Mordecai Ezekiel made a pilgrimage to Mexico. The primary economic adviser to Secretary Wallace, Ezekiel had also been a longtime advocate for fair distribution in the USDA's programs, especially for southern sharecroppers.[26] Discussing with Ambassador Daniels the inconclusive attempt to lend USDA planners to La Laguna a year earlier, Ezekiel grew convinced that "there is much in the experience with agricultural organization and education in the United States that would be of great value to our Mexican friends."[27] The New Deal, he thus believed, should be more generous in sharing its agrarian blueprints. Returning to Washington, Ezekiel pushed the USDA to pay the salaries of agency specialists lent to Mexico, and by the following summer, he was successful.[28] Equally enthusiastic was Wallace, who believed that the USDA's rehabilitation, credit, and education efforts of the late 1930s neatly dovetailed with the dramatic land reform that Cárdenas had pioneered in La Laguna. "Where large tracts of land are being divided and placed in the hands of individual settlers," Wallace wrote to Daniels, "we hope that [New Deal] agricultural extension work will be helpful in aiding those settlers to make the most effective use of their tracts."[29]

Finance minister Suárez, on learning of the USDA's offer to fund the partnership, was "very much gratified" and "would appreciate it very much if [USDA chief Wallace] could arrange it."[30] In July 1938, the USDA selected Walter E. Packard of the FSA to serve as the New Deal's emissary to La Laguna.[31] Packard was a unique figure. A classmate of Wallace's at Iowa State College, he had during the 1920s worked in Mexico, eventually becoming a high-ranking member of the National Irrigation Commission in the Calles era. His four years in Mexico earned him a deep sympathy with the agrarista cause, and Packard described the revolution as "one of the great agrarian adjustments of history" that will "enable [Mexico's] people to enjoy the full fruits of their labor."[32] He even came to know the socialist painter Diego Rivera, who later described Packard as "a true friend of Mexico."[33] When Roosevelt took office, Packard enthusiastically enlisted in the USDA, rising to direct the Rural Resettlement Division of Tugwell's Resettlement Administration and then serving in the FSA's Land Utilization Program. He was therefore a perfect candidate to bridge the two nations' converging efforts of rural social engineering. Packard would not be the only US national staffing the state effort in La Laguna, as several US engineers consulted on matters of dam construction and irrigation.[34] But he was alone in his undue influence on the politically sensitive work of organizing ejidal production in Cárdenas's highly publicized agrarian experiment. Though the US and Mexican archival record is silent as to the specifics of Packard's participation, his invitation and presence in the hallowed ground of La Laguna speaks to agrarismo's broad geographic imaginary.

The USDA's participation in La Laguna showcased the Cárdenas government's surprising eagerness to enlist New Deal experts in the crafting of its agrarian program. Yet if such exchanges brought a southward flow of rural social engineers, they also enabled a series of pilgrimages to observe US agrarian experimentation during the Roosevelt years. None, arguably, was more evocative of the cross-border collaboration in rural reform than the career of Ramón Fernández y Fernández.

Born to a middling family in the northern state of Zacatecas in 1906, Fernández saw his childhood disrupted by the violence of the revolution. In 1922, he moved to Mexico City in pursuit of education, earning a bachelor's degree in agriculture from the National School of Agriculture at Chapingo in 1928, and then an advanced degree in agricultural economics from the Universidad Nacional Autónoma de México (National Autonomous University of Mexico, UNAM) in 1930. As a Chapingo and UNAM student, Fernández grew deeply politicized in his understanding of Mexico's agrarian problems, inspired by agrarismo's demand for rural social justice. During the 1930s, he sought to wed his political commitments to his technical training. In that decade he served both as a statistician and economist in the federal Agriculture Department—where he played a fundamental role in the 1930 agrarian census that would later serve as a primary motivation for Cardenista land reform—and as the propaganda secretary of the Liga de Agrónomos Socialistas (League of Socialist Agronomists).[35] Yet Fernández's attention to the social politics of agriculture was not confined to Mexico. During the 1930s, he also followed the US government's simultaneous attempt to remake its countryside, collecting USDA publications on topics such as changing land tenure and rural resettlement.[36]

In 1938, Fernández sought a closer engagement with US agrarianism when he applied to give a paper at the Fifth International Conference of Agricultural Economists, hosted that August at Macdonald College in Montreal, Quebec. His paper, an examination of Mexican land reform since the revolution, was accepted, and Fernández traveled through the United States for the first time to attend the conference. At Macdonald, Fernández must have felt somewhat out of place, as he was the only participant not arriving from the United States, Canada, or Europe. But as Fernández hoped, he had unlimited opportunity at the conference to engage with the social vision of the agrarian New Deal, whose leadership was well represented at the Montreal meeting. Over the week, he rubbed shoulders with and heard speeches from Wilson, Ezekiel, Carl Taylor of the BAE, and even Secretary of Agriculture Wallace, who addressed the conference on its final day.[37] When Fernández gave his presentation, titled "The Mexican Agrarian Reform," he felt that his English was too halting to read the paper, and had a friend from Iowa State College deliver the address. Through his interpreter, Fernández told the crowd about how "the concentration of territorial property in the hands of a few has constituted a fundamental social problem" in Mexico, and that Cardenismo sought "the solution of the agrarian problem in order to satisfy the popular impulses." The New Dealers in the audience would likely sympathize.[38]

Fernández's encounter with US rural reform in 1938 sowed seeds that would later bear fruit. In 1942, as agrarismo was falling from political favor in Mexico, but while USDA social engineering was peaking under the FSA and BAE, Fernández sought a far longer stay in the United States to learn firsthand of the promise of those New Deal programs. That summer, he applied for a yearlong "in-service training program" at the BAE, recently instituted for candidates from Latin America.[39] Arriving in Washington, DC, in October of that year, Fernández drank deeply from the well of New Deal agrarian philosophy. He took courses at the USDA's Graduate School, an institution that had been founded in 1921 to train federal employees, but was much expanded and reenergized with the 1930s' "cultural turn" in the USDA along with its nascent sensitivities to the social impact of agricultural and agrarian policy.[40]

In time, however, Fernández grew frustrated with the bookishness of social scientists who rarely left Washington, DC. He desired instead to see how action programs functioned in the countryside, and hence transferred to the FSA to study "credit problems more nearly related to those in his own country," as the US embassy noted. During 1943, Fernández began a monthslong tour of the rural counties most affected by New Deal reform. He studied the laboratory of Greene County, Georgia, where Arthur Raper and fellow rural sociologists challenged the social stratification of a plantation district; he learned of cooperative farm communities in the Mississippi Delta; and in Arkansas, where he stayed longest, he worked closely with FSA officials in rural credit. As the FSA weathered its most vicious attacks in late 1942 and early 1943, Fernández clipped articles from Arkansas newspapers that both praised and damned the bureau as it approached its institutional death.[41]

While the FSA did not survive the political attacks of 1943, Fernández bore its strategies back to Mexico. At the National School of Agriculture, he taught a course in 1945 titled Agricultural Credit in the United States, and commissioned his students to study New Deal programs in soil conservation and equitable rural lending.[42] He also lobbied Mexico's agricultural leadership to study the value of US models for rural rehabilitation. Describing his year in the United States to his former teacher at Chapingo and then secretary of agriculture Marte R. Gómez in 1945, Fernández confessed that he sympathized deeply with the "revolutionary faith" of the FSA's directors. Having seen the "results of their work[,] my sympathy was transformed into enthusiasm," and Fernández described his "natural impulse ... to push a campaign to have our own Farm Security."[43] What impact he may have had on Gómez is difficult to gauge. Yet what is certain is that Fernández himself put his education to use in the following decades, serving as director of economic studies at the National Bank of Agricultural Credit in the mid-1940s and then at a similar post in the National Bank of Ejidal Credit from 1953 to 1964. Fernández's commitment to wedding agricultural credit and land reform even took him beyond Mexico's borders in later years, when he served as a consultant to Fidel Castro's early agrarian reform program in Cuba during 1959 and 1960.[44] Fernández's career, though perhaps unusual in its reach, testifies to the lasting influence of New Deal agrarianism across the Americas.

It was not only Mexican economists and social scientists who looked northward during the Roosevelt era. The New Deal's union of social conscience and modern technology similarly captivated those in the "hard" agricultural sciences, such as agronomists, engineers, plant breeders, and the like. Such borrowings came at a moment when Mexican agricultural science was dramatically expanding its influence and impact on the countryside. During the Porfiriato, agronomy was a neglected discipline with minimal impact on agricultural practice. While the National School of Agriculture had been founded in 1854 in Mexico City, student enrollments remained low throughout the nineteenth century. Managers of large haciendas, with access to abundant cheap labor, rarely saw reason to hire trained experts or mechanize production. And the corpus of agricultural science taught in Mexico was overwhelmingly of foreign import—initially from France, but increasingly from the United States by the dawn of the twentieth century—and was rarely attuned to the climatic and ecological particularities of Mexico's diverse agricultural zones.[45]

Social revolution presented unexpected opportunities for the fledgling field of agricultural science in Mexico. In the revolt that engulfed the 1910s, countless *agrónomos* allied with the agrarista cause, proclaiming the hacienda—which they deemed both exploitative and unproductive—as their common enemy. While genuine political sympathies undoubtedly inspired many revolutionary agronomists, desires for career advancement and state support were important motivations, and many sought to leverage political allegiances into paid positions. Their success in doing so varied enormously depending on the mercurial political atmosphere, and the conservative shift away from agrarismo during the 1920s' rule of Calles left many agronomists out in the cold—often literally. But with the rejuvenation of land redistribution and concomitant expansion of the rural state apparatus in the Cárdenas era, hundreds of agronomists found viable employment as surveyors, statisticians, teachers, and extension service staff. As they allied with the state and sought inclusion in the "revolutionary family" during the 1930s, Mexican agronomists championed their technical expertise as a necessary complement to agrarian reform and a primary ingredient to rural social justice.[46]

The rapid expansion and politicization of Mexican agronomy after 1910 poses a fundamental question: Was postrevolutionary agricultural science nationalist in character? Early scholars certainly assumed so, highlighting agronomists' rhetoric of national social revolution and anti-interventionism, alongside the fact that foreign landowners paid much of the price of land expropriation. Such accounts insist that Mexican agricultural science enjoyed a brief window of national autonomy between the blatant Eurocentrism of the Porfirian years and the dominance of US science that accompanied the green revolution in the 1940s and beyond.[47] In reality, though, there was far more continuity than change in Mexican agronomy's internationalist outlook. Even as agricultural scientists championed national sovereignty and a revolutionary agenda, they continued to borrow foreign methods and models, particularly from the United States.[48] Dozens of Mexican agronomists completed advanced degrees at US universities during the 1910s and 1920s, and the Sociedad Agronómica Mexicana (Mexican Agronomic Society, SAM) offered courses in English during the same period. When the federal agriculture department planned a major push to teach campesinos new cultivation methods in 1929, it mailed local agents a verbatim translation from the USDA's Extension Service handbook.[49]

But as the New Deal USDA incorporated a new emphasis on social, cultural, and ecological problems in the countryside, those earlier borrowings escalated in their frequency and impact. The newly founded Soil Conservation Service, led by liberal North Carolinian Hugh H. Bennett, attracted five prominent agronomists for a months-long internship during the early 1940s.[50] Eduardo Limón, perhaps the foremost maize breeder in Mexico, spent much of 1942 in North Carolina studying corn at a USDA experiment station there, as he felt that "general conditions in North Carolina resemble conditions in Mexico a great deal." Limón, along with the Soil Conservation

Figure 3.1. 1941 Roberto Montenegro painting of Henry A. Wallace and Centeotl, the Aztec god of maize. Ramón Fernández y Fernández Papers, box 180. Courtesy of the Biblioteca Luis González, Colegio de Michoacán.

Service interns, also took the opportunity of visiting the USDA in Washington, DC, and speaking with Henry A. Wallace, the foremost champion of coupling rural social reform to agricultural science during the Roosevelt years.[51]

Indeed, no New Dealer was more romanticized in Mexico than Wallace, who became somewhat of an idol among Mexico's revolutionary agronomists. His two-month tour of the nation in 1940 and public declarations of sympathy for Cárdenas's agrarian experiment provided additional fodder for his veneration. That admiration was made demonstrably clear in 1941, when the SAM, the primary professional organization of Mexico's agricultural scientists, planned a bold gesture of solidarity with the then vice president. That fall, César Martino, president of the SAM and Cárdenas's federal secretary of agrarian action, commissioned the renowned muralist Roberto Montenegro to paint a portrait of Wallace in a Mexican motif. Completed in September, the oil painting displayed Wallace alongside Centeotl, the Aztec god of maize.[52]

Figure 3.2. Henry A. Wallace receiving Roberto Montenegro's painting from the Sociedad Agronómica Mexicana, Washington, DC, October 1941. Ramón Fernández y Fernández Papers, box 180. Courtesy of the Biblioteca Luis González, Colegio de Michoacán.

Rather than mail the painting to their US ally, Martino—along with four other SAM members and Mexican agriculture chief Marte R. Gómez—elected to travel to Washington, DC, in October to personally present Wallace with their token of homage. Wallace, predictably, "infinitely appreciated" the present and SAM's gesture. As thanks, Wallace accompanied the group on a tour of the Beltsville Agricultural Experiment Station in rural Maryland, discussing the commonalities in US and Mexican agrarian reform and agricultural development. Writing later to Fernando Foglio Miramontes, the chief of Mexico's federal Agrarian Department, Wallace thanked his "brother agronomists" for the painting, which "represents very well my interest in Mexico and in maize, the plant with which Mexico has enriched the world."[53]

As demonstrated by the near apotheosis of Wallace, the economist Fernández's transnational career, the USDA's role in La Laguna, and the many other exchanges of the decade, it is undeniable that many of the key architects of Mexico's agrarian reform kept a watchful eye on New Deal efforts to overcome rural social problems. Agrarismo in the Cárdenas era—a program that has largely been understood in a strictly national context—therefore appears far more internationalist than assumed. Even as formal relations between the US and Mexican governments chilled when US nationals lost property to expropriation, the bond between liberal New Dealers and Cardenista reformers only grew stronger. And perhaps more than any other region, it was the US South and New Deal programs aimed at the South that most inspired cosmopolitan Mexican bureaucrats, social scientists, and agronomists.

Yet in dusting the fingerprints of the New Deal on Mexico's agrarian reform, looking to Mexican observers of US policy can only partially reveal the complexities of that entangled past. The New Deal also manifested itself in Mexico through the one US state actor who wielded the greatest power over the future of the Cardenista project: the elderly ambassador to Mexico City, Josephus Daniels, who would play an unpredictably pivotal role in enabling the agrarian reform of the 1930s.

North Carolina's New Deal Diplomat

Roosevelt's road to the White House was paved with promises of dramatic change. In the lowest depths of the economic crisis in 1932, US voters paid most attention to Roosevelt's plans for domestic economic recovery; indeed, Roosevelt prominently emphasized national over international concerns on the campaign trail. But he also promised a refashioning of the United States' global presence, particularly in regard to the Western Hemisphere. That posture was largely a response to what the incoming president saw as errors of the recent past. During the decade that followed World War I, Republican administrations in Washington—in spite of a rhetorical commitment to isolationism—oversaw numerous military interventions in Latin America and the Caribbean, often invited by US businesses that perceived threats to their profits and security. These frequent violations of national sovereignty sowed widespread resentment of the United States among a broad spectrum of Latin American society. As the Depression reshuffled national priorities and saddled business leaders with much of the blame for the economic crisis, Roosevelt seized an opportunity to reverse patterns of US intervention abroad. Just weeks after his 1933 inauguration, he made his first announcement of a diplomatic doctrine that promised the other American republics "neighborly cooperation in every form of human activity."[54]

Perhaps the Latin American nation most essential to Roosevelt's "good neighbor" rhetoric was Mexico. Diplomatic relations between the two nations had been exceedingly icy since the revolt against Díaz in 1910. Especially in the wake of the US Navy's occupation of Veracruz in 1914 and the

US Army's fruitless hunt for Pancho Villa in 1916–17, Mexicans across the political spectrum nurtured a smoldering animus toward the invasive Colossus of the North. US outrage over expropriated property during the 1920s provided another ingredient in the already-bitter stew. Meanwhile, the land border between the two nations hung in a purgatorial state of half war for nearly two decades after 1910. Roosevelt was thus eager to continue Herbert Hoover's efforts toward rapprochement that had been especially successful under Ambassador Dwight Morrow (1927–30). The selection of the US envoy to Mexico in 1933 was therefore a choice of extreme importance in the New Deal's diplomatic reinvention. And though few could predict it at the time, when Cárdenas renewed the push for agrarian reform and targeted the property of foreign landlords later in the decade, the US ambassador's dilemmas would become front-page news.[55]

With such high stakes for the future of US-Mexican relations, many observers were astounded when Roosevelt named Josephus Daniels, a seventy-one-year-old newspaper editor from Raleigh, North Carolina, to the post in spring 1933. Roosevelt and Daniels had a long personal and political relationship. During the Woodrow Wilson administration of the 1910s, Daniels had been secretary of the navy, and he appointed a young Roosevelt as his assistant secretary—the first government post for the New Yorker. In the following decade Daniels served as a political mentor for his former charge, schooling Roosevelt in the ways of the southern Democratic Party. While never himself a candidate for office, Daniels was a key opinion maker in the South, and the newspaper that he had edited since the 1890s, the *Raleigh News and Observer*, was the largest and most influential in his state. The *News and Observer*'s steadfast support for Roosevelt in the 1932 North Carolina Democratic primary and general election left Roosevelt politically indebted to Daniels.[56]

As a candidate for ambassador to Mexico, though, Daniels was a baffling choice. He had no diplomatic experience to speak of, which immediately made him an outsider among the career diplomats who populated the State Department. He also spoke no Spanish whatsoever, and would learn little during his decade in Mexico. But even beyond these eccentricities, there were three additional reasons why Daniels seemed an unwise choice in 1933. First, his earlier career in the US Navy made him toxic to many Mexicans. In 1914, Daniels had overseen the bloody US invasion of the port of Veracruz in an attempt to sabotage the rise of reactionary general Victoriano Huerta. While most Mexicans had little love for Huerta, they nevertheless detested this violation of their territorial sovereignty, and the memory of Veracruz loomed large in the public imagination as the worst example of imperial Yankee intervention. News of Daniels's selection as ambassador, then, spurred a violent uproar. Protesters stoned the US embassy in response, while the press was aflame with criticism. One student group declared that since Daniels had "violated the national sovereignty and honor" of Mexico, his appointment was an insult to the Mexican people.[57]

Second, for a diplomat chosen to work in a predominantly mestizo nation, Daniels had a well-deserved reputation as one of the most vocal white supremacists in the US South. Born during the Civil War and coming of age during Reconstruction, Daniels saw racial order and white control of southern society as fundamental to its progress. From his editorial desk at Raleigh's *State Chronicle* and then the *News and Observer* during the 1880s and 1890s, Daniels penned fiery columns about the necessity of rigid racial hierarchies and danger of racial mixing. Ironically, in the 1890s he warned that white and black intermarriage would "Mexicanize the South," revealing his early understanding of the United States' southern neighbor.[58] Daniels's racism grew especially pronounced when white rule perceived external threats. In the last years of the 1890s, as poor white farmers joined with black Republicans in a Populist alliance to overthrow conservative Democratic rule in North Carolina, Daniels and his allies waged a self-described "White Supremacy Campaign" to drive a wedge between those potential allies. The *News and Observer* eagerly stoked the flames of racial hatred by publishing incendiary articles on the alleged sexual exploitation of white women by black men. In November 1898, this campaign ignited a savage race riot in the city of Wilmington, North Carolina, where white mobs murdered dozens of blacks. That the massacre's blood stained Daniels's hands is undeniable, but he nonetheless clung to this racial orthodoxy for decades to come. When serving under President Wilson in the 1910s, Daniels was a key architect of formal racial segregation in the US Navy.[59]

Lastly, Daniels's political history raised questions as to how he would interpret agrarian revolt in Mexico—an issue of primary importance to US-Mexican relations in 1933. No stranger to the politics of rural discontent, Daniels had witnessed decades of strife over the future of North Carolina's countryside. Coming of age while King Cotton tightened its grasp on the region, and as slave plantations splintered into a patchwork system of tenancy and sharecropping, Daniels believed that a resurgent "New South" required a diversified, scientific agriculture that abandoned the feudalistic estates of the past. Unlike an older generation of conservatives, Daniels hoped to expand state power to aid farmers, whether through research, education, or credit. When agrarian political ferment struck North Carolina in the 1880s, the Jeffersonian Daniels sympathized with efforts to organize small white farmers, prompting one historian to dub Daniels a "radical agrarian." But Daniels's agrarianism had distinct racial limits. After all, the Populists that Daniels had dedicated so much energy to crushing in the "White Supremacy Campaign" of the 1890s represented an alliance between marginalized and dispossessed black and white farmers. Immediately thereafter, too, Daniels pushed for the electoral disfranchisement of both the white and black lower classes in the pursuit of political order. Yet in the decades that followed, Daniels displayed a growing discomfort with the rural status quo. He fretted about "a bad tenant system" and the "tremendous burden imposed upon the farmers by the credit system," and his editorials during the early twentieth century suggest considerable fluidity as he reconsidered the agrarian dilemmas of the US South.[60]

Despite these contradictions and the public outcry that followed Daniels's appointment as Mexican ambassador in early 1933, Roosevelt refused to reverse his decision. Though this seems perplexing, in many ways the president's paradoxical bond to Daniels reflected the larger relationship between progressives in the Democratic Party and US southern elites, with the latter remaining faithfully Democratic on Election Day though simultaneously hampering the party from moving leftward. Yet in Daniels's particular case, there were signs that the editor was no hidebound conservative by the 1930s. Having seen the progressivism of his hero Wilson torpedoed by Republican administrations during the 1920s, Daniels had begun to grow more outspoken in his populist rhetoric, frequently attacking monopoly interests and demanding state action on the part of industrial workers and poor farmers. As for his once-rabid racism, an uneasy silence from his editorial desk on such issues suggested a gradual moderation. Indeed, by 1933, Daniels likely struck Roosevelt as one of the South's most prominent liberals. In time, Daniels would surprise nearly everyone.[61]

In the weeks before leaving for Mexico City, Daniels traveled from Raleigh, North Carolina, to Washington, DC, to begin his education in Mexican history, politics, and culture. With his contradictory background, it is difficult to guess at how Daniels interpreted the Mexican agrarian struggle in early 1933. Still, it is likely that the formal education he received from the State Department was rather unsympathetic to the plight of the Mexican campesino. While Roosevelt was anxious to adopt a new stance toward Latin America through his much-publicized Good Neighbor policy, most of the State Department diplomatic staff members were remnants of an earlier era and were more eager to collect outstanding US debts than to romanticize peasant activists.[62] But Daniels did not receive his education in the State Department alone. In March 1933, just weeks before he departed for his post in Mexico City, his longtime friend George Foster Peabody—the New York–based, Georgia-born liberal philanthropist—suggested that Daniels meet with a young scholar, Frank Tannenbaum, to discuss the situation in Mexico.[63]

Tannenbaum—as the previous chapter detailed—was unmatched in his romantic admiration for Mexico's social revolution. Having spent much of the 1920s documenting the progress of agrarian reform in the Mexican countryside, Tannenbaum was one of the foremost US champions of the legitimacy of the Mexican Revolution. His published 1929 dissertation, *The*

Mexican Agrarian Revolution, was the first academic treatment of the revolt against Díaz, and its effusive support for land redistribution was hardly subtle. Tannenbaum thus imparted to Daniels in 1933 an interpretation of the revolution far different from that shared by the ambassador's peers in the State Department. On Peabody's suggestion, Tannenbaum mailed Daniels a copy of *The Mexican Agrarian Revolution* on March 21. The ambassador was so intrigued by Tannenbaum's "rare knowledge" that they met the following day in Washington for a "two hours talk."[64] The following week, Tannenbaum visited Daniels in Washington, DC, where Tannenbaum showed slides and short films taken from his earlier research journeys into rural Mexico to observe peasant schools and ejido farms.[65] Daniels effused to Tannenbaum that his impressions of Mexico were "gathered in a way that gives you a knowledge of the country and its people which could not be obtained in any other way."[66] Promising to read the dissertation on the train ride down into Mexico, Daniels also invited Tannenbaum to visit him as soon as he could.[67]

During his first year in Mexico City, Daniels underwent a dual education: he learned firsthand of the tempestuous politics of postrevolutionary Mexico, but all the while, with eyes northward, he became an ardent New Dealer. That fortunate simultaneity would forever transform his understanding of Mexican politics, his diplomatic career, and ultimately the course of Mexico's agrarian reform. Despite his distance from Washington, the ambassador paid close and sympathetic attention to the experimental measures of Roosevelt's first hundred days in 1933. He even took time to intervene in the president's favor when North Carolina conservatives dragged their feet in implementing reform measures.[68] In embracing the New Deal, Daniels also sought to push it further. He was fond of telling US visitors to the embassy in Mexico City that if he had any gripe with Roosevelt, it was that "he is too blamed conservative and I wished he would be more radical."[69] Captivated by reformism at home, it was thus no surprise that Daniels interpreted the platform of Mexico's revolutionary ruling party as a parallel of the New Deal. Formally accepting his appointment in April 1933 in Mexico City, Daniels declared that the United States and Mexico had both "embarked upon new and well-considered experiments with optimism born of courage."[70] Even though political boss Plutarco Elías Calles still dominated Mexico's ruling party, Daniels saw enough progressive rhetoric to warrant these frequent comparisons. "The aspirations of this government [in Mexico]," wrote Daniels to Roosevelt in late 1933, "are in line with those which our people are striving to attain."[71]

Daniels not only heard echoes of the New Deal in Mexico; he also saw shadows of the US South. The ambassador was particularly quick to draw commonalities between the land tenure system of Mexico and that of his home, as "we [southerners] know something about the evils of the tenant system and absentee landlordism." In trying to explain rural Mexico to his children in North Carolina, he translated "campesino"—literally meaning country person—into "tenant."[72] Discussing the historic lack of a strong tradition of rural public education in Mexico with a university professor, Daniels declared, "There is much in common between the southern States and Mexico."[73] Then, in November 1933, Daniels received his first visit—of many—from Tannenbaum, who was likewise eager to compare the US South and Mexico. Over Thanksgiving dinner at the embassy, Tannenbaum urged that Daniels accompany him on a journey to rural Indian villages outside the capital to demonstrate the successes of the revolution's evolving land and education policy. Daniels agreed, and three days later he joined the young scholar on a horseback tour of schools and ejido farms in an Otomí Indian community in the nearby state of Hidalgo. To Daniels, the voyage was "a revelation." As he wrote in his diary, "They are doing here on a smaller scale exactly what [educational reformers] did in North Carolina forty or fifty years ago in the beginning of our educational renaissance."[74]

Daniels's ubiquitous comparisons between the Mexican Revolution, New Deal, and US South—spurred in no small part by his young mentor Tannenbaum—would eventually give rise to a deeply sympathetic understanding of Mexico's political ferment. By the end of his first year as ambassador, Daniels had grown convinced that the push for land redistribution was not a case of creeping socialism or anti-US banditry, as many in the State Department believed, but a fundamental prerequisite to justice, peace, and democracy in Mexico. "Mexico can never really prosper until there is a larger opportunity for the average man to own land," he wrote Roosevelt in 1933, and "it is still rankling in the hearts of the many that the promise of land has materialized only in a comparatively small way."[75] The ambassador insisted that "Mexico was right in taking portions of big haciendas, and [deeding] them to the men who till the soil," despite the international property conflicts it would inherently lead to.[76] Yet Daniels's solutions for Mexico were always refracted through the prism of his experiences in the US South, evidenced when he told Roosevelt that "Mexico's safety is that its people 'live at home and board in the same place'"—referencing the "live at home" campaign of rural self-sufficiency that had swept the US South in the decade after the Populist movement.[77]

Daniels's dual metamorphosis as radical New Dealer and ally of the Mexican Revolution also permeated his deep-seated thinking on race, though in unpredictable ways. The rabid white supremacist who had once sneered at Mexico's racial mixing would during the 1930s describe indigenous Mexicans as a "hardy race ... in whose veins flows the blood that gave distinction to Montezuma and statesmanship to Juárez." The newspaper editor who had once provoked white men to murder their black neighbors over fears of miscegenation sympathetically declared that in Mexico, "the native race has

Figure 3.3. Josephus Daniels and his wife, Addie, in charro costumes, Mexico City, 1937. Frank Tannenbaum Papers, box 57. Courtesy of Columbia University.

played upon other races living alongside, imparting quite as much as it has received." The "future of Mexico," he likewise argued, "lies in the united co-operation of all elements who are proud to be called Mexicans, and in free-dom from race and class consciousness." This is not to suggest that overnight Daniels emancipated himself from a lifetime of racial prejudice. Like many other white foreigners in revolutionary Mexico, Daniels frequently essential-ized indigenous culture, and represented it as static and unchanging. "Yesterday, today, and tomorrow the Indian is and will be himself," Daniels wrote in 1935, "unchanged in fundamentals from the day his ancestors disputed the march of Cortez to Tenochtitlan." But in contrast to his blatant racism of the late nineteenth and early twentieth century, Daniels's rhetoric in 1930s' Mexico nonetheless suggests a dramatic about-face.[78]

This reeducation did more than reshape Daniels's diplomatic career in Mexico City; it also revised his understanding of agrarian politics in his home state and pushed him toward new solutions to the social inequalities that plagued the US South. On May 18, 1934, Daniels returned home to the United States for the first time in thirteen months to celebrate his seventy-second birthday with his family in North Carolina. In his honor, the Raleigh Chamber of Commerce threw him a birthday dinner, attended by the city's most prominent business elites. The dinner unexpectedly showcased a rein-vented Daniels. Arriving at the Sir Walter Raleigh Hotel, Daniels "[shook] hands with the Negro doorman who opened the door of his automobile"—a gesture so noteworthy that the *News and Observer* highlighted it twice in its reportage of the event.[79] Then later in the evening, in front of an audience of more than three hundred, Daniels pontificated on "what the United States might learn from its Southern neighbor ... a country we ought to be proud to have as a neighbor." Speaking on "the division of the great haciendas, and the enabling of men who had long tilled the soil to become owners of the land," Daniels told the presumably shocked crowd that "the next forward step in North Carolina and the South is to divide large plantations so that the large tenant class may own the soil they till."[80]

When Tannenbaum unexpectedly took steps to do exactly that in the following months—as explored in chapter 2—Daniels became a critical ally in the effort to translate Mexican agrarismo into the US South. When two recalcitrant North Carolina senators made a public show of opposition to the Tannenbaum-authored Farm Tenant Homes Act in spring 1935, the young scholar sought the aid of Daniels, whom he was certain would be "fully in sympathy with the bill."[81] Daniels, as Tannenbaum predicted, was a firm supporter and met with the North Carolinian politicians to push them for action. When one reversed his position, Tannenbaum was convinced that Daniels's support had been the key ingredient to their success.[82] And when the tenant bill stalled in the House during 1936, Daniels penned a long jeremiad to Roosevelt urging him to move faster on realizing US agrarian reform. "My repugnance to [landlessness has] been heightened by my knowledge that it had been the curse of Mexico," Daniels implored the president. "If tenancy continues to go forward by leaps and bounds in our country the time will come when peonage will be the curse of the United States as it has been of Mexico." When Roosevelt soon thereafter hastened the creation of the FSA, Daniels would see a realization of Mexico's promise for the United States.[83]

Yet the arena in which Daniels's increasingly radical, regionally inflected New Dealism came to bear most decisively was on Mexico's own agrarian reform. In 1933 and 1934, when the ambassador first developed sympathies for Mexico's rural dispossessed and government programs to aid them, the ruling party's push for land reform was largely rhetorical. Active redistribution had frozen in the long shadow of Calles, who in 1930 had declared that the ejido was a dead end for Mexico's agricultural development. As Calles's puppet presidents Abelardo Rodríguez and Cárdenas slowly broke free from his grasp, though, the expropriation of large estates became a primary plank in the revolutionary party's platform. And because so many of the estates marked for subdivision were foreign owned, agrarismo was a truly international struggle. Indeed, between 1927 and 1940, Mexican officials expropriated approximately 6.2 million acres of land belonging to US landowners, the lion's share of which was redistributed during the Cárdenas era. Such losses infuriated US absentee landlords ranging from newspaper magnate William Randolph Hearst to modest smallholders, many of whom led saber-rattling publicity campaigns and lobbied Washington for military action on their behalf in Mexico. Tasked with representing and defending these aggrieved landowners, the US embassy thus became a primary player in the fight for the future of Mexico's countryside. By 1936 and 1937, the ensuing crisis placed Ambassador Daniels at a crossroads, forcing him to choose between his nascent sympathies for the campesino and the State Department's demands that he protect US-owned estates in Mexico.[84]

A decade earlier—and certainly two decades later—a muscular Latin American nationalization campaign targeting US citizens would have surely invited military intervention. But to the great fortune of Mexican agrarismo, Cárdenas's resurgent radicalism coincided with Roosevelt's own leftward drift between 1935 and 1937, when the US president pushed through the most lasting social reforms of his administration. Bridging these two worlds was North Carolina's New Deal ambassador. Observing Cárdenas's revival of the revolution's promises to the campesino, Daniels was consistently unable to divorce US and Mexican politics. Writing to Roosevelt in 1938, Daniels declared, "Cárdenas has the same goal that you have set before yourself in the United States since you assumed the presidency."[85] To skeptical supervisors in the State Department, Daniels likewise sought to justify Cárdenas's expropriation campaign in US terms, arguing that the Mexican president was "even more strongly committed to land distribution under the Six-Year Plan than our Government is to the New Deal."[86] Daniels felt no discomfort sharing such analogies with Cárdenas himself; "the 'plan' of the Mexican Government," he told the president in 1935, "has many similar points with that which President Roosevelt is following."[87]

Cárdenas—a shrewd politician above all—was quick to note Daniels's eagerness for sympathetic comparisons and frequently seized on it for Mex-

ico's benefit. As early as 1935, Cárdenas told a predictably charmed Daniels
that "he wish[ed] he could give the New Deal of America to Mexico."[88] In
negotiating with the ambassador in late 1936 over land expropriations in
the Yaqui Valley of Sonora, the president asked "a personal favor" of Daniels
and Roosevelt, with their "interest in the forgotten man," that perhaps they
might aid "the great mass of the poor agrarian workers to own the land on
which they worked."[89] Whether such declarations were genuine or political
stagecraft is difficult to tell, but there is no doubt that Daniels swallowed it
whole. As the ambassador told Cordell Hull, his chief in the State Department, in 1940, Cárdenas "has a profound respect and admiration for President Roosevelt [and] regards his own policies as a Mexican New Deal."[90]

In private, Cárdenas realized full well the importance of Daniels's agrarian sympathies for the success of agrarismo. The North Carolinian's "effort
to identify with the true significance of our reforms," the president wrote a
friend in 1937, "has achieved more ... than any other ambassador could have
achieved with arrogance and demands."[91] As Cárdenas's son Cuauhtémoc
later recalled, his father "much appreciated Ambassador Daniels" along with
his "sympathy toward Mexico and its government."[92] Indeed, the ideological
congruence and tacit support of the US ambassador and President Roosevelt
provided an opening for extensive land reform in Mexico. As Cárdenas escalated the scale and scope of expropriation in 1937 and 1938, Daniels repeatedly wrote to Secretary of State Hull that Mexican social justice trumped
US property claims. "In all our dealings with Mexico," Daniels pled in late
1938, "we cannot lose sight of the fact that it has been the victim of exploitation by its own recreant officials and foreigners."[93] Though the conservative
secretary of state often saw Daniels's stubbornness as insubordination—he
fumed to a friend that same year that "Daniels is down there taking sides
with the Mexican Government"—Hull ultimately acquiesced, partially because growing tensions in Europe reshuffled State Department priorities.[94]
No historian has done more to reconstruct the tense diplomatic negotiations
between the State Department and Cárdenas government than John Dwyer,
who argues that Daniels consistently "sided with Mexico against the State
Department" as the agrarian diplomatic dispute heated up. Daniels "championed most Cardenista reforms," in Dwyer's telling, often infuriating State
Department "hard-liners" as millions of dollars of US-owned property was
nationalized. In the long history of US–Latin American relations, this Mexican diplomatic victory represented an undeniable watershed.[95]

Cárdenas's monumental reparto de tierras—division of lands—was
arguably the foundational moment in twentieth-century Mexican political
history. In addressing the revolution's long-neglected demands for agrarian
reform, Cárdenas granted new legitimacy to the ruling party's political machine, defusing popular unrest and laying the groundwork for sixty years of
unbroken party rule. Yet had the agrarista campaign not been mediated by

a New Dealer sympathetic to the social ills of landlessness and tenancy, it is difficult to guess how the hinge of the 1930s may have swung. By decade's end, at age seventy-eight, Daniels reflected, "The older I grow the more radically progressive I get."[96] There was more than a grain of truth in that declaration. In the Mexican culmination to his long political career, Daniels began to resolve some of the dilemmas that had haunted him for decades. The obsessive white supremacy that marked much of his adulthood gave way to a grudging acceptance of a mestizo nation. His hand-wringing about agrarian democracy and the distribution of wealth in the countryside—manifested in such contradictory ways in North Carolina—climaxed in the dramatic struggle for the ejido in the Cárdenas years. Along the way, the thread of his complex career unwittingly entwined the rural histories of the US South and Mexico.

***

During the restless years when Cárdenas and Roosevelt shared the public stage in North America, US and Mexican agrarian reformers both in and out of government conceived of their fight against rural inequality in transnational terms. The myriad comparisons that they made—between plantations and haciendas, between campesinos and sharecroppers—had a transformative effect on both movements for rural justice. In the United States, agrarian liberals in the USDA drew inspiration from Mexican revolutionary agrarismo, which played a decisive role in their radicalization. As the most prominent example, the FSA, perhaps the most redistributionist agency of the rural New Deal, grew from comparisons between the US South and revolutionary Mexico. Simultaneously, a score of influential rural leaders including Rexford Tugwell, M. L. Wilson, and Henry A. Wallace visited Mexico at the height of that nation's agrarian reform, observing its progress and gauging its applicability in the United States. Outside Washington, DC, nonstate actors such as the Southern Tenant Farmers' Union also relied on Mexican examples to push the boundaries of the US political spectrum.

Yet as this chapter has demonstrated, Mexican reformers too crossed national borders, both in person and spirit, when considering the future of their nation's countryside. The agrarian New Deal frequently served as a reference point when Cardenista bureaucrats planned the support systems that would accompany ejidal land grants after the drama of expropriation. The RA, FSA, and BAE each found admirers in postrevolutionary Mexico, and state planners solicited the advice of those agencies despite their government's nominal nationalism of the decade. Likewise, the foot soldiers of Cárdenas's rural project—agronomists, economists, statisticians, and social scientists of various stripes—displayed a surprising interest and at times reverence for the agrarian New Deal's leadership and evolving ideology.

Perhaps the most dramatic collision of New Deal and Cardenista ideology, however, could be found in the career of US ambassador to Mexico Josephus Daniels. As the US official in Mexico who wielded the greatest influence over the political future of the land redistribution project, Daniels proved to be one of Cárdenas's most reliable allies in pursuing a campaign of rural social leveling. Daniels's unexpected embrace of agrarismo grew in part from his steadfast commitment to the New Deal's advocacy for the "forgotten man," but it was likewise the product of decades of standing witness to the human misery of the plantation complex in the US South. Although Daniels had earlier been implicit in the construction of that status quo, in his elderly years he began to buck against it, resulting in unexpected political alliances. Yet Daniels's budding sympathies for agrarismo would have amounted to little had Cárdenas not skillfully exploited those instincts for the purposes of Mexico's national project. In nurturing Daniels's romantic parallels between the two nations' social reformism, Cárdenas displayed both his political genius and a deep sensitivity to US political and regional complexities.

Daniels's ubiquitous comparisons between the landscape of rural Mexico and his US South, though, would not only change the course of land redistribution in the 1930s. It would also give rise to perhaps the most decisive campaign to remake rural Mexico: the Rockefeller Foundation's green revolution in agricultural research and extension. Until now, this book has largely examined US and Mexican governmental attempts to promote rural social engineering and agricultural change. Yet nonstate actors, and particularly agents of US philanthropy, would have an equal, if not greater, impact on the shared future of the Mexican and US countryside. Acknowledging the winding, border-crossing career of the Rockefeller philanthropies—and the unlikely interlocutors like Daniels who made it possible—forces a dramatic reassessment of US-led "development" campaigns after World War II.

Chapter Four

ROCKEFELLER RURAL DEVELOPMENT
From the US Cotton Belt to Mexico

In late June 1941, three US agronomists loaded suitcases and scientific equipment into a green GMC Suburban Carryall station wagon in New York and set course for Mexico City. The three men—Paul C. Mangelsdorf, Richard Bradfield, and Richard Schultes—were apostles of US agricultural science at a moment when that field was dramatically expanding in influence. Mangelsdorf was a corn breeder who taught at Harvard University, Bradfield was a soil scientist at Cornell University, and Schultes was a graduate student of Mangelsdorf's at Harvard, where he studied economic botany. What brought them together and then bound them for Mexico was a seemingly simple mission. They traveled on behalf of the Rockefeller Foundation, the massive New York–based philanthropy, and sought to answer a pressing question: Could US agricultural methods be transplanted in Mexico for the benefit of its farmers?[1]

Driving southwest from New York, the team crossed the Mexican border at Nuevo Laredo. Over the next two and a half months, the three men traveled thousands of miles across sixteen states, surveying wildly diverse agricultural zones and filling notebook after notebook with wide-eyed observations. They interviewed hundreds of farmers, from humble campesinos to plantation managers, and heard conflicting stories about the past and future of Mexican agriculture. Near Ciudad Victoria in Tamaulipas, they participated in a state ceremony granting ejido plots to landless farmers, which deeply "impressed" them. Near Querétaro, they spoke to hacienda owners still "bitter about the revolution."[2] But what particularly struck the Rockefeller team were the low food crop yields that most small-scale farmers confronted at harvest time. At summer's end, the scientists reported to the Rockefeller Foundation that rural Mexico stood at a crossroads. They argued that in the wake of the land reform of the 1930s, the most significant bottleneck to Mexico's agricultural productivity was technological proficiency. With that in mind, the survey team unanimously recommended that the foundation pursue a program of agricultural research and extension in Mexico.[3]

The consequences of that decision would be staggering, both for Mexico and the planet as a whole. In 1943, the Rockefeller Foundation partnered with a sympathetic President Manuel Ávila Camacho to found the Mexican Agricultural Program (MAP), which sought to raise the standard of living in rural Mexico by improving the productivity of basic food crops. The program targeted a range of Mexican dietary staples, from maize and beans to wheat. Over the next decade, US agronomists alongside their Mexican counterparts collected seeds, bred new plant varieties, tested pesticides and fertilizers, and then disseminated their findings to a wide swath of Mexican farmers. It was a grueling effort with often-ambiguous results, but by the early 1950s the foundation boasted of success in raising certain crop yields. Mexico then became a springboard for globalizing this campaign. In 1950, Rockefeller planners initiated a similar program in Colombia, and then by 1957 moved to India; within a decade they had further expanded to the Philippines, Pakistan, and Vietnam.

In 1968, US Agency for International Development chief William Gaud memorably coined the term "green revolution" to describe the project of First World technical assistance to Third World farmers that the Rockefeller Foundation had initiated a generation earlier. In Gaud's eyes, this was a humanitarian, altruistic effort distinct from Soviet "red" and Iranian "white" revolutions, devoid of violence and politics. Yet by the time of its naming, the green revolution had become a key US weapon in the Cold War, promising to neutralize peasant radicalism and Communist sympathies by filling empty bellies. Whether it ultimately realized that promise is debatable, but that the green revolution remade the environmental and social fabric of the planet is undeniable. The campaign narrowed ecological diversity in its persistent promotion of monoculture; it triggered massive rural migrations in societies across the Global South, as peasant farmers uprooted by technopolitical enclosure movements became wageworkers in urban slums or on distant commercial farms; it contributed to a frenzy of urbanization whose future is yet unresolved. Of the many Western-led campaigns of "development" that defined the latter half of the twentieth century, the green revolution likely had the greatest impact on the landscape and population of our planet.[4]

From where did this sweeping global transformation arise? How did agriculture and rural poverty in a nation like Mexico come to be the concern of scientists and policy makers thousands of miles removed? If the green revolution has been the subject of intensive study by social scientists, economists, and—only recently—historians, its origins and motivations have barely begun to be explored.[5] Because of the campaign's ultimate prominence as a US Cold War strategy toward winning "hearts and minds" in the Third World, students of the green revolution have nearly all assumed that its provenance may be found in post-1945 geopolitics. In this view, a cadre of hubristic US internationalists, concerned with Soviet expansionism and intoxicated by recent advances in agronomy, sought to transplant an idealized US agriculture on a hungry Third World. Mexico was but the first of many poor nations in which this package was to be tested, with the Cold War providing the motivation and hybrid seeds, DDT, and synthetic fertilizer as the vehicle.[6]

In the pages that follow, I suggest that such an assumption dangerously distorts the origins of the green revolution and the impetus behind the Rockefeller Foundation's intervention in Mexican agriculture. Rather than being conceived beyond the borders of the United States in a Cold War crucible, the green revolution was born in the domestic laboratory of the early twentieth-century US South. In the world of Rockefeller philanthropy, the MAP was merely one in a succession of efforts designed to grapple with rural poverty and underdevelopment. The Rockefeller family organized its first philanthropic venture in 1903 under the General Education Board (GEB), an agency that explicitly targeted the regional poverty of the US Cotton Belt. From 1906 to 1914, the GEB oversaw an extensive attempt to remake southern agriculture and the socioeconomic organization of the countryside. Then, in the bleak years of the Great Depression, the Rockefeller philanthropies returned to the region, and grappled again with the technological, social, and environmental obstacles to regional growth.

When the Rockefeller Foundation established its influential Mexican program in 1943, therefore, its leaders explicitly modeled that project on earlier experiences within the United States. As one key architect of the MAP declared in 1941, Mexico in the wake of Lázaro Cárdenas's land reform would greatly benefit from "an adaptation of the General Education Board's Southern agricultural program to suit Mexican conditions."[7] In the view of these leaders, such an effort would rely on the transmittance of a portmanteau of agricultural technologies unavailable to the earlier campaign, but for any assault on poverty and underdevelopment to be successful, it must also consider human concerns. And in the eyes of foundation planners, the US Cotton Belt was a region that shared the social, economic, and environmental problems of Mexico as well as other poor rural nations, and they believed that the South's continuing struggle with poverty could teach valuable lessons. As previous chapters have demonstrated for the agrarian New Deal and Cardenista land reform, the green revolution too was a product of the frequent comparisons that marked the US-Mexican agrarian dialogue of the 1930s. And the US South, more so than any other part of the United States, decisively shaped its outcome.[8]

To acknowledge the importance of US regionalism abroad forces a reevaluation of that nation's global expansion in the post-1945 era.[9] Like many other US-led internationalist projects during the so-called American Century, the green revolution is commonly described as a campaign to "Americanize" Third World agriculture. Yet I argue that instead of one, there were *many* Americas that served as blueprints for agrarian transformation. Alabama and Iowa, for example, offered dramatically different models for rural reconstruction. In many ways, Alabama provided far more relevant lessons for fighting poverty in Mexico than Iowa ever could. With its history of economic colonialism, plantation agriculture, racial stratification, and the uneven distribution of land and wealth—trends quite familiar to the twentieth-century Global South—a place like Alabama more closely resembled the decolonizing republics of Asia, Africa, and Latin America. The careful selection of particular regional models, rather than blanket "Americanization," was thus crucial to the waging of the green revolution and countless other US development programs abroad.

Unearthing the regional US roots of development work in the Cold War Third World likewise does much to discredit characterizations of the US South in the first half of the twentieth century as disconnected, parochial, and isolated from national and global currents. Far too often, scholars have internalized the opinions of contemporary critics like H. L. Mencken, who caustically dismissed the South's religious fundamentalism, distrust of outsiders, and racial anxieties as utterly distinct from the United States and world beyond. Indeed, as US historiography has taken the so-called transnational turn in recent decades, southern history between Reconstruction's end and World War II has been largely untouched by such methodologies. Yet when we acknowledge the myriad ways that the era's diagnoses of and solutions for southern poverty were internationalized in the following decades, the South emerges as vital to global conversations about agrarian unrest, modernization, and economic growth.

This chapter turns away from the government bureaucrats, social scientists, and agrarian radicals who have until now populated this book's pages, in favor of a close analysis of US philanthropy and its profound impact on the North American—and ultimately global—countryside. I examine the Rockefeller philanthropies' winding road into Mexico, beginning at the dawn of the twentieth century and culminating in the establishment of the MAP in 1943. The chapter opens with the GEB's early and quixotic attempt to overcome rural poverty in the US Cotton Belt, exploring the competing visions that fractured its campaign. Measured by its lofty rhetoric, that program was undeniably a failure. Still, during the agrarian ferment of the 1930s, an unexpected alliance of US southern reformers—led notably by ambassador to Mexico Josephus Daniels—pushed the Rockefeller Foundation to replicate its earlier efforts in Mexico. By 1943, when the foundation formally partnered with the Mexican government to work in agricultural reform, that push would reach its successful climax.

On its heels, the following chapter examines the first decade of the Rockefeller program founded in 1943, tracing how comparisons and analogies to the US South continued to shape that campaign long after its birth. Along the way, the green revolution—that polarizing global phenomenon that has undeniably remade our planet's social and ecological landscape—appears more fluid, more rooted in historical contingency, and far more "American" than most scholars have assumed.

ROCKEFELLER PHILANTHROPY AND THE US SOUTH

In the years surrounding the turn of the twentieth century, it appeared as if the US South had rejoined the national fold. White southern troops fought alongside northerners in a common war for empire in the Caribbean and Pacific, the US Supreme Court upheld the legality of racial segregation, and for the first time since the 1860s, a southerner—Woodrow Wilson— captured the White House. "New South" boosters knelt at the altar of northern industry, while white veterans of the Union and Confederacy together embraced a nostalgic and whitewashed myth of why they had once fought.[10] Yet as the South and nation grew together, they also grew further apart. As roads, rails, and telegraph lines made neighbors of distant peoples, a growing chorus of northern voices began to call attention to the vast divide separating the industrial city and cotton South. Influential reformers and philanthropists such as Robert C. Ogden, John Fox Slater, and George Peabody saw in the South a benighted and squalid region, starved of capital, credit, and education. They noted its endemic public health problems and worried particularly about the dire poverty of black southerners, who had seen a steady erosion of their political and economic status since the end of Reconstruction. During the first decade of the century, hand-wringing over the "problem South" grew ubiquitous in northern elite circles.[11]

Alarm at the deprivation in the US South was especially pronounced as reformers looked to the region's countryside. Admittedly, city dwellers' anxieties about the failings of rural life were not restricted to the South in this era. In the wake of populism's political demise, urban progressives— represented best by the so-called Country Life movement—sought to address the imbalance between city and country that had energized the farmers' earlier revolt. But unlike the Grange or Farmers' Alliance, urban progressives worried that the US countryside's gravest problem was not external exploitation but rather its inability to keep pace with industrial modernity. Imagining farmers as stubborn conservatives that slowed national growth,

Country Life devotees proposed a remaking of the farm in the image of the city and factory. And in looking to the South, where sharecropping, mono-culture, soil erosion, and the shadow of the plantation sharpened percep-tions of decline and decay, reformers sounded a particularly urgent call for change.[12]

The twin anxieties of regional backwardness and rural torpor crystal-lized most decisively in the philanthropic career of the wealthiest man in the United States, John D. Rockefeller. It was in his family's early effort to remake the US southern countryside that—unwittingly—the seeds of the global green revolution would first be planted. As the executive of the be-hemoth Standard Oil Company, Rockefeller had in the late nineteenth cen-tury amassed a fortune of a scale unknown to the United States before the second industrial revolution. Like his contemporaries Cornelius Vanderbilt and Andrew Carnegie, Rockefeller believed in the necessity of philanthropy, informed by his evangelical faith and nagging fear of social upheaval in an age of growing inequality. Organized Rockefeller philanthropy had its ori-gins in 1901, when Rockefeller's son, John D. Jr., climbed aboard the "Mil-lionaire's Special" as it set course from New York into the US South. Given its name by skeptical southern journalists, the "Special" was a train excur-sion attended by the leading lights in northern philanthropy, chartered by retail magnate Robert Ogden to inspire interest in the South among a new generation of industrialist donors. What Rockefeller junior witnessed—endless cotton fields, dilapidated schoolhouses, and sharecroppers both black and white—would guide his career in the years to come; he later re-called the trip as "one of the outstanding events of my life."[13]

Rockefeller junior implored his father to take action, and Rockefeller senior obliged by chartering the GEB in January 1903 and endowing it with an unprecedented $53 million during its first decade.[14] While the board's publicly stated mission—like its name—was intentionally ambiguous, its leadership unanimously targeted the "needs of the people of our Southern States."[15] While Rockefeller junior provided the public face of the board's leadership, the primary architects of the GEB were two New York Baptist ministers who had long advised Rockefeller senior: Frederick T. Gates and Wallace Buttrick. Both had family roots in the evangelical abolitionist world of the mid-nineteenth century, and both were deeply concerned about the "situation in the South," as the former wrote the latter in 1901.[16] Like other northern elite reformers of the era, they shared a dark fascination with the chasm of difference that lay between their urban industrial world and the languishing cotton states. Yet Gates and Buttrick sympathized particularly with the desperate plight of the black southerner, whose uplift and educa-tion "presents a peculiar and special obligation."[17] That their concern for African Americans was deeply paternalist is undeniable; Buttrick himself wrote that "the one thing needed here is a white man with a deep sense of responsibility for these negroes."[18] Nevertheless, in an era termed the "nadir" of US race relations by scholars, the GEB's support for black education and economic advancement posed an undeniable challenge to the South's racial hierarchy.[19]

As their board's name suggested, Gates, Buttrick, and Rockefeller junior began their philanthropic effort in the schools and universities of the South. But in traveling throughout the region, they quickly came to realize that other obstacles preceded education. "We are interested in the schools of the South," Gates told fellow GEB officers in 1905, "but we ought to be interested chiefly in the soil of the South, which supports the school."[20] It was not long, therefore, before they turned their reform agenda to rural life and agriculture. Yet the GEB's leadership wisely acknowledged that social and economic structures contributed to farm poverty as much as environmental concerns. On a trip to Alabama in 1902, Buttrick noted that while "the land is old and worn out," equally disastrous was that "practically all of these farmers are slaves to the crop-mortgage system."[21] Targeting agriculture as the primary stumbling block to regional growth, the GEB's leadership soon confronted the entangled ills of soil erosion, tenancy, exploitative lending practices, competitive global cotton markets, and a racial hierarchy ordering them all. That intricate web invited few easy solutions. Unwilling to consider land reform or other forms of social leveling, Rockefeller planners sought an alternate strategy to break the chains of the cotton economy that submerged most southern farmers in poverty and dependence.[22]

Northern philanthropy had no monopoly on planning a reconstruction of the southern farm in this era. The US Department of Agriculture (USDA) had recently embarked on a similar mission, which would ultimately dovetail with the GEB's efforts and requires some explanation. Though merely a shadow of the juggernaut it would become by the New Deal, the USDA funneled substantial resources into fomenting an agricultural renaissance in the Cotton Belt at the turn of the century. Pioneering those efforts was Seaman A. Knapp, an elderly farm educator and Iowa agriculture professor who had grown wealthy speculating in Louisiana rice planting.[23] Knapp began his work for the USDA in 1898 as a bioprospector in Asia, seeking rice cultivars "better suited to the requirements of rice culture in the Southern states than those now in cultivation there."[24] His travels took him through China, Japan, India, and the Philippines in a curious inversion of the later green revolution. Returning to the United States in 1902, Knapp was appointed "Special Agent for the Promotion of Agriculture in the South" by the USDA's Bureau of Plant Industry, and tasked with establishing demonstration farms in Texas and Louisiana that would exhibit foreign seed varietals and encourage diversification away from cotton. Yet to Knapp and the USDA's great disappointment, such efforts were met with little local enthusiasm. Neither tenants nor landowners, either distrustful of government-paid "book farmers" or unable to apply their recommendations, paid much attention to the bureau's early demonstration efforts.[25]

What rescued Knapp from obscurity was the first Mexican immigrant to transform the US South: *el picudo*, the insect known in English as the boll weevil. The weevil had long plagued cotton growers in Mexico's northeast with its seemingly insatiable appetite for maturing plants, and during the 1890s it crept into Texas on the endless white blanket that covered the Gulf Coast. By the turn of the century, the terror among US cotton planters and sharecroppers who lay in the weevil's path was palpable. Knapp, hardly a novice to self-promotion, immediately saw in cotton's crisis an invaluable opportunity to popularize his demonstration work. Speaking to farmers in a newly apocalyptic tone, Knapp heightened their fears with dark forecasts of the weevil's ruin, in calculated preparation of his fall 1903 announce-ment that he had found a solution to their woes. On a few trial acres in Terrell, Texas, Knapp boasted that volunteers using his cultural method—burning the previous season's cotton stalks and planting early—had beaten the weevil in an infected county and reaped a record harvest of the fiber. While Knapp's declaration was overblown, if not downright deceptive, as Terrell actually saw no weevils that season, panicked cotton growers eagerly embraced it. Knapp's agents enlisted hundreds of volunteers the following year to demonstrate his method and convert their neighbors, and overnight Knapp became a darling of the southern press.[26]

While the hysterical boll weevil campaign was a stark departure from his prior diversification work, Knapp began his efforts to reconstruct cotton culture with a genuine belief that it could solve the rural South's many ills. With his roots in New York and Iowa, Knapp imagined farmers as a homo-geneous and egalitarian lot, and he clung to the belief that increased pro-duction would lift all boats. Thus, in late 1903 he insisted, "The Southern states must continue to grow cotton" as "it was still their best cash crop."[27] But as Knapp chased the weevil through the Deep South, he confronted a landscape torn by contradictions and structural inequalities. By 1905, he came to worry about the prevalence of "soils that have been depleted by continuous cropping of cotton."[28] In the Mississippi Delta in early 1906, Knapp observed with disdain "very large cotton plantations, the owners of which do not care to raise anything but cotton" and "actually object to hav-ing diversification taught to the tenants, because they fear that the tenants will become independent farmers and leave their employ."[29] Knapp came to particularly abhor the "dominant, oppressive, and insolent" crop lien sys-tem that chained tenants to landlords—and both to cotton monoculture—while "unblushingly swe[eping] the earnings of toil from the masses into the coffers of the few."[30] Therefore, not long after Knapp had promised to save cotton culture from the weevil's wrath, he had become a fundamental critic of it.

This conversion dramatically impacted his stewardship of the demonstration work, and would ultimately bring about a partnership with the Rockefeller philanthropies. As early as October 1904, Knapp proposed to the USDA a departure from the myopic emphasis on cotton, "allowing [its work] to include corn and a few other common crops" alongside an expansion to states east of the Mississippi River yet untouched by the weevil.[31] Knapp envisioned a sweeping reconstruction of southern agriculture with the feared insect as his vehicle, as "there is nothing but the plagues of Pharaoh or the American boll weevil that will oblige [large planters] to change their methods."[32] Yet in doing so, Knapp confronted serious obstacles. Interstate commerce laws restricted government intervention to weevil-infested states, and Knapp quickly discovered that the underfunded USDA could hardly bankroll the vast campaign he dreamed of. It was then that Knapp and his allies reached out to the Rockefeller philanthropies. In May 1905, the USDA's assistant secretary contacted the GEB's Gates for his aid. Gates was predictably enthusiastic that through their partnership, "something highly useful and important can be done for the South, along the lines of reclaiming their worn out soil and elevating their rural life."[33] In April 1906, the GEB and USDA signed a "memorandum of understanding" that formalized their partnership.[34] GEB funding would pay the salaries of USDA demonstration agents to work in non-weevil-infested states, where they would teach "better methods of farming in order to secure the bare necessities of life."[35]

Between 1906 and 1914, the GEB funneled nearly $1.2 million into Knapp's farm demonstration campaign.[36] Rockefeller money paid for hundreds of newly hired agents to enter counties in every state between Mississippi and Virginia, where they enlisted local volunteers to adopt a package of agricultural practices and show its potential to curious neighbors. That package was surprisingly sensitive to the ecological and socioeconomic contours of the rural South. Knapp's "Ten Commandments" of modern agriculture demanded "the judicious use of barnyard manure and legumes" and the "systematic rotation of crops" along with an emphasis on the "home production of food" to foster independence from creditors.[37] Knapp's agents enlisted both landowners and renters, and questionnaires mailed to participants reveal the leadership's sensitivity to agrarian class tensions. One 1908 survey inquired whether the demonstration work "enabled any of the small farmers to get out of debt to the merchants and bankers," and if "any perceptible number of tenants ... have been able to purchase farms."[38] Cotton and the weevil played significant roles during earlier years, but the GEB and Knapp's insistence on diversification ultimately shunted the white fiber to side stage, in favor of food crops like corn. After all, by 1909 Knapp was publicly arguing that "the single-crop system" and "large plantation" both "retard ... rural development and promote ... class distinctions against mass development."[39]

Figure 4.1. General Education Board corn demonstration in Mississippi, late 1900s or early 1910s. General Education Board Papers, series 1054, box 48, folder 559. Courtesy of Rockefeller Archive Center.

If Knapp and his agents displayed a surprising eagerness to critique the economic structures of the Cotton Belt, they gladly embraced the white South's racial order and its subordination of African Americans. Knapp's speeches are littered with disparaging statements about "an unlettered and previously subordinate race," whose "possession of lands as owners, renters, and occupiers" had "drive[n] out the better classes just as an inferior coinage usurps the place of the more valuable."[40] In pursuing the demonstration campaign, Knapp rarely displayed much sympathy to the plight of black farmers, confessing to his chief at the USDA that the impact of the work would be far reduced "if we include all the colored farmers."[41] Neither did his white agents seem concerned, as one noted from Mississippi, that "white men own the land and rent it to the darkies."[42] As was true of many southern demagogues of the early twentieth century, Knapp and his agents happily condemned moneyed interests but were careful to toe the color line.

Of the thousands of demonstration agents who fanned out across ten southern states between 1906 and 1914, many more received their paychecks from the GEB than from the USDA.[43] That fact prompts an important question: How much power and influence did the Rockefeller leadership wield over Knapp's work? Scholars have long accepted the GEB's insistent claim that it was merely a silent partner to the USDA, providing money and little else.[44] The archival record, however, reveals otherwise. For example, Buttrick demanded that Knapp's agents report personally to him, while Knapp was

Figure 4.2. South Carolina General Education Board corn demonstrator sits by his record-breaking harvest of 1910. General Education Board Papers, series 1054, box 48, folder 559. Courtesy of Rockefeller Archive Center.

required to present hiring decisions before the board.[45] Knapp frequently met with GEB officers and attended their board meetings in New York, where the Rockefeller leadership sought to shape the work undertaken on the ground: Gates pushed Knapp to prioritize corn over cotton, and chose the official name for their joint project.[46] It was no surprise, then, that Gates would describe "our agricultural work" to a fellow reformer with no mention of Knapp or the USDA, proud that "the seed seems to be growing and spreading wherever we have sown it."[47]

Perhaps the GEB's most significant influence on the agricultural demonstration work was its insistence that the campaign incorporate black southerners. Even before its partnership with the USDA, Rockefeller philanthropy had worked closely with Alabama's Tuskegee Institute and its agricultural chief George Washington Carver to implement practical means for extending agricultural research to black tenants, sharecroppers, and landowners.[48] Before 1906, Knapp had instructed his all-white agents to work with black farmers but he opposed hiring African Americans for the job. GEB pressure overturned this ban, and the USDA hired Thomas Campbell in 1906 as its first black demonstration agent. Knapp himself acknowledged that his "efforts to take up some work ... among the colored people" was due to the personal pressures of the Rockefeller leadership.[49] Such measures earned the

GEB bitter enemies in the region; for instance, the *Southern Farm Magazine* in 1907 maligned the "negroid tendencies" of the Rockefeller board and its "Africanizing of the South under the cover of philanthropy."[50] Yet despite the fiery backlash, the desegregation pushed by northern philanthropy was piecemeal at best. As late as 1912, the USDA employed only 31 black extension agents alongside 681 whites.[51]

For nearly a decade, Knapp, the USDA, and the Rockefeller philanthropies spoke of their campaign's impact on the rural South in millennial terms. The GEB declared that crop diversification and rising agricultural productivity had ushered in a "social and educational awakening" in the region, while Knapp boasted of "whole sections raised from poverty to prosperity."[52] Were such declarations warranted? Ultimately, the project's greatest accomplishment was the institutionalization of state power in rural people's lives. In May 1914, eyeing the popularity of the GEB-Knapp program, Congress passed the Smith-Lever Act, which created the Cooperative Extension Service within the USDA and expanded the reach of farm demonstration into every state of the union. That decision marked a fundamental turning point in the history of the US countryside. During the twentieth century, the Extension Service would serve as the primary conduit between federally funded agricultural research and practicing farmers. Largely eschewing the GEB's hand-wringing about poor farmers, racial minorities, and monoculture, extension agents partnered with wealthy commercial farmers to champion efficiency, mechanization, and an industrial ethos for farming, which reaped similar effects in the US countryside as later green revolutions would in the Global South.[53]

Yet as a solution to rural poverty, indebtedness, and soil erosion—the problems that had first drawn the Rockefeller philanthropies to the South—the demonstration campaign was a dismal failure. Whatever gains in diversification made during the 1900s and early 1910s were abandoned during the Great War, when cotton prices spiked upward in response to overseas demand. Farmers hopeful of quick profits rapidly returned fields once planted in corn, peanuts, and peaches to the white fiber. When the war's end brought a devastating crash in agricultural prices, those small farmers who had seen gains in the previous decade were the first to default on loans and lose their lands. In 1920, more southern farmers were tenants and sharecroppers than had been the case in 1900, and King Cotton continued to wash away the fragile skin of the South's topsoil. It was therefore no surprise when the New York radical Frank Tannenbaum toured the southern countryside in 1923, and expressed shock at the "white plague" of cotton monoculture and the "new slavery" it presided over. In his travels, Tannenbaum did not observe "any interest in the scientific upbuilding of the soil, rotation of crops, or the cultivation of legumes." Less than a decade after its climax, the sweeping farm demonstration campaign seemed to have left little trace on the rural South, and the region's downward spiral would only continue.[54]

To the GEB's leadership, the shortcomings of the farm demonstration work were compounded by the ignominy of their exit from government co-operation. Just as the Smith-Lever bill to create a national Extension Service awaited congressional action in spring 1914, the Rockefellers reluctantly captured the national spotlight after labor unrest at their family-owned Colorado Fuel and Iron Company resulted in the slaughter of nineteen pro-testers by the state militia. Public condemnations of the violence were deaf-ening. And as it became widely known that Rockefeller philanthropy had played a pivotal role in the farm demonstration work, the family's many critics funneled outrage at the Colorado massacre into the halls of Con-gress. During the Smith-Lever hearings, infuriated politicians denounced the Rockefellers' "silent empire" and money "red with human blood and dripping with human tears." Several senators pushed—unsuccessfully—to revoke the GEB's charter, but by the end of the debate Congress formally barred the GEB from any future government collaboration. To the board's leadership and Rockefeller family, such a public insult stung badly.[55]

What can we make of the Rockefeller philanthropies' decade-long effort to reconstruct US southern agriculture? Ultimately, the campaign contained many of the ironies that characterized later "development" work in the Global South. Much smoke and little fire marked the campaign, as its rhe-torical accomplishments far outpaced its physical achievements. It won supporters by promising the possibility of sweeping social and economic change through the adoption of technical expertise and its material coun-terparts, rather than the redistribution of land and wealth. Like the Cold War green revolution, the Rockefeller program in the US South fostered—as historian Nick Cullather writes of a later period—a "sheltering discourse of modernization protect[ing] it from the memory or imputation of failure."[56] Yet Knapp and the GEB's campaign also left behind an ambiguous legacy as to the potential human and environmental impact of agricultural reform. Their project began by solely emphasizing the increased production of cot-ton, but over time came to critique monocultural production and planta-tion economics. While hopeful that farmers who did not own their land would benefit from agricultural extension, neither Knapp nor the GEB risked a wholesale repudiation of local power structures. And no matter the Rockefellers' posturing to the contrary, the USDA actively excluded Af-rican Americans from the demonstration work and denied them its poten-tial benefits.

Despite these missteps and contradictions, the early twentieth-century campaign to transform the US southern countryside had a surprisingly long afterlife within the Rockefeller philanthropies. Into the 1960s, foundation leaders continued to describe the GEB's demonstration work as "still the best available answer to the problems of underdeveloped countries."[57] As Rockefeller planners in subsequent decades would remember it, the southern agricultural work imparted three practical lessons. First, it showed that skeptical farmers would only adopt new techniques after seeing their utility firsthand on a neighbor's plot. "The place to write [agricultural] knowledge," as Buttrick argued in 1907, "is on the soil," where it "will be read by the farmer and understood by him."[58] Second, the campaign revealed the compelling visual power of abundance—particularly as illustrated through the new medium of photography—and Rockefeller promotional materials of southern farmers standing beside record harvests closely resemble those distributed a half century later in Asia and Latin America. Lastly, the GEB's partnership with Knapp revealed that rural poverty was not merely the product of low crop yields but equally of intangible structural problems—represented in the US South by tenancy, exploitative lending practices, racial exclusion, and political disfranchisement. It was especially this last lesson that held the greatest potential value for agricultural reformers of later generations, although it would not always be followed.

The bridge between the GEB's reform of US southern agriculture and the global green revolution, however, was hardly foreordained. Indeed, few of the architects of the Rockefeller work in the Progressive era Cotton Belt imagined their campaign as a blueprint for similar efforts elsewhere. It was only through the unexpected encounters and exchanges between US and Mexican rural reform in the coming decades—coming to a head during the turbulent years of the 1930s—that the GEB's work in the US South would serve as a model for even more ambitious efforts in Mexico.

Bridging the US South and Global South

The Rockefeller philanthropies' first experiment with agricultural reform ended in disaster. After investing nearly a decade and a fortune into the USDA's campaign to remake the southern farm, the GEB was greeted with rebuke rather than recognition. Publicly excoriated for a perceived attempt to force its agenda on the government, the GEB was in 1914 forcibly barred from future federal cooperation. Not surprisingly, deeply felt resentment at the Smith-Lever catastrophe permeated the board's leadership and compelled a turn away from campaigns of social engineering. By the late 1910s, the GEB had retreated from direct interventions in southern society and economy, choosing instead to fund institutions of higher education. It was not long thereafter that the aging vanguard represented by Buttrick and Gates retired, replaced by younger leadership more likely to come from the ranks of Progressive social science than the clergy—many of whom believed the board should look beyond its narrow regional focus.[59]

As the GEB withdrew from its attempt to remake the US southern coun-tryside, though, other wings of Rockefeller philanthropy carried the torch. In 1909, Rockefeller senior gave $1 million to found the Rockefeller Sani-tary Commission for the Eradication of Hookworm Disease, diagnosing the South's dismal public health as an obstacle equal to agriculture. Armed with a nascent understanding of germ theory, the public health troops of the Sanitary Commission built latrines, purified water sources, and treated in-fected children and adults across the region. In contrast to the agricultural campaign, the hookworm project could quickly boast demonstrable results. Just five years later, its leadership triumphantly declared that the commis-sion's primary aim could be "deemed to have been accomplished."[60] It was the success and popularity of the public health work that compelled Rocke-feller senior to unveil the largest and most ambitious of his philanthropic institutions: the Rockefeller Foundation, chartered in 1913 with an endow-ment that made the GEB's appear paltry. Like its predecessor, the Rockefeller Foundation began its work in the US South, seeking to replicate the success of the hookworm campaign for other tropical diseases. During the 1910s, the foundation and its International Health Board (IHB) targeted yellow fever, malaria, and tuberculosis across the Cotton Belt, with much fanfare but more modest success.[61]

It was not long thereafter that ambitious Rockefeller leaders proposed that their US southern work in hookworm, malaria, and yellow fever be "made a world campaign."[62] Public health, therefore—not agriculture—served as the Rockefeller philanthropies' first vehicle for globalizing lessons learned in the incubator of the US South. In 1914, the foundation took its first steps beyond the boundaries of the United States when it forged an alliance with colonial administrators in London to initiate a hookworm treatment program in British Guiana. In the following decade, IHB officials established offices across the Caribbean, Latin America, Pacific Asia, and northern Africa. Though seemingly abrupt, the leap from public health work in the US South to destinations abroad came naturally to the Rockefeller philanthropies. In their theorization of the causes of tropical backwardness, poverty, and disease, Mississippi and Alabama spoke volumes about other Caribbean societies, and even countries as far away as India and Egypt. The US South, foundation planners believed, simply lay in the northern reaches of a global "hookworm belt" that stretched across the planet's tropical and semitropical regions. As such, doctors trained in the South often provided leadership abroad, seamlessly moving between plantation districts in Geor-gia, Cuba, and the Philippines. Public health work also built the foundation's first bridge to Mexico, when in 1920 the IHB partnered with the revolution-ary Mexican state to combat yellow fever in Veracruz and Tamaulipas.[63]

By the 1920s, the Rockefeller Foundation headquarters on Forty-Ninth Street in New York City was the central hub in a vast philanthropic network that stretched from the US South outward into the Caribbean world, and then across the globe to Asia and Africa. In pursuit of the "well-being of mankind throughout the world"—the Rockefeller Foundation's founding motto—thousands of evangelically minded US experts and reformers fanned out across a planet then largely parceled between colonial powers. As the tendrils of US informal empire extended into the world's far reaches in the early twentieth century, foundation philanthropy served as an undeniable vanguard.[64]

Despite the crucial role that agriculture played in shaping the Rockefeller family's philanthropic vision in its earliest years, farming attracted scant attention during the foundation's interwar campaigns. In contrast to the massive funding devoted to public health and education efforts, agriculture and rural life received a pittance of the foundation's time and energy between 1915 and 1940.[65] Just a decade later, such an imbalance would be hard to remember; indeed, by the 1960s, the Rockefeller Foundation was inseparable in the public sphere from its agricultural work worldwide. This decisive return to the foundation's agricultural roots was neither foreordained nor accidental—it was the product of the cross-pollination of US and Mexican agrarian politics during the 1930s. And leading the charge were two North Carolinians who should perhaps be recalled as the "fathers" of the green revolution: John A. Ferrell and Josephus Daniels.

Ferrell was a medical doctor and administrator for the Rockefeller Foundation's IHB, and his career perfectly exemplified the philanthropies' tight link between public health work in the US South and the greater Caribbean. He was born in 1880 to a middling family in Sampson County, North Carolina, an eastern plantation district where cotton and tobacco dominated the local economy. After working a few years as a rural teacher and then earning a degree in medicine at the University of North Carolina in 1907, Ferrell joined the Rockefeller Sanitary Commission to participate in the battle against hookworm in North Carolina. He saw in the Sanitary Commission both a professional opportunity and a chance to ease the suffering of poor rural residents of eastern North Carolina. By 1912, Ferrell was directing hookworm work in all the counties of his home state, and a year later he had risen to become associate director of the IHB.[66]

As the second in command of the IHB, Ferrell presided over the foundation's expansion of public health programs into Latin America. Crisscrossing the Caribbean basin during the 1920s, he coordinated the translation of US southern models into foreign context. When he first traveled to Mexico in 1927 to plan an expansion of the IHB program there, Ferrell described the small villages he visited as analogous to those he had observed in the US South. Praising the progress IHB workers and their allies in the Mexican public health service had made outside Mexico City, Ferrell declared, "So far as [the] number of pit privies is concerned, I might have been in North

Figure 4.3. John A. Ferrell of the Rockefeller Foundation's International Health Board. Rockefeller Foundation Papers, series 100, box 6, folder 152. Courtesy of Rockefeller Archive Center.

Carolina."[67] When he needed medical personnel in Mexico and elsewhere in Central America, he turned to staff members who had proven themselves working in the plantation districts of the US South.[68]

When Ferrell returned to Mexico in spring 1933, though, he grew convinced that public health reform alone was insufficient for combating rural poverty. Just as the Rockefeller philanthropies a generation earlier had sought to eradicate the hookworm alongside a reconstruction of agriculture, he believed that the foundation of the 1930s should also consider expanding its Mexican program beyond medicine. Meeting with Mexico's top ministers of agriculture and public health that March, Ferrell proposed that his foundation might aid the government in promoting "the advancement of agriculture," particularly through "demonstrations for elevating the standard of living."[69] Although the Mexicans politely declined to commit—likely because of the sharp politicization of agrarian affairs at the moment—on Ferrell's return to New York he pushed his superiors in the foundation to consider an expansion of their Mexican program. In response, Rockefeller Foundation vice president Selskar M. Gunn traveled to Mexico in 1934 to ascertain the possibility of broadening philanthropic work into agriculture and rural education. While sympathetic to the emerging agrarista campaign to undo the "evils which were inherent in the old plantation or hacienda plan of land tenure," Gunn worried that "Mexico is going through a violent attack of nationalism." Ultimately, the "uncertainties of the moment" meant that 1934 was "not a propitious time to consider expanding our present small program in Mexico." Ferrell's initiative was put on ice.[70]

The push for a Rockefeller agricultural program in Mexico would be revitalized by the second North Carolinian essential to the green revolution's early history: Daniels. Just weeks after Ferrell's 1933 visit to Mexico City, Franklin Roosevelt appointed Daniels as US ambassador, and the *News and Observer* editor moved from Raleigh to the Mexican capital. Daniels was Ferrell's senior by almost twenty years, and had first come to know the young doctor in the early years of the Rockefeller philanthropies' southern work. Curiously, Daniels was initially an angry opponent of the family's hookworm campaign, claiming in the pages of his newspaper that southerners should not "canonize Standard Oil Rockefeller" as he sought "to buy the appreciation of the people whom he has been robbing for a quarter of a century." Yet Daniels later admitted that he "got off on the wrong foot." Due in part to his conversations with Ferrell, a fellow North Carolinian who was leading the Rockefeller effort in his state, Daniels came to admit the "seriousness of the disease" and eventually "expressed [his] appreciation" for the foundation's public health work. Daniels and Ferrell remained in touch thereafter.[71]

In February 1935, Ferrell returned to Mexico City to review the foundation's public health work—his first visit since Daniels's diplomatic appointment. Rekindling their friendship at the US embassy that winter, Ferrell met with Daniels four times during his stay. In their long meetings, the two North Carolinians contrasted the social and economic problems of Mexico with their native region. This was hardly a surprise; after all, by 1935 Daniels had been comparing US southern and Mexican rural problems, along with the New Deal and Mexican Revolution, for nearly two years. "The situation in Mexico," Daniels told Ferrell, was "in many respects quite similar to that in the southern United States after the Civil War," though "the economic status of the ordinary Mexican family is probably a good deal worse than prevailed in the South." While "the South had its negro problem Mexico has the controversy between church and state," he concluded in an awkward juxtaposition. Yet as in the US South, Daniels argued that the "most urgent problem [in Mexico] involves raising the economic level of the people."[72]

Diagnosing similar dilemmas in the US Cotton Belt and Mexico, Daniels proposed that solutions for one might also prove effective for the other. Recalling the Rockefeller family's prior "activities carried on in the South to build it up economically," the ambassador wholeheartedly recommended an "adoption of the program supported by the General Education Board" in agriculture. Daniels believed such a campaign would "strengthen the present efforts of the [Cárdenas] Government" in land reform and agricultural development, and would eventually produce an "economic base high enough to permit taxes for the payment of services in public health, public education, public welfare, road building, etc." Ferrell, closely familiar with the GEB's agricultural campaign from his first decade with the Rockefeller philanthropies, was quick to agree. Working from Daniels's suggestions, Ferrell wrote a memorandum to his superiors at the foundation in which he proposed a program devoting between $25,000 to $100,000 a year "to aid the Government in developing demonstrations of agriculture and other activities intended to improve the economic wellbeing of families and communities." Mexican trainees might be sent to the United States for "studying procedures," then return home to "develop programs adaptable to Mexican conditions."[73] Ferrell also recommended that the foundation translate into Spanish and distribute "publications dealing with the rehabilitation of the U.S. South" as an "aid for Mexican agricultural and educational development."[74]

Daniels contributed his personal momentum to the proposal, too. On Ferrell's return to New York, the ambassador leaned on an influential friend of his, Raymond B. Fosdick, for support. Daniels had met Fosdick during the Great War, when the latter had been a close associate of President Wilson and undersecretary general of the League of Nations. By the 1930s, Fosdick was a key player in the Rockefeller philanthropic world as well as a prominent trustee of both the foundation and the GEB.[75] In Daniels's plea to Fosdick, he reiterated his belief that Mexico's "problems are somewhat similar to those we had in the South for several decades following the Civil War." Daniels therefore recommended the foundation pursue "some adaptation of the programs administered in the South by Buttrick, [IHB chief Wickliffe] Rose, and others" as such a move promised "real progress for Mexico." To lead the effort Daniels nominated Ferrell, as "his training with Buttrick and Rose and his actual participation in the South" prepared him well for "guiding a larger cooperative program in Mexico." Daniels also volunteered his embassy's support for any such venture. "[Ferrell] and I understand each other," Daniels assured Fosdick, "and [we] can work together for the development of cooperation in health and welfare movements for Mexico as we did for the development of the South."[76]

Yet to Daniels's and Ferrell's frustration, the Rockefeller Foundation evinced little interest in such suggestions. With most of the foundation's money and staff tied up in Asia and Europe, postrevolutionary Mexico seemed to pose greater risk than opportunity. There is no evidence that Fosdick responded to Daniels's exhortation, and Ferrell admitted several months later that he had "not been able to find a way for securing aid in this direction."[77] When Fosdick was elected president of both the Rockefeller Foundation and the GEB in 1936, the two allies renewed their efforts to convert him to their cause. Daniels wrote Fosdick in March of that year, insisting that he visit Mexico immediately to witness both the "great progress" made by the Cárdenas government in social policy and the opportunities for expanding Rockefeller aid.[78] Ferrell penned another memorandum to the new president calling for a "program of activities designed to improve economic conditions in Mexico" modeled on the work of "the General Education Board in the South from 1905 to 1914." He insisted that "two or three qualified persons might be sent to study [Mexico's] agricultural problems and possibilities and then outline broadly a constructive program."[79] Once again, however, their pleas fell on deaf ears. Eventually, Daniels grew bitter at the foundation's indifference toward and neglect of Mexico. In March 1937, he wrote angrily in his diary, "As [the Rockefellers] get millions here from oil fields they ought to do it; they expend millions of dollars in China to only a few thousand in Mexico."[80]

The Rockefeller Intervention in Mexican Agriculture

Daniels and Ferrell would only see their wishes fulfilled after two tectonic shifts reconfigured the political landscape within and beyond the foundation, opening new avenues for agricultural intervention. First, the Rockefeller philanthropies returned their attention to the problems of the rural US South. Second, global geopolitical unrest reoriented the foundation's agenda to suddenly emphasize Latin America and particularly Mexico.

Though Rockefeller philanthropy undeniably had its origin in anxieties about regional backwardness and the plight of rural African Americans, the late 1910s and 1920s had witnessed the group's steady retreat from strictly US southern concerns. The larger foundation had by then abandoned its original springboard, and even the explicitly regional GEB was by the late 1920s primarily funding colleges and universities outside the South.[81] Yet the Great Depression, which struck the Cotton Belt with an unmatched ferocity, would dramatically reverse this trend. After 1929, Rockefeller leaders grew increasingly worried that whatever gains made in the previous generation were being rapidly eroded by the economic collapse, especially among African Americans. Concerns about the stagnation and suffering of the US South reached a fever pitch by the mid-1930s, as activist sociologists like the University of North Carolina's Howard W. Odum publicized the region's myriad ills. Reflecting this heightened anxiety, in fall 1935 the GEB arranged a major conference titled Opportunities and Needs in the Southern States, where Odum and his collaborators spoke. The meeting signaled a symbolic return to the concerns that had originally fueled Rockefeller philanthropy, and was the first of many to come.[82]

Ultimately, it was the ascent of Raymond Fosdick, elected president of both the GEB and foundation in fall 1936, that brought the Rockefeller leadership full circle in revisiting the Cotton Belt. Fosdick firmly believed that the South remained a blighted region hungering for change. The GEB's new president embraced Odum's conclusion that Dixie was a rich land inhabited by poor people, and that shortsightedness, political demagoguery, and waste underlay this contradiction. Indeed, Fosdick upheld Odum's 1936 magnum opus *Southern Regions of the United States* as the "authoritative text on Southern conditions" that suggested all the "important issues in a program of rural reconstruction in the South."[83] It was therefore no surprise when in late 1936 Fosdick unveiled the GEB's New Southern Program, which would partner with the foundation in an "inter-department attack on the education and social problems of the South."[84] Over the next decade, Rockefeller philanthropy again grew synonymous with the impoverished region. Under the New Southern Program, the GEB served as a grant-making hub, funneling resources to reformers in academia and the federal government. The GEB breathed life into Odum's Institute for Research in Social Science, and it funded studies of land tenure at the University of Arkansas and small-scale rural industries at Clemson Agricultural College in South Carolina. Rockefeller money went toward agroecology in Senoia, Georgia, and trained African American "rural social engineers" in Tennessee and Alabama to work with the Farm Security Administration (FSA).[85]

Directly overseeing the New Southern Program after 1937 was a figure who would later play a prominent role in the foundation's Mexican campaign: Cornell University dean of agriculture Albert R. Mann. Born in Pennsylvania in 1880, Mann had studied agricultural economics with the renowned Liberty Hyde Bailey, whose humanistic approach to agriculture Mann shared. Despite his lack of southern roots or pedigree, Mann was endlessly curious about that region's agriculture, and since the early 1930s, he had worked with the Rockefeller philanthropies to publicize discrimination against black farmers along with the social and environmental failings of cotton culture.[86] While hardly a radical, Mann more than most economists was deeply concerned with agriculture's social and cultural context.

As the leader of the New Southern Program, he emphasized the importance of addressing "land economics, especially land tenure and utilization" as well as the persistence of "plantation folkways," which he believed "inhibit[ed] southern progress under present conditions."[87] Although he could hardly predict it at the time, such experience would decisively shape his later career in Mexico.

As stewards of a renewed program in southern rural reform, Fosdick, Mann, and other architects of Rockefeller philanthropy gained intimate knowledge of an agrarian world in crisis, cleaved by social and economic hierarchies, and haunted by its past. On their tours of the Cotton Belt in the late 1930s and early 1940s, they met black and white sharecroppers who described their insecurities; they saw an archaic agricultural system and the scarred landscape it produced.[88] Indeed, through the New Southern Program they grappled with the same difficult questions that would later shape the green revolution. What were the structural obstacles to overcoming rural poverty? How did power relations across the lines of race and class shape the organization of agriculture? And how could a small group of reformers hope to make a dent in social and economic patterns that were generations old? While predominantly observers in these early years, the Rockefeller leadership's engagement with the crisis of the Depression era South proved a lasting influence. When the foundation's leaders embarked on its Mexican agricultural intervention in 1943, they could draw on a generation of experience within the United States. Knapp's campaign in farm demonstration, then thirty years behind them, was an obvious precedent. Yet just as important were fresher memories of the Depression era South, and the zealous reformers in the New Deal and academia who challenged its status quo.

The philanthropies' return to the US South during the years of the Depression would decisively shape their pursuits of the 1940s. Nevertheless, the internal dynamics of Rockefeller bureaucracy alone cannot explain why the foundation chose Mexico as the site on which to transplant its program of rural uplift. Instead, that decision would stem from geopolitical ruptures far beyond its New York offices. By 1937, Japanese aggression imperiled the multiple Rockefeller programs in health and education on China's eastern coast, sending its agents fleeing. Thousands of miles westward, Adolf Hitler's invasion of Poland in 1939 likewise threatened the security of the foundation's vast investment in the European physical and social sciences. By 1940, therefore, the Rockefeller Foundation was in a state of limbo, desperate to address the global crisis, but restricted by the violence that was increasingly ensnaring Europe and Asia. It was no surprise then that the philanthropies rediscovered Latin America in the early years of World War II. Due in no small part to fears over Nazi expansion in the Western Hemisphere, Latin America became the target of vast US public and private outreach efforts in the early 1940s. In Washington, DC, Nelson Rockefeller's federal

Office of Inter-American Affairs sought to woo Latin American leaders with promises of aid and collaboration; Rockefeller's peers in philanthropy similarly looked southward.[89]

Mexico in particular seemed to offer a favorable political environment for US aid and anti-Axis efforts during the war. When Cárdenas's successor Ávila Camacho took power in December 1940, his promises of moderation, stability, and international cooperation eased many US anxieties from the 1930s. Ultimately, though, what tilted the scales in favor of a Rockefeller agricultural program in Mexico was a pilgrimage by the United States' most renowned agrarian New Dealer: Henry A. Wallace. As chapter 2 explored in some detail, former secretary of agriculture and vice president elect Wallace journeyed to Mexico in December 1940 to show US support at Ávila Camacho's contested inauguration. In his nearly two months in Mexico, Wallace traveled throughout the central plateau, speaking with common farmers in their ejido plots and surveying their stands of maize; he met with presidents, politicians, and agronomists.

Yet perhaps Wallace's most important contact in Mexico was Ambassador Daniels, whom he "got very well acquainted" with during his visit.[90] The two liberal New Dealers had known each other for years, but it was in late 1940 that they solidified their bond. Over several days at the embassy, the two men discussed the confluence of US and Mexican agrarian and agricultural reform. Just as Daniels had done with Ferrell, the ambassador compared the rural poverty of Mexico with that of the post-emancipation US South, insisting yet again that an agricultural demonstration project had the potential of reversing such ills. It was undoubtedly Daniels's pressure and persuasion that led Wallace to declare in mid-December, "The average ejidatario produces with his present technology less than the average share cropper in the South." Wallace also adopted Daniels's solution to that dilemma: that "one of the great foundations in the United States could render a great service by setting up a rather small experiment station designed both to discover and demonstrate more efficient methods of growing corn and beans."[91]

Nearly every account of the green revolution's origins argues that it was Wallace who provided the impetus and inspiration behind the Rockefeller Foundation's agricultural experiment in Mexico. Such an assumption is inviting, considering the vice president elect's interests and his statement above, and it has deeply shaped the historiography of the early green revolution.[92] The archival record, however, reveals no evidence for such a claim. Rather, Wallace merely contributed leverage to the two North Carolinians in fulfilling their push of more than half a decade. Though the former USDA chief was undoubtedly convinced of the necessity of Rockefeller action in Mexico by mid-December 1940, once he returned to the United States in January 1941 he took no action toward satisfying it. It was instead Daniels

Figure 4.4. Henry A. Wallace, Josephus Daniels, and their wives, Ilo and Addie, respectively, in Mexico City, December 1940. Lot 5376G. Courtesy of Library of Congress Prints and Photographs Division.

who provided the momentum in approaching the foundation's leadership once again.

In early January 1941, Daniels returned home to North Carolina to visit his family in Raleigh. Coincidentally, Ferrell was there that same week to attend an FSA conference on rural nutrition in the South. Encouraged by his discussions with Wallace in Mexico City, Daniels contacted Ferrell, and the two men convened at Daniels's home in Raleigh on January 12, 1941. As he had done earlier, Daniels insisted to Ferrell that Mexican "progress will be hastened by an adaptation to Mexican conditions of the activities of the Rockefeller Foundation boards in our southern states with respect to health, education, and agriculture." While their previous efforts had met with little success, Daniels assured Ferrell that they had found a well-placed ally in Wallace. Convinced that the vice president elect's sympathy for their plan provided new legitimacy, the ambassador urged Ferrell to approach the foundation's leadership once again.[93]

In the following week, Ferrell penned a program proposal that would ultimately serve as the blueprint of Mexico's green revolution. Titled "Aid to Mexico," the document began with a laundry list of that nation's social and economic shortcomings. "There are racial problems.... [T]he masses have been exploited by interests both within and without," and historically "there has been a failure to develop the human resources and to establish creditable standards of living for the underprivileged masses." To him and Daniels, "who for decades have been in close touch with the Southern states and their problems," it was evident that "the Mexican situation is similar to that which confronted the South following the war between the states." Due to these parallels, and because the "Rockefeller boards have aided substantially in the South over a period of forty years," Ferrell suggested the foundation pursue in Mexico "an adaptation of the General Education Board's Southern agricultural program." Yet Knapp's demonstration campaign was but one of many regional models that Ferrell believed might succeed in Mexico. He was equally optimistic about "the type of assistance given by the Farm Security Administration," encompassing "small loans, ... guidance in carrying out a prescribed program" of planting, and "supervision by farm agents and home economists." The US South's recent history, Ferrell insisted, revealed that there "is a precedent for government aid to the poor agricultural families."[94]

Yet Ferrell acknowledged that rural Mexico was neither a tabula rasa lacking history nor a mirror image of the US South. Mexico was not a place of stasis but instead of recent transformation, namely because of "the social revolution that has gained momentum for the past twenty years." Indeed, in his proposal Ferrell evinced a surprisingly sympathetic portrayal of recent Cardenista reforms. "The general plans Mexicans have evolved for the advancement of education and agriculture," Ferrell observed, were "soundly conceived and as good as could be provided for dealing with Mexican conditions." As justification for this argument, Ferrell—stunningly—included with his report the book *Democracy Comes to a Cotton Kingdom*, the 1940 portrayal of La Laguna's land reform written by Clarence Senior of the Southern Tenant Farmers' Union. Ferrell, therefore, saw Rockefeller aid as complementary—rather than contradictory—to the Cardenista vision of a just and productive countryside.[95]

Ferrell's proposal, with Wallace's symbolic stamp of approval, received a far more enthusiastic response among the foundation's leadership than previous efforts. On reading Ferrell's report, President Fosdick immediately made plans to discuss it with Vice President Wallace. Wallace, Fosdick, and Ferrell met on February 3 in Washington, DC, to debate the possibilities of foundation aid to Mexican agriculture. Wallace assured Fosdick that he was optimistic about the prospects of such a program, though he insisted that it must target corn and beans, Mexico's "principal foods," and that it would be most effective if "located on the plateau [surrounding Mexico City] where the population is dense." The agrarian New Dealer was likely pleased when Fosdick and Ferrell suggested a program of "aid to small farmers along the line of the subsistence homestead projects and the Farm Security Administration." Wallace nevertheless warned the foundation to tread carefully in Mexico, as the Rockefeller name might be linked in popular memory with "the oil industry, expropriated property, and the attendant controversies."[96]

With momentum building, the foundation's leadership met in New York on February 18 to formally consider a Mexican agricultural program. Represented in the meeting were the many diverse wings of Rockefeller philanthropy: President Fosdick sat alongside Ferrell, the project's instigator, and the heads of the foundation's Divisions of Natural Sciences and Social Sciences. Yet perhaps the most instrumental figure in the room was Albert Mann, then head of the GEB's New Southern Program and in the words of one colleague, "the only person on the 55th floor ... who really knew anything about agriculture."[97] Fosdick opened the meeting by emphasizing Mexico's need "for specialists and demonstrations such as the G.E.B. did in our South twenty years ago," aimed toward making "a contribution to the standard of living." Mann, as the resident expert on agriculture, laid out what he saw as the primary needs of the Mexican program, arguing that the "demonstration of existing knowledge" might prove the most effective approach. Likely remembering the Knapp campaigns, Mann suggested demonstrating "simple method[s] of selection of seed stocks" alongside "comparative variety trials which do not require any extension of basic research." By the meeting's end, Fosdick—weighing Mann's experience leading such programs in the United States—tasked the GEB chief with the next step of preparing a longer memorandum on the "agricultural approach to Mexico."[98]

The document Mann prepared two days later provided abundant evidence that its author was relying on his prior engagement with both the US South and New Deal programs targeting southern poverty. Any effort to improve Mexican agriculture, Mann argued, should pursue a two-pronged strategy. First was the "strengthening of basic scientific foundations" through the training of Mexican scientists in the basic agricultural sciences, such as soil chemistry, plant breeding and genetics, and plant pathology. Then, too, that "long-time procedure" should be accompanied by a more immediate campaign of extending "established knowledge of improved farm practices through demonstrations [to] persons of limited schooling," as exemplified best by the "Farm Security Administration in the United States." Both campaigns, insisted Mann, "must be indigenous and arise out of native abilities, native plant and animal stocks, and the cultural characteristics of the people." To undertake such an effort, Mann recommended that the foundation send two experts down to Mexico for a preliminary survey. The first should be a plant scientist, but the second ought to be well versed in social and economic studies, familiar with "special undertakings of the Farm Security Administration type." This balance of expertise was crucial to Mann's formulation of a program.[99]

As the foundation's leadership pondered how to proceed in Mexico, the North Carolinian Ferrell lent his personal effort to shaping the program under consideration. In mid-March 1941, he traveled to Mexico—where he would spend more than two weeks—to meet with Daniels again and investigate the possibilities of Rockefeller aid in agriculture. In Mexico City, Ferrell told the ambassador about his program proposal, which Daniels approved as "illuminating and interesting."[100] Ferrell went to the National School of Agriculture in the state of México as well as several rural normal schools in Mexico City and Michoacán, surveying the state of agriculture in between. Like Mann, Ferrell insisted to his foundation superiors that a program "supplying guidance and instruction in simple terms which the poor farmers in remote communities can understand" must accompany any pure research program. As his memories of the US South reaffirmed, "practical, simple demonstrations along elementary lines" would "hasten a better day for the Mexicans."[101]

Weighing Mann and Ferrell's suggestions, in April 1941 the foundation's leadership reconvened to appoint a so-called Survey Commission that would travel that summer for a lengthy examination of Mexico's agricultural problems. The foundation chose three men to make the trip: Elvin C. Stakman, a plant pathologist specializing in wheat who was then teaching at the University of Minnesota and had some experience working in Mexico; Harvard University's Paul Mangelsdorf, a corn breeder who had written extensively on the historical origins of maize and its social context; and Richard Bradfield, a soil scientist at Cornell University who had spent his career working with both synthetic and organic fertilizers. The selection of solely agronomists for the commission, in spite of Mann's insistence that the foundation appoint a social scientist or agricultural economist, was born from pressure within the Rockefeller Foundation's Division of Natural Sciences, which would provide the institutional home for the Mexican program. The Division of Natural Sciences leadership, not surprisingly, was far less interested in agriculture's social and economic context. Yet Mann bargained a compromise in securing the appointment of Mangelsdorf, who had worked extensively in East Texas with corn varieties appropriate to poor farmers during the 1930s—research that Mann "had been quite impressed with." Indeed, as the following chapter will reveal, Mangelsdorf would later play the most fundamental role in translating the lessons of the Depression era US South into Mexican context.[102]

In summer 1941—as this chapter's opening pages illustrated—Stakman, Bradfield, Mangelsdorf, and Mangelsdorf's graduate student Richard Schultes trekked nearly five thousand miles across rural Mexico in their GMC station wagon. The report they composed at summer's end revealed their sympathy for both the ejido and its small-scale cultivators. "There are some who assert that the relatively low status of agricultural productivity in Mexico is the fault of the ejidal system," observed the three writers, "and that improvement cannot be brought about as long as it exists." Among the large landholders they had met with, this was a ubiquitous observation. But they believed that "the first part of the assertion certainly is oversimplification and the second part is very probably not true." The main problem of Mexican agriculture, they claimed, was not its social organization in the post-Cárdenas era but rather its lack of effective techniques of cultivation. Mexican reformers' "social zeal," therefore, "should not be curbed but their scientific zeal must be increased.... Revolution must be followed by evolution," the Survey Commission members asserted, and in developing a package of scientific techniques appropriate to the ejidatarios, they hoped to strengthen the position of smallholders across Mexico.[103]

Yet how would they achieve this goal? The survey team's plan for improving peasant cultivation techniques was oriented toward the twin crops of corn and beans. The team suggested three concrete strategies toward boosting food crop cultivation: improvement of the soil, the introduction of new plant varieties, and the management of diseases and pests. In discussing maize, the survey team—and particularly Mangelsdorf, the group's corn expert— was rather skeptical of the promises of hybridized corn seed, a political technology that will be examined in far greater depth in the following chapter. Such seed, the three scientists argued, "must be purchased anew each year, and the small farmer in Mexico has neither the cash nor the initiative to do so." If hybrid corn was ever to make an impact among common farmers, they claimed, it had to be distributed by the ejidal banks to smallholders without the interference of commercial seed companies. Such a verdict would have sweeping consequences. But the men's sensitivity to social and economic inequalities also had its limits. They diagnosed the poverty of Mexico's soils as a major obstacle to rural welfare, but as a remedy emphasized the importance of synthetic, commercial fertilizers that were beyond the reach of most Mexican farmers.[104]

In the Survey Commission's report, the foundation's leadership believed it had arrived at a workable blueprint for the reconstruction of Mexican agriculture. That document should be understood as a patchwork quilt knit by many hands. It contained elements from the two North Carolinians who initiated the push for a Mexican program and looked back at Knapp's demonstration work in the US Cotton Belt as a replicable precedent. It showed the fingerprints of GEB New Southern Program leaders such as Fosdick and Mann who looked for inspiration in the New Deal's agrarian program in the southern states. Equally, it was influenced by the three agronomists who digested these earlier efforts, and their vision for an agricultural program did not always converge with the Rockefeller planners they partnered with. But whatever unanswered questions or competing visions lay within that blueprint would have to await resolution on the ground in

Mexico, for the foundation moved quickly to realize its plan. In December 1941 the GEB's Mann and Division of Natural Sciences chief Frank B. Hanson presented the Survey Commission's report to the foundation's board of trustees, which approved it unanimously.[105] The following July, the foundation hired Jacob George Harrar, a young plant pathologist and former student of Stakman who had experience working in both Puerto Rico and Virginia, as the local director to administer the planned program in Mexico. Finally, in October 1942, Fosdick reached out to Marte R. Gómez, President Ávila Camacho's agriculture secretary, to begin formal negotiations for a partnership in agricultural reform.

Writing twenty-five years later in their celebratory memoir *Campaigns against Hunger*, Bradfield, Stakman, and Mangelsdorf remembered a neat transition from the foundation's US work into Mexico. "What most urgently needed to be done in 1941 in Mexico was fairly obvious," they recalled.[106] In truth, great uncertainties marked this leap. That the Mexican government would embrace Rockefeller collaboration was uncertain; how the foundation might fare in the turbulent currents of post-Cardenista politics was entirely unknown. Likewise, the contrasting agrarian visions of the diverse groups that drafted the 1941 Rockefeller blueprint coexisted uncomfortably and would force difficult choices in their practical application in Mexico. Over the next decade, countless questions demanded answers, and on their resolution hung the fate of rural Mexico and much of the planet's countryside.

***

The desire to transform agriculture and its human practitioners had animated Rockefeller philanthropy since its inception at the dawn of the twentieth century, but nearly all studies of the green revolution begin in 1943 with the foundation's experiment in Mexico. As this chapter has shown, such an instinct neglects a far deeper history that helps to explain the origins of US "development" efforts abroad. Rather than a product of Cold War geopolitical anxieties, the Rockefeller-led green revolution had its roots in the early twentieth-century US South, a region that served as a domestic laboratory for philanthropic antipoverty efforts. Though few of its architects could have predicted it, the GEB's partnership with Knapp and the USDA between 1906 and 1914 provided the model that would inspire proponents of Mexican rural transformation in the 1930s and 1940s.

Yet the agricultural demonstration work undertaken by the GEB in the early twentieth century presented no neat or easily replicable model. Its long-term impact on boosting agricultural production or reversing agrarian poverty was negligible, as any observer of the Depression years could attest. Contrasting prescriptions for a healthy countryside similarly fractured the campaign. The USDA started its southern work as a desperate attempt to save cotton culture from the threat of the boll weevil, but over time Knapp—alongside Buttrick and Gates of the GEB—came to realize that the structural obstacles of lending, landownership, and monoculture were far more powerful in reproducing southern poverty than declining crop yields. By the campaign's later years, Knapp and his allies promoted a surprisingly emancipatory agenda in the Cotton Belt that sought to foster diversification, ecological conservation, and rural autonomy. That their campaign failed—and that it was wholly incomplete in its neglect of African Americans and most tenant farmers—is undeniable. Nevertheless, its failure did not dampen future generations' genuine belief that practical farm demonstrations represented a novel and effective solution to rural backwardness and poverty.

During the 1930s, the lively exchange between US and Mexican agrarian reformers supplied the connective tissue that would compel the Rockefeller philanthropies to transplant the GEB's ambiguous agenda on Mexico. Of primary significance was US ambassador Daniels, a contradictory figure whose long career entwined the US and Mexican plantation belts. For much of that decade, Daniels had actively drawn comparisons between the plight of the dispossessed US sharecropper and the Mexican campesino, juxtaposing the rural dilemmas facing Cárdenas era Mexico with those of the New Deal Cotton Belt. A vocal supporter of agrarista land redistribution, he came to believe that technical and scientific aid from the United States would bolster the fledgling ejido. The Rockefeller philanthropies, with their US southern experience and moral debt to Mexico arising from Standard Oil's history of petroleum extraction, could in Daniels's view best render this service. Ferrell—a fellow North Carolinian—would join Daniels in pushing the Rockefeller Foundation to translate southern lessons into postrevolutionary Mexico.

Daniels and Ferrell's initial efforts toward realizing such a leap floundered, failing to resonate among Rockefeller planners who had largely abandoned the US South and saw more risk than opportunity in politically tumultuous Latin America. But as the ravages of the late Depression returned the Cotton Belt to the philanthropies' drafting board, and as world war inspired a nascent interest in the other American republics, new avenues linking the US South and Mexico suddenly opened. With the GEB's Fosdick and Mann providing the guidance, in 1941 the Rockefeller Foundation seriously considered the proposal that Daniels and Ferrell had then championed for more than half a decade. Following the North Carolinians' conclusion that the US South offered valuable experience toward a reconstruction of Mexican agriculture, the foundation's leadership drew on the GEB's lessons and the more recent agrarian New Deal in proposing strategies for raising Mexico's rural standard of living. After an intensive survey verified Daniels and

Ferrell's assertion that US technical assistance might substantially benefit small-scale Mexican farmers, the foundation set in motion a program that would ultimately have vast global consequences.

Whether the proposed MAP would in 1943 replicate the missteps and shortcomings of the Rockefeller philanthropies' earlier experiments in agricultural reform remained uncertain. Would the effort favor the disfranchised marginal farmers who represented Mexico's rural majority, or would it partner exclusively with large landowners? Would it exclude indigenous cultivators, as the GEB effort had marginalized black southerners? Would a Rockefeller program in Mexico emphasize increased production above all or seek patterns of fair distribution? Would it favor staple monoculture or diversification? That US regional models had given birth to Mexico's green revolution was undeniable, yet whether such blueprints would continue to shape its course—and if so, how—was far less clear. The Rockefeller program's dramatic first decade in Mexico would resolve many of these unanswered questions.

Chapter Five

GREEN REVOLUTIONS
US REGIONALISM AND THE MEXICAN AGRICULTURAL PROGRAM

IN SPRING 1941, as the Rockefeller Foundation's leadership weighed the feasibility of an agricultural intervention in Mexico, it solicited the advice of several academic experts on Mexico and Latin American agriculture. One was Carl O. Sauer, a geographer at the University of California who specialized in the US Southwest and Mexico. In contrast to the rather sycophantic responses that accompanied his, Sauer delivered a biting rebuke to the foundation's proposed plan of action:

> A good aggressive bunch of American agronomists and plant breeders could ruin the native resources for good and all by pushing their American commercial stocks.... Mexican agriculture cannot be pointed toward standardization on a few commercial types without upsetting native economy and culture hopelessly. *The example of Iowa is about the most dangerous of all for Mexico.* Unless the Americans understand that, they'd better keep out of this country entirely.[1]

Students of the green revolution widely cite Sauer's critique as a prophetic warning of the dangers of US scientific hubris and evangelism abroad.[2] Indeed, the geographer's conclusions are often indistinguishable from the sharply critical scholarship on the green revolution by social scientists and humanists during the past generation. In their telling, First World agricultural aid to Third World farmers was a quintessential example of what political scientist James C. Scott called "high modernism," or the myopic transplanting of US imperial science on incompatible agrarian societies. Scholars frequently follow Indian environmentalist Vandana Shiva in denouncing the "violence" of the green revolution, revealing how the imposition of Western plant cultivars decimated indigenous genetic diversity, how large commercial growers dispossessed smallholders unable to adopt new technologies, and how pesticides and synthetic fertilizers laid waste to tropical ecologies.[3] Even twenty-first-century champions of a second green revolution for Africa acknowledge the failings of that project's first iteration.

Bill Gates of the Gates Foundation, speaking in 2009, could not deny the "excesses of the original Green Revolution," which had prescribed "too much irrigation [and] fertilizer," and brought a "consolidation of farms that could crowd out small-holder farmers."[4]

It is hardly my aim to discredit these carefully documented and persuasive critiques of the green revolution. Admittedly, in its mature phase of the 1960s and 1970s, that campaign was a social and ecological catastrophe, and no apologia for its many missteps will be found here. Yet as a historian, I am skeptical of assumptions that the metaphoric serpent in the garden was present at the green revolution's creation. The eagerness to paint Sauer as a soothsayer neglects an important contradiction: Did the Rockefeller Foundation truly seek to remake Mexico from "the example of Iowa"? Sauer later confessed that he had "his back up" to the plan because he believed that it was the Iowan Henry A. Wallace who had initiated it.[5] John A. Ferrell, the North Carolina doctor who alongside US ambassador to Mexico Josephus Daniels had in fact spurred the foundation into action, knew better. "That which has been suitable for Iowa" could not "be superimposed on Mexico," agreed Ferrell when he responded to Sauer's criticism three days later. But Ferrell insisted that "in the Southern States the development of sound agricultural practices was undertaken as the best method of combating poverty," and in Mexico he believed that a similar program seeking "more efficient production" along with "wise diversification of crops should improve the nutritional and economic standards among the families on the farms."[6]

The complexities of US regionalism, as it turns out, had a profound but largely unacknowledged impact on the first decade of Mexico's green revolution. Contrary to Sauer's assumption, the Rockefeller Foundation began its influential experiment in Mexican agriculture convinced that the troubled past and present of the US South—not that of an idealized Midwest—could provide useful lessons for staging a campaign of rural uplift in Mexico. Knowing the sharecropper's struggle at home, Rockefeller planners thought they could reach the ejido farmer in Mexico. This chapter demonstrates how in its first years of operation, the Rockefeller program consistently acknowledged the dangers of introducing technologies unsuited to the social and economic context of the Mexican countryside. Rather than a high modernist imposition ignorant of local particularities, the green revolution started with a distinctly "low modernist" sheen in its coupling of expert-led rural planning with a sensitivity toward agrarian class divisions, subsistence economics, and revolutionary politics. Midwife to such peasant-friendly planning was the lived experience of agrarian inequality in the US Cotton Belt.[7]

Curiously, when historians of US expansion and empire have acknowledged the role of the US South as a model for "Americanization" abroad, that has rarely made those campaigns appear more socially conscious or sensitive to local complexities. Andrew Zimmerman, Mary Renda, Paul Kramer, and many others have each revealed the invidious ways that Jim Crow segregation, racial pseudoscience, and white supremacy were translated from the fin de siècle US South into countless regions across the globe. This is a fundamental part of the story of US global expansion in the twentieth century, yet the US South was defined by divisions beyond race. It was also torn by inequalities in landownership, economic power, and political rights, and in many ways Dixie bore great resemblance to stratified postcolonial societies of the Global South. When US development planners abroad acknowledged that their target societies shared these historic inequalities with the Cotton Belt, they were less likely to treat those societies as composed of "people without history," in anthropologist Eric Wolf's memorable words.[8]

Yet the Rockefeller program's emphasis on small-scale farmers was not solely a product of philanthropic wisdom and beneficence. The foundation's agricultural experiment was at heart a partnership with the revolutionary party of Lázaro Cárdenas, and I argue below that the enduring agrarista footprint on the Mexican state likewise played a crucial role in ensuring that Rockefeller philanthropy benefited recent land reform grantees. To scholars of twentieth-century Mexico this may seem surprising, because in most accounts 1940 was when the Mexican Revolution "got off of its horse and into a Cadillac," as memorably expressed by contemporary journalist Carlos Denegri.[9] By such logic, 1940 marked the simultaneous decline of a revolutionary state dedicated to social justice and the ascent of a regime devoted to rapid urbanization and industrialization. This monochromatic narrative, however, misses the unscripted possibilities of the era. Cárdenas and Manuel Ávila Camacho (1940–46) were cut from different political cloth, without doubt. But to assume that the 1940 succession brought an overnight repudiation and reversal of Cardenismo conceals a history far more fluid. Though Ávila Camacho did slow active land redistribution—as Cárdenas himself had done after 1938—his administration remained committed to fortifying the fledgling ejido and ensuring its permanence. It was therefore no surprise that the *Avilacamachista* agriculture secretary who oversaw the Rockefeller program, Marte R. Gómez, was a former Zapatista who as governor of Tamaulipas in the 1930s had redistributed a million and a half acres of land. Any history of the early green revolution, then, must consider both continuity and change in the Mexican political landscape.[10]

Mexico's revolutionary heritage and the Rockefeller Foundation's experience in the US South ensured that for much of the 1940s, the architects of the collaborative effort to remake Mexican agriculture were insistent that its fruits go to the impoverished rural majority. Yet by the last years of that decade, two entwined transformations of national and international scope eroded this early alliance with the campesino. The growing emphasis of the

Mexican state on urban industrialization dried up funding for projects meant to enable or expand the ejido sector, as bureaucrats sought political peace in the countryside rather than peasant stability. Similarly, the intruding pressures of the Cold War pushed foundation planners toward rapid and demonstrable results in Mexico that could be applied elsewhere in the nascent Third World. Along the way, the experimental attempt to work with Mexican smallholders on their terms fell victim to a more sensational program partnering with large, commercial farmers eager to adopt industrial technologies. As the US southern model fell from favor, one born from a romanticized Midwest took its place, with sweeping consequences for both Mexico and the globe.

This chapter narrates the formative first decade of the Rockefeller Foundation's Mexican Agricultural Program (MAP) along three avenues. First, I explore the tempestuous political atmosphere of early 1940s' Mexico to answer a simple question: Why would the Mexican state under Ávila Camacho, in an era of significant nationalistic fervor, partner with a controversial US philanthropy in hoping to resolve the meaning of its agrarian revolution? The answer has much to do with the politicization of production and anxieties over the ejido's ability to feed the nation. Seeking resolution of this tense debate, the Ávila Camacho government and Rockefeller Foundation joined to found the MAP in early 1943. The second part of the chapter examines how in its first five years, that program—relying on prior experience in the US South—tailored its agricultural research and extension work to the needs of poor ejido farmers in the central plateau surrounding Mexico City. Rejecting the US gospel of commercial hybrid seed for maize farming, Rockefeller plant breeders proposed alternative methods more appropriate to farmers who lacked irrigation, large acreages, and ready capital. Such an approach engendered resistance both within and without the philanthropy, but remained central to the MAP for years. Whether that strategy could produce a rapid explosion in yields and productivity—not simply sustain campesino cultivators—increasingly became the concern of both foundation and Mexican state planners in the later years of the decade. The final part of the chapter looks at the twilight of peasant-friendly development in the face of national and global mandates to prioritize material abundance over the health and stability of the countryside.

Politicizing Agricultural Production in 1940s' Mexico

When Cárdenas handed the reins of presidential power to his successor Ávila Camacho in December 1940, he had left an indelible footprint on rural Mexico. In the popular mythology of the time, Cárdenas had redeemed the revolution by fulfilling the promises that had mobilized rural revolt a generation earlier. More than any of his predecessors, Cárdenas incorporated peasant voices within the machinery of his party and fostered the sentiment among rural people that the government was responding to their needs. His greatest achievement, with little doubt, was his redistribution of nearly fifty million acres of land as ejidos to be worked by the formerly dispossessed. Cardenista land reform represented the climax of a generation-long struggle to remake the Mexican countryside; the Rockefeller Foundation was hardly the first to try its hand at rural uplift.

Still, when Cárdenas left office in 1940, the future of the ejido remained uncertain. The whirlwind redistribution campaign of the late 1930s, waged rapidly to disorient and overwhelm its many opponents, had rarely paused to consider the land reform's impact on agricultural production. Credit, irrigation, and machinery often failed to accompany ejidal grants except in the few regions that Cárdenas had designated as flagships of the land reform. The timing of land grants rarely conformed to the natural cycles that farmers were bound to in planting and harvesting their crops, which meant that it frequently took several seasons for former hacienda lands to be returned to production. Without doubt, the sudden shake-up in land tenure did bring a great deal of dislocation and confusion, and Cárdenas's political opponents seized on this trauma as they sought to discredit the ejido as a productive economic unit. Rather than dry academic statistics, questions of productivity and efficiency were wound up with the smoldering legacy of a social revolution.

By the last years of Cárdenas's term, two opposing sides battled over the future of Mexican agriculture, and their debate would set the parameters for agrarian politics in the 1940s. On one side were the opponents of the land reform project, made up predominantly of large landowners, the clergy, and business interests. While this coalition had resisted land redistribution since the revolution had erupted, by the late 1930s it had substantially revised its oppositional rhetoric. Acknowledging that it would be politically impossible to turn back the clock to the Porfiriato, such critics instead aimed to discredit the recently expanded ejidal sector as a danger to national food security. While earlier conservative pundits had maligned the ejido as radical or un-Mexican, opponents of land reform in the late Cárdenas and Ávila Camacho years turned to a critique of redistribution clothed in the seemingly neutral language of efficiency and production. The "true agrarian problem," claimed one 1938 editorial in the Mexico City newspaper Excélsior, was not land but rather the "scarcity of agricultural production" in the wake of redistribution. With "uncertainty and mistrust" permeating the countryside, and a new class of uneducated campesinos attempting to take the place of the hacendado, the editorial warned, corn shortages were sure to follow.[11] US wartime restrictions on southbound agricultural exports exacerbated such anxieties. Among the ejido's opponents, it became commonplace to blame wartime shortages on "the failure of the campesinos to intensify their agricultural production," as one editorial from early 1942 did, accusing a large proportion of ejidal recipients of "preferring to surrender to indolence" rather than working their fields.[12]

On the other side of the political spectrum were the champions of the ejido, represented on the public stage by politicians, teachers, and particularly agronomists. Indeed, many of those trained in agricultural science joined the agrarista cause in the wake of the revolution. The very names of their professional organizations of the era—the Liga de Agrónomos Socialistas (League of Socialist Agronomists), Bloque de Agrónomos Revolucionarios (Block of Revolutionary Agronomists), and Frente Revolucionario de Agrónomos Mexicanos (Revolutionary Front of Mexican Agronomists)—reflected their marriage of science and politics. In stark contrast to their political adversaries, these defenders declared that the ejido was an institution worth investing in. If science and technology were extended to ejidatarios, this group fervently claimed, their small plots would far exceed the productivity of the old hacienda. The hacienda needed to be eliminated not only because of its social failings but also because it "represents the medieval epoch in agriculture," as one editorialist accused in 1936, using "no more equipment than a few oxen and a wooden plow."[13] Mexican agriculture clung to "antiquated processes and methods," claimed the agronomist Marco Antonio Durán in 1942. To overcome this unfortunate situation, Durán pleaded that Mexico's agronomists, "identifying with the Mexican Revolution and the campesinos, should put all their strength into solving ... the enormous problem that destiny has presented us." That problem, as Durán and his peers recognized, was to raise the productivity of the land reform's recipients.[14]

No figure better understood this dilemma than Marte R. Gómez, perhaps the most prominent of the revolutionary agronomists—and later a key collaborator of the Rockefeller Foundation. Born in the northern state of Tamaulipas, Gómez enrolled at Mexico City's National School of Agriculture on the eve of the revolution. When the revolt broke out, he left to join Emiliano Zapata's southern army and later admitted that it was in those heady days that "the agrarista ideal fired my spirit."[15] When Gómez returned to finish his agronomy degree, such a spirit continued to animate his career. Gómez's political education in the crucible of the revolution taught him that peasants deserved to own the soil they tilled, agricultural production had to be modernized for the sake of efficiency, and cooperativism was the key that would make the first two possible. Unlike some agrarista intellectuals who solely championed collectivism and wished to eliminate all forms of land tenure outside the ejido, Gómez believed cooperation between individually worked ejidos and private farmers would enable smallholders to acquire modern technologies and negotiate commercial markets. Gómez implemented this philosophy in the 1920s as state secretary of agriculture in Tamaulipas, but the rightward turn under President Plutarco Elías Calles forced him out of politics, even leading to an exile in France between 1930 and 1932.[16]

The Cardenista renaissance of the later 1930s reopened political doors that had been closed to the revolutionary agronomists, and Gómez was no exception. Pledging an aggressive land redistribution campaign, he was elected governor of his home state in 1936, a post that he held until 1940. During those years, he oversaw the subdivision of hundreds of large estates, totaling 1.5 million acres of farmland granted to nearly 20,000 ejidal beneficiaries in Tamaulipas.[17] Following redistribution, Gómez led an aggressive campaign to endow the newly granted ejidos with credit, machinery, and agricultural education. He staged his flagship demonstration of ejidal cooperativism at El Mante, a wealthy sugar plantation district bordering Veracruz, which Gómez eagerly showed to Wallace in December 1940 as he escorted the US vice president elect down to Mexico City.[18] Yet Gómez's emphasis on cooperative rather than collective farming earned him enemies among the most radical of agronomists, who believed that private farms could never exist in harmony with state-granted ejidal plots. The governor disagreed, revealing that even among the agronomists who supported land redistribution, there were bitter divisions.[19]

Gómez's proven commitment to investing the ejido with technology, credit, and education made him an attractive candidate to head up the agriculture secretariat under Ávila Camacho, who asked Gómez to join his cabinet in late 1940. Ávila Camacho's cabinet selection is a matter of no small importance, because countless scholars view the 1940 transfer of power as the most decisive turning point in postrevolutionary Mexican history, particularly on the agrarian question. Such an interpretation, however, simplifies a much more protracted and unscripted process. Reading backward into time the Mexican state's neglect of rural inequality during the 1950s and 1960s, too many historians have assumed that the ruling party's transition away from agrarismo was a foreordained affair. While Cárdenas's successor did shift gears in his pursuit of agricultural development, Ávila Camacho's stress on intensifying production on existing ejidos, as opposed to granting new ones, was not merely a cover for undoing the land reform project. Instead, Gómez seems to best reflect the ambivalent position of the new administration. Never a rigid doctrinaire, he sought to work within the realm of the possible. His goal, like many of his fellow revolutionary agronomists, was to redeem the ejido by making it a productive economic unit.[20]

Presidential rhetoric in the early years of Ávila Camacho's term reflected the strategic tightrope on which the ruling party balanced. The president and his cabinet sought to convince the public that even though they were slowing land redistribution, they were strengthening existing ejidos by endowing them with the support systems that Cárdenas never had time to establish. It was no easy task, but the president did it by skillfully blending the social propaganda of the revolution and an econo-scientific emphasis on productivity. At a public event memorializing the death of Zapata in Cuautla, Morelos, in April 1941, Ávila Camacho declared that "lands wrongfully unproductive" were the "antithesis not only of Zapata, but all of the heroes who fought to open a road to justice."[21] Equally illustrative was his exhortation to the National Confederation of Peasants in 1943 that the most compelling way of "demonstrating that the ejido system provides its fruits is to visibly augment [its] yields." To do so, Ávila Camacho pressured campesinos to practice cultivation with "the stick and the plow and not—as some farmers believe—with this pistol or the rifle," thus explicitly beseeching rural people to renounce the militarized agrarian politics of the 1930s and adopt the production-oriented social consensus that he sought to foster in the 1940s.[22] Such statements testify to a depoliticizing instinct within the party, but taken in their historical context they were not merely a rhetorical foil for selling out the peasantry.

After 1940, the Ávila Camacho government moved rapidly in turning rhetoric into action. Critiquing Cárdenas's organization of the agriculture secretariat as ineffective, Gómez disbanded the Agrónomos Regionales, the underfunded extension service that had sent a few dozen agronomists around the country to teach farmers modern methods, and closed several experiment stations he deemed unproductive.[23] In 1942, Ávila Camacho announced the first annual Plan de Movilización Agrícola, or Agricultural Mobilization Plan. The plan pinpointed antiquated production methods as the primary obstacle to the ejido's productivity, and pledged to distribute iron plows and chemical fertilizer to as many campesinos as it could, while setting production goals for twenty food and fiber crops.[24] On paper, the plan looked quite impressive. To US vice president Wallace, Gómez proudly claimed that Ávila Camacho's assault on the nation's agricultural shortcomings was "the most ambitious that in the history of Mexico has ever been attempted," and he may well have been correct.[25]

In spite of these monumental efforts, Ávila Camacho's government could not banish the persistent specter of food scarcity, and press reports of corn shortages were common in the early years of the decade.[26] Such shortfalls stemmed from both environmental and political factors. In part, poor weather and the failure of seasonal rains during 1941 and 1942 cut corn supplies and resulted in a price spike. But in contrast to conservatives who blamed scarcities on Cardenista land reform, the political culprit lay with Mexico's wartime cooperation with the United States. Seeking warmer relations with the Roosevelt government, Ávila Camacho had agreed to aid the US war effort by growing "strategic crops" that could not be produced north of the border, such as guayule rubber and castor beans for oil production, in

Figure 5.1. Jalisco farmers receiving iron plows under the Plan de Movilización Agrícola, 1943. Secretaría de Agricultura y Fomento, "Informe de labores Sept. 1943—Aug. 1944," Manuel Ávila Camacho Papers, box 1001, folder 606.3/97. Courtesy of the Archivo General de la Nación.

exchange for discounted US agricultural machinery. Between 1941 and 1943, the Mexican state devoted large swaths of federal land to such crops and encouraged their cultivation among northern farmers. What neither government expected, however, was the profound impact that the climbing price of rubber and oilseed crops would have on Mexican corn production, which had rarely been profitable in prior years. Seduced by high prices, farmers rapidly turned former grain land over to oilseed and fiber production. As corn production fell and food prices rose, George Messersmith, the US ambassador who replaced Daniels in late 1941, admitted that "we have been at least partially instrumental in disorganizing Mexican agricultural economy." Therefore, at the very moment when the revolutionary state sought to prove that the ejido was a productive economic unit, it faced additional extranational challenges.[27]

In his first few years as agriculture secretary, Gómez found himself assailed from all sides, and quieting conservative hysteria about the land redistribution's role in reducing agricultural production was one of his primary objectives. Publicly, Gómez assured crowds that the "well-worn charge" of food scarcity was nothing but a political ploy to "discount the Agrarian Reform," and that rising prices were only the product of unscrupulous speculators.[28] Privately, though, during 1941 and 1942 he acknowledged the crisis and prepared for the real possibility of widespread hunger, seeking to ease the political blow of scarcities should they arrive.[29] Through Wallace, he pressured for the availability of US corn imports should a serious shortage arise.[30] Gómez convinced Ávila Camacho to found the Nacional Reguladora y Distribuidora (National Regulatory Distribution Corporation), a federal agency that was chartered to oversee the storage, transportation, and marketing of all basic food grains.[31] Then, as a last recourse, Ávila Camacho wrote personal letters to every state governor beseeching them to raise corn yields to avert political catastrophe.[32]

It was in the midst of this desperate struggle to demonstrate the productivity of the fledgling ejido that Gómez received the Rockefeller Foundation's request to begin a cooperative program in agricultural improvement. It was not surprising that it perked his attention. Gómez had first heard of the philanthropy's interest in Mexican agriculture from his friend Wallace in March 1941, but it was only in October of 1942 that the foundation made its formal offer of aid.[33] Gómez was well aware of the Rockefeller philanthropies' earlier work, describing to Ávila Camacho in 1942 how they had sought to "improve the conditions of life of the rural population of the Southern States of the American Union," noting that the Rockefeller family's General Education Board (GEB) had "pushed for agricultural education and were the ones who brought extension work to its apogee."[34] In speaking with the foundation's representatives, Gómez grew convinced that their vision of rural development did not clash with his. As one early member of the Rockefeller scientific team remembered, "The government realized that the yield of the ejidos was going down rather than up, and that something must be done about it."[35] Gómez believed that sympathetic US science might aid in this effort, and told the foundation's president Raymond Fosdick that he embraced their collaboration "with great enthusiasm."[36]

In partnering with a political wing that was actively seeking to bolster the land tenure complex established by Cárdenas, the Rockefeller Foundation decisively took sides in the heated debate over the future of Mexico's countryside. With two generations of experience addressing small-scale farmers' ills in the US South, the Rockefeller philanthropies hoped to transplant such lessons in defense of the beleaguered Mexican ejido. The first years of that effort garnered significant success, revealing that the green revolution started with motivations far different from commonly remembered.

The American South and Mexican Maize

In early February 1943, Rockefeller representative J. George Harrar arrived in Mexico City to realize a program whose planning stretched back nearly a decade. What was once distant fantasy was rapidly becoming concrete. As

Harrar's superiors had negotiated with the Ávila Camacho government, the Rockefeller-led MAP—known locally as the Oficina de Estudios Especiales (Office of Special Studies)—would constitute a branch of Gómez's agriculture secretariat. Its initially modest headquarters of one building and a few acres of test plots were to be located on the National School of Agriculture's Chapingo campus, forty kilometers east of the capital in the state of México. Gómez's selection of Chapingo to house the Rockefeller program was rather symbolic, as it was on those grounds that he had begun his education as both agronomist and agrarista. The campus was a former hacienda that had belonged to one of Díaz's lieutenants but had been expropriated during the early days of the agrarian reform. The old chapel, now a monument to the revolution, was graced by one of Diego Rivera's most famous murals, where the school's motto was proudly displayed: "Here we teach the exploitation of the soil, not the man."[37]

Though the MAP was formally anchored in the Mexican agriculture secretariat, the foundation leveraged a fair deal of autonomy to pursue its research agenda. The local director for the effort would be the thirty-seven-year-old Harrar, a plant pathologist trained at the University of Minnesota. At the program's inauguration in 1943, Harrar was the only permanent employee of the MAP, but he was guided by the foundation's New York–based Advisory Committee, composed of Elvin C. Stakman, Richard Bradfield, and Paul C. Mangelsdorf, the same three senior agronomists who had surveyed Mexican agricultural possibilities for the foundation in 1941. With the MAP located in the foundation's Division of Natural Sciences, its interim director Frank B. Hanson served as the formal head of the Mexican program, although he rarely intervened in its administration. Instead, the Advisory Committee's "three musketeers"—as they were often called within the Rockefeller sphere—dictated policy while Harrar was tasked with implementing it. Stakman himself accompanied Harrar in early 1943 and remained in Mexico two months, helping to launch their research efforts and hire additional personnel. The aim of the program reflected the resolutions adopted in 1941: the MAP would emphasize basic research and complement it with practical demonstration, with the ultimate goal of raising the productivity of essential food crops, primarily corn and beans.[38]

Juxtapositions of the US South and Mexico had given birth to the MAP, and they would continue to shape the early years of its operation. That became abundantly clear in the early hiring of personnel, wherein a majority of new staff had experience in poor rural regions of the South. Harrar, the local director, had worked in southwestern Virginia for most of the 1930s. In seeking a soil scientist, the Advisory Committee's Bradfield favored one candidate because "he was brought up on a farm in the Ozark Mountains and would probably be more sympathetic with the problems of the poorer farmers of Mexico."[39] The MAP's first hire was its corn breeder, Edwin Wellhausen, an Oklahoman recruited from the West Virginia Experiment Station in September 1943. That pick was so unorthodox that the geographer Carl Sauer and botanist Edgar Anderson wrote to the foundation expressing their surprise at the "selection of a bearer of light from West Virginia," a "backward American region" that they suggested—tongue in cheek—might instead benefit from "Mexican missionaries" of agriculture.[40] The second Rockefeller hire in early 1944 was William Colwell, a soils specialist who was working at North Carolina State College in Raleigh; he was joined in 1945 by Lewis M. Roberts, the team's second corn breeder and a native of the East Texas Cotton Belt who had trained at Texas A&M.[41]

The New York leadership of the early MAP, like the local staff, was similarly drawn from the philanthropies' prior and ongoing campaigns in US regional reform. Particularly important was Albert R. Mann, the agricultural economist who had spearheaded the GEB's New Southern Program since the late 1930s. In April 1943, Mann became the first Rockefeller administrator to travel to Chapingo to oversee the newly founded program since "there seems no doubt that at least part of the Mexican picture is not too different from some of the more backward agricultural parts of our own South," as one of his colleagues then noted.[42] Mann was then catapulted to the forefront of the Mexican program's leadership in 1945 when Hanson, interim chief of the Division of Natural Sciences, died unexpectedly in July and left the MAP without a formal director. It was not long before Rockefeller Foundation president Fosdick approached Mann, then arranging his retirement from the GEB after eight years of leading its southern program, to offer him the leadership of the MAP. Having already bridged US and Mexican rural development for several years, Mann eagerly accepted the position of deputy director of agriculture with "primary responsibility" for leading the MAP by 1946.[43]

Yet more than any other member of the Rockefeller team, it was the US southern experience of botanist and corn breeder Paul Mangelsdorf that would most dramatically impact the foundation's early program in Mexico. Like his colleagues Stakman and Bradfield, Mangelsdorf had declined a permanent on-site appointment with the MAP, serving instead as a member of the agricultural Advisory Committee that set program policy as well as periodically reviewed Harrar and his team's work. But after the foundation had serious trouble finding a permanent corn breeder in early 1943 and subsequently saw its work on Mexican maize improvement stalled, Mangelsdorf agreed to secure a leave of absence with his employer, Harvard University, and spent summer and fall 1943 in Chapingo. In those months, he laid the groundwork for a corn-breeding program that would ultimately be taken over by the full-time breeder, Wellhausen, who joined the team in September. As the premier architect of the MAP's corn-breeding program, unanimously deemed Mexico's most important food crop by foundation leaders, Mangelsdorf thus wielded unparalleled influence over the entire project's course.

Born in 1899 in Kansas, Mangelsdorf earned his PhD in botany at Harvard with an emphasis on corn. But rather than returning to work in the Midwest, as many other corn specialists did, the young Mangelsdorf took a job during the late 1920s at the Texas Agricultural Experiment Station in College Station, in eastern Texas. Relocating there brought him to a rural landscape far different from that of Kansas and Massachusetts. East Texas in the 1920s was a racially segmented world of sharecroppers and cotton farms, where small cultivators grew corn in modest quantities, primarily for home consumption. Compared to the relatively homogeneous rural Midwest that Mangelsdorf had grown up in, east Texas posed staggering new challenges.[44]

Mangelsdorf remained in east Texas for thirteen years, from 1927 until 1940. During that period, he witnessed a veritable revolution in the US cultivation of corn, which requires some explanation. In 1927, nearly all US corn farmers planted their crop from last year's seed, choosing varieties based on yield, aesthetics, and hardiness. They drew on a deep well of multigenerational, place-based knowledge in selecting seeds, and as any visitor to a rural county fair could attest, it was a practice farmers took pride in. But when Mangelsdorf left Texas in 1940, nearly all farmers in the midwestern Corn Belt annually purchased seed from commercial vendors like Pioneer Hi-Bred and DeKalb. Fueling this switch was a new agricultural technology: double-cross hybrid corn. Born from early twentieth-century experimentation in Mendelian genetics, the double-cross hybrid was the product of extensive inbreeding and the crossing of inbred strains, which yielded a significantly larger ear than did nonhybrid varieties. On the farm, however, higher yields came at a high price. In addition to paying for seed—an entirely novel practice—farmers found that if they replanted the kernels of a double-cross hybrid, its offspring would not exhibit the "hybrid vigor," or increased size, of the first generation. As such, if farmers wanted to continue reaping the benefits of hybridized seed, they had to return to their breeder every spring for a new infusion of seed. This was a convenient fact for the seed companies, which now sat on top of a multimillion-dollar industry. The mechanics of capitalist accumulation were built into the double-cross hybrid, and not accidentally.[45]

From his vantage point in east Texas, Mangelsdorf curiously watched hybrid corn's meteoric rise—on a trajectory that was nothing short of staggering. In 1933, hybrid seed was planted on 0.4 percent of US cornfields; by 1945, that number had risen to 90 percent, with concentrations even higher in the Midwest.[46] But among Mangelsdorf's neighbors in the southern Cotton Belt, the gospel of hybridization did not have the same appeal. As he recalled, his constituents "were predominantly small farmers, and they were not [as] receptive to change as the farmers of west Texas who farmed on a much larger scale." To make the transition to planting hybrids, cultivators needed cash and capital, which most sharecroppers and tenants lacked. After visiting and speaking with farmers across his region, Mangelsdorf grew convinced that double-cross hybrid corn did not have universal application. He was deeply skeptical "whether or not we could ever get the small Texas farmer to pay out $10 or $12 a bushel for hybrid corn and whether we could keep him from saving his own seed and buying new seed every year."[47]

But if double-cross hybrids were unsuitable for east Texas tenants and smallholders, Mangelsdorf insisted that his constituents could still benefit from recent revolutions in plant genetics. During the 1930s, he had come under the sway of Merle T. Jenkins, an unconventional corn specialist at the USDA's Bureau of Plant Industry. Jenkins had gained some renown championing what he called "synthetic" maize, based on the same Mendelian genetics that underwrote the double-cross method but with a major difference. In contrast to hybrids that were commonly inbred multiple generations to "purify" genetic traits before they were crossed, with the convenient consequence of reducing the yield of the second generation so that farmers could not effectively replant seed, Jenkins attempted to inbreed corn strains only one or two generations before crossing them. That strategy produced higher-yielding plants, yet they were open pollinated—that is, unlike the conventional double-cross hybrid, their yield would not greatly decline in subsequent generations. Despite the contradictory name, synthetics were in fact more "natural" than double-cross hybrids; they also adapted better to new environments because of their uncontrolled reproduction.[48]

The implications of Jenkins's method were revolutionary. With synthetic seed, farmers could nearly match the yields of their double-cross-hybrid-planting neighbors, but without having to annually repurchase seed, thus preserving both their autonomy and pocketbook. Had the US Corn Belt embraced this alternative technology, that region's history would likely have taken a far different course. Such possibilities were smothered, however, by the steadfast resistance of seed companies and their allies in land grant university research, which ensured that most US experiments with synthetics during the interwar period occurred on paper as opposed to in the field.[49] But in 1930s' east Texas, where double-cross hybrids struggled to take root, Mangelsdorf saw an opportunity to test the promise of open-pollinated maize. As one of Jenkins's foremost disciples, Mangelsdorf devoted himself to breeding and distributing synthetics, which he believed were more appropriate to the stratified social landscape of east Texas than double-cross hybrids. In November 1939, he joined Jenkins in organizing the First Southern Corn Improvement Conference in New Orleans, where Mangelsdorf served as both executive committee chair and Texas' state representative. In his report to the conference, Mangelsdorf argued emphatically that "hybrid corn would never be used as extensively in the South as in the Corn Belt."[50]

It is hardly surprising, therefore, that as Mangelsdorf arrived in Chapingo in summer 1943 to forge the MAP's maize-breeding program, he instantly began drawing parallels between the socioeconomic limitations of Mexican farmers and those he had known in the east Texas Cotton Belt. The ejidatarios of central Mexico, he concluded, were not so different from the tenants of the southeastern United States. Seeking affirmation, he wrote to Jenkins for advice on drafting "some kind of immediate program for Mexico," suggesting the breeding and distribution of synthetics as the wisest course of action.[51] His former mentor eagerly agreed that "the present economic status of most [Mexican] farmers would seem to preclude the possibility of hybrid corn."[52] Indeed, the longer Mangelsdorf remained in Mexico, the more he grew convinced that what he had seen during his "fourteen years in Texas" was "quite similar to the present situation in Mexico." Double-cross hybrid corn might be viable in a "country with a reasonably uniform agriculture, like our state of Iowa," but Mexico offered no such possibilities. Open-pollinated synthetic maize, Mangelsdorf concluded, was far better suited to the political economy of the Mexican countryside.[53]

Mangelsdorf expected his Mexican collaborators to wholly embrace such a strategy, and was shocked when not all did. In particular, the MAP's pursuit of synthetic maize came into conflict with Eduardo Limón García, one of the nation's most renowned corn breeders, employed at the federal experiment station in León, Guanajuato. Trained in Chapingo but having earned a master's degree at Iowa State College in 1935, Limón had a romantic devotion to the double-cross hybrid. His breeding work in the early 1940s was dedicated exclusively to breeding such plants using strains imported from the United States, and his relations with the MAP grew stiff and formal.[54] Mangelsdorf, convinced that double-cross hybrids were poorly suited for practical application in the Mexican countryside, reached out to the agriculture secretariat's leadership in hopes of intervention. In December 1943, at the tail end of his residence in Chapingo, he wrote to agriculture undersecretary Alfonso González Gallardo to express his doubt whether double-cross hybrid corn "will fill the needs of the small farmer whose maize culture is limited to producing a crop sufficient to feed himself and his family." While there was "undoubtedly a place for hybrid corn of this type among the larger planters," Mangelsdorf insisted that his regional experience within the United States could teach valuable lessons in Mexico:

> Hybrid maize has not been especially successful in the Southern part of the United States where conditions are more nearly comparable to those of Mexico than are those of the Corn-Belt. Where acreages are small, where maize is not ordinarily a cash crop but is grown primarily for home consumption, it is difficult ... to educate the farmer to purchase new seed each year.[55]

Mangelsdorf's pressure on the Mexican agriculture secretariat bore surprising fruit. When that bureau prepared its annual report in 1944, its authors reprinted lengthy portions of Mangelsdorf's December 1943 letter,
citing its "very valuable opinions." In presenting the secretariat's priorities
for future work in corn improvement, the report likewise ranked synthetics
first, "so that the farmer who does not perceive the advantages of hybrid
corn or does not have the resources to buy or barter for such seed year after
year can at least reproduce it and obtain it without having to sacrifice a large
percentage of his production."[56] Agriculture chief Gómez took to the public
sphere to caution farmers—many of whom were seduced by rumors of hybrid wonders—that such seed presented no silver bullet. Double-cross hybrids, Gómez warned, were expensive, delicate, and required new seed yearly,
while "synthetic varieties are very similar to hybrids in yield [but] do not
require the annual change of seed."[57] Thus, throughout the Ávila Camacho
administration, the agriculture secretariat prioritized the breeding and distribution of synthetics given that double-cross hybrids were not "in the immediate reach of the common farmer," as the bureau's mouthpiece concluded
in 1946.[58]

During the first years of its operation, therefore, the MAP displayed a
surprising sensitivity to the ejido farmers it was tasked to aid. Rather than
blindly imposing an idealized US agricultural model aimed solely at boosting productivity, the Rockefeller Foundation's leadership digested its long
experience within the fractured US South to plan a research program tailored to the economic limitations of smallholders. At center stage was the
maize-breeding effort inaugurated by Mangelsdorf and continued by resident agronomist Wellhausen after 1944, which began to distribute synthetic
seed to Mexican farmers by 1947.[59] With steady support from the foundation's leadership, the MAP's maize program departed from the US scientific
mainstream in pursuit of alternatives rejected north of the border.[60] Such
experimentation impressed even the most stubborn skeptics of Rockefeller
intervention in Mexico. When Carl Sauer—who had memorably foretold
the disastrous consequences of US meddling in Mexican agriculture—visited
Chapingo in early 1945, he concluded that Wellhausen gave "the impression of feeling his way intelligently into his problem," hardly "unaware of
the cultural medium in which [he is] working."[61]

If the campaign for synthetic maize represented the cornerstone of the
Rockefeller program's socially conscious rural development, other wings of
the MAP also complemented it.[62] Soil fertility research, led by the Advisory
Committee's Bradfield and the recently hired Colwell, strove to "find inexpensive and feasible methods of increasing yields" of primary food crops. In
practice, this meant a reduced stress on high-priced commercial fertilizers
in favor of boosting soil fertility "with a minimum expense to the farmer,"
particularly through the planting of green manures such as vetch and clo-

Figure 5.2. Lázaro Cárdenas, Henry A. Wallace, and Marte R. Gómez touring the Rockefeller crop test plots at Chapingo, September 1946. Archivo Hermanos Mayo, envelope 225. Courtesy of the Archivo General de la Nación.

ver, crop rotation, and composting.[63] And under the leadership of former GEB chief Mann, the MAP in 1946 broke ground on a coordinated program of demonstration and extension—work that had previously been neglected. That year, the Advisory Committee planned to host regular field days in Chapingo in hopes of reaching "the leaders of the ejidos, the agricultural teachers, [and] the leaders in the Ejidal Bank."[64]

Nothing better evoked the Rockefeller program's smallholder sympathies and alliance with revolutionary Mexico than a symbolic visit to Chapingo in 1946 from two legendary agrarian icons: Lázaro Cárdenas and Henry Wallace. Orchestrated by Mann, the reunion testified to the fusion of transnational political ideologies that had initially given birth to the MAP. Wallace, then secretary of commerce under Harry Truman, was eager to return to Mexico after his 1940 tour and accepted Mann's invitation.[65] Cárdenas, having never visited the ongoing project, was equally curious.[66] On September 7, Wallace, Cárdenas, and agriculture chief Gómez convened in Chapingo. The three men—the agrarian New Deal's foremost champion, the immortalized patron of Mexico's land reform, and the former Zapatista—together walked the grounds of the Rockefeller Foundation's experiment station. In the test plots where synthetic maize was being grown for distribution to ejido farmers, Cárdenas and Wallace heard of the unconventional breeding strategies pursued by the foundation's staff. Wallace recalled in his diary that "most of the corn-belt inbred strains of corn are not adapted to Mexican conditions"; Cárdenas similarly expressed marvel at the promise of "this class of crops."[67]

The 1946 meeting of Cárdenas, Wallace, and Gómez in Chapingo's synthetic maize field represented the high-water mark of the early green revolution. Up to that point, the Rockefeller Foundation's intervention in Mexican agriculture had sought to democratize the fruits of modern agronomy—a mission born from the lessons of the US South and guided in no small part by the social ideologies of those three distinguished visitors: the agrarian New Deal, Mexican agrarismo, and the marriage of science and revolutionary politics. But rather than marking a new chapter in socially conscious rural reform, the symbolic reunion of 1946 represented a closing of the book. Agrarian activism in both countries was then waning, not waxing. Just ten days after Wallace returned from Mexico, he was dismissed from his commerce post for challenging Truman's Cold War entrenchment with the Soviet Union; it was the last political appointment Wallace would ever hold. By year's end, Gómez too stood outside the halls of government, removed from his post by the incoming presidential administration of Miguel Alemán (1946–52). And although Cárdenas's idolization among rural Mexicans would hardly diminish, the ejido experiment that he had long nursed saw its future imperiled during the increasingly conservative Alemán years.

As the political fortunes of Wallace, Cárdenas, and Gómez declined precipitously in the coming years, the peasant sympathies of the MAP followed their trajectory. That shift grew from internal and external pressures. Thrust into an escalating Cold War that rapidly polarized geopolitics, Rockefeller philanthropy sought to dovetail its work with the US State Department's global agenda. Within Mexico, the revolutionary ruling party under Alemán decisively turned its back on questions of rural social justice to favor food security for the nation's growing cities. Confronting the uncertainties of postwar planning, the Rockefeller leadership reconsidered the priorities of its experiment in Mexico. That reconfiguration entailed a neglect of both small-scale farmers and the earlier lessons of the US South.

The Decline of Peasant-Friendly Plant Breeding

The dawn of 1947 witnessed gathering storm clouds that presented a serious challenge to the established course of the foundation's agricultural intervention in Mexico. In particular, two sudden changes in leadership threatened to undermine the ejido-centered rural development program then being implemented: one within the philanthropies, and the other from within the Mexican state. How the MAP weathered that tempest would determine the future of the green revolution.

First, Albert Mann, the former GEB chief who was then overseeing the MAP as deputy director of agriculture, died suddenly in February, at the age of sixty-six. Mann had been a crucial proponent of translating US southern experience into the Mexican context, and he had recently spearheaded efforts to expand the extension apparatus of the MAP. Following Mann's unexpected death, the program's leadership went to Warren Weaver, a mathematician who had become director of the Division of Natural Sciences in 1932. During World War II, he had temporarily withdrawn from foundation service to work in the wartime US government's Office of Scientific Research and Development. Thus, in the crucial years when the MAP had been proposed and conceived, Weaver had either been absent or uninterested in the project; he later admitted to have "participated only in occasional discussions" of the early Mexican program. As Weaver had minimal experience in either agriculture or rural affairs, it was wholly uncertain where the new chief would lead the MAP.[68]

Second, the advent of the new year presented the Rockefeller Foundation with an unprecedented quandary: it confronted a complete turnover in Mexico's political leadership, following Alemán's inauguration in December 1946. That transfer of power caused much hand-wringing among the MAP's directors, who feared that earlier guarantees of state cooperation must be fully renegotiated with the incoming leadership. Those worries were largely unfounded, but Alemán did oversee a decisive shift in postrevolutionary agrarian policy. If the Ávila Camacho years had represented a protracted negotiation of the meaning of Cardenismo and its rural transformations, the Alemán era ushered in a "profound reversal of many central reforms of the Mexican Revolution," in the words of one historian.[69] Alemán was not subtle in his articulation of plans to turn away from the land reform project, declaring that continued redistribution promised "insecurity and consequent instability" of the agricultural sector.[70] During his first month in power, Alemán pushed through a series of reforms that revealed a clear departure from Ávila Camacho's moderation. He expanded protections against expropriation among large landholders and even amended the revolutionary sacred cow of the Constitution's Article 27, which mandated land reform.[71]

Such measures threatened the centrality of the ejido to the Mexican state's agricultural development project, of which the Rockefeller program was a part. But the most serious practical challenge to the MAP's socially conscious maize-breeding strategy came from an unexpected source. In the first week of January 1947, Alemán established a new federal agency to aid in boosting Mexico's food production: the Comisión del Maíz, or Corn Commission. With an enviable annual budget of four million pesos, the president tasked the Corn Commission with reproducing improved maize strains from the agriculture secretariat and distributing them to farmers across the

Figure 5.3. President Miguel Alemán inspecting seed to be distributed by the Comisión del Maíz, 1947. Archivo Enrique Díaz, Delgado y García, box 89, sub-box 11. Courtesy of the Archivo General de la Nación.

nation.[72] Among the Rockefeller team, the commission's announcement was initially welcomed, as it seemed to represent a long-awaited federal commitment to agricultural extension and outreach. But frustrations soon abounded, because the commission emphatically prioritized double-cross hybrid maize over open-pollinated varieties. An early news announcement of the commission's plans underscored the agency's emphasis on "hybrid and double hybrid maize types" because they "produce the greatest yields," and—in telling language—"would permit this crop, now uneconomical, to pay dividends and stimulate the campesino and farmer."[73]

The Corn Commission's strategy for transforming Mexican maize culture was thus at odds with the synthetic-oriented Rockefeller program, and relations between the two agencies grew increasingly tense. Stakman of the Advisory Committee resented what he saw as an attempt "to dominate virtually all agricultural work in order to benefit personally"; Mangelsdorf betrayed "little liking or respect" for the agency.[74] Such antagonisms flared when the commission regularly intervened in the MAP's breeding work. As the maize breeder Wellhausen later remembered, "The Corn Commission pointed out to me one day that what we should do was make hybrids which in advanced generations dropped very sharply so the farmers would discard them and not plant the seed ... and come back for new seed." In Wellhausen's eyes, "this would have been a mistake, because ... the majority of the farmers would have continued to plant advanced generation seed, or would have given up the use of this seed rather than going back for it every year." Frustrated with the commission's disregard for rural realities, Wellhausen concluded, "They want to stick to hybrids because they figure they can control hybrids 100 percent."[75]

Why indeed might Alemán's Corn Commission have been so adamant in its dedication to double-cross hybrid maize over open-pollinated varieties? Wellhausen's conclusion about "control" was blunt, but not entirely off the mark. Historians and social scientists, studying how Mexico's revolutionary ruling party constructed its legitimacy and power after 1940, have highlighted the importance of patron-client relationships in binding various social groups to the party through the expectation of patronage, services, and preferential treatment. Agriculture was no exception, and in weighing open-pollinated varieties and double-cross hybrids, the Corn Commission approached plant breeding in a different way than did the MAP. Synthetics, distributed to farmers once and then replanted indefinitely, were far less useful in fostering dependent relationships between corn farmers and the federal government. Double-cross hybrids, however, required annual replenishing and as such provided a mechanism for building rural reliance on state largesse. Just as US seed companies had chosen hybrids to yield economic profits through annual repurchasing, Mexico's Corn Commission likewise favored double-cross hybrids to yield political profits. Its career reflected that decision: in 1952, the last year of Alemán's term, the commission distributed 2,925 tons of hybrid seed alongside a mere 205 tons of open-pollinated varieties.[76]

In losing access to the Corn Commission as an effective avenue for distributing synthetic maize seed, the MAP's peasant-friendly breeding strategy suffered a serious disadvantage. Yet that failure was compounded by an ongoing struggle to convince farmers to adopt synthetic varieties. Not long after Mangelsdorf and Wellhausen's office released its first "Rocamex" *variedad sintética* (synthetic variety) maize strains in 1947 did it encounter skepticism among suspicious farmers around Chapingo. The MAP team had not expected campesino resistance to the high generational variability of synthetic plants—that the sizes, shapes, and appearance of maize grown from synthetic variety seed was rather unpredictable, even though the yield was higher than local varieties. Area farmers, as Wellhausen noted, "through a long period of selection, have developed very uniform varieties," and "didn't like the idea of having a variety which had long ears, and short ears, and big ears, and small ears."[77] This "imagined obstacle," as Wellhausen deemed it in frustration, was a significant hurdle and revealed the cultural limits of US scientific intervention even at its most socially sensitive.[78]

As the synthetic corn program hit unexpected bumps after 1947, MAP breeders devoted to a rival food crop pushed to dislodge maize as the keystone of the Rockefeller project. The plant that would ultimately eclipse corn in the MAP effort was wheat, and its ascent during the late 1940s signaled a dramatic departure from the socially conscious program of earlier years. Indeed, it sowed the seeds of a fundamentally different green revolution. Why? Wheat and corn represented opposite poles of the divided Mexican countryside at midcentury. Corn was raised nearly everywhere, but its primary production zone was in the densely populated central plateau surrounding Mexico City, where most farmers tended small rain-fed plots, often in ejidos, largely on the outskirts of cash economies. These cultivators had little access to irrigation, capital, or recent technological innovations, and their primary goal was not surplus or profit but instead security and subsistence. Larger commercial farmers in arid northern regions of the country, on the other hand, grew most of Mexico's wheat. Utilizing artificial irrigation and machinery, these farmers more closely resembled those of the US Midwest in their individualistic rural culture as well as participation in national and international markets.[79]

Yet maize and wheat were hardly equals in the Mexican diet of the 1940s: the former far outpaced the latter in terms of popular consumption and cultural significance. Corn tortillas and tamales, dietary staples of Mesoamerican civilization for thousands of years, provided the lion's share of calories and nutrition for Mexican campesinos and city dwellers alike. Wheat bread remained a rarity across most of the nation, the fare of the elite hacendado rather than the rural and urban masses. The Rockefeller Foundation's planners had readily acknowledged this imbalance between the two crops in drafting their initial program for Mexican agriculture, choosing to prioritize corn improvement, as "no crop is more closely tied up with the daily lives of the average Mexican farmer." In the Survey Commission's formative 1941 travel report, wheat was relegated to the sidelines, not even meriting designation as a principal crop variety.[80]

Therefore, Harrar and Stakman were quite surprised when, on their arrival in Mexico City in February 1943, agriculture secretary Gómez "rather unexpectedly" designated the improvement and pathology of wheat as "the most important single problem" confronting Mexican agriculture.[81] What rationale might have led Gómez to prioritize a crop then covering less than a tenth of Mexico's farmland? His insistence on wheat must be understood in light of the revolutionary government's racialized campaign to remake campesino life by targeting food, which historian Jeffrey Pilcher has called the "tortilla discourse."[82] Since the Porfirian era, modernizing elites blamed campesinos' diet of corn, beans, and chiles for stunting their physical and intellectual development, even suggesting that the consumption of corn inherently produced backward, dark-skinned people in contrast to strong and virile wheat-fed Europeans. Gómez, a native of the Mexican north where wheat production and consumption were more common, was well versed in such rhetoric. Gómez had earlier written of the "apathetic natures, sadness, indifference toward life, and short stature" of corn-fed southern Mexicans as compared to the "stronger and better built individuals" subsisting on wheat and dairy in the North.[83] In this way, Gómez's agenda in remaking Mexican agriculture targeted not simply food supply but race, culture, and biology, too.

Though the MAP leadership was privately "doubtful whether [wheat] actually is the most important single problem," it assured Gómez in early 1943 that its program would address improvement of that crop and solutions to its primary disease, *chahuixtle*, or rust.[84] Harrar, trained as a plant pathologist, promised to spearhead that effort. But Harrar's administrative and diplomatic duties as local director left him little time for other work, and during the MAP's first two years the wheat program lagged far behind the synthetic maize effort in progress and resources. To address this imbalance, in fall 1944 the Advisory Committee hired a second plant pathologist, Norman E. Borlaug, to breathe new life into the wheat-breeding program. Like Harrar, the Iowa-born Borlaug had been a doctoral student of Stakman's at the University of Minnesota. Yet Borlaug was otherwise an outlier among the MAP's Chapingo staff. He had no experience working in poor rural areas of the US South, as Harrar, Mangelsdorf, Wellhausen, and soils expert Colwell did. Borlaug also came to the MAP from a lucrative career in commercial agribusiness rather than public service, employed at E. I. DuPont de Nemours and Company during the war. With this background, it was not surprising that Borlaug viewed Mexican agriculture in a different light from his peers. Rather than sympathizing with Cardenista land reform, he summarily dismissed the ejido as a "built-in political hedge" against boosting production, as "small farm units are not economical."[85]

Such biases quickly manifested themselves in Borlaug's early wheat-breeding work in Chapingo. He began by importing hybrid strains from abroad, primarily from the United States, testing them in various central Mexican climates and altitudes.[86] Irrigation and heavy synthetic fertilization were essential to the performance of such plants, but this hardly concerned Borlaug, who spent far less time worrying about the practicality of his methods for poor Mexican farmers. Unlike his colleagues who had learned in the US South the dangers of universal models for agricultural transformation, Borlaug sought to re-create in Mexico his native and much-romanticized Midwest. It was therefore not surprising that when Carl Sauer visited Chapingo in 1945, he immediately noted the "pitfalls in the [MAP's] wheat campaign" and its emphasis on foods that only "the privileged fraction of the population can absorb."[87]

Yet Borlaug's most decisive break with the MAP's peasant orientation came in 1946, when he proposed an entirely new direction for the wheat program. Frustrated by the limitations of ejido farmers in central Mexico, where plots were relatively small, and wheat was rarely grown or eaten, Borlaug concocted a plan to relocate his efforts to the state of Sonora. In the arid wheat belt of northwestern Mexico, a full thousand miles from Chapingo, he dreamed of partnering with large commercial farmers who had easy access to investment capital and irrigation. But to Borlaug's bitter frustration, Harrar quashed this scheme. "The guts of our problem is here, in the poverty areas," the MAP's director reprimanded Borlaug. "The northern farmers [are] rich and [don't] need our help," Harrar observed. Borlaug bargained a compromise in arranging a brief annual leave during Chapingo's winter off-season to survey possibilities in Sonora, but Harrar promised him few resources and insisted that the wheat program remain anchored in central Mexican concerns.[88]

By 1947, the synthetic maize campaign and Borlaug's wheat program—each presenting sharply contrasting visions for rural progress—were locked in a struggle for the future of the green revolution. Ultimately, their contest would be settled by two broader transformations that ensnared the Rockefeller Foundation and tilted the game in favor of Borlaug.

The first was a deepening Cold War. After early standoffs between the United States and Soviet Union in western Europe during 1945 and 1946, the crossroads of the Cold War shifted southward to the decolonizing and postcolonial states of Asia, Africa, and Latin America. It was in these years that policy makers first spoke of a "Third World," that vast swath of humanity affiliated neither with the capitalist nor Communist blocs.[89] By the late 1940s, strategists in both Washington, DC, and Moscow began to pour vast resources into broadcasting their economic as well as social models as the Third World's surest path toward abundance and prosperity. Within US policy circles, the increasingly ubiquitous watchword motivating this global outreach was "development," an ambiguous and contradictory faith born from the belief that human social progress could be mapped on a linear path, and that "advanced" nations could speed the evolution of "backward" ones. Especially after President Truman declared in his 1949 inaugural address that the United States must "mak[e] the benefits of our scientific advances and our industrial progress available for the improvement and growth of underdeveloped areas," the politicization of Third World technical assistance rose to a fever pitch.[90]

Proceeding apace with the Cold War's advance into the nascent Third World was a dramatic resurgence in fears about global hunger and starvation. While US and European intellectuals had periodically revived Reverend

Thomas Malthus's prediction that population growth would ultimately out-pace natural resources, the famines and deprivations of World War II along with its immediate aftermath punctuated such apocalyptic forecasts. In the United States, two hugely influential books published in 1948—William Vogt's *The Road to Survival* and Fairfield Osborn's *Our Plundered Planet*—inflamed anxieties about the future of the planet's food security. Both Vogt and Osborn were conservationists, concerned with deforestation, erosion, and increasingly exploitative agricultural practices, and together they warned that the scarcities of the war might be not an aberration but rather a harbin-ger of crises to come.[91] Within the Rockefeller Foundation, the two books made a lasting impact. Warren Weaver, the Division of Natural Sciences chief overseeing the MAP after Mann's death, deemed that Vogt's *Road to Survival* "does seem to present very basic problems in a forceful way," and asked that the New York office purchase multiple copies for distribution.[92]

The converging tremors of the Third World Cold War and neo-Malthusian revival shook the Rockefeller Foundation to its core, and that ideological convulsion would alter the course of the MAP. Confronting an unfamiliar geopolitical terrain, the foundation's leadership felt a sudden urgency to extract from Mexico a universal, replicable model for feeding a world be-lieved to be on the brink of starvation and chaos. Mangelsdorf and Brad-field declared in 1948 that "the most critical problem which faces the world today is that of producing sufficient food to feed the world's population."[93] Such a statement stood in stark contrast to the Survey Commission's 1941 proposal, which found little evidence that Mexico was starving, but instead targeted rural poverty and the peon's "emancipation from overwhelming drudgery."[94] In 1950, Stakman asserted that Mexico was a crucial test site be-cause "the Western hemisphere may become the world's last refuge against communism," and therefore "it will be of tremendous importance for the United States to demonstrate that the democratic system is capable of assist-ing backward peoples."[95] Steeped in such rhetoric, it was not surprising that the foundation's leaders soon started to ponder whether the "pattern of procedure developed in Mexico" might "extend similar help in other Latin American countries."[96]

Yet what exactly was that "pattern of procedure"? In the latter half of the 1940s the MAP was torn between two competing visions: the peasant-friendly maize program and Borlaug's experimentation with wheat. As the foundation reconsidered its priorities and began to look beyond Mexico, that contradiction demanded resolution. Borlaug, sensing that Wellhausen was making slow progress boosting corn yields on ejido farms, started to lobby more aggressively for expanding his Sonoran work. In summer 1948, such pressure flared into open conflict when Harrar demanded that Borlaug abandon Sonora entirely as it was a distraction from the MAP's primary task in central Mexico. Borlaug, infuriated, resigned from the Rockefeller

Foundation and made plans to leave the country. Had this conflict occurred two or three years earlier, Borlaug would likely have left and become a mere footnote in the green revolution's history. But at the anxious crossroads of 1948, the senior Stakman decided to intervene on Borlaug's behalf, successfully pressuring Harrar to reverse his decision and funnel new resources into Mexico's northwest. The conflict marked a significant victory for Borlaug, while auguring trouble for the future of the MAP's socially conscious plant breeding.[97]

Stakman likely intervened on Borlaug's behalf in hopes that the wheat breeder might engineer an overnight miracle in Sonora, providing the foundation with sufficient fodder for expanding beyond Mexico and pledging its effort to the global Cold War. Borlaug would not disappoint. With far greater resources and his hands no longer tied by Harrar's insistence on reaching ejido farmers, Borlaug made rapid headway on breeding higher-yielding, rust-resistant wheat varieties. Fundamental to his success were cozy relationships with Sonora's largest entrepreneurial farmers, including Rodolfo Elías Calles, former governor of the state and son of 1920s' president Plutarco Elías Calles.[98] Borlaug also developed a close partnership with Richard Spurlock, the manager of a vast hacienda owned by the American Cyanamid Corporation, which was eager to capitalize on higher yields of wheat.[99] Such alliances with Mexico's agrarian upper crust bypassed the slow and grueling path chosen by the MAP's maize program. With like-minded, well-heeled collaborators to test and reproduce new strains of wheat, it was not long before Borlaug boasted of a wholesale revolution in Sonoran wheat production, and by 1951 he claimed that 70 percent of all the wheat grown in Mexico was planted from MAP cultivars. The maize program could hardly advertise such success.[100]

As Borlaug's star rose, wheat steadily eclipsed corn in both the MAP's planning and publicity. When Stakman argued in 1951 that the Mexican program could be "applied directly in other Latin American countries," it was based on his belief that "the improvement of Mexican wheats has been little short of astounding."[101] In a December 1949 interview with *Tierra*, the mouthpiece of the Mexican agriculture secretariat, Harrar bragged of new hybrid, rust-resistant wheats, mentioning only briefly the maize program's progress.[102] Though the corn-breeding team continued to experiment with peasant-friendly varieties during the new decade, with Wellhausen declaring as late as 1956 that "the development of synthetic varieties is the best program for all underdeveloped areas where corn is important," such work was increasingly a footnote rather than focal point of the program as a whole.[103] With few avenues to reproduce and distribute synthetic seed, as the federal Corn Commission excluded all but hybrid varieties, Wellhausen and his colleagues acknowledged political realities and turned more attention toward double-cross maize cultivars. By 1954, the MAP prepared thirteen hybrid corn varieties for distribution alongside one open-pollinated strain.[104]

The Rockefeller agricultural program in Mexico had initially been tailored to the peculiar postrevolutionary context of Mexico, inspired by the foundation's prior experience in the US South, but by the opening of the 1950s evidence of this legacy was fleeting. Once sympathetic to the ejido, the MAP leadership in 1951 dismissed the "hundreds of thousands of uneconomic farm units that are too small even to provide a subsistence for the families that are dependent on them."[105] Criticism of the nascent emphasis on large commercial farms was summarily dismissed. In late 1949, Rockefeller Foundation trustee and Dartmouth College president John S. Dickey visited Chapingo, and warned that the program could "introduce fresh economic disparities within the Mexican economy" and thereby "present political problems not now even dimly perceived by many Mexicans."[106] Dickey recommended an immediate socioeconomic study of such dilemmas, but Weaver was skeptical. The Division of Natural Sciences chief sardonically likened hiring social scientists to asking "the foreman of a line repair crew, sent out to splice a telephone cable broken in a storm, whether he wouldn't like to take along a couple of professors interested in the social impact of modern communications systems." The MAP was performing emergency work, Weaver implied, and asking it to pause for careful study would be impertinent and risky.[107]

Intoxicated by the perceived urgency of the Third World Cold War and looming food scarcities, and confident that it had a replicable model in Mexico, the Rockefeller Foundation leaped to transplant it elsewhere. In May 1950, the Colombian Agricultural Program began operation in Medellín, Colombia, and a similar agency opened its doors in Santiago, Chile, in April 1955. But perhaps most important, in 1957 the Rockefeller Foundation signed a cooperative agreement to work with the government of India, establishing offices in New Delhi. At that moment, the Cold War battle for South Asia was at high tide, and Rockefeller plant breeders worked hand in glove with the US State Department in assuring that every harvest of rice and wheat would go toward preventing a Communist revolution in the world's largest democracy. Their much-publicized success in forestalling Indian famine prompted further expansion. In 1960, the Rockefeller and Ford Foundations partnered to open the International Rice Research Institute in the Philippines, which would serve as an outpost for transforming risiculture across Southeast Asia, ever with a watchful eye toward US military involvement in Vietnam.[108]

As the Rockefeller Foundation aggressively globalized the lessons of the MAP across multiple continents in the 1950s, there was little doubt as to which of its competing visions it packaged for export. Dismissing the halting progress of the synthetic maize program, foundation planners favored a rapid increase in production even if it threatened to exacerbate agrarian class tensions. No longer did they view the Third World countryside as a counterpart to the plantation districts of Alabama or East Texas; they now saw it as

in particular expressed anxiety over the social costs of rural transformation. "In spite of the vast changes that had taken place throughout the country," Mangelsdorf recalled, "we couldn't see that the lot of the small farmer, the ejidatario, had changed very much." Indeed, smallholders were "gradually being squeezed out of the picture," just as "has happened in the United States." Well aware of the possibilities that the early Rockefeller program in Mexico had first suggested, Mangelsdorf undoubtedly felt some twinge of regret at this outcome.[112]

***

In the decade between 1943 and 1953, the Rockefeller Foundation's MAP— long considered the blueprint of the global green revolution—underwent a dramatic transformation. At its founding, the project represented an alliance between a philanthropy well versed in US rural poverty and a postrevolutionary government committed to endowing recent land reform grantees with credit, education, and appropriate technologies. Rather than pursuing increased food production at whatever cost, the US and Mexican architects of the MAP acknowledged that Mexico's fundamental challenge in 1943 was not hunger but instead the common farmer's lack of stability, security, and ability to improve their lot. Most illustrative of this understanding was the foundation's attempt to breed better varieties of maize, the single most important food crop in the nation. Rejecting the US gospel of double-cross hybrid corn as inappropriate to the social and economic context of Mexico's ejidal sector, Rockefeller planners experimented with alternative plant varieties spurned by US seed companies that promised to grant campesinos higher yields without sinking them into debt or eroding their independence. For several years, this peasant-friendly strategy occupied center stage in the collaborative effort to improve Mexican agriculture.

It was not long before resistance to such an approach arose from several quarters, however. With the political ascension of Alemán after 1946, federal efforts to preserve and stabilize the ejido sector lost ground while programs promising to boost food production and siphon the rural population to urban centers received top priority. If campesinos were to be "modernized" and made productive citizens, believed Alemán, it would occur in the city, not the countryside. The MAP's synthetic maize program would therefore curry little favor in the halls of government. Equally crippling of that approach was the escalating ideological struggle between the United States and Soviet Union during the late 1940s. Anxious about Communism's seductive appeal to dispossessed rural peoples the world over, US policy makers sought to rapidly demonstrate that technical assistance from the First World provided a surer path to prosperity and progress than the political slogans of the Second World. Such sentiments permeated the offices of the Rockefeller Foundation, lending a new urgency to the Mexican program while raising expectations that it would soon produce a speedy and replicable model for boosting food production. Pinned between an unsympathetic Mexican state and the global Cold War, the MAP's planners slowly abandoned the experimental maize program to prioritize the breeding of wheat, a crop capable of rapid improvements, but one rarely grown or eaten by peasant cultivators. Such a dismissal of smallholder agriculture would echo across the planet as the foundation exported its Mexican wheat program elsewhere in Latin America and ultimately to Asia in the years that followed.

Yet it is impossible to understand the rise and fall of peasant sympathies in the green revolution without acknowledging the significance of US regionalism to that history. To deem the MAP a blunt project of "Americanization" conceals far more than it reveals. The Rockefeller Foundation's intervention in Mexican agriculture was born from comparisons between Mexico's countryside and the plantation belt of the US South. Such juxtapositions likewise influenced the first years of the collaborative program in Mexico, motivating planners and plant breeders like Mann, Mangelsdorf, and Wellhausen to tailor technological solutions to the economic limitations of the smallholders who represented the rural majority. Grappling with power and inequality in the US Cotton Belt prompted the Rockefeller leadership to acknowledge that Mexico shared a similar history, and that any solution to rural poverty must acknowledge long-standing social divisions as well as the structures reproducing them. Such sensitivities, though, were relatively short lived. When the foundation hitched its wagon to Borlaug—an Iowan who understood Mexico's possibilities in light of an idealized Midwest and had little interest in challenging inequality—it betrayed the promise of its early experimentation. Indeed, the instinct to model Third World progress on an archetypal Midwest was then only beginning, as the international development apparatus that ballooned in influence during the 1950s and 1960s would continuously sweep away the political and historic complexities of regions it sought to remake. Our planet's social landscape today attests to the tragedy of such shortsightedness.

In the world of Rockefeller philanthropy, the influence of US southern models for rural growth and progress was on the wane by the last years of the 1940s. But this would hardly mean that Mexican planners and politicians ceased to look to the Cotton Belt when crafting programs to reshape their countryside. Instead, such juxtapositions came to a crescendo as the Mexican state after 1946 embarked on an unprecedented campaign of hydraulic rural development patterned explicitly after the New Deal's most renowned regional program: the Tennessee Valley Authority. The final chapter explores this last major attempt to bridge the agrarian politics of the United States and Mexico at midcentury.

Chapter Six

TRANSPLANTING "EL TENESÍ"
NEW DEAL HYDRAULIC DEVELOPMENT IN POSTWAR MEXICO

IN SPRING 1947, President Miguel Alemán made the first major Mexican state visit to the United States in nearly forty years. With all the pomp and circumstance that the young and flamboyant president demanded, his tour was meant to be a celebration of the warming relationship between the United States and Mexico after decades of tension and distrust. Confetti and crowds greeted him across the country. In Washington, DC, he addressed the US Congress; in New York, he spoke before the newly founded United Nations, riding in a parade organized in his honor. Yet after these expected visits to the political and economic centers of the United States, Alemán's tour took a surprising turn when he flew southward to Muscle Shoals, Alabama, and Chattanooga, Tennessee. What drew him to this corner of the US South were the most spectacular symbols of New Deal rural development: the works of the Tennessee Valley Authority (TVA), which had long captivated the Mexican president. On May 6, standing before the concrete leviathan of Chickamauga Dam on the Tennessee River north of Chattanooga, Alemán pondered this "great experiment, of which [Mexico] can and will take the greatest advantage." As his TVA hosts described their ambitious campaign to stem the waste of the region's human and natural resources, Alemán decided that his nation and the Tennessee Valley shared more than one might imagine. "The TVA plan," he excitedly told Chattanooga reporters, "can be fully applied to Mexico."[1]

In previous chapters, this book has explored how reformers and bureaucrats in the United States and Mexico during the years of the Great Depression and World War II eagerly exchanged models for rural reconstruction. Those models were wildly diverse, ranging from land expropriation and resettlement to agronomic research and social science planning. In that lively dialogue, Mexicans and US nationals drew consistent parallels between the agrarian problems of the US Cotton Belt and diverse hacienda zones of Mexico. Perhaps no strand of this web, though, was as highly publicized or dynamic in its remaking of nature and human life as the common campaign to transform river basins. During the 1930s and 1940s, the US South and southern Mexico were both the targets of vast federal attempts to harness waterpower and turn rivers into engines for economic growth as well as agrarian social change. In the South, the TVA, one of the most groundbreaking and controversial agencies of the New Deal, most famously undertook this effort. In Mexico, the ruling party after World War II pioneered a vast attempt to achieve a similar task through the so-called *desarrollo integral de cuencas*—integrated development of river valleys—that would dramatically reshape the society and economy of southern coastal Mexico.

This chapter will demonstrate that those two efforts were entangled and forged in relation to one another, particularly through Mexican intellectual borrowing from the US South. From the 1930s through the 1950s, the TVA served as a seductive model for Mexican state planners seeking to transform their countryside. Public comparisons between the Tennessee Valley and Mexico's tropical lowlands became ubiquitous after World War II, casually employed by bureaucrats and the press. Political icons as diverse as Lázaro Cárdenas and Alemán would make pilgrimages to the Tennessee Valley. Yet rather than a neat blueprint to be seamlessly replicated, the "TVA idea" was forever transformed as it struck the rocky shoals of Mexican postrevolutionary politics. The social and political ideology of Mexico's ruling party after 1940 alongside the nation's unique history of social revolution ensured that the transplanting of TVA models often refigured them beyond recognition. Indeed, few of the Mexican river valley projects undertaken as nominal replicas of the TVA resembled their progenitor.[2]

Such a disparity between rhetoric and reality poses a fundamental question: Considering the divergent results, why did the Mexican state so frequently invoke the TVA when promoting its domestic agenda? This chapter shows that Mexican planners made transnational comparisons because such analogies served to depoliticize a divisive project and conceal the inherent risks that their venture suggested. By imagining the TVA as a transformative juggernaut helmed by technicians rather than politicians—hardly an accurate portrait of the original agency—the Mexican government sought to reassure an increasingly skeptical public that its rural development campaign had a successful and replicable precedent. The economist Albert O. Hirschman later diagnosed such "pseudo-imitation" as a common instinct in the practice of development, where "ventures that are 90 percent indigenous initiative and 10 percent imitation of a foreign model are regularly presented to the public as though the percentages were, in fact, reversed."[3]

Likewise, paeans to the TVA performed important ideological work at a crucial moment in Mexican political history. After Cárdenas's transformative presidency of 1934–40, the increasingly conservative leadership of the ruling party began to turn its back on campesinos to favor business stability, industrialization, and urbanization. The revolution, it declared, was to be institutionalized. In doing so, party leaders sought models for rural development that retained a nominal commitment to social justice, but favored increased production over fair distribution, and technocracy over democracy. The TVA came to serve in that role. With its rhetoric of combating poverty, disease, and "backwardness" through the rationalization of natural resource use, the TVA provided a convenient cover for the ruling party's effort to roll back the redistributive politics of the Cárdenas years. This grew partially from the inherent conservatism of the TVA itself: by diagnosing a wild and untamed river as the source of regional poverty, rather than uneven social and economic relationships, it turned attention away from the structural roots of both US southern and then Mexican inequality.

Yet even with conservative Mexican planners at the helm, exactly how US strategies in rural development would be adapted remained unpredictable. Explicit comparisons with the Tennessee Valley prompted the establishment of two river valley commissions in 1947: the Comisión del Papaloapan and Comisión del Tepalcatepec, targeting river valleys in coastal southeastern and southwestern Mexico, respectively. Despite their genesis in the same year and their common intellectual precursor, the two were fundamentally different undertakings. The former was Alemán's pet project, a quixotic, grandiose, and ill-conceived effort to remake the landscape and society of the Papaloapan River basin while simultaneously monumentalizing the ruling party's power and legitimacy. The latter, however, was proposed and led by none other than Mexico's most renowned champion of campesino interests, Lázaro Cárdenas, who believed that his commission should buttress the cooperative agricultural system enshrined by the 1930s' land reform. The contrasting careers of the Papaloapan and Tepalcatepec projects, alongside their successes and failures, reveal that the TVA was a fluid intellectual export that could be reinvented to justify diverse political agendas.

The pages that follow will explore the colliding worlds that made it possible for Mexican politicians to speak of replicating a US river valley nearly two thousand miles removed. I begin by reviewing the origins and first decade of the TVA in the US South. Long before it was an influential development model in the Global South, the TVA was one of the most controversial agencies of the New Deal, torn by competing visions within and confronted by powerful enemies without. Only during World War II, as the heated political battles of the 1930s gave way to a more conservative consensus, would the agency resolve its inner tensions and look abroad with a new singularity of purpose. Following that, I examine the role that the TVA occupied in the Mexican developmental imaginary from the 1930s through World War II. Seeking a successful model to combat lingering agrarian problems in rural Mexico, the Mexican state was seduced by the seeming likeness of the southern US and tropical coastal Mexico. Beginning during Cárdenas's presidency but reaching an apex under Alemán, Mexican bureaucrats publicly advocated the imitation of New Deal river valley development. The latter half of the chapter turns to two specific applications of the "TVA idea": in the Papaloapan River basin of Oaxaca and Veracruz, and in the Tepalcatepec valley of Michoacán. The diverging missions of these two projects, and the differing ideologies of their leadership, reveal the unpredictable nature of the era's agrarian crossings.

The TVA and Rural Development

In the southeastern United States, the Tennessee River is rivaled in historical significance only by the Mississippi. With its headwaters in the Appalachian mountain valleys of northeastern Tennessee, the river flows southwest toward Georgia, dipping into northern Alabama for more than 200 miles before flowing northward again and finally emptying into the Ohio River near Paducah, Kentucky. Along that 650-mile path, dozens of tributaries reach out like capillaries, creating a river valley basin that encompasses more than 40,000 square miles. For millennia, the river bore many fruits for its human neighbors, particularly as a source of food and a commercial artery, but it rarely conformed to the wishes and desires of its residents. During seasons of heavy rain, the Tennessee frequently flooded, claiming countless lives and farms; in years of drought, it bared rocky shoals and became nearly impossible to navigate.[4]

An unpredictable waterway, however, was only the first of the Tennessee Valley's problems after the Civil War. Despite the wealth of land, water, and timber resources in the river's basin, the region was one of poorest in the United States. This poverty was born in part from the scarcity of cash and credit that plagued the entire postbellum US South, but it was exacerbated by the extractive, semicolonial industries that dominated the valley, whether mining and logging in mountain and forest regions, or the cotton monoculture of northern Alabama and western Tennessee. Most of the valley's residents were farmers in the early twentieth century, and the region's agricultural zones were diverse: white smallholders dominated the more mountainous northeastern portions, while northern Alabama and western Tennessee more closely resembled Deep South plantation counties. In total, 11 percent of the valley's population was African American, although most black residents were concentrated in western regions. On the eve of the New Deal, rates of farm tenancy in some of the valley's cotton-growing zones neared 70 percent, and soil erosion was rampant. To many contemporary observers, the Tennessee Valley was a symbol of deprivation and backwardness.[5]

Around the turn of the twentieth century, government bureaucrats and business boosters came to believe that the fickle wildness of the Tennessee

River, rather than social and economic inequalities, was the primary obstacle to regional growth. Such impulses climaxed during World War I, when the US federal government began planning what would be the largest concrete dam in the world, Wilson Dam, for the purpose of generating electricity to produce nitrates for wartime explosives. Located on the Tennessee River's rocky path through northwestern Alabama in Muscle Shoals, Wilson Dam was never completed during the war and ran into political troubles afterward. The project languished during the 1920s as public and private forces battled for its control, and the dam was only partially operational when the Great Depression started. The debacle in Muscle Shoals revealed that the marriage of federal planning, technical prowess, and regional uplift was hardly a guaranteed recipe for success.[6]

While attempts to bring social and economic change to the Tennessee Valley by means of water control were at least a generation old by the 1930s, it is difficult to deny the singular importance of Franklin D. Roosevelt to those efforts. Entering the White House in spring 1933 with a popular mandate to combat the Depression by any means necessary, Roosevelt unveiled a bewildering array of experimental programs during his first several months in office. Few were more ambitious than his vision for the Tennessee Valley. Roosevelt was long familiar with the rural poverty of the US South, and a January 1933 visit to Muscle Shoals convinced him that the Tennessee River could serve as the backbone of a regional antipoverty program. In April of that year, Roosevelt presented a bill to Congress to charter a government corporation that he dubbed the TVA. The authority, in Roosevelt's proposal, would transcend traditional geopolitical boundaries, and address the problems of a "complete river watershed involving many States and the future lives and welfare of millions." It would operate a refashioned facility in Muscle Shoals, but more important, it would construct several more hydroelectric dams upriver and administer a distribution of their fruits to local people. The TVA was to be a showcase of the possibilities of state planning. After the bill rapidly passed the House and Senate in the spring, Roosevelt signed it in May 1933. As a piece of public policy, the TVA Act was unprecedented: it centralized power in an autonomous agency that answered only to the president, and made that agency responsible for planning the society and economy of a vast multistate region.[7]

Notwithstanding its lofty rhetoric, the language of the bill that Roosevelt signed was deliberately vague, and it was left up to a three-member board of directors to determine exactly what sort of change the TVA would pursue in the valley. The chair of that board, and the most significant policy maker during the agency's first years, was Arthur E. Morgan. A hydraulic engineer from Ohio, Morgan was deeply influenced by the utopian socialism of Edward Bellamy and believed that small, self-sustaining agrarian communities coupled with localized industry could serve as an antidote to what he saw as the chaos of urban civilization. Despite his training as a technician, Morgan was most interested in the human problems of the Tennessee Valley. He believed those problems were not a product of the region's isolation, as many observers assumed of Appalachia, but instead of its external exploitation and blind adherence to individualism over communalism.

Morgan's romantic idealism was balanced out by his two colleagues on the board: Harcourt A. Morgan and David Lilienthal. Harcourt Morgan—of no relation to Arthur—was the board's agricultural expert, trained as an entomologist. As the president of the University of Tennessee and its land grant agricultural school, Harcourt Morgan was far more comfortable in partnering with the valley's larger and wealthier farmers. But Arthur Morgan's most formidable counterweight on the TVA board was Lilienthal, an Indiana lawyer. The youngest board member, Lilienthal had already earned a reputation as a prominent champion of public power, having fought the collusion of private utilities against consumer interests in the Midwest. To Lilienthal, electrification was the panacea for the valley's ills, but unlike Arthur Morgan, he saw it as a means to the ultimate goal of urbanization, industrialization, and creating consumers who would participate in a national market. Lilienthal entertained few of Morgan's sympathies for agrarian subsistence.[8]

From day one, the TVA's leadership was bitterly divided, but Roosevelt's insistence that they focus on short-term results ensured a temporary ceasefire. In the heady first years of its operation, despite feuds and rivalries, the agency left a profound footprint on the Tennessee Valley. In its first decade, the TVA hired thousands of people to construct sixteen new multipurpose dams on the Tennessee River and its tributaries, moving more than a hundred million cubic yards of concrete, rock, and soil. Dams created massive reservoirs, which both tamed the river for navigability and forcibly pushed out tens of thousands of former residents. But dams represented only the tip of the iceberg: the TVA's leadership pursued the principle of "integrated development," insisting that poverty could only be overcome by simultaneously attacking all angles of a social problem. Therefore, the agency complemented dams with hundreds of miles of highways and railroads, alongside thousands of miles of electric lines. Fertilizer plants powered by hydroelectricity synthesized nitrogen from the atmosphere and sold their products at low prices to local farmers, seeking to revive exhausted and eroded soils. TVA public health employees also penetrated rural communities to wage war on malaria and other preventable diseases. This vast bureaucracy, otherwise fractured by state lines and jurisdictional divisions, answered only to TVA headquarters in Knoxville, and the agency's power was palpable.[9]

But as the TVA gathered momentum during the 1930s, the contradictory philosophies of its leaders threatened to tear it asunder. During the first few years of the agency's operation, Arthur Morgan had largely attempted to run the authority on his own, ignoring or silencing the voices of his two colleagues on the board. The imprints of Morgan's developmental vision were most prominently displayed in the model community of Norris, Tennessee, which he designed to balance subsistence agriculture with decentralized home industry. Morgan was also instrumental in forging cooperative organizations among Appalachian farmers to overcome what he saw as the destructive spirit of economic competition. By 1935, however, Lilienthal and Harcourt Morgan began to actively resist their marginalization, and to Arthur Morgan's great frustration, Lilienthal proved to have far more political acumen than the chair. Whereas the technocratic Morgan had cultivated few political alliances at the local and national level, believing his work to be above that realm, Lilienthal proved a skilled public spokesperson for his own TVA vision. Publicly ridiculing Morgan's emphasis on community and cooperation as "basket-weaving," Lilienthal went on the offensive by 1937. In time, the vicious battle for TVA's future erupted beyond the agency's boardrooms, threatening to humiliate the entire Roosevelt administration. At a moment when the New Deal had no shortage of enemies, the president decided in 1938 to fire Arthur Morgan, who had become a political liability.[10]

Now in the driver's seat, Lilienthal rapidly began to expunge Morgan's legacy from the operation and memory of the TVA. In 1944, he solidified his position as the intellectual architect of his agency when he penned *TVA: Democracy on the March*, a work that would be instrumental in forging its lasting myth. Marked by bold, audacious rhetoric, *Democracy on the March* was Lilienthal's epic tale of the TVA's accomplishments. Propelling the agency, in his telling, was a unified and coherent ideology: "the TVA idea" was singular rather than plural. Its mission was apolitical, transcending the "extremes of 'right' and 'left'" because "rivers have no politics," and their development should be determined by "dependable technical decisions." Yet as the book's title suggests, the TVA in Lilienthal's imagination was democratic as opposed to technocratic, fed by grassroots participation and local voices. Above all, it was transformative: just over a decade after the agency began to excavate rock and pour concrete, the Tennessee Valley's "worn-out cotton fields and rows of tenant shacks" were replaced by "the undulation of neatly terraced hillsides" and booming industry. The book would ultimately be translated into dozens of languages and sell hundreds of thousands of copies worldwide, and in the postwar years it was widely touted as the singular source required to understand the agency's work.[11]

As a work of polemic, *Democracy on the March* was highly persuasive and effective. But it was hardly an accurate depiction of the agency's first decade. In the hopes of making the TVA palatable to post-Depression US voters and seductive to international observers, Lilienthal simplified and streamlined a history far more contingent and ambiguous. Arthur Morgan appears nowhere in the text, and Morgan's emphasis on fostering independent agrarian communities is similarly absent. The social, economic, and racial context of the Tennessee Valley is barely broached, while "the people" meant to benefit from TVA uplift are almost exclusively portrayed as a homogeneous white mass. The bitterness and frustration of the nearly 130,000 residents displaced by dam reservoirs are given two scant pages of recognition. Additionally, the book's insistence on the apolitical or even antipolitical nature of the TVA downplayed Lilienthal's consistent attention to building alliances in Washington, DC, and the fundamentally political choices of selecting dam locations. Perhaps most problematically, though, *Democracy on the March*'s rapturous portrayal of the Tennessee Valley's metamorphosis in the course of one short decade far exaggerated the TVA's actual accomplishments. As several critics have claimed, by the late 1930s the agency had made an insubstantial impact on income and wages, and though wartime spending dramatically improved the socioeconomic index of the valley, it did so equally in regions of the South removed from TVA investment.[12]

Yet to most of the book's readers at home and abroad, *Democracy on the March* presented a compelling morality tale. Lilienthal distilled a decade of competing visions into a single sentence: his TVA stood for the conquest of nature through the marriage of centralized planning, technical know-how, and democratic rhetoric. Two primary ambitions motivated Lilienthal to write the book. First, he sought to defend an increasingly besieged liberalism at home, sustaining the New Deal into the postwar era. But most important, Lilienthal looked beyond the United States to a larger global task that he called "world reconstruction." Anticipating the growing geopolitical importance of the decolonizing states of Asia, Africa, and Latin America, he believed that US technical assistance to these nations might aid their leaders as they navigated between the political extremities of right and left.[13]

In predicting that the future of the TVA lay beyond the United States, Lilienthal proved prescient. Even though the agency would substantially scale back its domestic social agenda after World War II, becoming—in the words of one observer—little more than a "glorified Power Company," both Lilienthal and the TVA's international reputations ballooned during the early Cold War. As several recent works have detailed, the TVA became one of the United States' most significant intellectual exports after World War II, when nations as far-flung as Afghanistan, China, Colombia, India, and Vietnam each sought to replicate an imagined TVA blueprint, often with unpredictable consequences. Whether its residents knew it or not, the Tennessee Valley and its image would touch the lives of countless millions worldwide.[14]

Of all the world's observers that turned their eyes to this New Deal experiment in the US South, few came earlier, more frequently, or with more enthusiasm than those from Mexico. Beginning not long after water flowed through the first TVA dam in 1936, Mexican observers charted the agency's successes and failures, and considered the potential value of its technosocial engineering. As one of the most prominent strands of the US-Mexican agrarian dialogue, the intellectual exchange of river basin development models would profoundly reshape the Mexican countryside to an extent rivaled only by the green revolution.

Paths to Mexico

The desire to manipulate water resources was hardly new to twentieth-century Mexico. With its geography marked by astounding contrasts in precipitation, particularly between its dry and dusty North, temperate central plateau, and tropical South, Mexican hydraulic engineering efforts since independence manifested themselves in many guises. While mid-nineteenth-century liberal politicians had begun efforts to rationalize and order the natural landscape, it was especially during the Porfiriato that the government undertook projects to turn natural resources to national advantage. In those years, Mexico City received particular attention, where engineers sought to drain surrounding lakes to expand residential areas. Equally important, though, was the arid North. Fearing US encroachment and domination in sparsely populated border states, nineteenth-century Mexican politicians hoped to use irrigation as a way to develop cultivable land and attract commercial farmers to settle the region. Therefore, by the turn of the century, canals, dikes, wells, and even dams became increasingly common in northern states like Sonora, Sinaloa, Coahuila, and Durango. Dam projects in the Porfiriato were nevertheless often small-scale undertakings backed by private firms or state governments, rather than by federal investment from Mexico City. Before the 1920s, the government did not truly wield a class of trained engineers familiar with large-scale dam construction.[15]

The coming of the Mexican Revolution brought a renewed faith in hydraulic development, but the political meaning of those projects would prove quite malleable. For many revolutionary leaders of the 1910s and 1920s, dam projects were attractive because irrigation and land reclamation might forestall more radical approaches to the smoldering problem of landlessness. Francisco Madero, who initiated the revolt against Porfirio Díaz but had never looked sympathetically toward land redistribution, had been a firm proponent of federal dam building in northern Mexico even before 1910. Similarly, for 1920s' president Plutarco Elías Calles, who dramatically expanded the state's role in overseeing hydraulic engineering in 1926 when he founded the Comisión Nacional de Irrigación (National Irrigation Commission), dams were a means to foster a productive agrarian middle class that would defuse tensions between hacendados and landless laborers.[16]

As peasant activism heated up in the 1930s, however, with campesino groups demanding that a *reparto de aguas* (distribution of water) accompany any reparto de tierra (distribution of land), Lázaro Cárdenas oversaw a dramatic shift in the revolutionary rhetoric of water control. Unlike his predecessors, he married the image of the high modernist dam to the push for land reform symbolized by Emiliano Zapata. When in 1936 Cárdenas expropriated productive cotton estates in La Laguna, the most sweeping exercise in agrarian reform during his presidency, he simultaneously unveiled plans for a high dam on La Laguna's Nazas River to democratize its waters. The Lázaro Cárdenas Dam, claimed the president in his decree for the land expropriation, would provide the "indispensable hydraulic complement" to the cooperative ejidos being granted to former tenants and wageworkers. And it was not the only such effort: the dam in La Laguna stood alongside four others initiated in the late 1930s. By the end of Cárdenas's presidency, there was a growing public linkage between large government dams and the land reform campaign.[17]

Fervent nationalist rhetoric pervaded Mexican hydraulic engineering projects, yet paradoxically those efforts were frequently dependent on extranational expertise, particularly from the United States. Because the Mexican North shared the arid ecology of the US West, leaders from Díaz onward had regularly solicited US technical assistance. Even in 1930s' La Laguna, where US nationals lost thousands of acres of land to expropriation, the chief superintendent in constructing the Lázaro Cárdenas Dam was one Henry Thorne, a New York engineer. Many leading Mexican engineers, too, had US experience: Adolfo Orive Alba, a key figure who would lead the National Irrigation Commission in the 1930s and 1940s, had trained with the Bureau of Reclamation in the US West. This ongoing discourse between the United States and Mexico on the question of water management is significant, but it differed from the later dialogue that would center on the TVA. First of all, this earlier exchange was almost exclusively technical, rarely broaching human and social problems. Second, these borrowings never commanded the same popular recognition that the TVA model did, as most Mexican leaders in the revolutionary era avoided public homage to US models.[18]

But when Roosevelt's New Deal ramped up its dam construction campaign and wedded it to a rhetoric of uplifting the downtrodden, it was no surprise that more and more Mexicans started to look northward for inspiration. By the late 1930s, observations of the TVA's undertaking in the US South began to appear in the popular press. A 1938 editorial in Mexico City's *El Nacional* gushed about New Dealer Pare Lorentz's recent film *The River*, whose viewing "shake[s] one to the deepest roots of our being." Seeing in the film how the TVA attempted to remedy the waste of the Tennessee Valley, the author could not avoid "refer[ring] mentally to our own country," where problems of water control—although in terms of scarcity—were equally compelling.[19] Likewise, in 1940 the Mexico City newsmagazine *Nuevo Orden* sympathetically deemed the TVA a "lesson in socialism." Exploring how "capitalism was impotent to solve the problems" of the land and people of the Tennessee Valley, the essay enumerated—with obvious admiration—the TVA's multipronged efforts to remake the nature and culture of the valley. "The future of civilization," concluded the writer, could well "depend on the possibility of transforming the social tangle of the private corporation [and] developing it socially by democratic means."[20]

Mexican curiosity toward the TVA was not limited to the press. The Cárdenas administration, too, paid increasing attention to what was happening in the Tennessee Valley. When in 1938 Cárdenas commissioned a study of how other world governments were wrestling with the economic crises of the decade, his advisers named the "electrification of the Tennessee Valley" as one of the most significant accomplishments of the US New Deal.[21] In conversations with his US compatriot Frank Tannenbaum, Cárdenas spoke regularly of his regard for the TVA and other rural New Deal agencies.[22] Such interest among the highest ranks of the Mexican government would translate into a series of northward pilgrimages in the late 1930s. During the Cárdenas years, representatives from the National Irrigation Commission, Federal Electricity Commission, and International Waters Commission all toured the TVA region.[23]

The Cárdenas administration's interest in the Tennessee Valley, however, was overshadowed by that of the incoming regime of Manuel Ávila Camacho, which oversaw not only a significant escalation in missions to the TVA but also began to consider a direct application of its lessons to Mexican river valleys. Yet for Ávila Camacho, the political impulses behind river basin development differed significantly from those that had motivated Cárdenas. In La Laguna and elsewhere, Cárdenas had seen hydraulic engineering as complementary to his strategy of resolving agrarian strife by redistributing land to the rural population. For Cárdenas's successor, in contrast, river control made possible an entirely different solution: redistributing the rural population across the land, especially to sparsely settled regions in coastal southern Mexico. In spring 1941, Ávila Camacho announced plans for a national "march to the sea," which sought to relocate farmers from the crowded central plateau to the "fertile lands of the coast." As he slowed land redistribution in the 1940s, Ávila Camacho proposed tropical settlement as an alternative safety valve to agrarian discontent. And because such an effort would require "sanitary and health measures, the opening of communications, and the reclamation and drainage of swamps," hydraulic engineering would be essential to its success.[24]

In this pursuit of a "march to the sea," the TVA would serve the Ávila Camacho regime as a powerful rhetorical symbol. In November 1941, not long after announcing plans for coastal settlement, the president commissioned a study of the "works being undertaken by the Tennessee Valley Authority," as there "exists a special interest in knowledge of this particular topic."[25] It was not long before the previous trickle of Mexican state visitors to the Tennessee Valley grew to a flood. More than twenty pilgrims representing five wings of government made the trip between 1940 and 1946, usually staying several days in either Tennessee or Alabama.[26] The Ávila Camacho administration also orchestrated a long-term, detailed study of the TVA's accomplishments. In summer 1941, Mexican ambassador to Washington Francisco Castillo Nájera contacted TVA chair Lilienthal with hopes that the authority might host a group of Mexican engineers for an extended period to "study the methods that you have applied in Tennessee."[27] Lilienthal was excited, and promised to provide the visitors with official titles along with funding to pay for their room and board while studying with the TVA.[28] Matching Lilienthal's enthusiasm was that of Adolfo Orive Alba, chief of the National Irrigation Commission. By early winter 1942, Orive Alba selected six employees from his agency to spend half a year studying a diverse array of TVA projects.[29]

In May 1942, the six commission engineers—Gabriel Oropeza Mendoza, Armando Bravo, Manuel Navarro Novelo, Salvador Mérigo Jané, José Yépez, and Ignacio Alcocer—arrived in Knoxville to begin their residency. They met immediately with Lilienthal, notifying him that their months in the valley were to "equip them for similar work the Mexican government is projecting." Ever the evangelist, the TVA chair eagerly described to them how "the Esperanto of the 'TVA idea'" had the millennial potential to "whip the problem of poverty." As Lilienthal wrote in his diary, the six seemed enraptured: "It was great to see the expression on their faces."[30] Their first six weeks in Tennessee were spent in the classroom, where TVA employees prepared an elaborate orientation to the agency's history as well as the "geographic and economic setting in which it operates."[31] In essence, they received a crash course in US southern history. The six read University of North Carolina sociologists Rupert Vance and Howard Odum's portrayal of the shocking inequalities of the Cotton Belt, alongside W. J. Cash's *The Mind of the South*. After learning of the problems of tenancy and soil erosion, they embarked on field trips to observe both change and continuity in the valley's social landscape.[32] From the weekly technical reports the engineers submitted to the National Irrigation Commission, it is difficult to reconstruct how they interpreted the society and culture of Tennessee and Alabama, but it is certain that as nonwhite residents of Jim Crow Knoxville they faced discrimination.[33] The six engineers, despite being professionals in their twenties and thirties, were frequently described by the TVA staff as "boys," reflecting a white southern practice common in talking about African Americans.[34]

Figure 6.1. Engineers Armando Bravo and José Yépez at Fort Loudoun Dam, Lenoir City, Tennessee, in August 1942. Image no. KX-01839. Courtesy of the Tennessee Valley Authority.

The urgency with which Mexican officials looked to the TVA for inspiration dramatically increased in 1944, when one of the worst floods in several generations struck Mexico's southeastern coastal plain. Heavy summer rainfall in the southern reaches of the Sierra Madre Oriental sent an unprecedented rush of water into the river valleys of Oaxaca and Veracruz. Most severely affected was the Papaloapan River, which winds through the mountainous downslopes of northern Oaxaca and into the humid *tierra caliente*— hot lands—of central Veracruz. In September 1944, the Papaloapan overflowed its banks, inundating nearly eight hundred square miles of farmland and several towns. In Tuxtepec and Cosamaloapan, major population centers along the river's course, several hundred residents drowned when floodwaters as high as eight feet consumed the cities' neighborhoods. The agricultural economy of the region was crippled for months to come. President Ávila Camacho, touring the Papaloapan basin on an emergency visit that October, confronted a bleak panorama of squandered life and land.[35]

The Papaloapan Valley would become the primary point of comparison and exchange with the Tennessee Valley, although juxtapositions between the two were often tenuous. The Papaloapan basin encompassed nearly eighteen thousand square miles and contained 1.1 million residents in 1950—about half the size of the Tennessee Valley with a quarter of its population on the eve of the New Deal. The Papaloapan Valley's geographic contrasts paralleled those of the TVA region: the lower basin nearest the Gulf of Mexico was tropical land near sea level, while the upper basin was mountainous and cooler. As in the Tennessee Valley, geographic contrasts mapped onto contrasts in political economy and culture. In the more isolated and mountainous upper basin, lying predominantly within the state of Oaxaca, indigenous groups such as the Mazatecs and Mixtecs had long resisted state incursions, and their agricultural economy was rooted in the cultivation of maize and beans. In the Veracruzan lower basin, however, plantation agriculture dominated. Especially along the Papaloapan River, large-scale sugarcane and banana haciendas had been established during the Porfiriato, many owned by the US Standard Fruit and United Fruit companies. But if regional variations and colonial economics in the Papaloapan basin suggested some parallels to the Tennessee Valley, the Papaloapan region's agrarian politics revealed gaping contrasts. The lowlands of Veracruz witnessed one of the most radical—though largely unsuccessful—peasant movements of the revolutionary period, and in the Oaxacan upper basin, communal landholding continued to define rural life into the 1940s.[36]

The catastrophic flood of 1944 unexpectedly placed the Papaloapan River at center stage in the Mexican state's nascent campaign to use hydraulic engineering to resolve rural social problems. Ávila Camacho had previously spoken in ambiguous terms about a proposed "march to the sea," but after 1944 the Papaloapan basin became the primary site in demonstrating how that would be accomplished. In October 1944, at the end of his tour of the devastated region, the president declared that his administration would study, plan, and execute a "construction of works" in the Papaloapan basin that sought to both prevent future flooding and oversee a "foundation laid in order that the entire territory be developed in keeping with its potential economic possibilities." To accomplish this goal, the president suggested a multipronged campaign of dredging, damming, irrigation, rural electrification, and planned settlement. The Papaloapan was to be a showcase of Mexican state planning.[37]

Though Ávila Camacho was the first to broach plans for a remaking of the Papaloapan, the primary force behind the project was Miguel Alemán, his secretary of the interior (*secretario de gobernación*). Alemán was a native of Veracruz, born in the town of Sayula, on a tributary of the Papaloapan River. A pivotal but understudied political figure, Alemán was a key architect of the increasingly conservative postrevolutionary Mexican state. He had cut his teeth as Veracruz's governor during the Cárdenas years. Although Alemán loyally followed the 1930s' president's lead on questions of land and oil expropriation, he firmly believed that Mexico's future lay in industry, and that federal investment in public works would accomplish this goal.[38] More than any of his contemporaries, Alemán was seduced by the developmental potential of large dams. When he unveiled his presidential campaign in a late 1945 speech, he pledged that if elected, he would carry to fruition Ávila Camacho's plans for the Papaloapan Valley, "a region of our nation of unlimited economic possibility." Such a project would necessitate the "creation of a decentralized organism with sufficient authority and economic resources to simultaneously attack the problems of a region in its multiple aspects." In the same speech, Alemán made his inspiration abundantly clear: he was "taking advantage of the experience of the United States, where with much success was realized the program known as the 'System of the Tennessee Valley.'"[39]

As government planning for the Papaloapan basin escalated in the late Ávila Camacho years, two prominent pilgrimages tightened the web that entwined this river valley with the Tennessee. The first was Lilienthal's visit to Mexico in December 1945. On what was ostensibly a long vacation, the TVA chair made contact with Mexican government officials, and arranged for visits to ongoing dam and irrigation projects. As he toured the countryside of central Mexico, Lilienthal marveled at the visible links already established between his agency and the Mexican state. In the "remote back country," Lilienthal remembered, "I encountered not only former TVA engineers and young Mexicans who had trained with TVA, but construction equipment purchased from us, with the letters 'TVA' still on the trucks and gondolas." Lilienthal's most important meeting during the trip, however, was with Alemán and Orive Alba. The presidential candidate and irrigation minister excitedly described to the TVA chair "their dreams for the development, along TVA lines, of the basin of the Papaloapan River."[40] Lilienthal was predictably captivated and promised the two men that he "would act as a counselor on any phases of the Papaloapan project which are similar to the Tennessee."[41]

The second exchange would bring Ávila Camacho's agriculture minister Marte R. Gómez—who had already served as a critical go-between in the Rockefeller Foundation's entry into Mexican agriculture—to the Tennessee Valley. Trained as a hydraulic engineer himself, Gómez had long been fascinated by the TVA, and "what we can learn from [it] for the development of the Mexican irrigation systems and our agricultural regions."[42] Not long after Lilienthal's visit to Mexico, Gómez flew to Knoxville in April 1946 to visit Norris and Fontana Dams, meet with the TVA's board, and tour demonstration farms.[43] At a Knoxville banquet given in his honor, a humbled Gómez admitted to attendees that "to visit the Tennessee works is to deal with one of the most promising fulfillments of our time…. Everywhere in the world there are poor farmers," he observed, and "all of us must help him if we do not want that within the frontiers of each country there be depression and public malaise, revolution maybe."[44] As was clear from Gómez's words, the social rhetoric of Cardenismo was in retreat by 1946. A Mexican TVA, in Gómez's formulation, would not be a revolutionary dam—it would *prevent* further revolution in the countryside. By 1946, though, such declarations were not unorthodox within the Mexican ruling party.

FROM THE TENNESSEE TO THE PAPALOAPAN

The dialogue between the Mexican state and the TVA, begun under Cárdenas and accelerated under Ávila Camacho, would reach its apex when Alemán was sworn in as president in December 1946. As Mexico's first elected civilian head of state since 1911, Alemán signaled a dramatic reversal of Cardenista radicalism at a moment when many historians agree that the Mexican Revolution took a hard right turn.[45] That transition was evident in Alemán's inaugural address, where he paid lip service to revolutionary ideals of social justice, but emphasized administration by technical experts rather than populist generals, safety and stability for business, and above all, economic growth. In looking to rural Mexico, Alemán signaled that the pursuit of "peace in the countryside" would define his agrarian program. The administration's primary goal would be to increase agricultural production, with the hopes of raising the "very low level of life" that plagued the nation's nearly thirteen million rural residents. To achieve such a goal, the president stressed the primary importance of irrigation programs and the settlement of new lands, which might "resolve the problem of peasant overpopulation in certain regions." While unnamed, the Papaloapan project was the obvious arena where this vision would be showcased.[46]

In the first months of his presidency, Alemán took three decisive steps to realize his plans for the Papaloapan River basin. First, he overhauled the federal bureaucracy of water management to make possible a grand project that would combine hydraulic and social engineering. Under previous administrations, the TVA's principle of "integrated development" was practically impossible to pursue. Even though the National Irrigation Commission was an unusually powerful federal organ, its activities were restricted to agriculture, while any efforts to improve potable water supplies lay with the health and public welfare ministry, flood control with the ministry of public works, ejido formation with the Departamento Agrario, and so forth. Therefore, one of Alemán's first presidential decrees was to unravel this restrictive jurisdictional hierarchy by forging the Secretaría de Recursos Hidráulicos (Secretariat of Hydraulic Resources) from the ashes of the irrigation bureau. Just as Roosevelt's chartering of the TVA had wrested control of its jurisdiction from individual states and other government bureaus, the water secretariat would command unprecedented powers of central organization and autonomy. To oversee this new federal juggernaut, Alemán chose Orive Alba, the former irrigation chief under Ávila Camacho.[47]

Second, in February 1947, Alemán created the Comisión del Papaloapan, a dependent agency of the Secretariat of Hydraulic Resources that would coordinate and realize the president's ambitious plans for remaking the river valley of his home state. The commission, much like the TVA, would constitute "a managerial organism" possessing "unity of action in both its technical and administrative aspects." It would employ "its broadest powers [to] serve as a solid foundation for the progress of this vast region, promoting agriculture through irrigation and the generation of energy through utilization of the [Papaloapan] river's great volume and power."[48] El Nacional, the ruling party's mouthpiece, described the commission's goals in more direct and blunt language: the president's effort will "allow 600,000 campesinos to live where there are now 170,000," "incorporate a backward indigenous group into civilization," and ultimately, "convert a destructive force into a servant of man."[49]

Lastly, the president undertook his own pilgrimage to see the works of the TVA in person. In seeking inspiration for the Papaloapan project, Alemán added Alabama and Tennessee to the itinerary for his US visit in April 1947. In advance of his arrival, he sent a technical team—including the chair of the Papaloapan Commission, Reynaldo Schega, and the project's executive secretary, Eduardo Chavez—to spend a week and a half studying the region.[50] The president himself flew to Chattanooga on May 5 after visiting Washington, DC. Over the next two days, Alemán took a whirlwind tour of the TVA works.[51] On the morning of May 6, the president and his party of technical experts visited Chickamauga Dam north of Chattanooga. In the dam's powerhouse, Alemán marveled at turbines a dozen feet tall and waxed philosophical on the wonder of rural electrification. "Mexico has a problem similar to the one facing the Tennessee Valley before TVA developments came," he told Chattanooga reporters, and his administration hoped to solve those problems "the same way you did."[52] Leaving the dam, Alemán candidly confessed to Mexico City press representatives in his party that "this can be done on the Papaloapan."[53]

The most important stop on the tour, however, came in Muscle Shoals, where Alemán was shown how the TVA remade not only the valley's landscape but also its social and economic fabric. After a roundabout flight to see Fontana, Wheeler, and Guntersville Dams from the air, the party landed in Muscle Shoals on the afternoon of May 6. After touring Wilson Dam, they drove into the countryside of northern Alabama, where TVA officials insisted Alemán see the human face of rural development. Their destination was a demonstration farm run by the white Locker family, which had once resided on the property as cotton sharecroppers. As the Lockers enthusiastically told Alemán, TVA phosphate fertilizers and crop diversification

Figure 6.2. President Miguel Alemán (fourth from left) standing beside Chickamauga Dam, Chattanooga, Tennessee, May 6, 1947. Image no. KX-02828-A6. Courtesy of the Tennessee Valley Authority.

had restored both soil and dignity, as the Lockers had purchased the land to become independent owners. Cotton, the white scourge that had once plagued the family and kept it in debt, was nowhere to be seen, replaced instead by legumes, grasses, and livestock. Alemán was deeply impressed. "That is the sort of thing we hope to do soon in Mexico," the president told the elder Locker. "We have much land in my country which is as worthless as that which you have improved, and what you have shown me here today will be most valuable to us in planning the same kind of program in Mexico."[54]

Alemán was not alone in drawing parallels between the US South and rural Mexico; US and Mexican journalists were equally persistent. Alabama's *Huntsville Times* declared that "Mexico has many problems that are identical with our own," highlighting wild rivers, arid land, and farming "by the most primitive methods."[55] The *Birmingham News* observed that the "gutted, erosion-marked waste land" that characterized pre-TVA northern Alabama was "similar in many respects to much of the land in [Alemán's] native country."[56] In Mexico City, press accounts during and following the presidential visit informed readers of the history of the TVA, including maps

Figure 6.3. President Miguel Alemán with a family of former sharecroppers in Muscle Shoals, Alabama, May 6, 1947. Image no. KX-02828-A1. Courtesy of the Tennessee Valley Authority.

of the upper US South as well as large photos of dams and the countryside they purported to have transformed. Millennial pronouncements abounded; one reporter insisted that the TVA represented "the greatest work undertaken to tame the blind and devastating forces of the planet," while another observed that a region that was "once a wasteland is now a garden."[57] The Mexican press at times alluded to the social vision of the TVA, but that vision emerged rather muddy. While one journalist noted that the TVA had spawned "new industries whose benefits have gone directly to the poorer classes," most others eschewed discussions of class and poverty to highlight electrification, agricultural productivity, and improved public health.[58] And among nearly all Mexican press accounts, journalists made a seamless jump from the Tennessee Valley to the river valleys of southern Mexico. "Alemán will make, on the Papaloapan, a replica of the Tennessee Valley," announced one headline in *Excélsior*.[59]

Hydraulic resources chief Orive Alba, who became the most vocal proponent of translating US southern models for Mexican use, only encouraged such facile comparisons. In an interview with *El Universal* on his return to Mexico City in May 1947, Orive Alba explained that "the works of the

Figure 6.4. Front page of Mexico City's *Novedades*, May 7, 1947. The headline proclaims "This is what Mexico needs, says Mr. President in front of the Tennessee works." Accessed at the Biblioteca Miguel Lerdo de Tejada.

Tennessee Valley can serve as an example for executing a similar task on the river valley of the Papaloapan."[60] In speaking of the "similar characteristics" that bound together the two river valleys, he emphasized hydroelectric potential above all. As had been true in the US South, it was cheap electricity that "will come to completely transform the agricultural-production landscape [of the Papaloapan basin] and extraordinarily raise the standard of living of its inhabitants."[61] But in drawing analogies between the two regions, Orive Alba also molded the TVA myth to suit the Alemán administration's unique desires. "Look," he asked reporters, "at the Tennessee Valley before the initiation of these works, fourteen years ago—there too were sparsely populated areas like those in the Papaloapan; they grew and formed the foundation for new farms."[62] In seeking to bolster the government's coastal settlement program, Orive Alba imagined a TVA with a usable past, strategically neglecting that over- versus underpopulation had been the primary problem broached by the TVA.

Nevertheless, these too-neat analogies must have engendered resistance and blowback, possibly from nationalist quarters or those who saw the juxtaposition as spurious, because just weeks later the administration made a tactical reversal. In a June 1947 speech before the Mexican Association of

Engineers and Architects that was later serialized in several newspapers under the title "The Tennessee and President Alemán Face the Papaloapan," the hydraulic resources minister awkwardly backpedaled from earlier analogies. Frustrated by the "erroneous assessments of some writers," Orive Alba sought to elucidate in his speech "the essential differences between the Tennessee and our river to erase once and for all the notion that the Papaloapan will be a copy of what was done on the Tennessee."[63] For the first time, Orive Alba admitted that there were fundamental divergences between the two: the Tennessee Valley was "an overpopulated zone, under cultivation for many years, with soils eroded and impoverished by the monoculture of cotton," where in turn "the level of life was very low in comparison to the average level of the United States." The Papaloapan basin, on the other hand, "is essentially a virgin zone, sparsely populated, with uneroded and very fertile soils."[64] But in spite of those differences, the true debt of the Papaloapan Commission to the TVA lay with its creation of a "decentralized organism that would concern itself with resolving the problems of that river."[65] In Orive Alba's opinion, it was the bureaucratic organization and multipronged integrated development approach of the TVA that would prove most useful in Mexico.

With his public disavowal of the neat replicability of the US South in southern Mexico, Orive Alba insisted that the Papaloapan Commission was more than a cheap imitation of the TVA. That such a declaration succeeded in divorcing the Tennessee and Papaloapan in the public eye is unlikely, however, and press comparisons between the two only continued.[66] What is certain is that the relationship between the TVA and the Alemán government only grew closer in the following years, particularly through the steady southward flow of TVA staff. Mexican requests for TVA personnel began immediately after Alemán became president in 1946, as Orive Alba wrote to Lilienthal twice in the first two months of his term, seeking to hire a geologist and hydroelectric engineer.[67] Then, during Alemán's tour of the Tennessee Valley in May 1947, the president's team negotiated with the TVA to send "a brigade of *técnicos*"—technicians—to advise dam projects in Mexico.[68] TVA employees, too, hearing of opportunities in Mexico, wrote to the Alemán administration seeking work on the Papaloapan project.[69] Such interest on both sides ultimately led to multiple personnel exchanges. In summer 1948, the TVA's chief geologist, Berlen O. Moneymaker, spent several weeks in the Papaloapan basin surveying and reporting on dam site possibilities.[70]

Some personnel exchanges, like Moneymaker's, were brief, while others lasted several years. The Mexican career of Gerard H. Matthes, a hydraulic engineer and TVA consultant who had begun his career working with Arthur Morgan on the Miami Conservancy District in Ohio, was one such example. Matthes had extensive experience with flood control in the US South, having done consulting work in the 1930s and 1940s with both the TVA and Army Corps of Engineers' Mississippi River Commission. In December 1947, Orive Alba sent word to Matthes with an offer to employ his services in flood prevention in southern Mexico, as the Papaloapan project "presents certain problems of a similar character as the Mississippi does."[71] That Orive Alba followed engineering projects on the Mississippi River in addition to the Tennessee suggests that his eye on the US South transcended even the TVA. The chief of the water secretariat hoped that Matthes might lend his expertise to the so-called rectification of the Papaloapan River—an attempt to cut channels in the most winding loops of the river to minimize flood potential. Matthes agreed, and over the next four years spent several months in the Papaloapan basin, overseeing a massive effort to redirect the path of the river. His observations and reports were predictably riddled with comparisons between the hydrology and society of the Papaloapan and the Tennessee and Mississippi river valleys.[72]

As the Papaloapan Commission roared into action after 1947, moving untold tons of earth and concrete while commanding thousands of laborers, engineers, and bureaucrats, TVA visitors to the Papaloapan basin marveled at the parallels between their two respective projects. Roland Wank, the renowned TVA architect that designed the authority's first dams, decided after a 1951 visit to the Papaloapan that "it would do the hearts of TVAers [sic] good to know how much their example has accomplished" in Mexico.[73] Earl D. Hale, an employee in the TVA Information Office, toured the Papaloapan basin in early 1952, and was "amazed at the similarity in the Mexican approach to their problems and our own ideas in the Tennessee Valley."[74]

Such neat comparisons, however, pose a fundamental question: What exactly did the Papaloapan Commission achieve, and how closely did it resemble the TVA? To most observers, the clearest parallel between the two was the Miguel Alemán Dam, the largest dam in Mexico when completed in 1955 and similar in appearance to the concrete gravity dams of the TVA. Absorbing the largest share of the commission's expenditures, the Miguel Alemán Dam obstructed the flow of the Río Tonto, a major tributary of the Papaloapan, and in turn created a massive reservoir in mountainous Oaxaca. Yet unlike the TVA, the primary purpose of the dam was not the generation of electricity, which only began haltingly in 1960, but rather flood control in the lower basin. Flood control also motivated the second most expensive engineering project on the Papaloapan, which was the building of multiple cutoffs to "rectify" the twisting bends of the river. Together, the dam and the cutoffs were quite successful in stemming the Papaloapan's frequent floods as well as stabilizing industry and agriculture in the Veracruzan coastal plain. Still, the lower basin's security came at the expense of the Oaxacan upper basin, as the Miguel Alemán Dam displaced more than twenty thousand Mazatec Indians that commission anthropologists then resettled and attempted to "Mexicanize." Considering the prominent involvement of Alemán—a native of the Veracruzan lowlands, and hardly a champion of indigenous autonomy and independence—this was not a surprise.[75]

The Papaloapan project also departed from the TVA in its secondary goal of planned settlement. Spurred by the federal campaign to siphon rural residents from Mexico's densely populated central plateau toward the tropical coast, the Papaloapan Commission invested millions of pesos in infrastructure to attract potential settlers. Essential to that goal was the construction of a new city along the banks of the Papaloapan River intended to house workers and bureaucrats—unsurprisingly named Ciudad Alemán— which planners dreamed would grow to be a major metropolis. To link the new city to the valley and nation, the commission built hundreds of miles of highways throughout the upper and lower basin—in many places, the first paved roadways ever constructed. While new roads were successful in penetrating formerly isolated rural communities, the commission's grandiose plans for Ciudad Alemán never materialized. Built to house 150,000 residents, the city was planned with little regard to the population patterns of the valley and never grew to that size, rendering absurd the wide federal highways that intersected within the city. While the dashed dreams of Ciudad Alemán were perhaps the most visible failure of the colonization campaign, plans for developing new agricultural zones confronted similar obstacles. After a brief flurry of publicity and investment, efforts to use the Papaloapan River as a major source of irrigation were discontinued in 1952 by the incoming administration of Adolfo Ruiz Cortines.[76]

Perhaps most significantly, however, the Papaloapan project diverged in dramatic ways from the TVA in its socioeconomic and political impact. Neither of the TVA's key architects, Arthur Morgan nor Lilienthal, would have been comfortable with the transformations wrought in the Papaloapan basin. Morgan, insistent on the value of preserving small-scale communities that balanced industry and agriculture, would have been repelled by the commission's persistent dedication to an ideal of bigness. Indeed, the greatest beneficiaries of the Papaloapan project were large-scale agribusinesses in the lower basin, and the concentration of wealth in the valley grew more uneven in the years of the commission's work. Lilienthal might have applauded Alemán and Orive Alba's success in integrating isolated rural communities into a national market, but he would have seen little evidence that it was done in a democratic or participatory manner, as he had insisted on in *Democracy on the March*. Like other wings of the burgeoning one-party state in Mexico, the Papaloapan Commission was marked by paternalistic clientelism above all, and the development apparatus had little room for citizen input.[77] Orive Alba himself later confessed that his commission was ultimately "a state within a state" that "really ruled" the region.[78] Political scientist James C. Scott has argued that an ideological faith in order, legibility, and control initially motivated the TVA, but that its "high modernist scheme was brought to ground" by a resistant civil society in the United States.[79] The power that the Papaloapan Commission wielded is proof that such civil resistance was largely absent in southern Mexico.

In the end, the similarities between the Papaloapan project and TVA were largely rhetorical and cosmetic. What Alemán and Orive Alba directly borrowed from the TVA was its autonomous bureaucratic apparatus along with its mandate that regional development be a coordinated campaign to reinvent economy, ecology, and society. Beyond that, the two projects were largely distinct. Yet Alemán's pet project in Veracruz and Oaxaca was not the only river basin commission born from juxtapositions of the TVA. Just weeks after the government revealed plans to remake the Papaloapan in the image of the Tennessee, Mexico's most renowned champion of the campesino, Lázaro Cárdenas, spearheaded efforts to undertake a sister project in the Tepalcatepec River basin of Michoacán. The surprisingly distinct program that he pursued, along with the transnational pilgrimages that energized it, reveal that river valley development in Mexico was just as diverse and contradictory as in the United States.

A Cardenista TVA?

For decades after leaving the presidency in 1940, Cárdenas cast an unmatched shadow on Mexican politics. Unlike the popular heroes of the revolution's violent years, notably Emiliano Zapata and Pancho Villa, Cárdenas survived his historical moment and refused to retreat from the public eye, oftentimes to the irritation of his successors. In the years following his presidency, Cárdenas performed an awkwardly dual role. On the one hand, he sought to preserve the legitimacy of the one-party state that he had done so much to enthrone during his years in the presidency. On the other hand, he served as the veteran sage of the Mexican Left, nudging party rhetoric toward campesino and worker interests, and not infrequently playing the role of gadfly to the Mexico City political elite. After quietly serving as secretary of national defense during World War II in a gesture of support for the succeeding Ávila Camacho regime, Cárdenas began to make his presence felt in national politics. Though his inscrutable public persona after 1940 earned him the nickname of "the Sphinx of Jiquilpan," after his hometown, behind the scenes Cárdenas became a major player on the Left.[80]

In April 1947, on the heels of Alemán's announcement of plans for a massive federal effort to transform the Papaloapan river valley, Cárdenas wrote the new president with a bold proposal. With their common goal of "escalating the agricultural and industrial development of the country,"

Cárdenas offered his "personal effort" to establish and oversee a similar program in Michoacán's Tepalcatepec basin.[81] The Tepalcatepec River, which drains the southwestern corner of Mexico's central plateau into the Pacific Ocean, somewhat resembled the Papaloapan. Both valleys were marked by a contrast between mountainous, densely settled upper basins and fecund lower basins home to large haciendas, but otherwise underpopulated, rife with disease, and lacking in infrastructure. Both river valleys witnessed the dramatic rise of plantation agriculture in their hot lowlands during the Porfiriato. In their revolutionary history, however, the two differed significantly. While Veracruzan peasant leagues in the Papaloapan had been largely unsuccessful in their attempt to break up large plantations, in Michoacán the agraristas of the Tepalcatepec lowlands found a welcome ally in native son Cárdenas. In 1938, Cárdenas dramatically expropriated the productive estates of the Italian Cusi family at Nueva Italia and Lombardía, and subdivided them among nine thousand ejidatarios, marking the tierra caliente of the Tepalcatepec Valley as one of the most prominent national examples of land reform.[82]

As his proposal to Alemán attested, Cárdenas's commitment to the Tepalcatepec basin endured long after his presidency. His 1947 prescriptions for the remaking of the valley resembled Alemán's earlier pronouncements for the Papaloapan, but they also showcased their author's longtime commitment to ejido agriculture and campesino interests. Primarily, Cárdenas recommended a unified public health and road construction program to colonize tropical lowlands and relieve the "overpopulation that exists in ejidal centers" elsewhere in Michoacán. But alongside such overtures to the president's new "program of production," Cárdenas believed a river valley commission on the Tepalcatepec could bolster the land reform gains of the 1930s. As a lack of federal investment and shortage of credit had "made more difficult the situation of the campesino class," Cárdenas implored that the Tepalcatepec Valley receive an infusion of funding from the National Bank of Ejidal Credit and a new legion of teachers to staff rural schoolhouses.[83] Alemán, likely weighing the political clout and near-mythical stature of the former president, promised Cárdenas that he would initiate studies of the project's feasibility.[84]

In his proposal to Alemán, Cárdenas did not explicitly cite the TVA as an inspiration in planning works for the Tepalcatepec basin. Indeed, throughout his career, Cárdenas was reticent to publicly acknowledge influences from the United States. It is nevertheless certain that the TVA was on his mind when he drafted plans for Michoacán in spring 1947. As previously demonstrated, Cárdenas had entertained an interest in the Tennessee Valley since the 1930s, born from conversations with Frank Tannenbaum and agriculture secretary Marte Gómez.[85] To his young son Cuauhtémoc, Cárdenas often spoke sympathetically of the TVA's effort to "bring better living conditions and provide opportunities."[86] After TVA chair Lilienthal visited Mexico in 1945, Cárdenas wrote him to praise "your important work in the Tennessee Valley" that "will be of great benefit" to the agricultural regions of Mexico.[87] Likewise, press reportage on Cárdenas's plan for the Tepalcatepec insisted that like Alemán's project on the Papaloapan, it too drew inspiration from the "exemplary work of unified development of a natural region accomplished in the Tennessee Valley."[88]

Prompted by Cárdenas, in May 1947 President Alemán unveiled plans for a second river valley commission, charged with the "planning and construction of necessary works for the integrated development of the natural resources of the extensive valley of the Tepalcatepec River."[89] On June 1, he publicly appointed Cárdenas as the *vocal ejecutivo*, or chair, of the project.[90] Among Mexican conservatives, the news provoked uproar, as it evidenced the return of the hated Cárdenas to a significant position of power. Particularly incensed was *El Universal* editorialist Rafael Zubarán Capmany, who expressed "profound surprise" at the appointment of Cárdenas, a figure he judged a "destructive spirit inspired by social doctrines." In the eyes of Zubarán, "To execute technical work one needs to be a *técnico*, and General Cárdenas is not that." Yet to justify his critique of the appointment, the editorialist called on the TVA, whose "prohibition of politics in its administration" might serve as a model. According to Zubarán, "Every corner of the United States protested whenever anyone, however powerful, attempted to inject political considerations into the operations of TVA"—and Mexico should follow suit. His critical comparison revealed how the fluid TVA myth could be put to dramatically different uses within Mexico.[91]

Despite such rebuffs, the Tepalcatepec project would go on to become one of the most important development projects in postrevolutionary Mexico. With far less fanfare than the Papaloapan project, during the late 1940s and 1950s Cárdenas oversaw a vast construction campaign in the lowlands of Michoacán. Roads were of foremost significance. Cárdenas believed they would link productive ejidatarios to a national market, and by 1950 the commission had built more than twenty highways in the basin. Hydraulic engineering was also essential, but in contrast to the Papaloapan Commission's gigantism—which poured untold money into the construction of one showcase dam—Cárdenas oversaw the building of smaller irrigation dams paired with canals to extend water to distant farms. By 1961, the Tepalcatepec Commission claimed to have opened irrigation to more than two hundred thousand acres, benefiting primarily ejidal farmers. Accompanying infrastructure investments was one of the most sweeping public health campaigns in Mexican history, an effort that largely eradicated once-rampant tropical diseases such as malaria and tuberculosis. As Cárdenas frequently claimed to visitors and reporters, his commission's work held the "key to the future of the ejidos," and if its lessons were nationalized, "sooner or later all agriculture of Mexico would be managed cooperatively."[92]

Curiously, Cárdenas's stewardship of the Tepalcatepec project drew him closer to the Tennessee Valley and ultimately compelled him to make his first visit to the United States. In January 1954, already having led the Tepalcatepec Commission for seven years, Cárdenas sent word to Knoxville that he was "planning to take some time by May to visit [the] T.V.A."[93] While he ultimately postponed that trip, Cárdenas's interest in the agency lingered. In October 1955, he acknowledged in his diary that "the industrial region of Tennessee" was one of the "works that interest me in the United States," and he hoped to personally see them "in the next year."[94] But in advance of his own journey to the United States, in 1957 Cárdenas tasked his twenty-three-year-old son, Cuauhtémoc, to investigate the achievements of the Tennessee Valley. Born in 1934, the year his father became president, Cuauhtémoc trained as a civil engineer at the Universidad Nacional Autónoma de México (National Autonomous University of Mexico, UNAM) and received his undergraduate degree in 1955. On behalf of the Tepalcatepec and Federal Electricity Commissions, the younger Cárdenas traveled to the Tennessee Valley with two of his UNAM classmates in August 1957.[95] The three Mexican engineers spent ten days in Knoxville, visiting a variety of TVA projects. To Cuauhtémoc, the journey was an eye-opener. Writing to TVA chair Herbert Vogel after his trip, the young engineer described his awe at the "magnificent work you are developing and in which you have been successful."[96] Privately, though, Cuauhtémoc was shocked by the system of racial segregation he witnessed in Tennessee, remembering well the "signs saying 'Entry of Negroes Prohibited.'"[97]

In early 1959, the elder Cárdenas finally realized a trip he had by then been considering for nearly twenty years. On February 2, Cárdenas and his son, joined by a cadre of friends and fellow engineers, arrived in Knoxville to visit the TVA's headquarters. In the following two days, the group visited Fort Loudoun Dam on the Tennessee River, southwest of Knoxville, and toured demonstration test farms in nearby Loudoun County.[98] With the TVA leadership, Cárdenas discussed at length their "mutual problems in the development of natural resources."[99] At the authority's headquarters, they sat down for a viewing of the 1944 propaganda film *The Valley of the Tennessee*, which described how integrated development had rescued "a neglected people living in a ruined land" who had once "struggle[d] to scratch a bare living from the reluctant soil." Seeing the valley and its ongoing struggle with poverty made a deep impression on the group. One TVA employee noted that the visiting Mexicans "appeared to be tremendously interested and impressed by what is being done in this region," while also insisting that "some of us visit Mexico to see what they are trying to accomplish in the way of integrated resource development there."[100]

To Cárdenas, who had kept a curious eye on the TVA for decades, the trip was revelatory. Writing in his diary, Cárdenas decided that the "system of the Tennessee has demonstrated with its affirmative results the beneficence of

Figure 6.5. Cuauhtémoc Cárdenas and Lázaro Cárdenas with TVA chair Herbert Vogel in Knoxville, Tennessee, February 3, 1959. Image no. KX-03914. Courtesy of the Tennessee Valley Authority.

its organization." Yet in drawing such a conclusion, the director of the Tepalcatepec project was looking more toward the future than the past. "If the same system were introduced in [Mexico] and other countries, on a national scale, it would take a definitive step toward the solution of the social-economic problems that affect each one," aiding the impoverished "who lack that which is most indispensable for their subsistence."[101] In the hydraulic social engineering of the TVA, Cárdenas saw a solution to the problems that continued to plague the Mexican countryside. By 1959, however, Cárdenas understood Mexico's struggle as interchangeable with that of "other countries" rather than a product of its own particular history and culture—a declaration that would have been unlikely in earlier years.

Such comparisons to the Tennessee Valley were not merely philosophical musings, because Cárdenas would continue to play an active role in leading Mexican river valley development. In 1961, President Adolfo López Mateos merged the Tepalcatepec Commission into a newly founded Comisión del Balsas, a far larger agency that sought to address the economic problems of the entire eight-state Balsas River region, within which the Tepalcatepec was merely one of many tributaries. López Mateos, judging Cárdenas's popular-

Figure 6.6. Lázaro Cárdenas (front row, right) crossing Fort Loudoun Dam, Lenoir City, Tennessee, February 3, 1959. Image no. KX-03918. Courtesy of the Tennessee Valley Authority.

ity in Michoacán as an asset in bolstering the project's legitimacy, appointed him as chair of the new venture. In the nine years before Cárdenas died in 1970, he and Cuauhtémoc, who served as a chief engineer, directed the economic development of a region that included millions of inhabitants. While resembling the Tepalcatepec Commission in bureaucratic organization, the Balsas project departed from the earlier agency's stress on agricultural development, favoring instead industrial growth. Under Cárdenas's direction, the commission built several large hydroelectric dams on the Balsas to generate electricity for a much-touted steel plant in Las Truchas, Michoacán. And all the while, Cárdenas kept a steady watch on the lessons of the TVA. In 1962, he wrote to Knoxville headquarters with a request for agency publications and that "a group of people from Tennessee could visit [the Balsas], so that we might hear your observations and receive suggestions from your acknowledged experience."[102]

Considering Cárdenas's highly prominent role in the Mexican Revolution's agrarian reform, many looked hopefully to the Tepalcatepec and Balsas experiments for a demonstration that the ejido could represent a viable future for the nation's agriculture. They would be largely disappointed. Despite continued efforts by both commissions to ensure that the fruits of federal investment went to ejidatarios, the biggest beneficiaries of the agricultural boom were private owners. Much of this resulted from external pressures beyond the control of the commissions themselves. Because most ejido farmers were dependent on the state for capital and technical instruction, they were obliged to plant the crops prescribed for them. In the Tepalcatepec basin as elsewhere nationally, that meant a primary emphasis on export crops, particularly limes, melons, and cotton, whose acreage skyrocketed in Michoacán's tierra caliente during the 1950s and 1960s. But the ecology of the lowlands, favorable to countless insect and disease threats, ensured that such crops would require intensive chemical pest management and mechanized cultivation. While many ejidatarios attempted to adapt to this changing world, credit and institutional support were rarely sufficient, and most could not compete with private commercial farmers. In turn, ejido farmers increasingly rented their lands—illegally—to larger, private farmers who managed them and reaped their harvest, while former occupants abandoned their plots. Therefore, in Michoacán, the Cardenista dream of a productive and contented rural proletariat would slowly perish, neglected and starved by an apathetic state and hostile political atmosphere.[103]

The Mexican state's infatuation with river valley development grew from a particular moment in national and global history, when reformers captured the public imagination with millennial promises that science, state planning, and the domination of nature could perfect human societies. The Papaloapan project, along with later river basin programs created in its image—the Río Fuerte and Río Grijalva Commissions of 1951—grew from that instinct, as did the Tepalcatepec project to a lesser degree. Yet that moment was fleeting, and a generation after their charter, many of the ambitious projects proposed in the Alemán years had lost their luster. Their environmental and social costs, frequently outweighing their demonstrable benefits, grew difficult to justify to a public disillusioned with grandiose development schemes. With Cárdenas's death in 1970, the state folded the Balsas Commission into the agriculture secretariat, effectively liquidating it. The Papaloapan project stumbled through the 1960s and 1970s with reduced funding until the government disbanded it in 1982. In the eyes of neoliberal politicians, the functions of those programs would be best served by private enterprise. But across the landscape of rural southern Mexico, the projects' legacy was indelible, recorded in concrete monuments and a human geography forever remade.

***

In the three decades following the onset of the Great Depression, the US and Mexican governments both diagnosed the river valley as a basic geographic container for overcoming poverty and underdevelopment in regions believed to be internal economic peripheries. With a near-utopian faith in the union of hydraulic science and centralized state planning, they poured untold resources into remaking these vast regions. Roosevelt's New Deal empowered the muscular TVA to intervene in the culture, economy, and society of the US South. Born from conflicting ideologies, in its first decade the TVA struggled to define its social mission while simultaneously overseeing one of the most transformative construction projects of the twentieth century. By the end of World War II, a steady urge to resolve US southern poverty through rapid urbanization and industrialization eclipsed the agency's earlier emphasis on rehabilitating small-scale agriculture. After the war, conservative criticism and an increasingly hostile political atmosphere ensured that the TVA would assume a defensive stance at home. But its apostles, particularly former chair Lilienthal, took their evangelism abroad to Cold War battlegrounds in the nascent Third World. As TVA leaders believed, the fruits of integrated rural development in the US South had matured, and now their seed must be cast to the wind.

Postrevolutionary Mexico would provide fertile soil for those seeds to sprout, where heads of state both before and after the revolution had considered hydraulic engineering as a solution to social and political problems. If TVA evangelicals like Lilienthal imagined that a transplanting of US southern solutions in southern Mexico would be neat or linear, though, they would be consistently frustrated. Figures across the Mexican political spectrum considered the utility of the TVA blueprint after 1933, but ultimately those most attracted to it were conservatives who hoped to turn a corner from the agrarian redistribution and radicalism of earlier decades. In the "TVA idea," politicians like Alemán saw an alternative solution to the enduring dilemma of rural poverty and insecurity, and one that also promised to strengthen state power and legitimacy. Their plan, which they believed would satisfy land hunger in much of central Mexico, was to colonize and populate the sparsely settled lowlands of the tropical South. Although this goal departed dramatically from that of the TVA, Mexican leaders in the 1940s consistently drew reference to that agency and its supposedly apolitical past to silence critics as well as reassure skeptics. But as shown by the Papaloapan project, the state's best-funded and most renowned attempt at rural development, that effort hardly proved a workable solution to the tensions and inequalities within the Mexican countryside. Ultimately, the Papaloapan experiment evidenced all the stereotypical patterns of *proyectismo*, that development cycle common to Latin America—and the United States— that saw sanguine early pronouncements followed by costly mistakes, waning state interest, and ultimate abandonment.[104]

Yet the *Alemanista* Right was not the only political wing that looked to the Tennessee Valley for lessons in rural reconstruction. Cárdenas, the most prominent voice for agrarian social justice in midcentury Mexico, spearheaded his own river valley project in Michoacán beginning in 1947. In stark contrast to the gigantism of the Papaloapan Commission, Cárdenas sought to build infrastructure to foster the growth and productivity of land reform plots granted during the 1930s. Quite frequently, his Michoacán project resembled the early but often-forgotten aspirations of the TVA under Arthur Morgan. Yet in an era when the Mexican state pursued industrialization and increased production at whatever cost, boasting on the global stage of a Mexican Miracle, such efforts were ultimately shunted to the political margins.

The dialogue between US and Mexican reformers on river valley development was part of a much longer conversation sparked by the economic crash of 1929. Yet in many ways, the TVA exchange represented an end rather than a beginning. During earlier years, in the direct wake of capitalism's apparent failure, the parameters of agrarian and agricultural reform were far broader and more inclusive in both nations, and it was during the radical 1930s that Mexican ideas found traction in US politics. But by the late 1940s, as economic recovery increasingly rehabilitated liberal capitalism and the political center shifted rightward on both sides of the border, the avenues of equal exchange between the two narrowed. The one-sidedness of the river valley dialogue, flowing primarily from the United States to Mexico, was exemplary of this. After the 1950s, as politicians turned a cold shoulder to debates on the socioeconomic and cultural consequences of agricultural change, fewer and fewer observers drew parallels between the US and Mexican countrysides. For many, the two seemed impossibly distant, and few could remember a moment when their fates had been so closely interwoven.

EPILOGUE

THE YEARS following World War II brought a giddy sense of possibility to many in the United States and Mexico. Politicians and the press heralded the dawn of a new era, eagerly embracing peace, economic growth, and a renewed sense of social stability. But to Rubén Jaramillo and Ned Cobb, the postwar years brought disappointment and a growing sense of betrayal. Both were veterans of the agrarian political ferment of the 1930s. Jaramillo had been a dedicated agrarista who, in collaboration with president Lázaro Cárdenas, headed up the Emiliano Zapata Cooperative Society of sugar growers, established in 1938 in the south-central state of Morelos. Cobb was a black Alabama farmer who had early in the decade joined his state's Share-croppers' Union to halt the eviction of landless cultivators—an act of resis-tance that earned him a bullet in the leg and twelve years in prison. During the turbulent Depression era, the two saw a dramatic expansion of state power in the countryside, and both were hopeful that this transformation promised a brighter future for tillers of the soil.

By the time the war years drew to a close, however, much of that hope had vanished. After Cárdenas left office, Jaramillo bitterly observed how the postrevolutionary government marginalized poor rural people, co-opting and compartmentalizing peasant demands in pursuit of political stability rather than social justice. "Campesinos work themselves to death," he fumed in 1946, while "our exploiters sit in their comfortable offices without a care." Meanwhile, Cobb returned to Alabama after more than a decade behind bars to find that government intervention had fundamentally transformed farming, but it largely favored the white, wealthy, and landed who could afford the machines and chemicals promoted by federal agents. By then, nearly all the New Deal's promises to the rural poor had lapsed. Yet Cobb refused to leave the land, as so many of his neighbors were then doing, even as "it become plumb impossible" to "make a livin on a one-horse farm if cotton was your crop." He clung to the soil, "a mule farmin man to the last," but could not dissuade his children from abandoning rural Alabama for the uncertainties of northern city life. If Cobb resigned to a muted acquies-cence, Jaramillo chose to openly confront the leadership he believed had betrayed him. In the coming years, he and hundreds of followers alternated between electoral challenges and armed revolt, coming to a climax in the brutal 1962 murder of Jaramillo, his wife, and their three children at the hands of government troops.[1]

In many ways, Cobb and Jaramillo were exceptional figures. Cobb's early radicalism was rare by US standards, as was his adamant refusal to abandon the small farm. Jaramillo, too, was a renowned firebrand from a notably radical state, and his violent end elicited unusual shock. Nevertheless, in both of their lives were wound up the fates of millions of others in the US and Mexican countryside. Not long after World War II, the stormy public debate over rural poverty and the human impact of agricultural change tapered off in each nation. As conservatives silenced dissenting voices by means of force or compromise, it would be concerns of productivity—not inequality—that dominated the next generation of rural policy making. This political enclosure wrought profound changes. In the latter half of the twentieth century, US and Mexican farming came to be the domain of experts and corporations rather than common people, whose mules and plows were replaced by diesel tractors, six-row cultivators, and petrochemicals. Millions who had formerly tended the soil as tenants, ejidatarios, peons, and sharecroppers were painfully uprooted in the process, particularly in the densely settled rural landscapes of central Mexico and the US Southeast. These refugees would leave behind their parents and grandparents' world during the 1950s and 1960s to swell the ghettoes and shantytowns of booming cities, whether in Detroit, Los Angeles, or Mexico City. Along the way, rural poverty was hardly alleviated; it was simply exported to the cities. In Mexico, this sweeping transformation has largely been understood as a manifestation of the global green revolution. Few observers have adopted that model to understand the remaking of the rural United States, though such an artificial distinction conceals far more than it reveals.

The agrarian histories of the US and Mexico once again ran strikingly parallel. But if the shared trajectories of the long 1930s had elicited a lively dialogue across the border, far fewer such exchanges could be found in the century's latter half. Small farmers in the US and Mexico would instead suffer their fate in solitude, isolated by nationalisms born from the Cold War and an ever-hardening intellectual border separating First World from Third World. If rural people in either nation ceased to look to the plight of the other, this hardly minimized their common ground, though. These last pages consider those histories, both convergent and divergent.[2]

The postwar retreat from the agrarian experimentation of the 1930s stemmed from the consolidation of conservative power in the one-party political regimes that dominated the US South and Mexico. The US Democratic Party took a rightward turn on the national stage after World War II, but nowhere was it more pronounced than in the southern states, where the party had long had a choke hold on the electoral process and continued to do so until the late 1960s. Fearful of growing resistance to Jim Crow segregation and the new militancy of black soldiers returning from the war, the southern Democratic elite after 1945 closed ranks and excommunicated its internal dissenters. Liberal New Dealers like Florida's Claude Pepper, Georgia's Ellis Arnall, or Alabama's Lister Hill either lost their seats or were forcefully shoved back into the fold. The reactionaries who rose to speak for the region in the postwar era—politicians like James Eastland of Mississippi and Strom Thurmond of South Carolina—were united in their opposition to any federal intervention that might threaten white supremacy. Armed with nascent Cold War rhetoric, southern Democrats rejected the New Deal's social engineering as "Communistic" or "Soviet" in nature.[3]

Such political transitions were especially felt in the federal bureau that wielded the greatest power over the US countryside: the US Department of Agriculture (USDA). Between 1940 and 1950, the personnel and guiding philosophy of that agency underwent a dramatic reinvention. In the last years of the war and immediately thereafter, the USDA actively hemorrhaged the idealistic social scientists who had served as the architects of the agrarian New Deal. Those who took their place were figures like Jamie Whitten, a Mississippi planter-politician who held the chair of the Agricultural Appropriations subcommittee in the House of Representatives from 1949 to 1994, serving from that post as a "shadow Secretary of Agriculture," as the *New York Times* observed. Whitten believed that if the rural South were to become a lean and efficient producer of food and fiber, it had to trim the fat represented by unproductive farmers who were unable to adapt to the changing times. He and his like-minded peers in the USDA displayed little sympathy for the tenants and sharecroppers who faced marginalization in the postwar years. Whitten was representative of a nascent southern political elite that courted federal assistance for economic growth, but favored regional development over human development—in other words, the enrichment of place over people.[4]

In Mexico, the ruling party's pivot away from rural social reform was protracted in comparison to the United States, due to the greater political mobilization of Mexican country people and stubborn resilience of agrarista ideals. Yet over time, the state's march toward a productivist versus redistributionist ethos was just as certain. By 1938, Cárdenas slowed the pace of land expropriation, shifting emphasis toward federal investment in credit, irrigation, and education for existing ejidos. Manuel Ávila Camacho furthered this reorientation after 1940, but also offered large landholders new promises of exemption from expropriation, in hopes of reviving business confidence in the state. By the time Ávila Camacho rebranded his Mexican Revolutionary Party as the Partido Revolucionario Institucional (Institutional Revolutionary Party, PRI) in 1946, a whole host of party mechanisms were in place to co-opt and contain campesino discontent. His successor, Miguel Alemán, confirmed rumors that the PRI had turned away from the ejido as the building block of Mexico's agricultural future. In the wake of crop shortages during the tense war years, the ruling party declared that efficiency, productivity, and food security were to be the supreme goals of agrarian policy, not economic leveling.[5]

Having taken the reins of rural policy making, conservatives in both nations then harnessed the muscular power of federal intervention to transform the political economy of the countryside. In Mexico, the PRI leadership funneled vast sums into projects of agricultural "modernization" from the 1940s through 1970s, but such investment did not flow evenly across the segmented Mexican countryside. Some funding streams trickled into the coastal tropics, such as with the TVA-style river valley commissions, yet the flood of federal spending targeted the coastal northwest and northern border states, where large landowners cultivated cash crops for national and international markets. In the north, government aid bankrolled massive hydraulic engineering projects of which the primary beneficiaries were commercial farmers. Between 1941 and 1970, the six border states of the north plus coastal Sinaloa received more than 55 percent of all state irrigation spending, despite containing a far smaller percentage of the country's population. Complementing water management was the extension of cheap credit for private farmers along with the subsidization of agricultural machinery and petrochemicals. This steady shower of federal largesse on the northern states resulted in a flowering of the agribusiness sector. It was here that observers on the international stage began to speak of a Mexican Miracle in agriculture during the postwar years; it was here that the Rockefeller Foundation's Norman Borlaug registered his greatest successes in the improvement of wheat.[6]

As the commercial farmers of northwestern Mexico enjoyed a deluge of federal support, the vast majority of the nation's cultivators, concentrated in central-southern Mexico and tilling far smaller plots, thirsted desperately for their share. The state's persistent withholding of funding to small-scale farming in general and the ejido sector in particular was hardly accidental. Instead, it constituted the primary thrust of the postrevolutionary state's agrarian policy during the Cold War era: the routinization of paeans to revolutionary social justice and simultaneous deprivation of the land reform sector's economic lifeblood. Until the 1990s, the PRI dared not publicly revoke its ideological link to radicals like Zapata and Cárdenas, yet behind the scenes party officials actively dismantled the agrarista project. Starved of support systems, ejido cultivators saw their productivity stagnate while their well-funded competitors in agribusiness boasted of a revolution in yields, spurring economists to further denigrate the agrarian experiment for its perceived inefficiency.[7]

Federal intervention in US southern agriculture was similarly selective in its transformation of the countryside, dovetailing consistently with the wishes of the landed elite. In the 1940s and 1950s, the New Deal state further tightened its grip on the practice of US farming, but those government programs that survived the conservative assaults of the war years did not target rural inequality and poverty; they but sought to foster economies of scale in the agribusiness sector. In the US South, federal aid proved essential to the consolidation of a refashioned plantation agriculture, which proceeded in distinct stages. First, assistance from Washington, DC, allowed planters to abolish the compromise of sharecropping in favor of rural wage labor. Fundamental to this transition was the land allotment program of the Agricultural Adjustment Administration and its successor, the Agricultural Stabilization and Conservation Service. Designed to boost prices by limiting cultivated acres, the two agencies ultimately paid landlords to evict their tenants and rehire them as seasonal hourly labor. County-level committees oversaw the allotment program's administration, and local elites ensured that federal benefits did not disturb the racial and class hierarchies of the rural South.[8]

Yet wage labor alone did not satisfy planters' mandate for a low-cost, pliable, and seasonally reliable workforce. As farmworkers began to protest their abysmal pay, and especially as black southerners demanded political and economic rights, southern landlords responded by seeking the literal dehumanization of cotton culture. Federal research and subsidies for machinery and petrochemicals would accomplish precisely that in less than a decade. By the late 1940s, tractors and mechanical cotton pickers were growing ubiquitous on the largest plantations, financed in no small part by USDA land allotment paychecks. But even with the planting and harvesting of cotton mechanized, landlords still required human labor for the weeding or "chopping" of the crop during the late spring and early summer. With the 1950s' advent of herbicides such as 2,4-D, a chemical pioneered and perfected on federal experiment stations across the South, that final obstacle was removed. The rural demand for cheap and dependable human muscle—a demand that had shaped the course of southern history for centuries— vanished in a few short years, and the subsequent transformation was dizzying. The sharecropper shacks that had dotted the rural landscape for generations were quickly abandoned to decay, replaced by centralized neoplantations dependent on tractors, mechanical pickers, and chemicals.[9]

US and Mexican bureaucrats unfalteringly promoted their vision of agricultural transformation as the neutral and inevitable by-product of "modernization," but such rhetoric concealed the starkly political agenda that underlay rural policy making. In Mexico, the conscious decision to favor highly capitalized northwestern agriculture weakened the political and economic foundations of agrarismo, placating business interests and forestalling a revival of redistributionist promises to the rural poor. Federal development entrusted Mexico's economic future to agribusinesses and urban industrialists as opposed to ejido farmers. In the US South, the burgeoning black rights struggle likewise sharpened the political significance of agricultural change. Across the Cotton Belt in the 1950s and 1960s, white elites wielded their control of local USDA committees as a weapon to punish advocates of desegregation and equal rights. Cooperation between white supremacist Citizens' Councils, the USDA Extension Service, and the American Farm Bureau Federation was hardly uncommon. Not coincidentally, the mechanization and chemicalization of agriculture uprooted rural African Americans at the very same moment that they started to achieve their primary legislative successes.[10]

Hardly fooled by official rhetoric, sharecroppers and campesinos recognized their exclusion from state policy, and fought tooth and nail to challenge it. Poor farmers in the US South scrawled countless letters to the USDA to protest that "you havent done one thang for little farmers," as one Alabamian fumed in 1956. Rural African Americans who had been victims of USDA discrimination filed lawsuits to redress past wrongs, though few such cases were settled in a timely fashion, and black farmers confronting foreclosure and eviction had little time to await the slow grind of legal bureaucracy. In postrevolutionary Mexico, agrarian discontent boiled over in 1952 with a leftist challenge to PRI presidential hegemony, spearheaded by Miguel Henríquez Guzmán. The *Henriquistas* claimed strong support in the countryside, where many hoped their candidate would revive the promise of Cardenismo, but official tallies of the July election handed a clear victory to Alemán's handpicked successor. When thousands of Henriquistas gathered in Mexico City's Alameda to protest the perceived election fraud, security forces opened fire on the crowd, killing dozens. The futility of formal political challenge pushed many agrarian radicals toward violent revolt. In 1950s' Morelos, Rubén Jaramillo led rural rebels in the name of Zapata; in the 1960s and 1970s, guerrilla fighter Lucio Cabañas and his Party of the Poor protested the betrayal of the Mexican Revolution. Both men and countless of their followers were ultimately murdered by federal counterinsurgency forces.[11]

Although some farmers in the United States and Mexico took up pens or rifles to contest their marginalization, most judged open resistance too risky and quietly abandoned their land. Indeed, the technopolitical transformation of agriculture in the postwar decades resulted in a rural enclosure movement of unprecedented scale and scope. Hundreds of thousands of displaced campesinos from central and southern Mexico migrated to the new agricultural hubs of Sinaloa and Baja California, arriving hat in hand as wageworkers. Millions more fled failing ejidos for growing metropolises. The breakneck expansion of Mexico City's population—counting less than 3 million in 1950, but home to more than 20 million by the new century— was a testament to the wholesale evacuation of the countryside. In the rural United States, out-migration and mechanization had been proceeding since the early twentieth century, yet nowhere was it as accelerated or sudden as in the postwar Cotton Belt. From the 1940s through the 1960s, more than 11.5 million southerners left their home region, and most were former farmers. Particularly shocking was the rapid decimation of black agriculture after World War II. In 1940, there were nearly 700,000 US farms operated by African Americans, located overwhelmingly in the South; by 1969, there were 87,000. As in Mexico, most of these rural exiles found new homes in the slums of industrial cities, whether in Los Angeles, Detroit, or Boston.[12]

Mere statistics, however, cannot communicate the vast impact of these human migrations. In the United States, the postwar southern diaspora fundamentally rewove the social, cultural, and political fabric of the entire nation. The rapid acceleration of the black Great Migration effectively nationalized the struggle for racial equality. As long-disfranchised rural refugees swelled urban ghettos, they vocally demanded their share of US affluence. In turn, middle-class whites fled the city for sprawling, federally subsidized suburbs, cultivating new political ideologies that would refigure US conservatism. When frustrations mounted in the most marginalized black communities, fiery riots erupted during the 1960s, and the "urban crisis" of that decade was intimately bound to the agrarian crisis of earlier years. Yet not all the consequences of the great southern out-migration were marked by strife. New syncretic cultural forms grew from the blending of rural and regional traditions with urban diversity; rock and roll, country music, rhythm and blues, and other popular musical forms can each trace their roots to the southern diaspora.[13]

In Mexico, rural enclosures made Mexico City into the world's largest metropolis during the late twentieth century—a "monstrous inflated head, crushing the frail body that holds it up," in the words of writer Octavio Paz. Located in the densely populated, corn-growing central plateau, the capital was the natural destination for the millions of rural people uprooted by the high modernist green revolution and simultaneous federal neglect of the ejido sector. Yet rather than colonizing the inner city, as rural migrants did in the United States, campesino refugees to Mexico City built vast squatter villages on the hilly outskirts of the Federal District, where an informal economy in food, goods, and services provided them with meager livelihoods. By the 1980s, Mexico City was not only the world's largest city but also one of its most unequal. The city's astounding growth and dominance would forever transform national politics and Mexican cultural identity. Music, film, and literature reflected the heartbreaking yet hopeful transition of rural people into rapidly expanding urban spaces. Actor Mario Moreno's Cantinflas character and Pedro Infante's *ranchera* songs each immortalized the plight of transplanted and bewildered rural migrants.[14]

The demographic purge of Mexico's countryside also laid the groundwork for a vast surge in the migration of Mexicans to the United States—an issue that would both polarize and further entwine the two nations. As Mexican state planners in the postwar years abandoned the Cardenista agrarian experiment in favor of subsidized agribusiness, they foresaw a vast exodus from country to city and instituted safety valves to minimize its political volatility. The bracero program, initiated in 1943 as an emergency wartime measure that would send Mexican agricultural labor to the United States, was extended indefinitely after the war. In the eyes of the PRI leadership, braceros would bring back modern agricultural techniques to Mexico after their time in the United States, but the program also served to keep unemployed rural people from swelling Mexican cities. By the time the United States ended the bracero program in 1964, extralegal migrants would increasingly follow the paths blazed by government-sponsored migration. The PRI sought to counteract the migrational pull of the United States by inviting US companies to establish roots in Mexican soil, demarcating free trade maquiladora zones on the northern border where US firms would hire Mexican workers in Mexico. Yet those opportunities were insufficient in and of themselves to dissuade border crossings. During the 1960s and 1970s, as rural migrants realized that opportunities in urban Mexico were limited, they fled to the cities and industrial farms of California and Texas in larger and larger numbers each year.[15]

Rather than isolated phenomena, the US and Mexican rural enclosures during the third quarter of the twentieth century would serve as precursors of the global transformations to come. The migratory routes and marginal lives of uprooted US and Mexican farmers foreshadowed the making of what scholar Mike Davis has called a "planet of slums," as much of Asia, Africa, and Latin America followed similar paths toward breakneck and ramshackle urbanization. In 1950, there were eighty-six cities globally that could count more than one million inhabitants; by the second decade of the twenty-first century, there were more than five hundred. In 1950, 29 percent of humanity resided in cities; in 2008, the United Nations announced that the scales had tipped and a majority of the planet's population was then urban. The lion's share of this explosion came in the so-called Third World, and particularly in nations that actively pursued projects of agricultural "modernization" patterned on the global green revolution. That the United States and Mexico served as a sort of dress rehearsal is therefore not surprising, considering both were instrumental in the honing of the green revolution model.[16]

Witnessing the unprecedented decimation of *minifundia*—small farms—across the globe during the last century, many observers have concluded that this transformation was inevitable: a foregone conclusion or unavoidable waypoint in humanity's march toward an urban and industrial modernity. Such a verdict provides comforting nostrums to those reaping the fruits of this wrenching change and a convenient dismissal of its critics. But as this book has demonstrated, the destruction of peasant agricultures was the product of political choices, not free market economics or technological determinism. State intervention and the calculated withholding of government favor proved most pivotal in the success of mechanized, chemical-dependent, single-crop latifundia. Yet this model's future success in clothing and feeding the world is far from certain. The green revolution and its ideological cousins were undeniably successful in producing an overabundance of cheap food and fiber, but in an era of anthropogenic climate change, where the dwindling supply of both fossil fuels and fresh water looms larger each year, such gains may be fleeting. Likewise, the viability of our risky experiment in mass urbanization, prompted by the violent uprooting of billions of rural people, is only now beginning to be determined.

What is entirely certain, however, is that past and future dilemmas over land, food, water, and population were not and will not be segregated by the artificial dichotomies of Global North and Global South, of First World and Third World. The United States and Mexico, nations long understood on opposing sides of those binary divisions, grappled with strikingly analogous agrarian transformations during the twentieth century. Unprecedented social movements that confronted dispossession and inequality in the countryside shook both nations and both witnessed ruling regimes that intermittently embraced agrarian rebels but abandoned them when politically opportune. In time, each saw the rise of an expert class that sought to wield social and biological science to remake agriculture and rural life. The transformations of the US and Mexican countryside did not merely run parallel, though; they frequently intersected. In the new millennium, few remember that era of convergence. Yet to respond to the environmental and demographic challenges of the coming century, it may be imperative that we do.

NOTES

INTRODUCTION

1. Gloria Anzaldúa, *Borderlands/La Frontera* (1987; repr., San Francisco: Aunt Lute Books, 1999), 25.

2. Clarence Senior to J. R. Butler, May 23, 1939, reel 11, Southern Tenant Farmers' Union Papers (microfilm), Southern Historical Collection, University of North Carolina at Chapel Hill.

3. H. L. Mitchell and Farish Betton, "Land and Liberty for Mexican Farmers," July 1939, reel 12, Southern Tenant Farmers' Union Papers.

4. On the USDA training program and Fernández's participation, see George Messersmith to Ezequiel Padilla, June 2, 1942, and Alfonso González Gallardo to Ezequiel Padilla, June 25, 1942, both in III-2459-3, Archivo Histórico de la Secretaría de Relaciones Exteriores, Tlatelolco, Mexico City.

5. George Messersmith to Ezequiel Padilla, July 13, 1943, III-2459-3, Archivo Histórico de la Secretaría de Relaciones Exteriores. On the publications Fernández picked up on his tour of the US South, see "Greene County, Georgia: The Story of One Southern County," box 88, and "By-laws of Mileston Community, Inc., Tchula, Holmes County, Mississippi," box 52, both in Ramón Fernández y Fernández Papers, Biblioteca Luis González, Colegio de Michoacán, Zamora, Michoacán, Mexico.

6. Ramón Fernández y Fernández to Marte R. Gómez, March 6, 1945, Cartas, 1945, D-G, Marte R. Gómez Papers, Archivo Marte R. Gómez, Lomas de Chapultepec, Mexico City (hereafter Gómez Papers).

7. Even more so than Cardenismo, the rural New Deal was a profoundly conflicted affair. In this book, I distinguish between what I call the "agricultural" New Deal and the "agrarian" New Deal. The former came earlier and was far more conservative; its most representative legislation was the price control crop subsidy program of the Agricultural Adjustment Administration, which lives on—in revised form—to the present day. The agricultural New Deal was most concerned with boosting incomes for wealthier commercial farmers and stabilizing commodity prices. In contrast, the agrarian New Deal—which slowly began to take shape after 1935—concerned itself with the cultural, economic, and environmental poverty of the vast underclass of rural people that populated much of the US countryside, and was most concentrated in the cotton South. It was the architects of the agrarian New Deal—not the agricultural one—that looked toward Mexico, and it was the agrarian New Deal that most engaged Mexican observers. Chapter 2 will explore this distinction further.

8. On the important distinction between transnational and comparative history, see Micol Seigel, "Beyond Compare: Comparative Method after the Transnational Turn," *Radical History Review* 91 (Winter 2005): 62–90.

9. Kiran Klaus Patel, *The New Deal: A Global History* (Princeton, NJ: Princeton University Press, 2016), 67. The two most important works here are Daniel T. Rodgers, *Atlantic Crossings: Social Politics in a Progressive Age* (Cambridge, MA: Belknap Press of Harvard University Press, 1998), chap. 10; Patel, *The New Deal*. Though both are deeply researched works of scholarship, they prioritize US exchange with Europe above all. Rodgers is explicit in restricting his lens to

the North Atlantic; Patel is far more sensitive to parallels and influences deriving from Asia, Africa, and Latin America. Patel, however, still leans heavily toward Europe, especially Germany, Great Britain, France, and the Soviet Union. This is hardly a critique: white, professional-class New Dealers undoubtedly paid closer attention to those nations and saw them as more likely to contribute models. Indeed, within the national New Deal, it is hard to argue that Mexico should be given similar attention. But when considering the New Deal's particular vision for the US South, Mexico's proportional influence much increases, meriting intensive study.

10. Throughout this book I employ "South" and "southern" to designate the US southeast, specifically the states of South Carolina, Mississippi, Florida, Alabama, Georgia, Louisiana, Texas, Virginia, Arkansas, North Carolina, Kentucky, Missouri, and West Virginia. This geographic container does not include southwestern states such as California, Arizona, New Mexico, and so forth.

11. The borderlands historiographical tradition is wildly diverse and more than a century old, ranging back to the pioneering work of Herbert E. Bolton. For a recent overview of this body of literature in the context of transnational history, see Ramón A. Gutiérrez and Elliott Young, "Transnationalizing Borderlands History," *Western Historical Quarterly* 41 (Spring 2010): 26–53. For the best recent works in this vein, see Karl Jacoby, *The Strange Career of William Ellis: The Texas Slave Who Became a Mexican Millionaire* (New York: W. W. Norton, 2016); John Weber, *From South Texas to the Nation: The Exploitation of Mexican Labor in the Twentieth Century* (Chapel Hill: University of North Carolina Press, 2015); Geraldo L. Cadava, *Standing on Common Ground: The Making of a Sunbelt Borderland* (Cambridge, MA: Harvard University Press, 2013); Ruben Flores, *Backroads Pragmatists: Mexico's Melting Pot and Civil Rights in the United States* (Philadelphia: University of Pennsylvania Press, 2014); Rachel St. John, *Line in the Sand: A History of the Western U.S.-Mexico Border* (Princeton, NJ: Princeton University Press, 2011); Samuel Truett, *Fugitive Landscapes: The Forgotten History of the U.S.-Mexico Borderlands* (New Haven, CT: Yale University Press, 2006); Benjamin H. Johnson and Andrew Graybill, eds., *Bridging National Borders in North America: Transnational and Comparative Histories* (Durham, NC: Duke University Press, 2010); Samuel Truett and Elliott Young, eds., *Continental Crossroads: Remapping U.S.-Mexico Borderlands History* (Durham, NC: Duke University Press, 2004). In recent years scholars have stretched the borderlands geography far beyond the Mexican North and US Southwest; see, for example, Michael Innis-Jiménez, *Steel Barrio: The Great Mexican Migration to South Chicago, 1915–1940* (New York: New York University Press, 2013). As for the US South, no book has done more to integrate that region within the borderlands tradition than Julie M. Weise, *Corazón de Dixie: Mexicanos in the U.S. South since 1910* (Chapel Hill: University of North Carolina Press, 2015).

12. The memorable words are H. L. Mencken's, cited in George B. Tindall, *The Emergence of the New South, 1913–1945* (Baton Rouge: Louisiana State University Press, 1967), 210.

13. On the US South's global linkages after Reconstruction, see Andrew Zimmerman, *Alabama in Africa: Booker T. Washington, the German Empire, and the Globalization of the New South* (Princeton, NJ: Princeton University Press, 2010); Erin Elizabeth Clune, "From Light Copper to the Blackest and Lowest Type: Daniel Tompkins and the Racial Order of the Global New South," *Journal of Southern History* 76, no. 2 (2010): 275–314; Stephanie R. Rolph, "The Citizens' Council and Africa: White Supremacy in Global Perspective," *Journal of Southern History* 82, no. 3 (2016): 617–50; Stephanie Hinnershitz, "The 'Little Brown Brother' in the Jim Crow South: Race, Sex, and Empire in *State of Georgia v. Fortunatio Annunciatio* (1932)," *Journal of*

Southern History 82, no. 3 (2016): 549–78; Andrew C. Baker, "Race and Romantic Agrarianism: The Transnational Roots of Clarence Poe's Crusade for Rural Segregation in North Carolina," *Agricultural History* 87, no. 1 (2013): 93–114; Elizabeth Herbin-Triant, "Southern Segregation, South Africa–Style: Maurice Evans, Clarence Poe, and the Ideology of Rural Segregation," *Agricultural History* 87, no. 2 (2013): 170–93; Natalie Ring, *The Problem South: Region, Empire, and the New Liberal State, 1880–1930* (Athens: University of Georgia Press, 2012). Recent literature scholarship has also pushed in this direction. See John Wharton Lowe, *Calypso Magnolia: The Crosscurrents of Caribbean and Southern Literature* (Chapel Hill: University of North Carolina Press, 2016); Jon Smith and Deborah Cohn, eds., *Look Away! The U.S. South in New World Studies* (Durham, NC: Duke University Press, 2004).

14. An exhaustive list would be far too long to include here, but for a recent sampling see Sven Beckert, *Empire of Cotton: A Global History* (New York: Alfred A. Knopf, 2014); Walter Johnson, *River of Dark Dreams: Slavery and Empire in the Cotton Kingdom* (Cambridge, MA: Belknap Press of Harvard University Press, 2013); Matthew Karp, *This Vast Southern Empire: Slaveholders at the Helm of American Foreign Policy* (Cambridge, MA: Harvard University Press, 2016); Rebecca J. Scott, *Degrees of Freedom: Louisiana and Cuba after Slavery* (Cambridge, MA: Belknap Press of Harvard University Press, 2005); Matthew Pratt Guterl, *American Mediterranean: Southern Slaveholders in the Age of Emancipation* (Cambridge, MA: Harvard University Press, 2008); Jeffrey Kerr-Ritchie, *Rites of August First: Emancipation Day in the Black Atlantic World* (Baton Rouge: Louisiana State University Press, 2007); Edward Bartlett Rugemer, *The Problem of Emancipation: The Caribbean Roots of the American Civil War* (Baton Rouge: Louisiana State University Press, 2009). For rare works on Mexico within those same circuits, see Todd W. Wahlstrom, *The Southern Exodus to Mexico: Migration across the Borderlands after the Civil War* (Lincoln: University of Nebraska Press, 2015); Andrew J. Torget, *Seeds of Empire: Cotton, Slavery, and the Transformation of the Texas Borderlands, 1800–1850* (Chapel Hill: University of North Carolina Press, 2015); Sarah E. Cornell, "Americans in the U.S. South and Mexico: A Transnational History of Race, Slavery, and Freedom, 1810–1910" (PhD diss., New York University, 2008); Sarah E. Cornell, "Citizens of Nowhere: Fugitive Slaves and Free African Americans in Mexico, 1833–1857," *Journal of American History* 100, no. 2 (2013): 351–74.

15. For further evidence of this silence, through a historiographical review of the US South's global entanglement, see Peter Kolchin, "The South and the World," *Journal of Southern History* 75, no. 3 (2009): 565–80. Kolchin found few examples of studies exploring the century after Reconstruction, in stark contrast to the avalanche of studies on the eighteenth and nineteenth centuries. There are, however, several scholars in the more traditional field of diplomatic history that have demonstrated how US southern diplomats and lawmakers played an outsized role in US foreign policy. See, in particular, Joseph A. Fry, *Dixie Looks Abroad: The South and U.S. Foreign Relations, 1789–1973* (Baton Rouge: Louisiana State University Press, 2002); Joseph A. Fry, "Place Matters: Domestic Regionalism and the Formation of American Foreign Policy," *Diplomatic History* 36, no. 3 (June 2012): 451–82; Tennant S. McWilliams, *The New South Faces the World: Foreign Affairs and the Southern Sense of Self, 1877–1950* (Baton Rouge: Louisiana State University Press, 1988); Alfred O. Hero, Jr., *The Southerner and World Affairs* (Baton Rouge: Louisiana State University Press, 1965).

16. Rodgers, *Atlantic Crossings*.

17. For the numerous works that locate development's origins in 1940s' Cold War concerns, see Arturo Escobar, *Encountering Development: The Making and Unmaking of the Third World* (Princeton, NJ: Princeton University Press, 1995); Michael Latham, *Modernization as Ideology:*

American Social Science and "Nation Building" in the Kennedy Era (Chapel Hill: University of North Carolina Press, 2000); Gilbert Rist, *The History of Development: From Western Origins to Global Faith* (London: Zed Books, 2002); Nils Gilman, *Mandarins of the Future: Modernization Theory in Cold War America* (Baltimore: Johns Hopkins University Press, 2003); David C. Engerman, Nils Gilman, Mark Haefele, and Michael E. Latham, eds., *Staging Growth: Modernization, Development, and the Global Cold War* (Amherst: University of Massachusetts Press, 2003); Amy L. Staples, *The Birth of Development: How the World Bank, Food and Agriculture Organization, and World Health Organization Changed the World, 1945–1965* (Kent, OH: Kent State University Press, 2006). For two primary exceptions, which both locate its origins in the intellectual ferment of the 1930s, see David Ekbladh, *The Great American Mission: Modernization and the Construction of an American World Order* (Princeton, NJ: Princeton University Press, 2010); Daniel Immerwahr, *Thinking Small: The United States and the Lure of Community Development* (Cambridge, MA: Harvard University Press, 2015).

18. The Gaud quotations are from Sigrid Schmalzer, *Red Revolution, Green Revolution: Scientific Farming in Socialist China* (Chicago: University of Chicago Press, 2016), 2. On the green revolution's geopolitical, social, and environmental repercussions across the world, see, primarily, Raj Patel, "The Long Green Revolution," *Journal of Peasant Studies* 40, no. 1 (2013): 1–63; Nick Cullather, *The Hungry World: America's Cold War Battle against Poverty in Asia* (Cambridge, MA: Harvard University Press, 2010); John H. Perkins, *Geopolitics and the Green Revolution: Wheat, Genes, and the Cold War* (New York: Oxford University Press, 1997). On the tipping of the rural-urban scale, see United Nations Population Fund, "State of World Population 2007: Unleashing the Potential of Urban Growth," accessed February 26, 2016, https://www.unfpa .org/sites/default/files/pub-pdf/695_filename_sowp2007_eng.pdf.

19. A deeper historiographical review may be found in chapter 4, but for a few influential examples of this common interpretation of the Mexican Agricultural Program, see Cynthia Hewitt de Alcantara, *Modernizing Mexican Agriculture: Socioeconomic Implications of Technological Change, 1940–1970* (Geneva: UN Research Institute for Social Development, 1976); Deborah Fitzgerald, "Exporting American Agriculture: The Rockefeller Foundation in Mexico, 1943–1953," *Social Studies of Science* 16, no. 3 (1986): 457–83; Angus Wright, *The Death of Ramón González: The Modern Agricultural Dilemma* (Austin: University of Texas Press, 1990); Perkins, *Geopolitics and the Green Revolution*; Joseph Cotter, *Troubled Harvest: Agronomy and Revolution in Mexico, 1880–2002* (Westport, CT: Praeger, 2003). For two important exceptions, see Cullather, *The Hungry World*; Jonathan Harwood, "Peasant Friendly Plant Breeding and the Early Years of the Green Revolution in Mexico," *Agricultural History* 83, no. 3 (2009): 384–410.

20. John A. Ferrell, "Aid to Mexico: Continued Support of Public Health Services; Aid Also toward Measures in the Field of Agriculture; Possibly Special Activities in the Field of Education," January 27, 1941, folder 3814, box 561, series 323, 1941 stacks, record group 2, Rockefeller Foundation Archives, Rockefeller Archive Center, Tarrytown, New York.

21. Marte R. Gómez, "Memorandum para el Señor Presidente de la República sobre el funcionamiento de la Fundación Rockefeller y enumeración de las actividades que desearía realizar en México en materia de producción agrícola," September 21, 1942, Documentos Oficiales, 1942, vol. II, Gómez Papers.

22. C. Vann Woodward, "The Irony of Southern History," *Journal of Southern History* 19, no. 1 (1953): 3–19.

23. H. L. Mitchell and Farish Betton, "Land and Liberty for Mexican Farmers," July 1939, reel 12, Southern Tenant Farmers' Union Papers.

CHAPTER ONE: PARALLEL AGRARIAN SOCIETIES

1. Edward Ayers, *The Promise of the New South: Life after Reconstruction* (New York: Oxford University Press, 1992), 249–51; Robert McMath, *Populist Vanguard: A History of the Southern Farmers' Alliance* (Chapel Hill: University of North Carolina Press, 1975), 107–9; Samuel Proctor, "The National Farmers' Alliance Convention of 1890 and Its 'Ocala Demands,'" *Florida Historical Quarterly* 28, no. 3 (1950): 161–81 (quotations are from 179).

2. John Womack, *Zapata and the Mexican Revolution* (New York: Vintage Books, 1968) (quotations are from 402).

3. In this chapter and throughout the book, I use "plantation" and "hacienda" interchangeably to describe centrally managed, large-scale, single-crop landholding. There is a long debate about distinctions between the two. Recently, Jürgen Osterhammel claimed that the nineteenth-century plantation was defined by its modernity, tight linkages to global capital and consumption, and innovation in cultivation and conservation techniques, while the hacienda in the same era tended to be a relic from earlier days and thus insular, feudalistic, averse to market forces, and geared toward self-sufficiency rather than export. See Jürgen Osterhammel, *The Transformation of the World: A Global History of the Nineteenth Century* (Princeton, NJ: Princeton University Press, 2014), 682–85. In the US and Mexican context, however, this distinction holds little water. US southern plantations of the post-emancipation era, with a vast and cheap labor supply, rarely invested in mechanical or biological innovations until after World War II; likewise, many Mexican haciendas in the same era catered aggressively to global markets and implemented "modern" labor regimentation techniques.

4. For the major works in comparative history of the US South, see Frank Tannenbaum, *Slave and Citizen: The Negro in the Americas* (New York: Alfred A. Knopf, 1946); George M. Fredrickson, *White Supremacy: A Comparative Study in American and South African History* (New York: Oxford University Press, 1981); John Cell, *The Highest Stage of White Supremacy: The Origins of Segregation in South Africa and the American South* (New York: Cambridge University Press, 1982); Eric Foner, *Nothing but Freedom: Emancipation and Its Legacy* (Baton Rouge: Louisiana State University Press, 1983); Peter Kolchin, *Unfree Labor: American Slavery and Russian Serfdom* (Cambridge, MA: Harvard University Press, 1987); Rebecca J. Scott, *Degrees of Freedom: Louisiana and Cuba after Slavery* (Cambridge, MA: Belknap Press of Harvard University Press, 2005). For a transnational approach, see Andrew Zimmerman, *Alabama in Africa: Booker T. Washington, the German Empire, and the Globalization of the New South* (Princeton, NJ: Princeton University Press, 2010); Edward Bartlett Rugemer, *The Problem of Emancipation: The Caribbean Roots of the American Civil War* (Baton Rouge: Louisiana State University Press, 2009); Walter Johnson, *River of Dark Dreams: Slavery and Empire in the Cotton Kingdom* (Cambridge, MA: Belknap Press of Harvard University Press, 2013); Matthew Karp, *This Vast Southern Empire: Slaveholders at the Helm of American Foreign Policy* (Cambridge, MA: Harvard University Press, 2016).

5. For a few notable exceptions, see Gregory P. Downs, "The Mexicanization of American Politics: The United States' Transnational Path from Civil War to Stabilization," *American Historical Review* 117, no. 2 (2012): 387–409; Sarah E. Cornell, "Americans in the U.S. South and Mexico: A Transnational History of Race, Slavery, and Freedom, 1810–1910" (PhD diss., New York University, 2008), though only the dissertation's epilogue grapples seriously with the post-emancipation period; Julie M. Weise, *Corazón de Dixie: Mexicanos in the U.S. South since 1910* (Chapel Hill: University of North Carolina Press, 2015), though Weise does not discuss Mexico's

domestic political history at length. Likewise, I am not the first to place the US South's agrarian transformation of the late nineteenth century in global context. More than a decade ago, Steven Hahn gestured toward this in his influential *A Nation Under Our Feet: Black Political Struggles in the Rural South from Slavery to the Great Migration* (Cambridge, MA: Harvard University Press, 2003), chap. 9. Sven Beckert has more recently done so in *Empire of Cotton: A Global History* (New York: Alfred A. Knopf, 2014), chaps. 10–11.

6. For the most insightful critique of comparative history's shortcomings, see Micol Seigel, "Beyond Compare: Comparative Method after the Transnational Turn," *Radical History Review* 91 (Winter 2005): 62–90.

7. Though this chapter will not emphasize it, during this turbulent era, observers in the United States and Mexico did keep a close eye on the instability and disorder of their neighbor, and understood their own predicament in comparative context. See, in particular, Downs, "The Mexicanization of American Politics."

8. On the political stabilization of Mexico in the Díaz years and the coup against Lerdo, see Gilbert M. Joseph and Jürgen Buchenau, *Mexico's Once and Future Revolution: Social Upheaval and the Challenge of Rule since the Late Nineteenth Century* (Durham, NC: Duke University Press, 2013), chap. 2; Paul H. Garner, *Porfirio Díaz: Profiles in Power* (New York: Longman, 2001); Laurens B. Perry, *Juárez and Díaz: Machine Politics in Mexico* (DeKalb: Northern Illinois University Press, 1978); José C. Valadés, *El Porfirismo: Historia de un régimen* (Mexico City: Universidad Nacional Autónoma de México, 1977). On the culture of the Porfirian elite, see William Beezley, *Judas at the Jockey Club and Other Episodes of Porfirian Mexico* (Lincoln: University of Nebraska Press, 1987).

9. For a classic work on Reconstruction and its slow end, see Eric Foner, *Reconstruction: America's Unfinished Revolution, 1863–1877* (New York: Harper, 1989). On white violence and its impact, see George Rable, *But There Was No Peace: The Role of Violence in the Politics of Reconstruction* (Athens: University of Georgia Press, 1984). For a recent account of the protracted military withdrawal from the South, see Gregory P. Downs, *After Appomattox: Military Occupation and the Ends of War* (Cambridge, MA: Harvard University Press, 2015). For a synthetic essay on the question of continuity and change in the South's political elite from the antebellum to post-Reconstruction years, see James Cobb, "Beyond Planters and Industrialists: A New Perspective on the New South," *Journal of Southern History* 54, no. 1 (1988): 45–68. There were state-by-state variations in leaders' espousal of New South ideology, but by the 1880s it was clear that a new regional ethos had emerged.

10. For two contrasting accounts of the economic development philosophy of the New South Democrats, see Dwight B. Billings, *Planters and the Making of a "New South": Class, Politics, and Development in North Carolina, 1865–1900* (Chapel Hill: University of North Carolina Press, 1979); Jonathan M. Wiener, *Social Origins of the New South: Alabama, 1860–1885* (Baton Rouge: Louisiana State University Press, 1978). On the place of yeoman farmers before and after the Civil War, see Steven Hahn, *The Roots of Southern Populism: Yeoman Farmers and the Transformation of the Georgia Upcountry, 1850–1890* (New York: Oxford University Press, 1983); Joseph P. Reidy, *From Slavery to Agrarian Capitalism in the Cotton Plantation South: Central Georgia, 1800–1880* (Chapel Hill: University of North Carolina Press, 1992); Adrienne Monteith Petty, *Standing Their Ground: Small Farmers in North Carolina since the Civil War* (New York: Oxford University Press, 2013).

11. On the divided Mexican countryside and Porfirian plans of economic development, see Jesús Gómez Serrano, "Mitos y realidades del latifundismo porfiriano: Una aproximación

regional desde Aguascalientes," in *Mexico in Transition: New Perspectives on Mexican Agrarian History, Nineteenth and Twentieth Centuries*, ed. Antonio Escobar Ohmstede and Matthew Butler (Mexico City: CIESAS, 2013); Daniela Marino and María Cecilia Zuleta, "Una visión del campo: Tierra, propiedad y tendencias de la producción, 1850–1930," in *Historia económica general de México: De la Colonia a nuestros días*, ed. Sandra Kuntz Ficker (Mexico City: Colegio de México, 2010); Raymond B. Craib, *Cartographic Mexico: A History of State Fixations and Fugitive Landscapes* (Durham, NC: Duke University Press, 2004); Alan Knight, *The Mexican Revolution, Volume 1: Porfirians, Liberals, and Peasants* (New York: Cambridge University Press, 1986), chap. 1; Paul Hart, *Bitter Harvest: The Social Transformation of Morelos, Mexico, and the Origins of the Zapatista Revolution, 1840–1910* (Albuquerque: University of New Mexico Press, 2005); Alejandro Tortolero, *De la coa a la máquina de vapor: Actividad agrícola e innovación tecnológica en las haciendas mexicanas, 1880–1914* (Mexico City: Siglo Veintiuno Editores, 1995); Richard Weiner, *Race, Nation, and Market: Economic Culture in Porfirian Mexico* (Tucson: University of Arizona Press, 2004). For an important historiographical review of the Díaz regime, see Mauricio Tenorio Trillo and Aurora Gómez Galvarriato, *El Porfiriato: Herramientas para la historia* (Mexico City: Fondo de Cultura Económica, 2006).

12. On the closing of the commons in the US South, see especially Steven Hahn, "Hunting, Fishing, and Foraging: Common Rights and Class Relations in the Postbellum South," *Radical History Review* 26 (1982): 37–64; Hahn, *The Roots of Southern Populism*, chap. 7.

13. For the land statistic, see William Beezley, *Mexicans in Revolution, 1910–1946: An Introduction* (Lincoln: University of Nebraska Press, 2009), 4. For a classic examination of the hacienda and its social contract in colonial Mexico, see François Chevalier, *Land and Society in Colonial Mexico: The Great Hacienda* (Berkeley: University of California Press, 1963). On more recent historiographical debates, see Arnold Bauer, "Modernizing Landlords and Constructive Peasants in the Mexican Countryside," *Mexican Studies / Estudios Mexicanos* 14, no. 1 (1998): 191–212; Eric Van Young, *Writing Mexican History* (Stanford, CA: Stanford University Press, 2012), chap. 1. On the ejido and its prerevolutionary ambiguities, see Mikael Wolfe, "The Sociolegal Redesignation of *Ejido* Land Use, 1856–1912," in *Mexico in Transition: New Perspectives on Mexican Agrarian History, Nineteenth and Twentieth Centuries*, ed. Antonio Escobar Ohmstede and Matthew Butler (Mexico City: CIESAS, 2013). On the privatization of communal lands in Mexico, see especially Craib, *Cartographic Mexico*; Knight, *The Mexican Revolution, Volume 1*, chap. 3. On the internal tensions within pueblos over land privatization, see Emilio Kourí, *A Pueblo Divided: Business, Property, and Community in Papantla, Mexico* (Stanford, CA: Stanford University Press, 2004).

14. C. Vann Woodward, "New South Fraud Is Papered by Old South Myth," *Washington Post*, July 9, 1961, E3. Woodward's *Origins of the New South, 1877–1913* (Baton Rouge: Louisiana State University Press, 1951) began the long debate about the colonial economics of southern development. For a rejoinder, see Gavin Wright, *Old South, New South: Revolutions in the Southern Economy since the Civil War* (Baton Rouge: Louisiana State University Press, 1986). On the politics of southern economic "colonialism," see Joseph J. Persky, *The Burden of Dependency: Colonial Themes in Southern Economic Thought* (Baltimore: Johns Hopkins University Press, 1992).

15. Mark Wasserman, *Pesos and Politics: Business, Elites, Foreigners, and Government in Mexico, 1854–1940* (Stanford, CA: Stanford University Press, 2015), 8. Historians disagree over the levels of foreign ownership in the Porfirian Mexican economy. In *Empire and Revolution: The Americans in Mexico since the Civil War* (Berkeley: University of California Press, 2002), John

208 • Notes to Pages 19–21

Mason Hart contends that the level of US and British control of the Mexican economy was staggering. Knight in *The Mexican Revolution* and Wasserman in *Pesos and Politics* are skeptical of such claims. On the Hearst holdings in northern Mexico, see John Mason Hart, *Revolutionary Mexico: The Coming and Process of the Mexican Revolution* (Berkeley: University of California Press, 1987), 47–48; Hart, *Empire and Revolution*, 179–80. On Rosalie Evans and her hacienda, see Timothy J. Henderson, *The Worm in the Wheat: Rosalie Evans and Agrarian Struggle in the Puebla-Tlaxcala Valley of Mexico, 1906–1927* (Durham, NC: Duke University Press, 1998).

16. For the rail statistics, see Ayers, *The Promise of the New South*, 9; John H. Coatsworth, *Growth against Development: The Economic Impact of Railroads in Porfirian Mexico* (DeKalb: Northern Illinois University Press, 1981), 4. On the construction and importance of railroads to Porfirian Mexico, see Coatsworth, *Growth against Development*, especially chap. 6; Teresa Van Hoy, *A Social History of Mexico's Railroads: Peons, Prisoners, and Priests* (Lanham, MD: Rowman and Littlefield, 2008). On the US southern case, for the best explorations of the power of the railroads in transforming rural life, see Ayers, *The Promise of the New South*; Barbara Young-Welke, *Recasting American Liberty: Gender, Race, Law, and the Railroad Revolution, 1865–1920* (New York: Cambridge University Press, 2001).

17. On debt and rural transformation in the US South, see Hahn, *The Roots of Southern Populism*; Wright, *Old South, New South*. On the advent of sharecropping in the New South era, see Charles S. Aiken, *The Cotton Plantation South since the Civil War* (Baltimore: Johns Hopkins University Press, 1998), especially chaps. 1–2.

18. On debt peonage and the Porfirian hacienda, see Knight, *The Mexican Revolution, Volume 1*, chap. 3; Henderson, *The Worm in the Wheat*, chap. 2.

19. On the making of US southern racial ideology after emancipation, see Joel Williamson, *A Rage for Order: Black/White Relations in the American South since Emancipation* (New York: Oxford University Press, 1986); Hahn, *A Nation Under Our Feet*. On race and indigeneity in Porfirian Mexico, see Weiner, *Race, Nation, and Market*; Beezley, *Judas at the Jockey Club*; Alan Knight, "Racism, Revolution, and Indigenismo: Mexico, 1910–1940," in *The Idea of Race in Latin America, 1870–1940*, ed. Richard Graham (Austin: University of Texas Press, 1990). I do not mean to suggest that there existed a biracial spectrum solely of white and black (in the United States), or white and Indian (in Mexico), as there were thousands of Mexican and Mexican Americans in the western peripheries of the Cotton Belt, and even more Afro-descended Mexicans in the Gulf states, in addition to European, Chinese, and Middle Eastern immigrants. Yet in regional and national discourse, those populations were often ignored as they complicated the dominant narrative of race and national belonging. See Neil Foley, *The White Scourge: Mexicans, Blacks, and Poor Whites in Texas Cotton Culture* (Berkeley: University of California Press, 1997); Cornell, "Americans in the U.S. South and Mexico"; Weise, *Corazón de Dixie*; Moon-Ho Jung, *Coolies and Cane: Race, Labor, and Sugar in the Age of Emancipation* (Baltimore: Johns Hopkins University Press, 2006); Elliott Young, *Alien Nation: Chinese Migration in the Americas from the Coolie Era through World War II* (Chapel Hill: University of North Carolina Press, 2014).

20. Henry W. Grady speech to the New England Society of New York, December 21, 1886, cited in Ferald J. Bryan, *Henry Grady or Tom Watson? The Rhetorical Struggle for the New South, 1880–1890* (Macon, GA: Mercer University Press, 1994), 105.

21. John Kenneth Turner, *Barbarous Mexico* (1910; repr., Austin: University of Texas Press, 1969), 25. For the wage and life expectancy statistics, see Joseph and Buchenau, *Mexico's Once and Future Revolution*, 25.

22. George K. Holmes, "Peons of the South," *Annals of the American Academy of Political and Social Sciences* 4, no. 2 (1893): 74.

23. Charles H. Otken, *The Ills of the South* (New York: G. P. Putnam, 1894), 21.

24. Womack, *Zapata and the Mexican Revolution*, 402; C. Vann Woodward, *Tom Watson, Agrarian Rebel* (New York: Macmillan, 1938), 120, 115. Any comparisons between the two undeniably shatter if considering Watson's postpopulist career, in which he became a bitter race-baiting xenophobe; it is only the younger radical Watson that I consider here as a parallel to Zapata.

25. On US populism, for the best representation of this first school, see John D. Hicks, *The Populist Revolt: A History of the Farmers' Alliance and the People's Party* (Minneapolis: University of Minnesota Press, 1931); Woodward, *Tom Watson, Agrarian Rebel*. On the Mexican Revolution, for two early romantic interpretations, see Frank Tannenbaum, *The Mexican Agrarian Revolution* (New York: Robert Brookings Institution, 1929); Jesús Silva Herzog, *Breve historia de la Revolución Mexicana* (Mexico City: Fondo de Cultura Económica, 1966).

26. For major revisionist works on each revolt, see Richard Hofstadter, *The Age of Reform: From Bryan to F.D.R.* (New York: Vintage Books, 1955); Ramón Eduardo Ruiz, *The Great Rebellion: Mexico, 1905–1924* (New York: W. W. Norton, 1980); Romana Falcón, *El agrarismo en Veracruz: La etapa radical, 1928–1935* (Mexico City: El Colegio de México, 1977); Arturo Warman, *Y venimos a contradecir: Los campesinos de Morelos y el estado nacional* (Mexico City: Ediciones de la Casa Chata, 1976).

27. For the major postrevisionist works on each revolt, see Lawrence Goodwyn, *Democratic Promise: The Populist Moment in America* (New York: Oxford University Press, 1976); Knight, *The Mexican Revolution, Volume 1*. Of those two, Knight does a far better job in acknowledging regional variation and the impossibility of discussing a singular Mexican Revolution. Goodwyn's major shortcoming lies in his sometimes-myopic emphasis on southern and Great Plains farmers. For the most powerful recent challenge to Goodwyn, see Charles Postel, *The Populist Vision* (New York: Oxford University Press, 2007), which highlights California grower cooperatives rather than Cotton Belt farmers threatened by the crop lien, and draws dramatically different conclusions about their motivations and achievements. I follow the lead of these postrevisionists, and do not believe that either the Mexican or US agrarian revolts were singular, national movements that can be neatly compared and contrasted. Stretched across a vastly diverse national landscape, monolithic understandings of either US populism or the Mexican Revolution collapse under their own weight. Therefore, this chapter prioritizes the histories of rural insurgency in regions dominated by the plantation and responding to similar patterns of dispossession. The following explication of US populism is exclusively focused on the Cotton Belt, where former yeomen and freedpeople in the post-Reconstruction era revolted against the plantation nexus. Kansas and California, while crucial sources of national populist ideology, were so distinct from Cotton Belt populism as to warrant their exclusion. Likewise, within Mexico I stress the revolutionary experiences of regions that confronted similar plantation structures, like Morelos, La Laguna, and the Yucatán Peninsula.

28. Andrés Molina Enríquez, *Los grandes problemas nacionales* (Mexico City: A. Carranza e Hijos, 1909). On Molina's life and intellectual development, see Stanley F. Shadle, *Andrés Molina Enríquez: Mexican Land Reformer of the Revolutionary Era* (Tucson: University of Arizona Press, 1994). For a close analysis of Molina's romantic and often-misguided assumptions about the pueblos and their long-term influence, see Emilio Kourí, "Interpreting the Expropriation of Indian Pueblo Lands in Porfirian Mexico: The Unexamined Legacies of Andrés Molina Enríquez," *Hispanic American Historical Review* 82, no. 1 (2002): 69–117.

29. Woodward, *Tom Watson, Agrarian Rebel*, 187; Ayers, *The Promise of the New South*, 271. On the early years of the Texas Farmers' Alliance, see Goodwyn, *Democratic Promise*, chaps. 2–3; McMath, *Populist Vanguard*, chaps. 1–2; Ayers, *The Promise of the New South*, chap. 9. On Watson and his early rhetoric, see Woodward, *Tom Watson, Agrarian Rebel*, chaps. 9–10. On the popularity and significance of the Farmers' Alliance in the 1880s' Deep South, see Hahn, *The Roots of Southern Populism*; Ayers, *The Promise of the New South*; Barton C. Shaw, *The Wool-Hat Boys: Georgia's Populist Party* (Baton Rouge: Louisiana State University Press, 1984); McMath, *Populist Vanguard*; Connie L. Lester, *Up from the Mudsills of Hell: The Farmers' Alliance, Populism, and Progressive Agriculture in Tennessee, 1870–1915* (Athens: University of Georgia Press, 2006); William W. Rogers, *The One-Gallused Rebellion: Agrarianism in Alabama, 1865–1896* (Baton Rouge: Louisiana State University Press, 1970); Mark V. Wetherington, *The New South Comes to Wiregrass Georgia, 1860–1910* (Knoxville: University of Tennessee Press, 1994); James M. Beeby, *Revolt of the Tar Heels: The North Carolina Populist Movement, 1890–1901* (Jackson: University Press of Mississippi, 2008). While each of these works draws differing conclusions about the radicalism and biracialism of the alliance movement, the majority of them agree that the normative participant was a middle- to lower-class farmer who felt threatened or had recently lost land to the expanding plantations.

30. Hahn, *The Roots of Southern Populism*, 283. For the membership statistic, see Ayers, *Promise of the New South*, 220. On the tenuous place of black southerners in the Farmers' Alliance, see James M. Beeby, ed., *Populism in the South Revisited: New Interpretations and New Departures* (Jackson: University Press of Mississippi, 2012); Hahn, *A Nation Under Our Feet*, chap. 9; Omar H. Ali, *In the Lion's Mouth: Black Populism in the New South, 1886–1900* (Jackson: University Press of Mississippi, 2010); Gerald H. Gaither, *Blacks and the Populist Movement: Ballots and Bigotry in the New South* (Tuscaloosa: University of Alabama Press, 2005).

31. On Madero and the earliest phases of agrarian revolt, see Knight, *The Mexican Revolution, Volume 1*, chaps. 3–4; Hart, *Revolutionary Mexico*, chap. 8; Joseph and Buchenau, *Mexico's Once and Future Revolution*, chap. 3.

32. On Zapata's early career and the revolt in Morelos, see Womack, *Zapata and the Mexican Revolution*; Warman, *Y venimos a contradecir*. On the regional variations of revolt and the importance of liminal spaces, see Knight, *The Mexican Revolution, Volume 1*, chap. 3.

33. On the splintering of Madero's revolutionary faction, see Knight, *The Mexican Revolution, Volume 1*, chaps. 5–6.

34. Womack, *Zapata and the Mexican Revolution*, 404. For a full text of the Plan de Ayala, see ibid., 400–404. For an analysis of the ideological goals of Zapata and his allies, see Knight, *The Mexican Revolution, Volume 1*, 309–14.

35. Proctor, "The National Farmers' Alliance Convention of 1890 and Its 'Ocala Demands,'" 179. For a full text of the Ocala Demands, see ibid. On the meeting and its conflicted nature, see Ayers, *The Promise of the New South*, chap. 10. On its impact in one state, see Rogers, *The One-Gallused Rebellion*, chap. 9.

36. On the slow decline of the alliance and the political defeats of the Populists, see Ayers, *The Promise of the New South*, chap. 11; Goodwyn, *Democratic Promise*, chaps. 13–16.

37. On the weakness of the alliance and Populists to address the divisions of race, see Shaw, *The Wool-Hat Boys*; Beeby, *Revolt of the Tar-Heels*; Glenda Gilmore, *Gender and Jim Crow: Women and the Politics of White Supremacy in North Carolina, 1890–1940* (Chapel Hill: University of North Carolina Press, 1996), chaps. 1–2.

38. On the Córdoba, Veracruz, "Klux clan," see Craib, *Cartographic Mexico*, 227–29.

39. On Villa and Obregón's role in his assassination, see Friedrich Katz, *The Life and Times of Pancho Villa* (Stanford, CA: Stanford University Press, 1998). On Zapata's downfall, see Womack, *Zapata and the Mexican Revolution*, chap. 10.

40. On the framing of the Constitution, see Hart, *Revolutionary Mexico*, 328–33; Knight, *The Mexican Revolution, Volume 2: Counter-revolution and Reconstruction* (New York: Cambridge University Press, 1986), 469–77; E. V. Niemeyer, *Revolution at Querétaro: The Mexican Constitutional Convention of 1916–1917* (Austin: University of Texas Press, 1974).

41. On the competing interpretations of the ejido before and after the drafting of the Constitution of 1917, see Wolfe, "The Sociolegal Redesignation of *Ejido* Land Use, 1856–1912"; Shadle, *Andrés Molina Enríquez*, chaps. 5–6; Niemeyer, *Revolution at Querétaro*, chap. 5; Ann L. Craig, *The First Agraristas: An Oral History of a Mexican Agrarian Reform Movement* (Berkeley: University of California Press, 1983), chap. 3; Knight, *The Mexican Revolution, Volume 1*, 422–23. On Molina's influence on Article 27, see Kourí, "Interpreting the Expropriation of Indian Pueblo Lands in Porfirian Mexico."

42. For the tenancy statistics, see US Special Committee on Farm Tenancy, *Farm Tenancy* (Washington, DC: Government Printing Office, 1937), 39. For the best synthesis of the closing of the southern political and racial system after the Populist revolt, see Ayers, *The Promise of the New South*, chaps. 12–15; Gilmore, *Gender and Jim Crow*.

43. On the Sonoran dynasty's stabilization of the Mexican Revolution, see Héctor Aguilar Camín, *La frontera nómada: Sonora y la Revolución Mexicana* (Mexico City: Siglo Veintiuno Editores, 1977); Tzvi Medin, *El minimato presidencial: Historia política del maximato* (Mexico City: Ediciones Era, 1982); Joseph and Buchenau, *Mexico's Once and Future Revolution*, chap. 5; Jürgen Buchenau, *The Last Caudillo: Álvaro Obregón and the Mexican Revolution* (New York: Wiley Blackwell, 2011); Jürgen Buchenau, *Plutarco Elías Calles and the Mexican Revolution* (Lanham, MD: Rowman and Littlefield, 2007).

44. Joseph and Buchenau, *Mexico's Once and Future Revolution*, 97–99.

45. On change and continuity in the agrarian struggle from the 1910s to 1920s, see Christopher Boyer, *Becoming Campesinos: Politics, Identity, and Agrarian Struggle in Postrevolutionary Michoacán, 1920–1935* (Stanford, CA: Stanford University Press, 2003); Craig, *The First Agraristas*; Warman, *Y venimos a contradecir*. On the contradictory role of the professional classes in promoting agrarian reform, see, in particular, Michael A. Ervin, "The 1930 Agrarian Census in Mexico: Agronomists, Middle Politics, and the Negotiation of Data Collection," *Hispanic American Historical Review* 87, no. 3 (2007): 537–70; Michael A. Ervin, "The Art of the Possible: Agronomists, Agrarian Reform, and the Middle Politics of the Mexican Revolution, 1908–1934" (PhD diss., University of Pittsburgh, 2002); Joseph Cotter, *Troubled Harvest: Agronomy and Revolution in Mexico, 1880–2002* (Westport, CT: Praeger, 2003), chap. 2; Craib, *Cartographic Mexico*, chap. 7.

46. For two competing interpretations of the Country Life movement, see David B. Danbom, *The Resisted Revolution: Urban America and the Industrialization of Agriculture, 1900–1930* (Ames: Iowa State University Press, 1979); Scott Peters and Paul Morgan, "The Country Life Commission: Reconsidering a Milestone in American Agricultural History," *Agricultural History* 78, no. 3 (2004): 289–316. I am far more convinced by the former.

47. On Progressive era legislation and its link to earlier Populist demands, see Danbom, *The Resisted Revolution*; Elizabeth Sanders, *Roots of Reform: Farmers, Workers, and the American State, 1877–1917* (Chicago: University of Chicago Press, 1999); Postel, *The Populist Vision*. For an important recent study of sexuality and biopolitics in the Progressive era farm programs, see

Gabriel N. Rosenberg, *The 4-H Harvest: Sexuality and the State in Rural America* (Philadelphia: University of Pennsylvania Press, 2016).

48. On the contradictions of southern Progressivism, see Dewey Grantham, *Southern Progressivism: The Reconciliation of Progress and Tradition* (Knoxville: University of Tennessee Press, 1983), especially chap. 10 on agriculture; William A. Link, *The Paradox of Southern Progressivism, 1880–1930* (Chapel Hill: University of North Carolina Press, 1992); Theodore Saloutos, *Farmer Movements in the South, 1865–1933* (Berkeley: University of California Press, 1960); Ayers, *The Promise of the New South*, chap. 15.

49. On northern philanthropy in the Progressive era South, see Eric Anderson and Alfred A. Moss, *Dangerous Donations: Northern Philanthropy and Southern Black Education, 1902–1930* (Columbia: University of Missouri Press, 1999); Mary S. Hoffschwelle, *The Rosenwald Schools of the American South* (Gainesville: University Press of Florida, 2006); John Ettling, *The Germ of Laziness: Rockefeller Philanthropy and Public Health in the New South* (Cambridge, MA: Harvard University Press, 1981); Theodore R. Mitchell and Robert Lowe, "To Sow Contentment: Philanthropy, Scientific Agriculture, and the Making of the New South, 1906–1920," *Journal of Social History* 24, no. 2 (1990): 317–40.

50. Although Washington has been much maligned since the civil rights era as an accommodationist, such an interpretation misses the narrow parameters of political possibility he confronted in the early twentieth century. On the Tuskegee vision for rural transformation, see Robert J. Norrell, *Up from History: The Life of Booker T. Washington* (Cambridge, MA: Belknap Press of Harvard University Press, 2009); Mark D. Hersey, *My Work Is That of Conservation: An Environmental Biography of George Washington Carver* (Athens: University of Georgia Press, 2011).

51. Frank Tannenbaum, "The Single Crop," *Century Magazine* 106, no. 6 (October 1923): 816, 825. For the roots of the characterization of this era as the "nadir" of black life, see Rayford Logan, *The Negro in American Life and Thought* (New York: Dial Press, 1954). On the climax of lynching in the fin de siècle years, see Fitzhugh Brundage, *Lynching in the New South: Georgia and Virginia, 1880–1930* (Urbana: University of Illinois Press, 1993).

52. On Calles's public declaration, see Jocelyn Olcott, "*Mueras y matanzas*: Spectacles of Terror and Violence in Postrevolutionary Mexico," in *A Century of Revolution: Insurgent and Counterinsurgent Violence during Latin America's Long Cold War*, ed. Gilbert Joseph and Greg Grandin (Durham, NC: Duke University Press, 2010), 67.

53. On the US South in the lean years of the 1920s, see Jack Temple Kirby, *Rural Worlds Lost: The American South, 1920–1960* (Baton Rouge: Louisiana State University Press, 1987), chap. 1; David Kennedy, *Freedom from Fear: The American People in Depression and War, 1929–1945* (New York: Oxford University Press, 1999), chap. 1. On rural out-migration in that period, see Isabel Wilkerson, *The Warmth of Other Suns: The Epic Story of America's Great Migration* (New York: Random House, 2010); James N. Gregory, *The Southern Diaspora: How the Great Migrations of Black and White Southerners Transformed America* (Chapel Hill: University of North Carolina Press, 2005). On soil erosion and southern environmental history, see Paul Sutter, *Let Us Now Praise Famous Gullies: Providence Canyon and the Soils of the South* (Athens: University of Georgia Press, 2015).

54. On the unfolding impact of the Great Depression in the US South and Mexico, see, respectively, Kennedy, *Freedom from Fear*, chaps. 2–4; Alan Knight, "The Character and Consequences of the Great Depression in Mexico," in *The Great Depression in Latin America*, ed. Paulo Drinot and Alan Knight (Durham, NC: Duke University Press, 2014). On the international

origins of the economic crisis, see Kiran Klaus Patel, *The New Deal: A Global History* (Princeton, NJ: Princeton University Press, 2016), 24–44.

55. On the escalation of radical agrarismo in Mexico, see Craig, *The First Agraristas*, chap. 4; Boyer, *Becoming Campesinos*, chap. 4; Joseph and Buchenau, *Mexico's Once and Future Revolution*, chap. 6. On the US South, see Robin D. G. Kelley, *Hammer and Hoe: Alabama Communists during the Great Depression* (Chapel Hill: University of North Carolina Press, 1990); Donald Grubbs, *Cry from the Cotton: The Southern Tenant Farmers' Union and the New Deal* (Chapel Hill: University of North Carolina Press, 1971); Jason Manthorne, "The View from the Cotton: Reconsidering the Southern Tenant Farmers' Union," *Agricultural History* 84, no. 1 (2010): 20–45.

56. Roosevelt has no shortage of biographical studies; I rely here mostly on Kennedy, *Freedom from Fear*, 94–104; Sarah T. Phillips, *This Land, This Nation: Conservation, Rural America, and the New Deal* (New York: Cambridge University Press, 2007), 59–74. In contrast, there is no English-language biography of Cárdenas beyond studies of his presidency; helpful is Amelia Kiddle, "Lázaro Cárdenas (1895–1970)," in *Iconic Mexico: An Encyclopedia from Acapulco to Zócalo*, ed. Eric Zolov (Santa Barbara, CA: ABC-CLIO, 2015).

CHAPTER TWO: SHARECROPPERS AND CAMPESINOS

1. Pablo Campos Ortiz to the Departamento de Publicaciones del Partido Nacional Revolucionario, January 17, 1935, III-63-2, Archivo Histórico de la Secretaría de Relaciones Exteriores, Tlatelolco, Mexico City (hereafter AHSRE). The Plan Sexenal was in fact written by the PNR, not Cárdenas himself, but served as the guiding document of his presidency.

2. On this point, see, in particular, Kiran Klaus Patel, *The New Deal: A Global History* (Princeton, NJ: Princeton University Press, 2016).

3. On immigration and deportation directly after the economic crash, see Abraham Hoffman, *Unwanted Mexican Americans in the Great Depression: Repatriation Pressures, 1929–1939* (Tucson: University of Arizona Press, 1974); Francisco E. Balderrama and Raymond Rodríguez, *Decade of Betrayal: Mexican Repatriation in the 1930s* (Albuquerque: University of New Mexico Press, 2006). Though nativism toward Mexicans and Mexican Americans persisted throughout the 1930s, particularly in the US Southwest, government-led deportation campaigns largely preceded the New Deal.

4. On Mexico's place in the debates on slavery and abolition in the nineteenth-century United States, see Karl Jacoby, *The Strange Career of William Ellis: The Texas Slave Who Became a Mexican Millionaire* (New York: W. W. Norton, 2016); Robert E. May, *Slavery, Race, and Conquest in the Tropics: Lincoln, Douglas, and the Future of Latin America* (New York: Cambridge University Press, 2013); Todd W. Wahlstrom, *The Southern Exodus to Mexico: Migration across the Borderlands after the American Civil War* (Lincoln: University of Nebraska Press, 2015); Sarah E. Cornell, "Americans in the U.S. South and Mexico: A Transnational History of Race, Slavery, and Freedom, 1810–1910" (PhD diss., New York University, 2008). On Mexico in the US imaginary during Reconstruction, see Gregory P. Downs, "The Mexicanization of American Politics: The United States' Transnational Path from Civil War to Stabilization," *American Historical Review* 117, no. 2 (2012): 387–409.

5. There is a vast literature on the US reverberations of the Mexican Revolution during the 1910s. See W. Dirk Raat, *Revoltosos: Mexico's Rebels in the United States, 1903–1923* (College Station: Texas A&M University Press, 1981); Benjamin Heber Johnson, *Revolution in Texas: How*

a Forgotten Rebellion and Its Bloody Suppression Turned Mexicans into Americans (New Haven, CT: Yale University Press, 2003); Gerald Horne, *Black and Brown: African Americans and the Mexican Revolution, 1910–1920* (New York: New York University Press, 2005); John A. Britton, *Revolution and Ideology: Images of the Mexican Revolution in the United States* (Lexington: University Press of Kentucky, 1995); Jaime Marroquín Arredondo, Adela Pineda Franco, and Magdalena Mieri, eds., *Open Borders to a Revolution: Culture, Politics, and Migration* (Washington, DC: Smithsonian Institution Scholarly Press, 2013).

6. On US pilgrimages to Mexico during the 1920s, see Helen Delpar, *The Enormous Vogue of Things Mexican: Cultural Relations between the United States and Mexico, 1920–1935* (Tuscaloosa: University of Alabama Press, 1992); Megan Threlkeld, *Pan American Women: U.S. Internationalists and Revolutionary Mexico* (Philadelphia: University of Pennsylvania Press, 2014); Mauricio Tenorio Trillo, "Stereophonic Scientific Modernisms: Social Science between Mexico and the United States, 1880s–1930s," *Journal of American History* 86, no. 3 (1999): 1156–87; Mauricio Tenorio Trillo, "The Cosmopolitan Mexican Summer, 1920–1949," *Latin American Research Review* 32, no. 3 (1997): 224–42; Jesus Velasco, "Reading Mexico, Understanding the United States: American Transnational Intellectuals in the 1920s and 1990s," *Journal of American History* 86, no. 2 (1999): 641–67; José E. Límon, *American Encounters: Greater Mexico, the United States, and the Erotics of Culture* (Boston: Beacon Press, 1998).

7. On the Good Neighbor policy, see Fredrick B. Pike, *FDR's Good Neighbor Policy: Sixty Years of Generally Gentle Chaos* (Austin: University of Texas Press, 1995); Michael R. Hall, "The Good Neighbor Policy and the Americas," in *A Companion to Franklin D. Roosevelt*, ed. William D. Pederson (Malden, MA: Wiley-Blackwell, 2011).

8. For examples of scholarship on the nonagrarian exchanges of the 1930s, see Delpar, *The Enormous Vogue of Things Mexican*; Tenorio Trillo, "Stereophonic Social Modernisms"; Ruben Flores, *Backroads Pragmatists: Mexico's Melting Pot and Civil Rights in the United States* (Philadelphia: University of Pennsylvania Press, 2014); Carlos Kevin Blanton, *George I. Sánchez: The Long Fight for Mexican American Integration* (New Haven, CT: Yale University Press, 2014); Michael Calderón-Zaks, "Debated Whiteness amid World Events: Mexican and Mexican American Subjectivity and the U.S. Relationship with the Americas, 1924–1936," *Mexican Studies / Estudios Mexicanos* 27, no. 2 (2011): 325–59; Wilbert Terry Ahlstedt, "John Collier and Mexico in the Shaping of U.S. Indian Policy: 1934–1945" (PhD diss., University of Nebraska, 2015); Guillermo Palacios, "The Social Sciences, Revolutionary Nationalism, and Interacademic Relations: Mexico and the United States, 1930–1940," in *Populism in Twentieth Century Mexico: The Presidencies of Lázaro Cárdenas and Luis Echeverría*, ed. Amelia Kiddle and María L. O. Muñoz (Tucson: University of Arizona Press, 2010); Dina Berger and Andrew Grant Wood, eds., *Holiday in Mexico: Critical Reflections on Tourism and Tourist Encounters* (Durham, NC: Duke University Press, 2010), particularly Berger's essay "Goodwill Ambassadors on Holiday: Tourism, Diplomacy, and Mexico-U.S. Relations."

9. National Emergency Council, *Report on Economic Conditions of the South* (Washington, DC: Government Printing Office, 1938), 1.

10. On the rural New Deal, see classic works such as Theodore Saloutos, *The American Farmer and the New Deal* (Ames: Iowa State University Press, 1982); Richard S. Kirkendall, *Social Scientists and Farm Politics in the Age of Roosevelt* (Columbia: University of Missouri Press, 1966); Sidney Baldwin, *Poverty and Politics: The Rise and Decline of the Farm Security Administration* (Chapel Hill: University of North Carolina Press, 1968); David Eugene Conrad, *Forgotten Farmers: The Story of Sharecroppers in the New Deal* (Urbana: University of Illinois Press, 1965).

See also more recent studies such as Charles Kenneth Roberts, *The Farm Security Administration and Rural Rehabilitation in the South* (Knoxville: University of Tennessee Press, 2015); Jess Gilbert, *Planning Democracy: Agrarian Intellectuals and the Intended New Deal* (New Haven, CT: Yale University Press, 2015); Sarah T. Phillips, *This Land, This Nation: Conservation, Rural America, and the New Deal* (New York: Cambridge University Press, 2007); Jess Gilbert, "Low Modernism and the Agrarian New Deal: A Different Kind of State," in *Fighting for the Farm: Rural America Transformed*, ed. Jane Adams (Philadelphia: University of Pennsylvania Press, 2003); Dona Brown, *Back to the Land: The Enduring Dream of Self-Sufficiency in Modern America* (Madison: University of Wisconsin Press, 2011); Randal S. Beeman and James A. Pritchard, *A Green and Permanent Land: Ecology and Agriculture in the Twentieth Century* (Lawrence: University of Kansas Press, 2001); Jason Michael Manthorne, "As You Sow: Culture, Agriculture, and the New Deal" (PhD diss., University of Georgia, 2013). For the few works that do acknowledge transnational exchanges but do not emphasize Mexico, see Patel, *The New Deal*; Daniel T. Rodgers, *Atlantic Crossings: Social Politics in a Progressive Age* (Cambridge, MA: Harvard University Press, 1998).

11. For examples of traditional diplomatic histories on the period, see Friedrich E. Schuler, *Mexico between Hitler and Roosevelt: Mexican Foreign Relations in the Age of Lázaro Cárdenas, 1934–1940* (Albuquerque: University of New Mexico Press, 1998); Stephen R. Niblo, *War, Diplomacy, and Development: The United States and Mexico, 1938–1945* (Wilmington, DE: Scholarly Resources Books, 1995). For a groundbreaking exception that explores how US agrarian sympathies enabled Mexican land redistribution, but does not attempt to explain how Mexican examples inspired US policies in the same period, see John J. Dwyer, *The Agrarian Dispute: The Expropriation of American-Owned Rural Land in Postrevolutionary Mexico* (Durham, NC: Duke University Press, 2008).

12. Two essays stand out in particular: Warren C. Whately, "Ejido or Private Property: Mexican and American Ways out of Rural Backwardness," *Agricultural History* 60 (Winter 1986): 50–61; Roger L. Ransom and Kerry Ann Odell, "Land and Credit: Some Historical Parallels between Mexico and the American South," *Agricultural History* 60 (Winter 1986): 4–31.

13. See, for example, Phillips, *This Land, This Nation*, 242–83; David Ekbladh, *The Great American Mission: Modernization and the Construction of an American World Order* (Princeton, NJ: Princeton University Press, 2010); Elizabeth Borgwardt, *A New Deal for the World: America's Vision for Human Rights* (Cambridge, MA: Harvard University Press, 2005); Daniel Immerwahr, *Thinking Small: The United States and the Lure of Community Development* (Cambridge, MA: Harvard University Press: 2015); Clifford Kuhn, *At the Crossroads: Arthur Raper, the South, and the World* (Chapel Hill: University of North Carolina Press, forthcoming).

14. I am not the first to distinguish between multiple rural New Deals. See, in particular, Gilbert, *Planning Democracy*; Phillips, *This Land, This Nation*; Mary Summers, "The New Deal Farm Programs: Looking for Reconstruction in American Agriculture," *Agricultural History* 74, no. 2 (2000): 241–57.

15. Gavin Wright, *Old South, New South: Revolutions in the Southern Economy since the Civil War* (Baton Rouge: Louisiana State University Press, 1986), 118.

16. On continuity and change in early twentieth-century sharecropping, see Charles S. Aiken, *The Cotton Plantation South since the Civil War* (Baltimore: Johns Hopkins University Press, 1998), chap. 2; Sven Beckert, *Empire of Cotton: A Global History* (New York: Alfred A. Knopf, 2014), chap. 10; Pete Daniel, *Breaking the Land: The Transformation of Cotton, Tobacco, and Rice Cultures since 1880* (Urbana: University of Illinois Press, 1985); Wright, *Old South, New*

South. On the out-migration of black southerners, see Isabel Wilkerson, *The Warmth of Other Suns: The Epic Story of America's Great Migration* (New York: Random House, 2010); James N. Gregory, *The Southern Diaspora: How the Great Migrations of Black and White Southerners Transformed America* (Chapel Hill: University of North Carolina Press, 2005); Alferdteen Harrison, ed., *Black Exodus: The Great Migration from the American South* (Jackson: University Press of Mississippi, 1991).

17. David E. Hamilton, *From New Day to New Deal: American Farm Policy from Hoover to Roosevelt, 1928–1933* (Chapel Hill: University of North Carolina Press, 1991).

18. Daniel, *Breaking the Land*, chap. 5; Conrad, *Forgotten Farmers*; Wright, *Old South, New South*.

19. Will W. Alexander to Stacy May, January 10, 1934, folder 3864, box 324, series 200, record group (hereafter RG) 1.1, Rockefeller Foundation Archives (hereafter RFA), Rockefeller Archive Center, Tarrytown, New York (hereafter RAC).

20. Edwin Embree to Edmund Day, November 2, 1933, and Norma Thompson to Will W. Alexander, January 25, 1934, both letters in folder 3864, box 324, series 200, RG 1.1, RFA, RAC. On Rosenwald schools, see Mary S. Hoffschwelle, *The Rosenwald Schools of the American South* (Gainesville: University Press of Florida, 2006).

21. On Embree's Mexican interests, see Edwin Embree to Dwight Morrow, May 1, 1928, folder 16, box 116, Julius Rosenwald Fund Papers, Special Collections and Archives, Franklin Library, Fisk University, Nashville, Tennessee. For a fuller examination of the US-Mexican dialogue on revolutionary education, see Flores, *Backroads Pragmatists*. Alexander and Embree each have useful biographies. See Wilma Dykeman and James Stokely, *Seeds of Southern Change: The Life of Will Alexander* (Chicago: University of Chicago Press, 1962); Alfred Perkins, *Edwin Rogers Embree: The Julius Rosenwald Fund, Foundation Philanthropy, and American Race Relations* (Bloomington: Indiana University Press, 2011). On networks of reformist southern liberals, see Patricia Sullivan, *Days of Hope: Race and Democracy in the New Deal Era* (Chapel Hill: University of North Carolina Press, 1996); John Egerton, *Speak Now against the Day: The Generation before the Civil Rights Movement in the South* (New York: Alfred A. Knopf, 1994).

22. On Peabody's Mexican career, see John Mason Hart, *Empire and Revolution: The Americans in Mexico since the Civil War* (Berkeley: University of California Press, 2002), 40, 52, 128, 137–38. On his philanthropic activities and early life, see Louise Ware, *George Foster Peabody: Banker, Philanthropist, Publicist* (Athens: University of Georgia Press, 1951). On Peabody's Warm Springs, Georgia, home and his Roosevelt connection, see ibid., 204–17, 230–49.

23. George Foster Peabody to Will W. Alexander, June 28, 1934, President's Personal File 660, Franklin D. Roosevelt Papers, Franklin Delano Roosevelt Presidential Library, Hyde Park, New York (hereafter Roosevelt Papers). Peabody sent this letter along to Roosevelt to let him know about the conference.

24. Evidence of Tannenbaum's attendance at Lake George is from his 1934 appointment book, July 28–30, box 57, Frank Tannenbaum Papers, Rare Book and Manuscript Library, Columbia University, New York (hereafter Tannenbaum Papers).

25. Frank Tannenbaum, *Darker Phases of the South* (New York: G. P. Putnam's, 1924). Most of the chapters of the book were first published in *Century Magazine* between April and December 1923. Tannenbaum is best known as a historian, and the most famous of his works is the classic comparative study *Slave and Citizen: The Negro in the Americas* (New York: Alfred A. Knopf, 1946). Several essays detail Tannenbaum's career from a number of angles, as either an activist or scholar, but none have fully captured his fascination with the US South or transna-

tional political activities in the 1930s. For the best analyses of his life and scholarship, see Elisa Servín, "Frank Tannenbaum entre América Latina y Estados Unidos en la Guerra Fría," *A Contra Corriente* 13, no. 3 (2016): 50–75, which primarily addresses the post-1945 years; Helen Delpar, "Frank Tannenbaum: The Making of a Mexicanist, 1914–1933," *The Americas* 45 (October 1988): 153–71; Jefferson R. Cowie, "The Emergence of Alternative Views of Latin America: The Thought of Three U.S. Intellectuals, 1920–1935," Duke-University of North Carolina Program in Latin American Studies Working Paper no. 3, Durham, 1992; Joseph Maier and Richard W. Weatherhead, *Frank Tannenbaum: A Biographical Essay* (New York: Columbia University Seminars, 1974); Virginia S. Williams, *Radical Journalists, Generalist Intellectuals, and U.S.-Latin American Relations* (Lewiston, NY: Edward Mellen, 2001), chap. 6; Alan Knight, "Frank Tannenbaum and the Mexican Revolution," *International Labor and Working-Class History* 77, no. 1 (Spring 2010): 134–53; Stephen J. Whitfield, "Out of Anarchism and into the Academy: The Many Lives of Frank Tannenbaum," *Journal for the Study of Radicalism* 7, no. 2 (2013): 93–124. On Tannenbaum's application to Amherst College, see W. H. Hamilton to Frank Tannenbaum, November 22, 1922, box 3, Tannenbaum Papers. Tannenbaum's country of birth is sometimes given as Poland; the confusion likely arises from two conflicting US passports, from 1933 (Austria) and 1938 (Poland), in box 57, Tannenbaum Papers.

26. Frank Tannenbaum, *The Mexican Agrarian Revolution* (Washington, DC: Robert Brookings Institution, 1929), 187, 404. On Tannenbaum's exchanges with Peabody during the writing of his thesis, see Frank Tannenbaum to George Foster Peabody, April 29, 1927, box 4, Tannenbaum Papers; Frank Tannenbaum to George Foster Peabody, June 26, 1929, folder 5, box 25, George Foster Peabody Papers, Library of Congress, Manuscript Division, Washington, DC (hereafter Peabody Papers).

27. Edwin Embree, "Schools in Mexico: A Report to the Trustees of the Julius Rosenwald Fund," July 6, 1928, folder 7, box 58, Julius Rosenwald Papers, Special Collections Research Center, University of Chicago Library, Chicago, Illinois; Flores, *Backroads Pragmatists*, 152–53.

28. Will W. Alexander, *Reminiscences of Will W. Alexander* (1952), Columbia University Oral History Research Office Collection, Rare Book and Manuscript Library, Columbia University, New York, 376–77.

29. Will W. Alexander to Stacy May, January 24, 1935, folder 3865, box 324, series 200, RG 1.1, RFA, RAC.

30. Alexander, *Reminiscences of Will W. Alexander*, 377. On the southern automobile tour, see Tannenbaum 1934 appointment book, December 5–21, box 57, Tannenbaum Papers.

31. Tannenbaum, *The Mexican Agrarian Revolution*, 189–90.

32. Frank Tannenbaum to Will W. Alexander, October 13, 1934, box 61, Tannenbaum Papers.

33. Edwin Embree to Frank Tannenbaum, October 25, 1934, box 25, Tannenbaum Papers.

34. Frank Tannenbaum, "A Program to Develop a New System of Rural Land Tenure," n.d. (written in late December 1934), folder 7, box 6, entry 177, RG 83: Records of the Bureau of Agricultural Economics, US National Archives and Records Administration II, College Park, Maryland (hereafter NA).

35. "Detailed Report on Expenditures, Committee on Negroes and Economic Reconstruction," February 2, 1935, folder 3865, box 324, series 200, RG 1.1, RFA, RAC.

36. Frank Tannenbaum to Will W. Alexander, December 26, 1934, box 61, Tannenbaum Papers. While Appleby's title of "assistant to the secretary" of the USDA may sound like a mere clerk, his job was an important formal position that placed him within the upper echelons of

218 • Notes to Pages 51–52

the policy making world in the USDA. On Davis and the evolving administration of the AAA, see Daniel, *Breaking the Land*, 100–106.

37. Frank Tannenbaum to Paul Appleby and Chester Davis, December 29, 1934, box 61, Tannenbaum Papers. On the early push to convince the USDA of the value of tenant legislation, see Baldwin, *Poverty and Politics*, chap. 5. Baldwin acknowledges the crucial role of Tannenbaum in these negotiations and that Tannenbaum had prior experience in Latin America, but he does not explore the extent to which Tannenbaum's understanding of Mexico shaped his vision of US agrarian reform.

38. Tannenbaum 1935 appointment book, January 8–9, box 57, Tannenbaum Papers. On Bankhead's background, see Baldwin, *Poverty and Politics*, 132–33; Jack Brien Key, "John H. Bankhead, Jr.: Creative Conservative" (PhD diss., Johns Hopkins University, 1964).

39. Will W. Alexander, Charles S. Johnson, Edwin Embree, and Frank Tannenbaum, "Rehomesteading on Small Farms (Especially Applicable to the Cotton States)," folder S.1800, box 2115, finding aid PI-191, entry 17-I, RG 16: Records of the Office of the Secretary of Agriculture, NA.

40. US Senate, Subcommittee on Agriculture and Forestry, 74 Cong., 1st Sess., *To Create the Farm Tenant Homes Corporation: Hearing on ... S.1800 ... , March 5, 1935* (Washington, DC: Government Printing Office, 1935), 1. See also "Bills and Joint Resolutions Introduced," S.1800, 74 Cong., 1st Sess., 79 Cong. Rec. (February 11, 1935), 1781–82.

41. Between the beginning of January and the end of April 1935, Tannenbaum had thirty separate meetings with the leadership of the USDA, such as Wallace, Bankhead, Wilson, Tugwell, Jerome Frank, Lewis C. Gray, and others. See entries in Tannenbaum's 1935 appointment book for January 8, 9, 11, 14, 15, 17, 18, 21, 25, 26, and 28, February 5, 7, 21, 25, and 27, March 4, 5, 6, 7, 12, 18, 19, 20, 25, 27, and 28, and April 11, 19, and 29, box 57, Tannenbaum Papers.

42. Frank Tannenbaum to the editor of the *New Republic*, April 22, 1935, box 25, Tannenbaum Papers, later published in part as Frank Tannenbaum, "More about the Bankhead Bill," *New Republic* 83, June 5, 1935, 104.

43. Will W. Alexander to George Foster Peabody, May 7, 1935, folder 2, box 47, Peabody Papers.

44. On contemporary US interest in northern European land programs, see Rodgers, *Atlantic Crossings*, chap. 8. In a published letter to the editor ("The Bankhead-Jones Bill," *Washington Post*, April 28, 1935, B7), Tannenbaum claimed that "Russia, Mexico and Spain" were inappropriate comparisons for the Bankhead bill, and that "the Irish land settlement acts and Denmark's conversion of a feudal into a democratic land system" were more apt. This was political theater, however. All the evidence presented above makes it clear that Mexico was Tannenbaum's primary source of inspiration, yet he knew the political dangers of such an acknowledgment in the public sphere.

45. Charles S. Johnson, Edwin R. Embree, and Will W. Alexander, *The Collapse of Cotton Tenancy: Summary of Field Studies and Statistical Surveys, 1933–35* (Chapel Hill: University of North Carolina Press, 1935), 64, 66, 69. For Tannenbaum's outline, see the untitled document beginning with "A series of tables, maps, and charts ... ," n.d., box 25, Tannenbaum Papers. This four-page outline, however rough, was kept intact for *The Collapse of Cotton Tenancy*.

46. Franklin D. Roosevelt cited in George Brown Tindall, *The Emergence of the New South, 1913–1945* (Baton Rouge: Louisiana State University Press, 1967), 416. On Eleanor Roosevelt's role, see Patrick J. Gilpin and Marybeth Gasman, *Charles S. Johnson: Leadership beyond the Veil in the Age of Jim Crow* (Albany: State University of New York Press, 2003), 110.

47. 74 Cong., 1st Sess., 79 Cong. Rec. (June 24, 1935), 9960.

48. Edwin Embree to Frank Tannenbaum, June 25, 1935, box 61, Tannenbaum Papers.

49. Frank Tannenbaum to George Foster Peabody, July 5, 1935, folder 5, box 48, Peabody Papers.

50. James G. Maddox, "The Bankhead-Jones Farm Tenant Act," *Law and Contemporary Problems* 4, no. 4 (1937): 434–55; Baldwin, *Poverty and Politics*, 150–54.

51. Will W. Alexander to Frank Tannenbaum, July 2, 1935, box 61, Tannenbaum Papers. For evidence of Alexander's offer to join the RA, see Will W. Alexander to Frank Tannenbaum, July 3, 1935, box 25, Tannenbaum Papers.

52. Frank Tannenbaum to George Foster Peabody, July 5, 1935, folder 5, box 48, Peabody Papers; George Foster Peabody to Franklin D. Roosevelt, September 15, 1935, President's Personal File 660, Roosevelt Papers.

53. Dykeman and Stokely, *Seeds of Southern Change*, 217–19, 221–23.

54. Frank Tannenbaum to Will W. Alexander, February 28, 1936, box 25, Tannenbaum Papers.

55. Frank Tannenbaum to John Bankhead, February 28, 1936, box 61, Tannenbaum Papers.

56. Gilbert Joseph and Jürgen Buchenau, *Mexico's Once and Future Revolution: Social Upheaval and the Challenge of Rule since the Late Nineteenth Century* (Durham, NC: Duke University Press, 2013), chap. 6. On the contested historiography of Cardenismo, see the following chapter.

57. David M. Kennedy, *Freedom from Fear: The American People in Depression and War, 1929–1945* (New York: Oxford University Press, 1999), 284–87; William E. Leuchtenburg, *Franklin D. Roosevelt and the New Deal, 1932–1940* (New York: Harper and Row, 1963), 190–96.

58. Henry A. Wallace, "The Secretary of Agriculture on Rural Poverty, 1937," in *Agriculture in the United States: A Documentary History*, ed. Wayne D. Rasmussen (New York: Greenwood Press, 1975), 3:2845. See also Henry A. Wallace, "Rural Poverty," January 23, 1937, folder 3, box 2640, entry 17-I, finding aid PI-191, RG 16, NA.

59. For the most influential scholarly works of the mid-1930s on southern rural life and tenancy, see Rupert B. Vance, *Human Geography of the South: A Study in Regional Resources and Human Adequacy* (Chapel Hill: University of North Carolina Press, 1932); Rupert B. Vance, *How the Other Half Is Housed: A Pictorial Record of Sub-Minimum Farm Housing in the South* (Chapel Hill: University of North Carolina Press, 1936); Arthur F. Raper, *Preface to Peasantry: A Tale of Two Black Belt Counties* (Chapel Hill: University of North Carolina Press, 1936); Charles S. Johnson, *Shadow of the Plantation* (Chicago: University of Chicago Press, 1934); Howard W. Odum, *Southern Regions of the United States* (Chapel Hill: University of North Carolina Press, 1936). On the impact of these books on the political climate of the day, see Manthorne, "As You Sow," especially chap. 4; George B. Tindall, "The Significance of Howard W. Odum to Southern History: A Preliminary Estimate," *Journal of Southern History* 24 (August 1958): 285–307.

60. On the transition from the Resettlement Administration to the FSA and the shuffling of personnel, see Roberts, The *Farm Security Administration and Rural Rehabilitation in the South*, 66–76; Dykeman and Stokely, *Seeds of Southern Change*, 221–23; Baldwin, *Poverty and Politics*, 120–23, 187–92.

61. Franklin D. Roosevelt to Henry A. Wallace, November 16, 1936, folder 1, box 2439, entry 17-I, finding aid PI-191, RG 16, NA. Roosevelt's turn toward tenancy was part of a larger emphasis on southern poverty and problems; see Bruce J. Schulman, *From Cotton Belt to Sunbelt:*

Federal Policy, Economic Development, and the Transformation of the South, 1938–1980 (New York: Oxford University Press, 1991), especially chap. 1.

62. Jess Gilbert, "Agrarian Intellectuals in a Democratizing State: A Collective Biography of USDA Leaders in the Intended New Deal," in *The Countryside in the Age of the Modern State: Political Histories of Rural America*, ed. Catherine McNicol Stock and Robert D. Johnston (Ithaca, NY: Cornell University Press, 2001), 233.

63. President's Committee on Farm Tenancy, *Farm Tenancy: Report of the President's Committee* (Washington, DC: Government Printing Office, 1937), 85.

64. Will W. Alexander to Frank Tannenbaum, February 26, 1937, folder AD-2T, box 14, entry 1, finding aid PI-118, RG 96: Records of the Farmers Home Administration and Its Predecessors, NA.

65. Bankhead-Jones Farm Tenant Act, 50 Stat. 522 (July 22, 1937). Admittedly, for the purposes of brevity, I am simplifying the legislative process that resulted in the passage of the Bankhead-Jones bill. For an exhaustive discussion of the months of political negotiation that gave birth to the 1937 Bankhead-Jones law, see Baldwin, *Poverty and Politics*, chaps. 5–6.

66. On the early operation of the FSA, see ibid., chap. 7.

67. Will W. Alexander to Frank Tannenbaum, July 15, 1937, box 61, Tannenbaum Papers.

68. "La situación del campesino norteamericano," *El Nacional*, July 24, 1937, clipping in box 12, Ramón Fernández y Fernández Papers, Biblioteca Luis González, Colegio de Michoacán, Zamora, Michoacán, Mexico. I choose not to translate the word "campesino" here because its use in reference to US agriculture is rather unusual. *Agricultor* or *aparcero*, meaning farmer and sharecropper, respectively, would be more expected.

69. Francisco Castillo Nájera, "Informe Reglamentario del C. Embajador de México en Washington, DC sobre el programa agrario del President Roosevelt," March 15, 1937, 31–24–8, AHSRE.

70. Rexford Tugwell to Franklin D. Roosevelt, August 26, 1937, President's Personal File 564, Roosevelt Papers.

71. Gilbert, "Agrarian Intellectuals in a Democratizing State," 231; Clifford M. Kuhn, "'It Was a Long Way from Perfect, but It Was Working': The Canning and Home Production Initiatives in Greene County, Georgia, 1940–1942," *Agricultural History* 86, no. 2 (Spring 2012): 69. See also Summers, "New Deal Farm Programs." On southern planters' bitter opposition toward the FSA, see Baldwin, *Poverty and Politics*, 262–94.

72. Courtenay Dinwiddie to Marte R. Gómez, April 17, 1942, Cartas, 1941, I-P, Marte R. Gómez Papers, Archivo Marte R. Gómez, Lomas de Chapultepec, Mexico City (hereafter Gómez Papers).

73. C. B. Baldwin, "Recommendations for Assistance to Central America, Panama, and Mexico," April 18, 1942, folder titled "AD-070, General," box 38, entry 2, finding aid PI-118, RG 96, NA.

74. Charles Kenneth Roberts, "Client Failures and Supervised Credit in the Farm Security Administration," *Agricultural History* 87 (Summer 2013): 368–90; Manthorne, "As You Sow," chaps. 4–6 (quotation in title of chap. 4). On the racial politics of eviction and access to FSA programs, see Jane Adams and D. Gorton, "This Land Ain't My Land: The Eviction of Sharecroppers by the Farm Security Administration," *Agricultural History* 83, no. 3 (Summer 2009): 323–51. For evidence of the limited impact of the FSA, see Manthorne, "As You Sow"; Neil Foley, *The White Scourge: Mexicans, Blacks, and Poor Whites in Texas Cotton Culture* (Berkeley: University of California Press, 1997), 181–82.

75. Quoted in Roberts, *The Farm Security Administration and Rural Rehabilitation in the South*, 194.

76. Pete Daniel, *Dispossession: Discrimination against African American Farmers in the Age of Civil Rights* (Chapel Hill: University of North Carolina Press, 2013), 76; Spencer D. Wood, "The Roots of Black Power: Land, Civil Society, and the State in the Mississippi Delta, 1935–1968" (PhD diss., University of Wisconsin at Madison, 2006).

77. See Jason Manthorne, "The View from the Cotton: Reconsidering the Southern Tenant Farmers' Union," *Agricultural History* 84, no. 1 (2010): 20–45; Donald Grubbs, *Cry from the Cotton: The Southern Tenant Farmers' Union and the New Deal* (Chapel Hill: University of North Carolina Press, 1971); Jack Temple Kirby, *Rural Worlds Lost: The American South, 1920–1960* (Baton Rouge: Louisiana State University Press, 1987), 259–71.

78. Clarence Senior to H. L. Mitchell, December 9, 1936, reel 3, Southern Tenant Farmers' Union Papers (microfilm), Southern Historical Collection, University of North Carolina at Chapel Hill (hereafter STFU Papers).

79. H. L. Mitchell to Clarence Senior, December 11, 1936, reel 3, STFU Papers. On the politics of land reform and agricultural development in La Laguna, see, in particular, Mikael Wolfe, *Watering the Revolution: An Environmental and Technological History of Agrarian Reform in Mexico* (Durham, NC: Duke University Press, 2017), chap. 1; Manuel Plana, "La cuestión agraria en la Laguna durante la revolución," *Historia Mexicana* 50, no. 1 (2000): 57–90; Jocelyn Olcott, *Revolutionary Women in Postrevolutionary Mexico* (Durham, NC: Duke University Press, 2005), 123–29; Deborah Cohen, *Braceros: Migrant Citizens and Transnational Subjects in the Postwar United States and Mexico* (Chapel Hill: University of North Carolina Press, 2011), 37–38.

80. Clarence Senior to H. L. Mitchell, December 14, 1936, reel 3, STFU Papers.

81. H. L. Mitchell to Clarence Senior, December 16, 1936, reel 3, STFU Papers. For Mitchell's letter to the Mexican labor organizers, see H. L. Mitchell to the "Federación De Trabajadores De La Region Lagunera" [*sic*], December 16, 1936, reel 3, STFU Papers.

82. On the historical geography of La Laguna, see Wolfe, *Watering the Revolution*. On the failed attempt to colonize the region with black labor, see Karl Jacoby, *The Strange Career of William Ellis: The Texas Slave Who Became a Mexican Millionaire* (New York: W. W. Norton, 2016), chap. 4. On the slogan "haciendas sin hacendados," see Alan Knight, "Mexico c. 1930–1946," in *The Cambridge History of Latin America, Volume II: Latin America since 1930, Mexico, Central America, and the Caribbean*, ed. Leslie Bethell (New York: Cambridge University Press, 1990), 24.

83. Clarence Senior to J. R. Butler, May 23, 1939, reel 11, STFU Papers.

84. Clarence Senior to Lázaro Cárdenas, June 3, 1938, 433/296, Lázaro Cárdenas del Río Papers, Archivo General de la Nación, Mexico City (hereafter Cárdenas Papers).

85. Clarence Senior, "Memo on Suggested Conference on the Cotton Labor Problem," February 27, 1939, reel 10, STFU Papers. For the invitation to the FSA staff, see H. R. to D. A. Young, June 16, 1939, folder titled "AD-070, Mexico," box 38, finding aid PI-118, entry 2, RG 96, NA.

86. H. L. Mitchell and Farish Betton, "Land and Liberty for Mexican Farmers," July 1939, reel 12, STFU Papers.

87. Carlos M. Peralta to Lázaro Cárdenas, December 13, 1939, and "Tierra y libertad para los campesinos mexicanos," July 1939, both in 404.1/706, Cárdenas Papers.

88. H. L. Mitchell and Farish Betton, "Land and Liberty for Mexican Farmers," July 1939, reel 12, STFU Papers.

89. Clarence Senior, *Democracy Comes to a Cotton Kingdom: The Story of Mexico's La Laguna* (Mexico City: Centro de Estudios Pedagógicos e Hispanoamericanos, 1940), 45.

90. Wolfe, *Watering the Revolution*, chap. 6 and epilogue.

91. Adam Cohen, *Nothing to Fear: FDR's Inner Circle and the Hundred Days That Created Modern America* (New York: Penguin, 2009).

92. See Kirkendall, *Social Scientists and Farm Politics in the Age of Roosevelt*; Saloutos, *The American Farmer and the New Deal*; Phillips, *This Land, This Nation*; Gilbert, *Planning Democracy*.

93. On Tugwell's early career and political philosophy, see Michael Namorato, *Rexford G. Tugwell: A Biography* (New York: Praeger, 1988); Bernard Sternsher, *Rexford Tugwell and the New Deal* (New Brunswick, NJ: Rutgers University Press, 1964); Gilbert, *Planning Democracy*, chap. 4.

94. Henry A. Wallace to Cordell Hull, September 25, 1935, folder 1, box 2170, finding aid PI-191, entry 17-I, RG 16, NA.

95. Josephus Daniels to Rexford Tugwell, November 6, 1935, General Correspondence, reel 64, Josephus Daniels Papers, Library of Congress, Manuscript Division, Washington, DC (hereafter Daniels Papers).

96. Francisco Castillo Nájera to the Secretaría de Relaciones Exteriores, September 27, 1935, III–313–11, AHSRE.

97. Rexford Tugwell to Josephus Daniels, September 27, 1935, General Correspondence, reel 64, Daniels Papers.

98. Daniels diary entry, October 11, 1935, Diaries, reel 6, Daniels Papers.

99. Josephus Daniels to Henry A. Wallace, October 11, 1935, Special Correspondence, reel 63, Daniels Papers.

100. Rexford Tugwell to Henry A. Wallace, August 31, 1937, folder titled "AD-070 Mexico," box 6, finding aid PI-118, entry 1, RG 96, NA.

101. Rexford Tugwell to Franklin D. Roosevelt, August 26, 1937, President's Personal File 564, Roosevelt Papers.

102. See Rexford Tugwell, *The Stricken Land: The Story of Puerto Rico* (New York: Doubleday, 1946); Michael Janeway, "The Wartime Quartet: Muñoz Marín, Tugwell, Ickes, and FDR," in *Island at War: Puerto Rico in the Crucible of the Second World War*, ed. Jorge Rodríguez Beruff and José L. Bolívar Fresneda (Jackson: University Press of Mississippi, 2015).

103. For a sympathetic portrayal of Wilson's career, see Gilbert, *Planning Democracy*.

104. Donald Blaisdell to Pedro d'Alba, December 3, 1938, folder 1, box 2789, finding aid PI-191, entry 17-J, RG 16, NA.

105. "México expuso su programa agrícola al subsecretario Wilson, de Estados Unidos," *Excélsior*, December 20, 1938, clipping from Pierre de L. Boal to Donald Blaisdell, March 6, 1939, folder 2, box 3048F, finding aid PI-191, entry 17-J, RG 16, NA.

106. On Wilson and Parrés's conversations, see Pierre de L. Boal to Cordell Hull, January 6, 1939, folder 2, box 145, 102.7502/93, RG 59: Records of the State Department, NA.

107. M. L. Wilson to A. C. Baker, January 10, 1939, folder 3, box 3121, finding aid PI-191, entry 17-J, RG 16, NA.

108. M. L. Wilson to José Figueroa, January 12, 1939, folder 1, box 3122, finding aid PI-191, entry 17-J, RG 16, NA.

109. M. L. Wilson to Dr. and Mrs. W. E. Stone, January 10, 1939, folder 1, box 3122, finding aid PI-191, entry 17-J, RG 16, NA.

110. On Wilson's push to start a program of mutual cooperation, see Laurence Duggan to Cordell Hull, May 3, 1939, folder 3, box 5189, 811.61212/233, RG 59, NA; Donald Blaisdell to Laurence Duggan, May 5, 1939, folder 3, box 5189, 811.61212/234, RG 59, NA.

111. Gilbert, *Planning Democracy*, 9.

112. On the planned Cárdenas visit, see Frank Tannenbaum to M. L. Wilson, August 6, 1942, box 17, Tannenbaum Papers; M. L. Wilson to Paul Appleby, August 12, 1942, folder 7, box 746, finding aid PI-191, entry 17-M, RG 16, NA. Cárdenas postponed and ultimately declined the invitation; he would only travel to the United States in 1959.

113. On Wilson's postwar global career, see Phillips, *This Land, This Nation*, 250–51; Immerwahr, *Thinking Small*; Gilbert, *Planning Democracy*, 260.

114. Wallace's life has been chronicled by a number of scholars: see, in particular, John C. Culver and John Hyde, *American Dreamer: The Life and Times of Henry A. Wallace* (New York: W. W. Norton, 2000); Edward L. and Frederick H. Schapsmeier, *Henry A. Wallace of Iowa: The Agrarian Years, 1910–1940* (Ames: Iowa State University Press, 1968); Edward L. and Frederick H. Schapsmeier, *Prophet in Politics: Henry A. Wallace and the War Years, 1940–1965* (Ames: Iowa State University Press, 1970); Russell Lord, *The Wallaces of Iowa* (Boston: Houghton Mifflin, 1947); Gilbert, *Planning Democracy*.

115. Henry A. Wallace, "Farmers and Machines," Henry A. Wallace Papers, University of Iowa microfilm, reel 22, Library of Congress, Manuscript Division, Washington, DC (hereafter Wallace Papers). On Wallace's role in the rural New Deal and his political evolution, see Saloutos, *The American Farmer and the New Deal*. For a revisionist interpretation, see Summers, "New Deal Farm Programs." On his southern tours, see Gilbert, *Planning Democracy*, 90–91.

116. Henry A. Wallace to Will W. Alexander, August 31, 1937, folder titled "AD-070, Mexico," box 6, finding aid PI-118, entry 1, RG 96, NA.

117. On the regular luncheons, see Henry A. Wallace to Vincenzo Petrullo, July 26, 1939, folder 5, box 3088, finding aid PI-191, entry 17-J, RG 16, NA. On Wallace's growing skills in Spanish, see Culver and Hyde, *American Dreamer*, 246.

118. On the transition from Cárdenas to Ávila Camacho and the 1940 election, see Friedrich Schuler, *Mexico between Hitler and Roosevelt: Mexican Foreign Relations in the Age of Lázaro Cárdenas, 1934–1940* (Albuquerque: University of New Mexico Press, 1998), chap. 8; Alan Knight, "The End of the Mexican Revolution? From Cárdenas to Ávila Camacho, 1937–1941," in *Dictablanda: Politics, Work, and Culture in Mexico, 1938–1968*, ed. Paul Gillingham and Benjamin T. Smith (Durham, NC: Duke University Press, 2014).

119. On the political struggle for the 1940 nomination, see Kennedy, *Freedom from Fear*, 456–57; Culver and Hyde, *American Dreamer*, chap. 11.

120. "A New Era of Friendship Dawns in United States—Mexico Relations," December 1, 1940, *Washington Post*, B5. On Wallace's decision to travel to Latin America during his break from politics, see Culver and Hyde, *American Dreamer*, chap. 13.

121. Josephus Daniels to Cordell Hull, December 3, 1940, folder 2, box 4112, 812.001 Camacho, Manuel A/122A, RG 59, NA.

122. Department of State memorandum on US visitors, December 5, 1940, folder 3, box 4112, 812.001 Camacho, Manuel A/122A, RG 59, NA.

123. On Tannenbaum's participation, see Tannenbaum diary entry, December 2, 1940, box 57, Tannenbaum Papers; Josephus Daniels appointment notes, December 2, 1940, Diaries, reel 7, Daniels Papers. On the friendship between Cárdenas and Tannenbaum, see Frank Tannenbaum, "Cárdenas: That Is the Way He Is," *Survey Graphic*, August 1937, 425–27.

124. On "El canción del ejido," see Josephus Daniels, "Revised Outline of Activities of Special Mission," November 30, 1940, folder 8, box 28, Josephus Daniels Papers, Duke University Rare Book, Manuscript, and Special Collections Library, Durham, North Carolina.

125. Henry A. Wallace, "Land Hunger in Mexico," *Wallaces' Farmer and Iowa Homestead*, March 22, 1941, 5; Henry A. Wallace, "Wallace in Mexico: Corn Growing South of the Border," *Wallaces' Farmer and Iowa Homestead*, February 22, 1941, 10.

126. Henry A. Wallace to Cordell Hull, December 16, 1940, reel 22, Wallace Papers.

127. Henry A. Wallace to Josephus Daniels, May 3, 1943, Special Correspondence, reel 64, Daniels Papers. As an example of Wallace's Latin American popularity, in 1948 dozens of prominent leftists in Mexico formed clubs to support his presidential run; see "Estudiantes, obreros y profesionales forman la Sociedad 'Amigos de Wallace,'" *Excélsior*, April 13, 1948, file N22418, Archivos Económicos, Biblioteca Miguel Lerdo de Tejada, Mexico City. On Wallace's global stance during his vice presidency and after, see Thomas W. Devine, *Henry Wallace's 1948 Presidential Campaign and the Future of Postwar Liberalism* (Chapel Hill: University of North Carolina Press, 2013); Graham White and John Maze, *Henry A. Wallace: His Search for a New World Order* (Chapel Hill: University of North Carolina Press, 1995); Culver and Hyde, *American Dreamer*, chaps. 15–16.

128. See the following sources for evidence of such pilgrimages. On Ezekiel of the USDA, see Mordecai Ezekiel to Josephus Daniels, September 27, 1937, General Correspondence, reel 70, Daniels Papers. On Wickard of the USDA, see Diary, July 5–22, 1942, box 20, Claude Wickard Papers, Franklin Delano Roosevelt Presidential Library, Hyde Park, New York. On Appleby of the USDA, see Henry A. Wallace to Cordell Hull, September 25, 1935, folder 1, box 2170, finding aid PI-191, entry 17-I, RG 16, NA. On Littell of the Justice Department's Lands Division, see Norman Littell to Marte R. Gómez, January 2, 1941, Cartas, 1941, I-P, Gómez Papers. On Bennett of the Soil Conservation Service, see George Messersmith to Henry A. Wallace, July 16, 1942, reel 23, Wallace Papers. On Collier of the Bureau of Indian Affairs, see Ahlstedt, "John Collier and Mexico in the Shaping of U.S. Indian Policy."

129. Delpar, *The Enormous Vogue of Things Mexican*, 55.

130. Phillips, *This Land, This Nation*, 242–83; Immerwahr, *Thinking Small*; Kuhn, *At the Crossroads*.

CHAPTER THREE: HACIENDAS AND PLANTATIONS

1. Adolfo Ruiz Cortines, "El 'Nuevo Trato' del Presidente Cárdenas," *El Universal*, July 15, 1938, file J03054, Archivos Económicos, Biblioteca Miguel Lerdo de Tejada, Mexico City. On Ruiz Cortines's political career, see Roderic Ai Camp, *Mexican Political Biographies, 1935–2009*, 4th ed. (Austin: University of Texas Press, 2011), 851–52.

2. Scholarship on the Cárdenas era can be grouped into three basic schools. The orthodox view, pioneered by early scholars such as Tannenbaum, saw Cárdenas as the popular fulfillment of Zapata and Villa's struggle for social justice that had been subdued during the 1920s. See, for example, Frank Tannenbaum, *Mexico: The Struggle for Peace and Bread* (New York: Alfred A. Knopf, 1950); Tzvi Medin, *Ideología y praxis de Lázaro Cárdenas* (Mexico City: Siglo Veintiuno Editores, 1972). Revisionist historians, on the other hand, suspicious of the state after the 1968 Tlatelolco massacre, dismissed Cárdenas as a pawn of a centralizing corporatist state that favored capitalist development over fair distribution. For the most prominent examples, see Arnaldo Córdova, *La política de masas del cardenismo* (Mexico City: Ediciones Era, 1974); Arturo Anguiano, *El estado y la política obrera del cardenismo* (Mexico City: Ediciones Era, 1975); Nora Hamilton, *The Limits of State Autonomy: Post-Revolutionary Mexico* (Princeton, NJ: Prince-

ton University Press, 1982). Yet both the orthodox and revisionist schools were largely focused on Mexico City, and looked to elite state actors as the agents of either salvation or betrayal. The postrevisionist school, which remains dominant today, has abandoned the romanticism of the orthodox school, but remains committed to the unprecedented and popular nature of 1930s' politics. Highlighting regional variegation, grassroots participation, and cultural politics, recent works have produced a more balanced and complex understanding of the era. See, in particular, Adrian A. Bantjes, *As If Jesus Walked on Earth: Cardenismo, Sonora, and the Mexican Revolution* (Wilmington, DE: Scholarly Resources Books, 1998); Adolfo Gilly, *El cardenismo, una utopía mexicana* (Mexico City: Cal y Arena, 1994); Jennie Purnell, *Popular Movements and State Formation in Revolutionary Mexico: The Agraristas and Cristeros of Michoacán* (Durham, NC: Duke University Press, 1999); Christopher R. Boyer, *Becoming Campesinos: Politics, Identity, and Agrarian Struggle in Postrevolutionary Michoacán, 1920–1935* (Stanford, CA: Stanford University Press, 2003); Raquel Sosa Elízaga, *Los códigos ocultos del cardenismo: Un estudio de la violencia política, el cambio social y la continuidad nacional* (Mexico City: Universidad Nacional Autónoma de México and Plaza y Valdés, 1996); Mary Kay Vaughan, *Cultural Politics in Revolution: Teachers, Peasants, and Schools in Mexico, 1930–1940* (Tucson: University of Arizona Press, 1997); Marjorie Becker, *Setting the Virgin on Fire: Lázaro Cárdenas, Michoacán Peasants, and the Redemption of the Mexican Revolution* (Berkeley: University of California Press, 1995); Jocelyn Olcott, *Revolutionary Women in Postrevolutionary Mexico* (Durham, NC: Duke University Press, 2005); Ben Fallaw, *Cárdenas Compromised: The Failure of Reform in Postrevolutionary Yucatán* (Durham, NC: Duke University Press, 2001). For historiographical overviews of the scholarly battle to define Cardenismo, see Luis Anaya Merchant, "El cardenismo en la Revolución Mexicana: Conflicto y competencia en una historiografía viva," *Historia Mexicana* 60, no. 2 (2010): 1281–355; Alan Knight, "Cardenismo: Juggernaut or Jalopy?" *Journal of Latin American Studies* 26 (February 1994): 73–107.

3. On international Marxist networks, see Barry Carr, *Marxism and Communism in Twentieth-Century Mexico* (Lincoln: University of Nebraska Press, 1992); Daniela Spenser, *The Impossible Triangle: Mexico, Soviet Russia, and the United States in the 1920s* (Durham, NC: Duke University Press, 1999); Friedrich Katz, *The Secret War in Mexico: Europe, the United States, and the Mexican Revolution* (Chicago: University of Chicago Press, 1981). On the Mexican state and world economic depression, see Friedrich Schuler, *Mexico between Hitler and Roosevelt: Mexican Foreign Relations in the Age of Lázaro Cárdenas, 1934–1940* (Albuquerque: University of New Mexico Press, 1998); Alan Knight, "The Character and Consequences of the Great Depression in Mexico," in *The Great Depression in Latin America*, ed. Paulo Drinot and Alan Knight (Durham, NC: Duke University Press, 2014). On Mexico promoting its reforms as a model, see Amelia Kiddle, *Mexico's Relations with Latin America during the Cárdenas Era* (Albuquerque: University of New Mexico Press, 2016).

4. For an excellent primary exception, see John J. Dwyer, *The Agrarian Dispute: The Expropriation of American-Owned Rural Land in Postrevolutionary Mexico* (Durham, NC: Duke University Press, 2008), which examines US-Mexican diplomatic negotiations over land in the 1930s, but explores neither the impact of Mexican land reform on the New Deal nor the extensive influence of US agrarian experimentation on Mexico. For a consideration of Soviet Marxism's influence on agrarismo in La Laguna, see Carr, *Marxism and Communism in Twentieth-Century Mexico*, especially chap. 3. For an examination of irrigation from a similar angle, see Luis Aboites Aguilar, "The Transnational Dimensions of Mexican Irrigation, 1900–1950," *Journal of Political Ecology* 19 (2012): 70–80.

5. Knight, "The Character and Consequences of the Great Depression in Mexico," 225.

6. On the evolving agenda of Cárdenas's agrarian program, see Joseph Cotter, *Troubled Harvest: Agronomy and Revolution in Mexico, 1880–2002* (Westport, CT: Praeger, 2003), chap. 4; Mikael D. Wolfe, *Watering the Revolution: An Environmental and Technological History of Agrarian Reform in Mexico* (Durham, NC: Duke University Press, 2017); Nicole Mottier, "Ejidal Credit and Debt in Twentieth-Century Mexico" (PhD diss., University of Chicago, 2013); Christopher R. Boyer and Emily Wakild, "Social Landscaping in the Forests of Mexico: An Environmental Interpretation of Cardenismo, 1934–1940," *Hispanic American Historical Review* 92 (February 2012): 73–106; Gladys McCormick, *The Logic of Compromise in Mexico: How the Countryside Was Key to the Emergence of Authoritarianism* (Chapel Hill: University of North Carolina Press, 2016), chap. 1.

7. See, in particular, Ruben Flores, *Backroads Pragmatists: Mexico's Melting Pot and Civil Rights in the United States* (Philadelphia: University of Pennsylvania Press, 2014); Mauricio Tenorio Trillo, "Stereophonic Social Modernisms: Social Science between Mexico and the United States, 1880s–1930s," *Journal of American History* 86, no. 3 (1999): 1156–87; Jesus Velasco, "Reading Mexico, Understanding the United States: American Transnational Intellectuals in the 1920s and 1990s," *Journal of American History* 86, no. 2 (1999): 641–67.

8. On US-Mexican exchanges in the field of agricultural science before the 1930s, see Adolfo Olea-Franco, "One Century of Higher Agricultural Education and Research in Mexico (1850s–1960s), with a Preliminary Survey on the Same Subjects in the United States" (PhD diss., Harvard University, 2001); Cotter, *Troubled Harvest*.

9. Executive Committee of the Liga Nacional Campesina to Josephus Daniels, October 6, 1936, President's Personal File 86, Franklin D. Roosevelt Papers, Franklin Delano Roosevelt Presidential Library, Hyde Park, New York (hereafter Roosevelt Papers). "Peasant" is an imperfect translation of "campesino," which grows out of a Latin American context rather than a European one, but for the sake of convenience it will be used throughout.

10. Daniels diary entry, October 10, 1936, Diaries, reel 6, Josephus Daniels Papers, Library of Congress, Manuscript Division, Washington, DC (hereafter Daniels Papers).

11. Pedro de Alba to José Parrés, December 5, 1938, folder 1, box 2789, finding aid PI-191, entry 17-J, record group (hereafter RG) 16: Records of the Office of the Secretary of Agriculture, US National Archives and Records Administration II, College Park, Maryland (hereafter NA).

12. Francisco Castillo Nájera, "Datos sobre altos funcionarios del Gobierno Americano," March 11, 1938, 30–3–10, Archivo Histórico de la Secretaría de Relaciones Exteriores, Tlatelolco, Mexico City (hereafter AHSRE).

13. Fernando Foglio Miramontes to M. L. Wilson, January 21, 1939, folder 1, box 3122, finding aid PI-191, entry 17-J, RG 16, NA.

14. Alfredo Carduño Pombo to Alanís Patiño, August 18, 1935, III–63–2, AHSRE; Victor José Moya to the Bureau of Agricultural Economics, January 28, 1939, folder 9, box 454, finding aid PI-104, entry 19-B, RG 83: Records of the Bureau of Agricultural Economics, NA.

15. This quotation is from an early 1950s' interview Cárdenas gave to sympathetic US social scientists; see Henrik Infield and Koka Freier, *People in Ejidos: A Visit to the Cooperative Farms of Mexico* (New York: Frederick A. Praeger, 1954), 149.

16. Francisco Castillo Nájera to Will W. Alexander, December 23, 1937, III–72–1, AHSRE; C. B. Baldwin to Gonzalo Blanco Macías, June 2, 1941, folder titled "AD-070, Mexico," box 38, finding aid PI-118, entry 2, RG 96: Records of the Farmers Home Administration and Its Predecessors, NA.

17. Gilberto Flores Muñoz, *The New Deal and the Six Year Plan* (Mexico City: Publicaciones de la Secretaría de Acción Educativa del P.N.R., 1937), 6, 5, 4, 9. For information on Flores Muñoz's political appointments, see Camp, *Mexican Political Biographies*, 324.

18. On La Laguna's land reform, see Wolfe, *Watering the Revolution*; Olcott, *Revolutionary Women in Postrevolutionary Mexico*; Carr, *Marxism and Communism in Twentieth-Century Mexico*, chap. 3. The place of nationalism in the Mexican Revolution and its aftermath has been one of the most hotly debated questions in the historiography; for two diverging explanations, see Alan Knight, *The Mexican Revolution*, 2 vols. (New York: Cambridge University Press, 1986); John Mason Hart, *Revolutionary Mexico: The Coming and Process of the Mexican Revolution* (Berkeley: University of California Press, 1987).

19. Josephus Daniels to E. S. Askew, March 23, 1937, folder 1, box 648, Subject File—Mexico, Daniels Papers; Pierre de L. Boal to Josephus Daniels, December 23, 1936, folder 3, box 649, Special Correspondence, Daniels Papers.

20. Josephus Daniels to John Kerr, May 15, 1937, folder 1, box 648, Subject File—Mexico, Daniels Papers.

21. Ibid.

22. Josephus Daniels to Henry A. Wallace, December 28, 1936, Special Correspondence, reel 63, Daniels Papers.

23. For a summary of Daniels's exchange with Wallace, see Josephus Daniels to John Kerr, May 15, 1937, folder 1, box 648, Subject File—Mexico, Daniels Papers.

24. Suárez interviewed the USDA's Charles M. Davis in Mexico City; for details, see Josephus Daniels to John Kerr, March 23, 1937, folder 1, box 648, Subject File—Mexico, Daniels Papers. In Washington during April 1937, the Mexican minister met with Walter Packard and Van Buren Sharpe of the Resettlement Administration (the former was director of rural resettlement, and the latter was a candidate for the Mexican post); for details on the visit, see "Informe Reglamentario del C. Embajador de México en Washington, D.C. sobre funcionarios mexicanos que visitaron Washington," May 15, 1937, 31–42–8, AHSRE; John Kerr to Josephus Daniels, May 3, 1937, folder 1, box 648, Subject File—Mexico, Daniels Papers.

25. On the salary for the Resettlement Administration's candidate, see Van Buren Sharpe to Josephus Daniels, May 1, 1937, folder 1, box 648, Subject File—Mexico, Daniels Papers.

26. On Ezekiel's career, see Jess Gilbert, *Planning Democracy: Agrarian Intellectuals and the Intended New Deal* (New Haven, CT: Yale University Press, 2015); Richard S. Kirkendall, *Social Scientists and Farm Politics in the Age of Roosevelt* (Columbia: University of Missouri Press, 1966), especially 127, 152.

27. Mordecai Ezekiel to Josephus Daniels, November 17, 1937, General Correspondence, reel 70, Daniels Papers.

28. Mordecai Ezekiel to Josephus Daniels, June 6, 1938, General Correspondence, reel 71, Daniels Papers.

29. Henry A. Wallace to Josephus Daniels, July 14, 1938, folder titled "AD-070, Mexico," box 6, finding aid PI-118, entry 1, RG 96, NA.

30. Josephus Daniels to Henry A. Wallace, July 7, 1938, Special Correspondence, reel 63, Daniels Papers.

31. On Packard's selection, see Milo Perkins to Roy Hendrickson, July 18, 1938, folder titled "AD-070, Mexico," box 6, finding aid PI-118, entry 1, RG 96, NA; Josephus Daniels to Walter E. Packard, July 13, 1938, folder 52, box 14, Walter E. Packard Papers, Bancroft Library, University of California, Berkeley (hereafter Packard Papers).

32. Walter E. Packard, "The Agrarian Movement in Mexico," November 25, 1926, folder 3, box 7, Packard Papers.

33. Diego Rivera to Marte R. Gómez, March 31, 1941, Cartas, 1941, Q-Z, Marte R. Gómez Papers, Archivo Marte R. Gómez, Lomas de Chapultepec, Mexico City (hereafter Gómez Papers).

34. On the role of US technical advisers in La Laguna, see Aboites Aguilar, "The Transnational Dimensions of Mexican Irrigation"; Mikael Wolfe, "Bringing the Revolution to the Dam Site: How Technology, Labor, and Nature Converged in the Microcosm of a Northern Mexican Company Town, 1936–1946," *Journal of the Southwest* 53, no. 1 (2011): 1–31; Mikael Wolfe, "Yankee Technology and Nationalist Sensibilities: La Comisión Nacional de Irrigación in 1920s and 30s Mexico" (paper presented at the Latin American Studies Association Annual Meeting, Montreal, 2007).

35. For the biographical details on Fernández, see Leobardo Jiménez Sánchez, *Las ciencias agrícolas y sus protagonistas* (Chapingo, Mexico: Colegio de Postgraduados de la Universidad Autónoma de Chapingo, 1984), 1:142–43. On Fernández's position as a "socialist agronomist," see Liga de Agrónomos Socialistas to Manuel Ávila Camacho, December 21, 1940, box 159, Ramón Fernández y Fernández Papers, Biblioteca Luis González, Colegio de Michoacán, Zamora, Michoacán, Mexico (hereafter Fernández Papers). On the 1930 agrarian census and Fernández's role in it, see Michael A. Ervin, "The 1930 Agrarian Census in Mexico: Agronomists, Middle Politics, and the Negotiation of Data Collection," *Hispanic American Historical Review* 87, no. 3 (2007): 537–70.

36. See, for example, US Department of Agriculture, "A Graphic Summary of Farm Tenure," December 1936, box 3, Fernández Papers.

37. For the itinerary as well as a list of conference participants and their origin, see "Fifth International Conference of Agricultural Economists," August 21–28, 1938, box 153, Fernández Papers.

38. Ramón Fernández y Fernández, "The Mexican Agrarian Reform," August 1938, box 166, Fernández Papers.

39. On the exchange program and Fernández's participation, see George Messersmith to Ezequiel Padilla, June 2, 1942, and Alfonso González Gallardo to Ezequiel Padilla, June 25, 1942, both located in III-2459-3, AHSRE.

40. For evidence of Fernández's USDA Graduate School education, see Jiménez Sánchez, *Las ciencias agrícolas y sus protagonistas*, 145. On the Graduate School and its role in propagating a New Deal agrarian ethos, see Andrew Jewett, "The Social Sciences, Philosophy, and the Cultural Turn in the 1930s' USDA," *Journal of the History of the Behavioral Sciences* 49, no. 4 (2013): 396–427; Malcolm Rutherford, "The USDA Graduate School: Government Training in Statistics and Economics, 1921–1945," *Journal of the History of Economic Thought* 33, no. 4 (2011): 419–47.

41. George Messersmith to Ezequiel Padilla, July 13, 1943, III-2459-3, AHSRE. Fernández's explorations are also documented in the brochures and publications he collected on the road, which are now housed at the Colegio de Michoacán, Fernández Papers. See, for example, "Supervisor's Guidebook to Aid in Planning, Organizing, and Directing the County FSA Program," box 88; "Greene County, Georgia: The Story of One Southern County," box 88; "By-laws of Mileston Community, Inc., Tchula, Holmes County, Mississippi," box 52. Some sample news clippings are "Communal Farms Long Discredited," *Arkansas Democrat*, April 7, 1943, box 51, and "FSA System Condemned," *Arkansas Democrat*, April 15, 1943, box 153, both in the Fernández Papers.

42. For the course description, see Jiménez Sánchez, *Las ciencias agrícolas y sus protagonistas*, 147. For some examples of student papers, see Enrique Valdivia Muñoz, "¿Tiene importancia el crédito agrícola en la conservación de los suelos?" box 8, and Armando Huacuja, "Cooperativismo y cooperativas en los Estados Unidos," box 52, both in the Fernández Papers.

43. Ramón Fernández y Fernández to Marte R. Gómez, March 6, 1945, Cartas, 1945, D-G, Gómez Papers.

44. On Fernández's later career in Mexico and then his work in Cuba, see Jiménez Sánchez, *Las ciencias agrícolas y sus protagonistas*, 142, 157.

45. On Mexican agronomy's prerevolutionary career, see Olea-Franco, "One Century of Higher Agricultural Education and Research in Mexico," chap. 7; Cotter, *Troubled Harvest*, chap. 1; Michael A. Ervin, "The Art of the Possible: Agronomists, Agrarian Reform, and the Middle Politics of the Mexican Revolution, 1908–1934" (PhD diss., University of Pittsburgh, 2002), chap. 1.

46. On agronomists' postrevolutionary fates, see Cotter, *Troubled Harvest*, chap. 3; Rebeca de Gortari Rabiela, "Educación y conciencia nacional: Los ingenieros después de la Revolución Mexicana," *Revista Mexicana de Sociología* 49, no. 3 (1989): 123–41; Ervin, "The Art of the Possible," particularly the conclusion; Raymond B. Craib, *Cartographic Mexico: A History of State Fixations and Fugitive Landscapes* (Durham, NC: Duke University Press, 2004), chap. 7.

47. See, in particular, Cynthia Hewitt de Alcántara, *Modernizing Mexican Agriculture: Socioeconomic Implications of Technological Change, 1940–1970* (Geneva: UN Research Institute for Social Development, 1976); Bruce H. Jennings, *Foundations of International Agricultural Research: Science and Politics in Mexican Agriculture* (Boulder, CO: Westview Press, 1988).

48. On the absence of Mexican "scientific nationalism" in the revolutionary period, see Joseph Cotter, "The Origins of the Green Revolution in Mexico: Continuity or Change?" in *Latin America in the 1940s: War and Postwar Transitions*, ed. David Rock (Berkeley: University of California Press, 1994); Karin E. Matchett, "At Odds over Inbreeding: An Abandoned Attempt at Mexico / United States Collaboration to 'Improve' Mexican Corn, 1940–1950," *Journal of the History of Biology* 39, no. 2 (2006): 345–72.

49. On graduate education and the Sociedad Agronómica Mexicana's English course, see Cotter, *Troubled Harvest*, 86–90. On the translation of Extension Service guides, see "Acerca de programa de trabajos," March 18, 1929, folder 12C-113-1, box 3, Dirección General Agricultura y Ganadería, Records of the Secretaría de Agricultura y Recursos Hidráulicos (Group 215), Archivo General de la Nación, Mexico City.

50. Gonzalo Andrade Alcocer to Marte R. Gómez, January 1, 1943, Asuntos Oficiales, 1943, Gómez Papers.

51. Limón quote is from an undated *Raleigh News and Observer* article titled "Mexican Studying Agriculture Here," cited in Marte R. Gómez to Josephus Daniels, June 5, 1942, Cartas, 1942, A-F, Gómez Papers.

52. On Martino's political career, see Camp, *Mexican Political Biographies*, 611. On Martino and the SAM's commission of Montenegro, see Ines Amor to Francisco Castillo Nájera, September 30, 1941, folder 33, box 7, Archivo Particular de Francisco Castillo Nájera, AHSRE (hereafter Castillo Nájera Papers). On the composition of the painting, see Marte R. Gómez, "Memorandum que fue puesto en manos del Sr. Vicepresidente de los Estados Unidos," October 10, 1941, Cartas, 1941, Q-Z, Gómez Papers.

53. Henry A. Wallace to Manuel Ávila Camacho, October 14, 1941, and Henry A. Wallace to Fernando Foglio Miramontes, October 14, 1941, both letters found on reel 22, Henry A. Wallace

230 Notes to Pages 86–89

papers (microfilm), Library of Congress, Manuscript Division, Washington, DC. On the group trip to Washington to present the painting, see Francisco Castillo Nájera to Manuel Ávila Camacho, October 11, 1941, Cartas, 1941, A-Ch, Gómez Papers.

54. Michael R. Hall, "The Good Neighbor Policy and the Americas," in *A Companion to Franklin D. Roosevelt*, ed. William D. Pederson (Malden, MA: Wiley-Blackwell, 2011), 551. There is a vast literature on US intervention in Latin America between World War I and 1933; see, in particular, Alan McPherson, *The Invaded: How Latin Americans and Their Allies Fought and Ended U.S. Occupation* (New York: Oxford University Press, 2014); Greg Grandin, *Empire's Workshop: Latin America, the United States, and the Rise of the New Imperialism* (New York: Metropolitan Books, 2006). On the broad contours of the Good Neighbor policy, see Fredrick B. Pike, *FDR's Good Neighbor Policy: Sixty Years of Generally Gentle Chaos* (Austin: University of Texas Press, 1995).

55. On diplomatic tensions between the US and Mexico during the interwar period, see Linda B. Hall, *Oil, Banks, and Politics: The U.S. and Postrevolutionary Mexico, 1917–1924* (Austin: University of Texas Press, 1995); John Mason Hart, *Empire and Revolution: The Americans in Mexico since the Civil War* (Berkeley: University of California Press, 2002). On life in the border zone, see Rachel St. John, *Line in the Sand: A History of the Western U.S.-Mexico Border* (Princeton, NJ: Princeton University Press, 2011).

56. E. David Cronon, "A Southern Progressive Looks at the New Deal," *Journal of Southern History* 24 (May 1958): 151–76; Joseph L. Morrison, *Josephus Daniels: The Small-D Democrat* (Chapel Hill: University of North Carolina Press, 1966); Carroll Kilpatrick, ed., *Roosevelt and Daniels: A Friendship in Politics* (Chapel Hill: University of North Carolina Press, 1952).

57. Confederación Nacional de Estudiantes to Josephus Daniels, April 15, 1933, 24–1–8, AHSRE. On the reaction in Mexico to Daniels's appointment, see E. David Cronon, *Josephus Daniels in Mexico* (Madison: University of Wisconsin Press, 1960), 14–20; Lee A. Craig, *Josephus Daniels: His Life and Times* (Chapel Hill: University of North Carolina Press, 2013), 400; Josephus Daniels, *Shirt-Sleeve Diplomat* (Chapel Hill: University of North Carolina Press, 1947), 3–14.

58. *Raleigh News and Observer*, April 23, 1895, cited in Joseph L. Morrison, *Josephus Daniels Says: An Editor's Political Odyssey from Bryan to Wilson to F.D.R., 1894–1913* (Chapel Hill: University of North Carolina Press, 1962), 93.

59. On Daniels's racial politics, see Samuel L. Schaffer, "New South Nation: Woodrow Wilson's Generation and the Rise of the South, 1884–1920" (PhD diss., Yale University, 2010), chaps. 1 and 5; Craig, *Josephus Daniels*, chap. 4; Glenda Gilmore, *Gender and Jim Crow: Women and the Politics of White Supremacy in North Carolina, 1890–1940* (Chapel Hill: University of North Carolina Press, 1996), 65–66. On North Carolina politics and the Wilmington race riot, see Gilmore, *Gender and Jim Crow*, chap. 4; Gregory P. Downs, *Declarations of Dependence: The Long Reconstruction of Popular Politics in the South, 1861–1908* (Chapel Hill: University of North Carolina Press, 2011); James M. Beeby, *Revolt of the Tar Heels: The North Carolina Populist Movement, 1890–1901* (Jackson: University Press of Mississippi, 2008); David S. Cecelski and Timothy B. Tyson, eds., *Democracy Betrayed: The Wilmington Race Riot of 1898 and Its Legacy* (Chapel Hill: University of North Carolina Press, 1998).

60. Nathan Miller, *The U.S. Navy: An Illustrated History* (New York: Random House, 1977), 252; Josephus Daniels, *Editor in Politics* (Chapel Hill: University of North Carolina Press, 1941), 567–68. On Daniels's agrarian politics, see Craig, *Josephus Daniels*, chaps. 3–5; Morrison, *Josephus Daniels Says*, chap. 2.

61. On Daniels's political transformations in the 1920s, see Cronon, "A Southern Progressive Looks at the New Deal"; Morrison, *Josephus Daniels*, chap. 6. For an exploration of the difficult relationship between progressive Democrats and the South, see Ira Katznelson, *Fear Itself: The New Deal and the Origins of Our Time* (New York: W. W. Norton, 2013).

62. Schuler, *Mexico between Hitler and Roosevelt*, 40–41; Cronon, *Josephus Daniels in Mexico*, 76–81; Pike, *FDR's Good Neighbor Policy*.

63. George Foster Peabody to Frank Tannenbaum, March 20, 1933, box 4, Frank Tannenbaum Papers, Rare Book and Manuscript Library, Columbia University, New York (hereafter Tannenbaum Papers).

64. Josephus Daniels to George Foster Peabody, April 3, 1933, folder 1, box 43, George Foster Peabody Papers, Library of Congress, Manuscript Division, Washington, DC (hereafter Peabody Papers). On Tannenbaum mailing his dissertation, see Frank Tannenbaum to Josephus Daniels, March 21, 1933, box 1, Tannenbaum Papers.

65. Daniels diary entry, November 21, 1933, Diaries, reel 5, Daniels Papers.

66. Josephus Daniels to Frank Tannenbaum, March 23, 1933, box 1, Tannenbaum Papers.

67. Josephus Daniels to George Foster Peabody, April 3, 1933, folder 1, box 43, Peabody Papers; Josephus Daniels to Frank Tannenbaum, April 21, 1933, box 1, Tannenbaum Papers.

68. Daniels wrote North Carolina textile mill owners in 1934 beseeching them to accept collective bargaining with their workers; see Daniels diary entry, September 2, 1934, Diaries, reel 6, Daniels Papers.

69. Quoted in Cronon, "A Southern Progressive Looks at the New Deal," 152.

70. Daniels, *Shirt-Sleeve Diplomat*, 26. For inaugural address excerpts, see *Real Mexico*, folder 6, box 718, Speeches, Writings, and Related Material, Daniels Papers. John Dwyer's *The Agrarian Dispute* was the first work to highlight the primary importance of Daniels's role in the success of Cárdenas's campaign, and I am greatly indebted to it. Dwyer, however, does not delve deeply into Tannenbaum's key involvement, Daniels's agrarian career in the US South, or the impact Daniels would have on the agrarian New Deal.

71. Josephus Daniels to Franklin D. Roosevelt, October 14, 1933, Official File 23, Roosevelt Papers.

72. Daniels diary entry, February 2, 1935, Diaries, reel 6, Daniels Papers. Daniels's diary entries also served as letters home to his children in Raleigh.

73. Daniels diary entry, November 24, 1933, Diaries, reel 6, Daniels Papers.

74. Daniels diary entry, December 2, 1933, Diaries, reel 5, Daniels Papers. See also Daniels, *Shirt-Sleeve Diplomat*, 298–302.

75. Josephus Daniels to Franklin D. Roosevelt, May 2, 1933, Special Correspondence, reel 59, Daniels Papers.

76. Daniels diary entry, February 7, 1934, Diaries, reel 5, Daniels Papers.

77. Josephus Daniels to Franklin D. Roosevelt, January 29, 1934, folder 9, box 43, President's Secretary's File, Roosevelt Papers.

78. "Address of Josephus Daniels, American Ambassador, to the Members of the Tenth Seminar," July 13, 1935, folder 9, box 718, Speeches, Writings, Related Materials, Daniels Papers.

79. "Give Ambassador 'Good Neighbor' Welcome Here," *Raleigh News and Observer*, May 19, 1934, 1–2.

80. Daniels diary entry, May 18, 1934, Diaries, reel 5, Daniels Papers.

81. Frank Tannenbaum to Clarence Poe, April 24, 1935, box 61, Tannenbaum Papers.

82. On Daniels's meetings, see Will W. Alexander to George Foster Peabody, May 27, 1935, folder 2, box 47, Peabody Papers. On Tannenbaum crediting Daniels, see Frank Tannenbaum to W. T. Couch, May 29, 1935, box 25, Tannenbaum Papers.

83. Josephus Daniels to Franklin D. Roosevelt, September 28, 1936, Special Correspondence, reel 60, Daniels Papers.

84. For the acreage statistic, see Dwyer, *The Agrarian Dispute*, 159. On the US business community's response to land expropriation, see "U.S. Protests in Mexico," *New York Times*, October 17, 1937, 76; Hart, *Empire and Revolution*, chap. 12; Dwyer, *The Agrarian Dispute*, chap. 6.

85. Josephus Daniels to Franklin D. Roosevelt, October 29, 1938, folder 6, box 44, President's Secretary's File, Roosevelt Papers.

86. Josephus Daniels to Sumner Welles, November 6, 1937, folder 4, box 40, Sumner Welles Papers, Franklin Delano Roosevelt Presidential Library, Hyde Park, New York.

87. Lázaro Cárdenas, *Obras 1: Apuntes 1913–1940* (Mexico City: Universidad Nacional Autónoma de México, 1972), 1:324.

88. Daniels diary entry, April 14, 1935, Diaries, reel 6, Daniels Papers.

89. "Memorandum of Conversation of Josephus Daniels and Lázaro Cárdenas," December 15, 1936, folder 6, box 647, Subject File—Mexico, Daniels Papers.

90. Josephus Daniels to Cordell Hull, July 5, 1940, folder 2, box 1, Official File 146, Roosevelt Papers.

91. Lázaro Cárdenas to Francisco Castillo Nájera, October 29, 1937, folder 50, box 9, Castillo Nájera Papers.

92. Interview with Cuauhtémoc Cárdenas, June 3, 2016 (transcript in possession of author).

93. Josephus Daniels to Cordell Hull, September 3, 1938, folder 6, box 44, President's Secretary's File, Roosevelt Papers.

94. Quoted in Cronon, *Josephus Daniels in Mexico*, 216.

95. Dwyer, *The Agrarian Dispute*, 219, 202, 209. Dwyer's account provides unquestionable evidence that Daniels's agrarian sympathies made a major difference in the land negotiations of the 1930s, but Dwyer does not fully explore what led to Daniels's conversion. He makes brief note of how Daniels's New Dealism shaped his interpretation of revolutionary Mexico, but Daniels's agrarian background and regional perspective are barely broached.

96. Quoted in Cronon, "A Southern Progressive Looks at the New Deal," 152.

Chapter Four: Rockefeller Rural Development

1. On trip details, see Richard Bradfield to Paul C. Mangelsdorf, June 17, 1941, folder titled "Bradfield, Richard," box 2, Paul C. Mangelsdorf Papers, HUG (FP) 37.8, Harvard University Archives, Cambridge, Massachusetts. The team's fourth member, Elvin C. Stakman, joined the team at the Mexican border.

2. Richard Bradfield oral history, 1966, box 15, record group (hereafter RG) 13, Rockefeller Foundation Archives (hereafter RFA), Rockefeller Archive Center, Tarrytown, New York (hereafter RAC), 22, 25.

3. Elvin C. Stakman, Paul C. Mangelsdorf, and Richard Bradfield, "Agricultural Conditions and Problems in Mexico: Report of the Survey Commission of the Rockefeller Foundation," August–September 1941, folder 2, box 1, series 323, RG 1.1, RFA, RAC.

4. For the best recent summary of the green revolution's profound human and ecological consequences, see Raj Patel, "The Long Green Revolution," *Journal of Peasant Studies* 40, no. 1 (2013): 1–63. On the primary environmental impacts of the green revolution, see J. R. McNeill, *Something New under the Sun: An Environmental History of the Twentieth-Century World* (New York: W. W. Norton, 2000), 219–26; Angus Wright, *The Death of Ramón González: The Modern Agricultural Dilemma* (Austin: University of Texas Press, 1990). On the rash of urbanization that accompanied the green revolution, see Mike Davis, *Planet of Slums* (New York: Verso, 2006).

5. In the last three decades of the twentieth century, there was a massive outpouring of social science scholarship—much of it critical—on the human and ecological consequences of the green revolution across the globe. For a few prominent examples, see Lester R. Brown, *Seeds of Change: The Green Revolution and Development in the 1970s* (New York: Praeger, 1970); Harry M. Cleaver, "The Contradictions of the Green Revolution," *American Economic Review* 62, no. 1–2 (1972): 177–86; Kenneth A. Dahlberg, *Beyond the Green Revolution: The Ecology and Politics of Global Agricultural Development* (New York: Plenum Press, 1979); Cynthia Hewitt de Alcantara, *Modernizing Mexican Agriculture: Socioeconomic Implications of Technological Change, 1940–1970* (Geneva: UN Research Institute for Social Development, 1976); Andrew Pearse, *Seeds of Plenty, Seeds of Want: Social and Economic Implications of the Green Revolution* (Oxford: Clarendon Press, 1980); Bandhudas Sen, *The Green Revolution in India: A Perspective* (New York: John Wiley and Sons, 1974); Vandana Shiva, *The Violence of the Green Revolution: Third World Agriculture, Ecology, and Politics* (London: Zed Books, 1991); Wright, *The Death of Ramón González*; Akhil Gupta, *Postcolonial Developments: Agriculture and the Making of Modern India* (Durham, NC: Duke University Press, 1998). It was only at the end of the twentieth century that historians began to grapple with the origins and course of this influential development program, and the fundamental role that Mexico played. See, in particular, Joseph Cotter, *Troubled Harvest: Agronomy and Revolution in Mexico, 1880–2002* (Westport, CT: Praeger, 2003); Nick Cullather, *The Hungry World: America's Cold War Battle against Poverty in Asia* (Cambridge, MA: Harvard University Press, 2010); Deborah Fitzgerald, "Exporting American Agriculture: The Rockefeller Foundation in Mexico, 1943–1953," *Social Studies of Science* 16, no. 3 (1986): 457–83; Jonathan Harwood, *Europe's Green Revolutions and Others Since: The Rise and Fall of Peasant-Friendly Plant Breeding* (New York: Routledge, 2012); Gilberto Aboites Manrique, *Una mirada diferente de la Revolución Verde: Ciencia, nación y compromiso social* (Mexico City: Editorial Plaza y Valdés, 2002); David Kinkela, *DDT and the American Century: Global Health, Environmental Politics, and the Pesticide That Changed the World* (Chapel Hill: University of North Carolina Press, 2011), chap. 3; John H. Perkins, *Geopolitics and the Green Revolution: Wheat, Genes, and the Cold War* (New York: Oxford University Press, 1997); David A. Sonnenfeld, "Mexico's 'Green Revolution,' 1940–1980: Towards an Environmental History," *Environmental History Review* 16, no. 4 (1992): 28–52.

6. For examples of this narrative convention, see Fitzgerald, "Exporting American Agriculture"; Wright, *The Death of Ramón González*; Perkins, *Geopolitics and the Green Revolution*. Though much of Cullather's *The Hungry World* adheres to this narrative, it does explore the competing visions of the 1930s and 1940s.

7. John A. Ferrell, "Mexico: Memorandum from JAF [John A. Ferrell] to RBF [Raymond B. Fosdick]," January 27, 1941, folder 3814, box 561, series 323, 1941 Stacks, RG 2, RFA, RAC.

8. I am not the first to suggest that the US South served as a laboratory for US development thought in general and the Rockefeller Foundation's agricultural program in particular. Since the earliest academic research on the green revolution in the 1970s, a handful of scholars have

acknowledged—though nearly all in passing—that the Rockefeller philanthropies began their career in the US South. See, in particular, Harry M. Cleaver, "Origins of the Green Revolution" (PhD diss., Stanford University, 1975), which argued that the GEB's work in the US South served the Rockefellers as a model for later agricultural work in the Third World, but was almost entirely speculative and not based on archival research. Mexico receives little attention in Cleaver's study. In "Exporting American Agriculture," Fitzgerald makes brief reference to the Rockefellers' southern experience (in two pages), but she does not see its direct influence on the Mexican program. Likewise, a number of recent works in social science have argued that the post-emancipation Cotton Belt figured as a domestic incubator for diagnoses of and solutions for rural poverty and underdevelopment. See, in particular, Mona Domosh, "Practising Development at Home: Race, Gender, and the 'Development' of the American South," *Antipode* 47, no. 4 (2015): 915–41; Mona Domosh, "International Harvester, the U.S. South, and the Makings of International Development in the Early 20th Century," *Political Geography* 49 (November 2015): 17–29; David Nally and Stephen Taylor, "The Politics of Self-Help: The Rockefeller Foundation, Philanthropy, and the 'Long' Green Revolution," *Political Geography* 49 (November 2015): 51–63; Natalie Ring, *The Problem South: Region, Empire, and the New Liberal State, 1880–1930* (Athens: University of Georgia Press, 2012). While each of these studies brings valuable insight to the racialized and gendered perspectives on poverty that philanthropic planners honed in the early twentieth-century South, none are clear about how those early lessons impacted practical work in the Global South, often making intellectual leaps of faith from the century's early decades to later moments in the Cold War. All in all, no previous study has undertaken a thorough archival examination of both the Rockefellers' southern work and the MAP, nor sketched the connective tissue between the two. Notably, the two most prominent historical studies of the green revolution—Cullather's *The Hungry World* and Perkins's *Geopolitics and the Green Revolution*—make no mention of the foundation's prior work in the US South as an inspiration or influence.

9. Within the field of diplomatic history, several works have argued that politicians from the South have exercised a disproportionate influence on twentieth-century US foreign policy. See, in particular, Joseph A. Fry, *Dixie Looks Abroad: The South and U.S. Foreign Relations, 1789–1973* (Baton Rouge: Louisiana State University Press, 2002). For a recent review of literature in this vein, see Joseph A. Fry, "Place Matters: Domestic Regionalism and the Formation of American Foreign Policy," *Diplomatic History* 36, no. 3 (June 2012): 451–82. These works are exclusively concerned with formal state actors, however, neglecting individuals or institutions beyond the walls of government; development organizations are similarly overlooked.

10. On the symbolic reunion between northern and southern whites in the early twentieth century, see David Blight, *Race and Reunion: The Civil War in American Memory* (Cambridge, MA: Belknap Press of Harvard University Press, 2001); Nina Silber, *The Romance of Reunion: Northerners and the South, 1865–1900* (Chapel Hill: University of North Carolina Press, 1993); Samuel L. Schaffer, "New South Nation: Woodrow Wilson's Generation and the Rise of the South, 1884–1920" (PhD diss., Yale University, 2010).

11. On the growing divide between North and South at this supposed moment of reunion, see Ring, *The Problem South*.

12. On urban anxieties about the future of the countryside in an industrial nation, see David B. Danbom, *The Resisted Revolution: Urban America and the Industrialization of Agriculture, 1900–1930* (Ames: Iowa State University Press, 1979).

13. Quoted in Raymond B. Fosdick, *Adventure in Giving: The Story of the General Education Board* (New York: Harper and Row, 1962), 5. On the trip details, see Raymond B. Fosdick, *John D. Rockefeller, Jr.: A Portrait* (New York: Harper and Brothers, 1956), 116–19. On the dramatic rise of philanthropy in the industrial United States, see Lawrence Friedman and Mark McGarvie, eds., *Charity, Philanthropy, and Civility in American History* (New York: Cambridge University Press, 2003); Olivier Zunz, *Philanthropy in America: A History* (Princeton, NJ: Princeton University Press, 2012); John Ensor Harr and Peter J. Johnson, *The Rockefeller Century* (New York: Scribner's, 1988).

14. That amount was donated incrementally over the next decade, beginning with $1 million in 1902. See *The General Education Board: An Account of Its Activities, 1902–1914* (New York: General Education Board, 1915), 15–17.

15. Ibid., 216.

16. Frederick T. Gates to Wallace Buttrick, March 2, 1901, volume 348, Series L—Letterbooks, John D. Rockefeller Papers, Rockefeller Family Papers, RAC.

17. Wallace Buttrick, "After Fourteen Months of Study and Travel in the Southern States," May 12, 1903, folder 3176, box 304, series 1.2, General Education Board Papers (hereafter GEBP), RAC.

18. Wallace Buttrick, "Trip to Birmingham," July 4, 1902, folder 3176, box 304, series 1.2, GEBP, RAC.

19. On northern philanthropy's impact on black southerners, see Roy E. Finkenbine, "Law, Reconstruction, and African American Education in the Post-Emancipation South," in *Charity, Philanthropy, and Civility in American History*, ed. Lawrence Friedman and Mark McGarvie (New York: Cambridge University Press, 2003); Eric Anderson and Alfred A. Moss, *Dangerous Donations: Northern Philanthropy and Southern Black Education, 1902–1930* (Columbia: University of Missouri Press, 1999).

20. Joseph C. Bailey, *Seaman A. Knapp: Schoolmaster of American Agriculture* (New York: Columbia University Press, 1945), 215.

21. Wallace Buttrick, "Trip to Birmingham," July 4, 1902, folder 3176, box 304, series 1.2, GEBP, RAC.

22. Countless works have been written on the southern cotton economy in the early twentieth century. For an indispensable classic and newer global study, see, respectively, Pete Daniel, *Breaking the Land: The Transformation of Cotton, Tobacco, and Rice Cultures since 1880* (Urbana: University of Illinois Press, 1985); Sven Beckert, *Empire of Cotton: A Global History* (New York: Alfred A. Knopf, 2014).

23. As one of the most celebrated figures in US agricultural history, Knapp and his campaigns of the early twentieth century have received no shortage of scholarly attention. For two early and rather-uncritical examinations, see Bailey, *Seaman A. Knapp*; Roy V. Scott, *The Reluctant Farmer: The Rise of Agricultural Extension to 1914* (Urbana: University of Illinois Press, 1970). In later years, Knapp and his US southern campaign have been the target of a flood of revisionist scholarship, notably James C. Giesen, *Boll Weevil Blues: Cotton, Myth, and Power in the American South* (Chicago: University of Chicago Press, 2011), chaps. 1–2; Joan Malczewski, "Philanthropy and Progressive Era State Building through Agricultural Extension Work in the Jim Crow South," *History of Education Quarterly* 53, no. 4 (2013): 369–400; Theodore R. Mitchell and Robert Lowe, "To Sow Contentment: Philanthropy, Scientific Agriculture, and the Making of the New South, 1906–1920," *Journal of Social History* 24, no. 2 (1990): 317–40; Ring, *The*

Problem South, chap. 3; Judith Sealander, *Private Wealth and Public Life: Foundation Philanthropy and the Reshaping of American Social Policy from the Progressive Era to the New Deal* (Baltimore: Johns Hopkins University Press, 1997), chap. 2; Nally and Taylor, "The Politics of Self-Help." All these recent works, however, reconstruct the narrative of the Knapp campaigns from published sources or the GEB's incomplete archive at the Rockefeller Archive Center. I am the first to use the wealth of USDA and Bureau of Plant Industry sources at the National Archives in Maryland since Scott's 1970 book, which was essentially a hagiography.

24. James Wilson to Seaman A. Knapp, July 28, 1898, folder 5, box 30, entry 1, RG 54: Records of the Bureau of Plant Industry, Soils, and Agricultural Engineering, US National Archives and Records Administration II, College Park, Maryland (hereafter NA). On Knapp's findings, see Seaman A. Knapp, "Recent Foreign Explorations as Bearing on the Agricultural Development of the Southern States," *United States Department of Plant Industry Bulletin* 35 (February 14, 1903).

25. On Knapp's appointment as "Special Agent" and the early motivations for demonstration work, see Beverly Galloway to Seaman A. Knapp, August 20, 1902, folder 20, box 30, entry 1, RG 54, NA. For evidence that Knapp's early southern work had little to do with cotton and instead favored diversification, see A. J. Pieters to Beverly Galloway, October 10, 1903, folder 2, box 30, entry 1, RG 54, NA. That these initial farms failed is evidenced by the scarcity of archival documentation on their performance and their abandonment after the boll weevil campaign takes off. Giesen (*Boll Weevil Blues*, 18–19) suggests similarly.

26. On the boll weevil's history and myth, see Giesen, *Boll Weevil Blues*, especially chap. 1; Fabian Lange, Alan Olmstead, and Paul W. Rhode, "The Impact of the Boll Weevil, 1892–1932," *Journal of Economic History* 69, no. 3 (2009): 685–718.

27. Seaman A. Knapp to James Wilson, December 1, 1903, box 15, finding aid PI-191, entry 8, RG 16: Records of the Office of the Secretary of Agriculture, NA.

28. Seaman A. Knapp, "Suggestions to Special Agents," October 20, 1905, folder 3, box 29, entry 1, RG 54, NA.

29. Seaman A. Knapp to Beverly Galloway, April 25, 1906, folder 6, box 30, entry 1, RG 54, NA.

30. Seaman A. Knapp, "Better Conditions for Southern Farmers," April 1907, folder 10, box 2, Seaman A. Knapp papers, Southwest Collections and Special Collections Library, Texas Tech University, Lubbock (hereafter Knapp Papers).

31. Seaman A. Knapp to Beverly Galloway, October 4, 1904, folder 1, box 29, entry 1, RG 54, NA.

32. Seaman A. Knapp to Beverly Galloway, April 25, 1906, folder 6, box 30, entry 1, RG 54, NA.

33. Frederick T. Gates to Willet M. Hays (telegram), May 31, 1905, box 33, entry 8, finding aid PI-191, RG 16, NA. Nearly every historical account has suggested that the GEB reached out to the USDA rather than vice versa; however, the archival record does not support this. It may seem unusual for a federal agency to seamlessly petition private funding for public work, yet in Knapp's case it reflected continuity as opposed to change, as he had relied heavily on travel rebates from railroad companies to enable his peripatetic agents' work before then.

34. Minutes of the Meeting of the Executive Committee, April 20, 1906, box 23, series 3, GEBP, RAC.

35. Beverly Galloway to C. P. McCabe, March 17, 1906, folder 12, box 1, Knapp Papers.

36. On GEB spending, see "GEB Programs, 1902–1947," folder 3491, box 331, series 1.2, GEBP, RAC.

37. *The General Education Board*, 29.

38. "The Effect of the Farmers' Cooperative Demonstration Work upon Rural Conditions," attachment from Seaman A. Knapp to W. J. Apple, September 12, 1908, folder 14, box 1, Knapp Papers.

39. Seaman A. Knapp, "Causes of Southern Rural Conditions and the Small Farm as an Important Remedy," *Yearbook of the USDA* (1908): 311–20.

40. Ibid.

41. Seaman A. Knapp to Beverly Galloway, April 11, 1906, folder 6, box 30, entry 1, RG 54, NA. For a work that makes Knapp and his allies' dismissal and erasure of black farmers' contributions to the demonstration work powerfully clear, see Giesen, *Boll Weevil Blues*, chap. 2.

42. William Bamberge to Seaman A. Knapp, April 1, 1906, folder 6, box 30, entry 1, RG 54, NA.

43. When the weevil crossed state lines, the USDA took over funding for those states, but for the large majority of the period between 1906 and 1914, GEB agents outnumbered USDA-paid agents. Seaman A. Knapp, "Demonstration Work in Cooperation with Southern Farmers," *United States Department of Agriculture Farmers' Bulletin* 319 (1908): 7.

44. That claim was made most boldly in the often-cited *The General Education Board*. Yet this volume was entirely a public relations response to the fiery controversy that surrounded the 1914 Smith-Lever debates, when it was greatly in the interest of the GEB to disown its significant influence on government work.

45. On Buttrick asking for agent reports, see Seaman A. Knapp to William Bamberge, March 10, 1906, folder 3, box 30, entry 1, RG 54, NA. On hiring and GEB approval, see "Minutes of the Meeting of the Executive Committee," August 6, 1908, box 23, series 3, GEBP, RAC.

46. On Knapp attending GEB meetings, see Seaman A. Knapp to Beverly Galloway, November 21, 1906, folder 2, box 31, entry 1, RG 54, NA. On Gates emphasizing corn, see Frederick T. Gates to Seaman A. Knapp, March 10, 1906, volume 96, series L—Letterbooks, John D. Rockefeller Papers, Rockefeller Family Papers, RAC. On naming their program, see Frederick T. Gates to Seaman A. Knapp, June 11, 1907, volume 276, series L—Letterbooks, John D. Rockefeller Papers, Rockefeller Family Papers, RAC.

47. Frederick T. Gates to Horace Plunkett, October 14, 1908, folder 54, box 3, Frederick T. Gates Papers, RAC.

48. On Tuskegee and its agricultural vision under Carver, see Mark D. Hersey, *My Work Is That of Conservation: An Environmental Biography of George Washington Carver* (Athens: University of Georgia Press, 2011). On the GEB and its push to include black southerners in the demonstration work, see Earl W. Crosby, "The Roots of Black Agricultural Extension Work," *Historian* 39, no. 2 (1977): 228–47; Karen J. Ferguson, "Caught in 'No Man's Land': The Negro Cooperative Demonstration Service and the Ideology of Booker T. Washington, 1900–1918," *Agricultural History* 72, no. 1 (1998): 33–54.

49. Seaman A. Knapp to Rossa Cooley, May 25, 1909, folder 17, box 1, entry 3, RG 33: Records of the Extension Service, NA.

50. "Africanizing through 'philanthropy,'" *Southern Farm Magazine* 15 (November 1907): 7, 8.

51. For this statistic, see J. A. Evans to Beverly Galloway, March 29, 1912, folder 1, box 2, entry 2, finding aid PI-66, RG 54, NA. Under Knapp's stewardship, black agents could only instruct black farmers; in this sense the color line remained intact. On black southerners and extension work writ large, see Debra A. Reid, *Reaping a Greater Harvest: African Americans, the Extension Service, and Rural Reform in Jim Crow Texas* (College Station: Texas A&M University Press, 2007).

52. *The General Education Board*, 54; Seaman A. Knapp, "An Agricultural Revolution," *World's Work* 12 (July 1906): 7733.

53. On the institutionalization of the Extension Service and its impact on the rural United States, see Scott, *The Reluctant Farmer*; Deborah Fitzgerald, *Every Farm a Factory: The Industrial Ideal in American Agriculture* (New Haven, CT: Yale University Press, 2003); Gabriel N. Rosenberg, *The 4-H Harvest: Sexuality and the State in Rural America* (Philadelphia: University of Pennsylvania Press, 2016); Jim Hightower, *Hard Tomatoes, Hard Times: A Report of the Agribusiness Accountability Project on the Failure of America's Land Grant College System* (Cambridge, MA: Schenkman Publishing Co., 1973). On the Extension Service's failure to aid black farmers, see Pete Daniel, *Dispossession: Discrimination against African American Farmers in the Age of Civil Rights* (Chapel Hill: University of North Carolina Press, 2013); Reid, *Reaping a Greater Harvest*.

54. Frank Tannenbaum, "The Single Crop," *Century Magazine* 106, no. 6 (October 1923): 816, 822. For the tenancy statistic, see Gavin Wright, *Old South, New South: Revolutions in the Southern Economy since the Civil War* (Baton Rouge: Louisiana State University Press, 1986), 118. For a particularly revealing illustration of the ephemeral nature of prewar agricultural diversification in the South, see James C. Giesen, "'The Herald of Prosperity': Tracing the Boll Weevil Myth in Alabama," *Agricultural History* 85, no. 1 (Winter 2011): 24–49.

55. Sealander, *Private Wealth and Public Life*, 52, 53. On the Smith-Lever debates and denunciations of Rockefeller philanthropy, see ibid., 52–57. On the Ludlow massacre, see Thomas G. Andrews, *Killing for Coal: America's Deadliest Labor War* (Cambridge, MA: Harvard University Press, 2010).

56. Nick Cullather, "Miracles of Modernization: The Green Revolution and the Apotheosis of Technology," *Diplomatic History* 28, no. 2 (2004): 253.

57. Fosdick, *Adventure in Giving*, 61.

58. Wallace Buttrick, "Memoranda for an Address on Agricultural Education," April 1907, folder 7152, box 694, series 1.4, GEBP, RAC.

59. On the post-1914 career of the GEB, see Gerald Jonas, *The Circuit Riders: Rockefeller Money and Rise of Modern Science* (New York: W. W. Norton, 1989); Robert Kohler, *Partners in Science: Foundations and Natural Scientists, 1900–1945* (Chicago: University of Chicago Press, 1991). For two institutional accounts, see Fosdick, *Adventure in Giving*; "GEB Programs, 1902–1947," folder 3491, box 331, series 1.2, GEBP, RAC.

60. John Farley, *To Cast Out Disease: A History of the International Health Division of the Rockefeller Foundation, 1913–1951* (New York: Oxford University Press, 2004), 30.

61. On the southern hookworm campaign and its role in spawning further public health efforts, see John Ettling, *The Germ of Laziness: Rockefeller Philanthropy and Public Health in the New South* (Cambridge, MA: Harvard University Press, 1981); William A. Link, "Privies, Progressivism, and Public Schools: Health Reform and Education in the Rural South, 1909–1920," *Journal of Southern History* 54, no. 4 (1988): 623–42. On the southern roots of the malaria, yellow fever, and tuberculosis campaigns, see Farley, *To Cast Out Disease*.

62. Rockefeller Foundation's secretary Jerome Green in 1913, quoted in Farley, *To Cast Out Disease*, 4.

63. On the importance of southern regionalism to the Rockefeller Foundation's global public health campaigns, see Natalie Ring, "Mapping Regional and Imperial Geographies: Tropical Disease in the U.S. South," in *Colonial Crucible: Empire in the Making of the Modern American State*, ed. Alfred McCoy and Francisco Scarano (Madison: University of Wisconsin Press, 2009); Natalie Ring, "Inventing the Tropical South," *Mississippi Quarterly* 56, no. 4 (2003):

619–31. On the early global campaigns of the Rockefeller Foundation's IHB, see Steven P. Palmer, *Launching Global Health: The Caribbean Odyssey of the Rockefeller Foundation* (Ann Arbor: University of Michigan Press, 2010); Farley, *To Cast Out Disease*, chap. 7. On Rockefeller philanthropy in Mexico before the 1940s' agricultural program, see Anne-Emanuelle Birn, *Marriage of Convenience: Rockefeller International Health and Revolutionary Mexico* (Rochester, NY: University of Rochester Press, 2006); Armando Solórzano, "Sowing the Seeds of Neo-Imperialism: The Rockefeller Foundation's Yellow Fever Campaign in Mexico," *International Journal of Health Services* 22, no. 3 (1992): 529–54; Armando Solórzano, "The Rockefeller Foundation in Revolutionary Mexico: Yellow Fever in Yucatán and Veracruz," in *Missionaries of Science: The Rockefeller Foundation and Latin America*, ed. Marcos Cueto (Bloomington: Indiana University Press, 1994), 52–71.

64. For critiques of US philanthropy abroad, see Mark Dowie, *American Foundations: An Investigative History* (Cambridge, MA: MIT Press, 2001); Inderjeet Parmar, *Foundations of the American Century: The Ford, Carnegie, and Rockefeller Foundations in the Rise of American Power* (New York: Columbia University Press, 2012); Zunz, *Philanthropy in America*; Robert F. Arnove, ed., *Philanthropy and Cultural Imperialism: The Foundations at Home and Abroad* (Bloomington: Indiana University Press, 1982); Edward H. Berman, *The Ideology of Philanthropy: The Influence of the Carnegie, Ford, and Rockefeller Foundations on American Foreign Policy* (Albany: State University of New York Press, 1983).

65. There are two important exceptions worth noting here. In the mid-1920s, the International Education Board—founded in 1923 as the global wing of the GEB—sent Albert R. Mann, the dean of Cornell University's agriculture school, across the Atlantic Ocean for two years to exchange rural improvement strategies with agricultural reformers in Germany, Scandinavia, and central Europe. Mann would later play a key role in directing the MAP, but in doing so, he relied little on his European experience and far more on his extensive work in the US South with the GEB, which will be discussed later. On Mann's European career, see Jonathan Harwood, "Peasant Friendly Plant Breeding and the Early Years of the Green Revolution in Mexico," *Agricultural History* 83, no. 3 (2009): 387–89. Likewise, in the early 1930s the Rockefeller Foundation commissioned its vice president, Selskar M. Gunn, to undertake an agricultural improvement project in nationalist China. Through demonstrations, Gunn taught Chinese farmers the values of basic pest management, fertilization, and crop rotations. Gunn's campaign was poorly received and made little practical impact, and escalating civil war ultimately expelled Gunn and the Rockefeller Foundation from China by the decade's end. On Gunn's Chinese work, see, in particular, David Ekbladh, *The Great American Mission: Modernization and the Construction of an American World Order* (Princeton, NJ: Princeton University Press, 2010), chap. 1; Randall E. Stross, *The Stubborn Earth: American Agriculturalists on Chinese Soil, 1898–1937* (Berkeley: University of California Press, 1986); James C. Thomson, *While China Faced West: American Reformers in Nationalist China, 1928–1937* (Cambridge, MA: Harvard University Press, 1969). I choose to de-emphasize both the European and Chinese programs' influence on Mexico's green revolution because there is little archival evidence that either served the Rockefeller Foundation as a model; it was overwhelmingly the US South and Knapp's farm demonstration campaign that did. For example, when Gunn returned from China in the late 1930s, the foundation sent him not to Mexico but instead to the US South, where he studied the New Deal's evolving program of agrarian reform. See Selskar Gunn, "The Southeast: Notes and Comments on a Visit," May 1941, folder 4568, box 436, series 1.3, GEBP, RAC.

66. On Ferrell's role in the North Carolina hookworm program, see Ettling, *The Germ of Laziness*, 136; Birn, *Marriage of Convenience*, 122; John A. Ferrell, "The North Carolina Campaign against Hookworm Disease," *American Journal of Public Health* 2, no. 4 (1912): 253–57. On the agrarian history of the southeastern corner of North Carolina in which Ferrell came of age, see Adrienne Monteith Petty, *Standing Their Ground: Small Farmers in North Carolina since the Civil War* (New York: Oxford University Press, 2013).

67. "Notes concerning Dr. Ferrell's Trip to Mexico, 21 April to 2 May 1927," reel 1, Diaries of Officers: John A. Ferrell, RG 12.1, RFA, RAC.

68. For one example—of many—of Ferrell selecting candidates for Latin American work based on their US southern experience, see John A. Ferrell to Henry P. Carr, June 18, 1931, folder 474, box 58, series 323, RG 2, RFA, RAC. Carr was the field director of the International Health Division in Mexico, and was himself a doctor from southern Georgia.

69. "Notes on Dr. Ferrell's Trip to Mexico, March 15–April 21, 1933," folder 3778, box 558, 1933 stacks, RG 2, RFA, RAC; Ferrell conference with Gastón Melo, March 31, 1933, folder 2, box 1, series 323, RG 1.1, RFA, RAC.

70. Selskar M. Gunn, "Notes and Comments on a Visit to Mexico, Sept. 2–Nov. 15, 1934," folder 790, box 100, series 323, RG 2, RFA, RAC.

71. Josephus Daniels, *Editor in Politics* (Chapel Hill: University of North Carolina Press, 1941), 568–69.

72. John A. Ferrell, "Memorandum regarding Mexico and IHD Health Program," February 12, 1935, folder 3814, box 561, 1941 stacks, series 323, RG 2, RFA, RAC.

73. Ibid.

74. Charles Bailey to John A. Ferrell, February 22, 1935, folder 907, box 119, series 323, RG 2, RFA, RAC. In the letter, Bailey—the IHB's Mexican representative and Ferrell's host—summarizes what he and Ferrell had discussed earlier.

75. On Fosdick's early life and career, see Daryl L. Revoldt, "Raymond B. Fosdick: Reform, Internationalism, and the Rockefeller Foundation" (PhD diss., University of Akron, 1982); Cullather, *The Hungry World*, 28–30; Raymond B. Fosdick, *Chronicle of a Generation: An Autobiography* (New York: Harper and Brothers, 1958).

76. Josephus Daniels to Raymond B. Fosdick, March 5, 1935, folder 40, box 6, series 1.1, Josephus Daniels Papers, Southern Historical Collection at the Louis Round Wilson Library, University of North Carolina at Chapel Hill.

77. John A. Ferrell to Josephus Daniels, November 6, 1935, General Correspondence, reel 64, Josephus Daniels Papers, Library of Congress, Manuscript Division, Washington, DC (hereafter Daniels Papers).

78. Josephus Daniels to Raymond B. Fosdick, March 3, 1936, General Correspondence, reel 65, Daniels Papers.

79. John A. Ferrell memorandum to Raymond B. Fosdick, October 16, 1936, folder 63, box 10, series 323, RG 1.2, RFA, RAC.

80. Daniels diary entry, March 27, 1937, Diaries, reel 6, Daniels Papers.

81. See, for example, the list of activities in the *Annual Report of the General Education Board, 1928–1929* (New York: General Education Board, 1930).

82. "Conference on Opportunities and Needs in the Southern States," November 10, 1935, folder 4297, box 409, series 1.3, GEBP, RAC. On the impact of the Depression on the GEB, see Fosdick, *Adventure in Giving*, chap. 17.

83. Raymond B. Fosdick to Thomas Debevoise, March 15, 1938, folder 160, box 16, Rockefeller Boards, Rockefeller Family Papers, RAC; Howard W. Odum, *Southern Regions of the United States* (Chapel Hill: University of North Carolina Press, 1936).

84. Raymond B. Fosdick diary entry, May 6, 1938, Officer Diaries microfilm (digitized), RFA, RAC.

85. Details on various programs can be found in the GEB annual reports, 1937 through 1940. On the Georgia agroecology program, see S. B. Detwiler to Albert R. Mann, July 23, 1940, folder 2817, box 272, series 1.2, GEBP, RAC. On the partnership with the FSA, see Charles S. Johnson to Fred McCuistion, June 29, 1940, folder 4416, box 421, series 1.3, GEBP, RAC.

86. Albert R. Mann, "Report on Inspection of Negro Land-Grant Colleges in Certain States, and Visits to Hampton and Tuskegee Institutes," March 4, 1931, folder 3390, box 326, series 1.2, GEBP, RAC; Jackson Davis interview with Albert R. Mann, March 16, 1936, folder 3389, box 326, series 1.2, GEBP, RAC.

87. Albert R. Mann, "Some Background Observations for Southern Programs of the Rockefeller Boards," May 20, 1938, folder 212, box 26, series 900, RG 3.1, RFA, RAC.

88. On Mann and Fosdick's travels around the South, see Jackson Davis, "Trip Report," May 15, 1940, folder 5058, box 475, series 1.3, GEBP, RAC; John D. Rockefeller III, "Trip to Arkansas," October 7, 1940, folder 733, box 87, RG 5: John D. Rockefeller III Papers, Rockefeller Family Papers, RAC.

89. On the United States' renewed diplomatic concerns with Latin America during World War II, see Fredrick B. Pike, *The United States and Latin America: Myths and Stereotypes of Civilization and Nature* (Austin: University of Texas Press, 1992), 287–94. On the Office of Inter-American Affairs, see Monica A. Rankin, *¡México, La Patria! Propaganda and Production during World War II* (Lincoln: University of Nebraska Press, 2009); Claude C. Erb, "Prelude to Point Four: The Institute of Inter-American Affairs," *Diplomatic History* 9, no. 3 (1985): 249–69. On the Rockefeller Foundation's reorientation toward Latin America in the same era, see Raymond B. Fosdick, *The Story of the Rockefeller Foundation* (New York: Harper and Brothers, 1952), 184–85, 259–61.

90. Henry A. Wallace, *The Reminiscences of Henry A. Wallace* (1951), Columbia University Oral History Research Office Collection, Rare Book and Manuscript Library, Columbia University, New York, 1287–88.

91. Henry A. Wallace to Cordell Hull, December 16, 1940, reel 22, Henry A. Wallace Papers, University of Iowa microfilm, Library of Congress, Manuscript Division, Washington, DC.

92. The seeds of the Wallace origins myth were sown in foundation literature reflecting on the MAP's roots. See, for example, Fosdick, *The Story of the Rockefeller Foundation*, 184–85; Elvin C. Stakman, Richard Bradfield, and Paul C. Mangelsdorf, *Campaigns against Hunger* (Cambridge, MA: Belknap Press of Harvard University Press, 1967), 19–22. Most major scholarly works, though, have actively propagated the myth. See, for example, Cullather, *The Hungry World*; Wright, *The Death of Ramón González*; Patel, "The Long Green Revolution"; Kinkela, *DDT and the American Century*; Fitzgerald, "Exporting American Agriculture"; Servando Ortoll, "Orígenes de un proyecto agrícola: La fundación Rockefeller y la revolución verde," *Sociedades rurales, producción y medio ambiente* 4, no. 1 (2003): 81–96. For a notable exception, although it does not acknowledge the regional models or GEB experience that prompted Daniels and Ferrell's push, see Perkins, *Geopolitics and the Green Revolution*.

93. John A. Ferrell to George Payne, January 21, 1941, folder 2, box 1, series 323, RG 1.1, RFA, RAC.

94. John A. Ferrell, "Aid to Mexico: Continued Support of Public Health Services; Aid Also toward Measures in the Field of Agriculture; Possibly Special Activities in the Field of Education," January 27, 1941, folder 3814, box 561, series 323, 1941 stacks, RG 2, RFA, RAC.

95. Ibid.

96. John A. Ferrell, "Notes on Conference with Vice President Wallace, RBF, and JAF regarding Mexico—Its Problems and Remedies," February 3, 1941, folder 2, box 1, series 323, RG 1.1, RFA, RAC. See also Raymond B. Fosdick memorandum on conference with Henry A. Wallace, February 3, 1941, folder 70, box 11, series 323, RG 1.1, RFA, RAC.

97. Harry M. Miller oral history, interviewed by William C. Cobb, May 1967, box 19, RG 13, RFA, RAC, 16.

98. "Staff Conference," February 18, 1941, folder 2, box 1, series 323, RG 1.1, RFA, RAC. Fosdick also asked Frank Hanson, interim chief of natural sciences, to assist Mann on writing the memo on agriculture in Mexico. But because of other duties, Hanson did not do so, and Mann wrote the report alone.

99. Albert R. Mann, "Approach to a Possible Natural Science Program in Mexico with Special Reference to Agriculture," February 20, 1941, folder 70, box 11, series 323, RG 1.1, RFA, RAC.

100. Daniels diary entry, April 7, 1941, Diaries, reel 7, Daniels Papers.

101. John A. Ferrell, "Report by JAF on His Visit to Mexico," March–April 1941, folder 3814, box 561, series 323, 1941 stacks, RG 2, RFA, RAC.

102. Paul Mangelsdorf oral history, interviewed by William C. Cobb, 1966, RG 13, RFA, RAC, 45. It is worth mentioning that before organizing the Survey Commission, the foundation sent the Division of Natural Sciences zoologist Harry "Dusty" Miller to Mexico in March 1941 to scout the possibilities of a program in agriculture. In contrast to Daniels and Ferrell—and the later Survey Commission report—Miller in his report on the visit contemptuously dismissed the Mexican Revolution's agrarian program, and denigrated the average ejido farmer as stubborn, uncooperative, ignorant, and racially inferior. Large commercial farmers, Miller insisted, would be the only worthwhile partners in an agricultural program, and his report smacks of US hubris and arrogance. I underemphasize Miller and his report's significance, however, in the path toward Mexico because the Rockefeller Foundation's leadership did likewise; Fosdick, Mann, and their peers immediately acknowledged the Miller report's flaws and biases, and sent the Survey Commission to right these wrongs. See Harry Miller, "Mexican Log: Aspects of Agriculture in Mexico," March 28, 1941, folder 366, box 33, series 1.1, RG 6.13, RFA, RAC.

103. Elvin C. Stakman, Paul C. Mangelsdorf, and Richard Bradfield, "Agricultural Conditions and Problems in Mexico: Report of the Survey Commission of the Rockefeller Foundation," August–September 1941, folder 2, box 1, series 323, RG 1.1, RFA, RAC.

104. Ibid.

105. "Resolution on Survey of Agriculture in Mexico," December 3, 1941, folder 103, box 17, series 323, RG 1.2, RFA, RAC.

106. Stakman, Bradfield, and Mangelsdorf, *Campaigns against Hunger*, 36.

CHAPTER FIVE: GREEN REVOLUTIONS

1. "Comments by Professor Carl Sauer," February 10, 1941, folder 2, box 1, series 323, record group (hereafter RG) 1.1, Rockefeller Foundation Archives (hereafter RFA), Rockefeller Archive Center, Tarrytown, New York (hereafter RAC). Italics are mine.

2. For works that cite Sauer's critique of the foundation's Mexican program as illustrative of its original shortcomings, see Angus Wright, *The Death of Ramón González: The Modern Agricultural Dilemma* (Austin: University of Texas Press, 1990); Nick Cullather, *The Hungry World: America's Cold War Battle against Poverty in Asia* (Cambridge, MA: Harvard University Press, 2010); Joseph Cotter, *Troubled Harvest: Agronomy and Revolution in Mexico, 1880–2002* (Westport, CT: Praeger, 2003); Bruce H. Jennings, *Foundations of International Agricultural Research: Science and Politics in Mexican Agriculture* (Boulder, CO: Westview Press, 1988); Stephen A. Marglin, "Farmers, Seedsmen, and Scientists: Systems of Agriculture and Systems of Knowledge," in *Decolonizing Knowledge: From Development to Dialogue*, ed. Frédérique Appfel-Marglin and Stephen A. Marglin (New York: Oxford University Press, 1996).

3. James C. Scott, *Seeing Like a State: How Certain Schemes to Improve the Human Condition Have Failed* (New Haven, CT: Yale University Press, 1998); Vandana Shiva, *The Violence of the Green Revolution: Third World Agriculture, Ecology, and Politics* (London: Zed Books, 1991). For a few influential critical works on the green revolution that fall outside Mexico, see Arturo Escobar, *Encountering Development: The Making and Unmaking of the Third World* (Princeton, NJ: Princeton University Press, 1995); Akhil Gupta, *Postcolonial Developments: Agriculture and the Making of Modern India* (Durham, NC: Duke University Press, 1998); David Kinkela, *DDT and the American Century: Global Health, Environmental Politics, and the Pesticide That Changed the World* (Chapel Hill: University of North Carolina Press, 2011).

4. Raj Patel, "The Long Green Revolution," *Journal of Peasant Studies* 40, no. 1 (2013): 38.

5. Carl O. Sauer to Joseph Willits, March 12, 1941, folder 63, box 10, series 323, RG 1.2, RFA, RAC.

6. John A. Ferrell to Raymond B. Fosdick, February 13, 1941, folder 2, box 1, series 323, RG 1.1, RFA, RAC.

7. Jonathan Harwood pursues a strikingly similar argument about the dynamism and possibility of the early years of the green revolution in Mexico; see Jonathan Harwood, "Peasant Friendly Plant Breeding and the Early Years of the Green Revolution in Mexico," *Agricultural History* 83, no. 3 (2009): 384–410. But he credits such sympathies with inspirations from German plant-breeding efforts of the early twentieth century, though his evidence is more speculative than empirical as few of the MAP's staff members wrote of European similarities. The US South, however, turns up frequently in their correspondence. On low modernism, see Jess Gilbert, *Planning Democracy: Agrarian Intellectuals and the Intended New Deal* (New Haven, CT: Yale University Press, 2015), 8–9.

8. Eric Wolf, *Europe and the People without History* (Berkeley: University of California Press, 1982), x. Wolf's ruminations on the West's denial of history to the "rest" are brought to bear on the postwar development project most notably in James Ferguson, *The Anti-Politics Machine: "Development," Depoliticization, and Bureaucratic Power in Lesotho* (New York: Cambridge University Press, 1990). On race, the US South, and empire, see Mary Renda, *Taking Haiti: Military Occupation and the Culture of U.S. Imperialism, 1915–1940* (Chapel Hill: University of North Carolina Press, 2001); Paul Kramer, *The Blood of Government: Race, Empire, the United States, and the Philippines* (Chapel Hill: University of North Carolina Press, 2006); Andrew Zimmerman, *Alabama in Africa: Booker T. Washington, the German Empire, and the Globalization of the New South* (Princeton, NJ: Princeton University Press, 2010); Marilyn Lake and Henry Reynolds, *Drawing the Global Colour Line: White Men's Countries and the International Challenge of Racial Equality* (New York: Cambridge University Press, 2008); Erin Elizabeth Clune, "From Light Copper to the Blackest and Lowest Type: Daniel Tompkins and the Racial Order of the Global

New South," *Journal of Southern History* 76, no. 2 (2010): 275–314; Elizabeth Herbin-Triant, "Southern Segregation, South Africa–Style: Maurice Evans, Clarence Poe, and the Ideology of Rural Segregation," *Agricultural History* 87, no. 2 (2013): 170–93; Stephanie R. Rolph, "The Citizens' Council and Africa: White Supremacy in Global Perspective," *Journal of Southern History* 82, no. 3 (2016): 617–50; Natalie Ring, *The Problem South: Region, Empire, and the New Liberal State, 1880–1930* (Athens: University of Georgia Press, 2012).

9. William H. Beezley, ed., *A Companion to Mexican History and Culture* (Malden, MA: Blackwell Publishing, 2011), 453.

10. For a repudiation of the traditional 1940 division, see Susie Porter, "The Apogee of Revolution, 1934–1946," in *A Companion to Mexican History and Culture*, ed. William H. Beezley (Malden, MA: Blackwell Publishing, 2011), 453–67.

11. "El verdadero problema agrario," *Excélsior*, February 22, 1938, clipping from Josephus Daniels to Cordell Hull, February 28, 1938, 812.52/2597, reel 88, microfilm pub. M1370, RG 59: Records of the Department of State, US National Archives and Records Administration II, College Park, Maryland (hereafter NA).

12. Fernando Leal Novelo, "Grave problema agrario que indica falta de intensificación agrícola por parte de los campesinos," *Gráfico*, January 31, 1942, clipping from file A02059, Archivos Económicos, Biblioteca Miguel Lerdo de Tejada, Mexico City (hereafter BMLT).

13. Ramón Beteta, "La distribución de tierras," *El Nacional*, August 3, 1936, clipping from box 164, Ramón Fernández y Fernández Papers, Biblioteca Luis González, Colegio de Michoacán, Zamora, Michoacán, Mexico (hereafter Fernández Papers).

14. Marco Antonio Durán, "El aumento de la producción agrícola nacional," *México Agrario* 4, no. 1 (1942), 45, 50. On the long marriage between revolutionary politics and agricultural science after 1910, see Michael A. Ervin, "The Art of the Possible: Agronomists, Agrarian Reform, and the Middle Politics of the Mexican Revolution, 1908–1934" (PhD diss., University of Pittsburgh, 2002); Ramón Fernández y Fernández, *Chapingo hace 50 años* (Chapingo, Mexico: Escuela Nacional de Agricultura, 1976).

15. Marte R. Gómez to José Vasconcelos, August 11, 1923, in Emilio Alanís Patiño, ed., *Vida política contemporánea: Cartas de Marte R. Gómez* (Mexico City: Fondo de Cultura Económica, 1978), 1:23.

16. On Gómez's long career, see Michael A. Ervin, "Marte R. Gómez of Tamaulipas: Governing Agrarian Revolution," in *State Governors in the Mexican Revolution, 1910–1952: Portraits in Conflict, Courage, and Corruption*, ed. Jürgen Buchenau and William Beezley (Lanham, MD: Rowman and Littlefield, 2009); Gustavo Esteva, "Hosting the Otherness of the Other: The Case of the Green Revolution," in *Decolonizing Knowledge: From Development to Dialogue*, ed. Frédérique Appfel-Marglin and Stephen A. Marglin (New York: Oxford University Press, 1996), 249–78.

17. Ervin, "Marte R. Gómez of Tamaulipas," 129.

18. On Wallace's stop at El Mante, see Josephus Daniels to Cordell Hull, December 3, 1940, folder 2, box 4112, 812.001 Camacho, Manuel A/97, RG 59, NA.

19. On the Mexican Far Left's critique of Gómez, see, in particular, Emilio López Zamora, *La situación del distrito de riego de El Mante* (Mexico City: Liga de Agrónomos Socialistas/Editorial Ramírez Alonso, 1939); Ervin, "Marte R. Gómez of Tamaulipas," 133–34.

20. On Gómez working within the "art of the possible" see Ervin, "Marte R. Gómez of Tamaulipas"; Ervin, "The Art of the Possible." For a recent exception to the neglect of the Ávila Camacho years that also acknowledges the unpredictability of that era, see Halbert Jones, *The*

War Has Brought Peace to Mexico: World War II and the Consolidation of the Post-Revolutionary State (Albuquerque: University of New Mexico Press, 2014).

21. Manuel Ávila Camacho, "Texto del discurso pronunciado por el C. Presidente de la República, el 10 de abril de 1941, durante la ceremonia efectuada para conmemorar la muerte del caudillo Gral. Emiliano Zapata," General Don Manuel Ávila Camacho, 1940–45, Marte R. Gómez Papers, Archivo Marte R. Gómez, Lomas de Chapultepec, Mexico City (hereafter Gómez Papers).

22. Manuel Ávila Camacho, "Discurso pronunciado en el Palacio de Bellas Artes con motivo del quinto aniversario de la fundación de la Confederación Nacional Campesina," November 19, 1943, folder 708.1/37, box 1185, Manuel Ávila Camacho Papers, Archivo General de la Nación, Mexico City (hereafter Ávila Camacho Papers).

23. Cotter, *Troubled Harvest*, 151–52.

24. Secretaría de Agricultura y Fomento, "Plan de Movilización Agrícola," June 1942, box 143, Fernández Papers.

25. Marte R. Gómez to Henry A. Wallace, March 31, 1942, Documentos Oficiales, 1942, Vol. II, Gómez Papers.

26. For press reports on corn scarcities in the early Ávila Camacho years, see "El problema del maíz," *Novedades*, August 29, 1941, clipping from file P12675, Archivos Económicos, BMLT; "El gran problema," *Gráfico*, August 9, 1943, clipping from file P12409, Archivos Económicos, BMLT.

27. George Messersmith to Philip Bonsal, October 4, 1943, folder 4, box 4148, 812.5018/87, RG 59, NA. Mexican critics were also cognizant of this dilemma; see "El fracaso de nuestra agricultura," January 25, 1944, *Ultimas Noticias de Excélsior*, clipping from file A02059, Archivos Económicos, BMLT. On the US-Mexican agricultural cooperation of the wartime years and its consequences for Mexican food production, see Enrique C. Ochoa, *Feeding Mexico: The Political Uses of Food since 1910* (Wilmington, DE: Scholarly Resources Books, 2000), chap. 4; Mark Finlay, *Growing American Rubber: Strategic Plants and the Politics of National Security* (New Brunswick, NJ: Rutgers University Press, 2009), chap. 5; Stephen R. Niblo, *War, Diplomacy, and Development: The United States and Mexico, 1938–1945* (Wilmington, DE: Scholarly Resources Books, 1995), 93–95.

28. Marte R. Gómez, "Discurso que el ingeniero Marte R. Gómez pronunció en la comida de los Rotarios," November 1942, Discursos de Marte R. Gómez, Gómez Papers.

29. On Gómez's acknowledgment of corn shortages and rising prices to colleagues in government, see Marte R. Gómez to the Director Gerente del Banco Nacional de Crédito Agrícola, March 31, 1942, Documentos Oficiales, 1942, Vol. II, Gómez Papers.

30. On Gómez using claims of Mexican wartime sacrifice to secure favors from the US government, see, in particular, Marte R. Gómez to Henry A. Wallace, March 30, 1943, Cartas, 1943, T-Z, Gómez Papers.

31. Ochoa, *Feeding Mexico*, 74–76.

32. For the letter that went out to every state's governor, see Manuel Ávila Camacho to Rodolfo T. Loaiza (and others), January 20, 1944, folder 545.2/83, box 760, Ávila Camacho Papers.

33. Henry A. Wallace to Marte R. Gómez, March 7, 1941, Cartas, 1941, Q-Z, Gómez Papers. For the formal offer, see Raymond B. Fosdick to Marte R. Gómez, October 1, 1942, folder 63, box 10, series 323, RG 1.2, RFA, RAC.

34. Marte R. Gómez, "Memorandum para el Señor Presidente de la República sobre el funcionamiento de la Fundación Rockefeller y enumeración de las actividades que desearía

realizar en México en materia de producción agrícola," September 21, 1942, Documentos Oficiales, 1942, Vol. II, Gómez Papers.

35. Edwin J. Wellhausen Oral History, June 1966, RG 13, RFA, RAC, 166.

36. Marte R. Gómez to Raymond B. Fosdick, October 17, 1942, Documentos Oficiales, 1942, Vol. II, Gómez Papers.

37. In Spanish, the verb "explotar" has a slightly different meaning than "exploit" in English. When applied to human beings, it does connote the same negative, imbalanced relationship that is implied in the English, but when applied to land or soil, it more closely means to "cultivate," with fewer negative implications. On Chapingo and the national significance of Rivera's mural there, see Jennifer Krzyminski Younger, "Utopía Mexicana: Diego Rivera's Program for Chapingo Chapel, 1924–1927" (PhD diss., University of Maryland, 1999).

38. On the launching of the MAP and its organization, see Elvin C. Stakman, Richard Bradfield, and Paul C. Mangelsdorf, *Campaigns against Hunger* (Cambridge, MA: Belknap Press of Harvard University Press, 1967), chap. 3; Elvin C. Stakman, "Report on Agricultural Activities in Mexico," May 20, 1943, folder 60, box 10, series 323, RG 1.2, RFA, RAC.

39. Richard Bradfield to Frank Hanson, January 7, 1943, folder titled "Bradfield, Richard," box 2, HUG (FP) 37.8, Paul C. Mangelsdorf Papers, Harvard University Archives, Cambridge, Massachusetts (hereafter Mangelsdorf Papers).

40. Carl O. Sauer to Joseph Willits, August 23, 1943, folder 6, box 1, series 323, RG 1.1, RFA, RAC; Anderson letter, dated August 19, 1943, enclosed in Sauer's letter to Willits.

41. On the recruitment of Colwell and Roberts, alongside their biographical information, see Stakman, Bradfield, and Mangelsdorf, *Campaigns against Hunger*, 40–42.

42. Frank Hanson to Jacob George Harrar, April 8, 1943, folder 4, box 1, series 323, RG 1.1, RFA, RAC. On Mann's 1943 trip to review the program, see Albert Mann, "Observations in Mexico," April 25, 1943, folder 1909, box 201, series 1.2, General Education Board Papers (hereafter GEBP), RAC.

43. "Memorandum on NS Agricultural Program in Mexico," March 8, 1946, folder 11, box 2, series 323, RG 1.1, RFA, RAC. On Mann's acceptance of the post, see Warren Weaver memorandum on Albert Mann, November 27, 1945, folder 10, box 2, series 323, RG 1.1, RFA, RAC. On Mann's formal title, see Warren Weaver to Raymond B. Fosdick, April 18, 1946, folder 11, box 2, series 323, RG 1.1, RFA, RAC.

44. On the cotton regions of east Texas at this time, see Neil Foley, *The White Scourge: Mexicans, Blacks, and Poor Whites in Texas Cotton Culture* (Berkeley: University of California Press, 1997).

45. On hybrid corn along with its political and economic consequences, see Jack R. Kloppenburg, *First the Seed: The Political Economy of Plant Biotechnology, 1492–2000* (New York: Cambridge University Press, 1988); Deborah Fitzgerald, *The Business of Breeding: Hybrid Corn in Illinois, 1890–1940* (Ithaca, NY: Cornell University Press, 1990); Deborah Fitzgerald, "Farmers Deskilled: Hybrid Corn and Farmers' Work," *Technology and Culture* 34, no. 2 (1993): 324–43; Noel Kingsbury, *Hybrid: The History and Science of Plant Breeding* (Chicago: University of Chicago Press, 2009), chap. 10.

46. Fitzgerald, *The Business of Breeding*, 220. Much of that explosion in acreage was due to New Deal programs such as the Agricultural Adjustment Administration (AAA), which paid cash—a relative rarity in the US countryside—to farmers who removed cropland from cultivation. Of course, when farmers invested that cash in hybrid seed to make their reduced acreage far more productive, this sabotaged the AAA's stated mission of lowering supply. This was but one of the many paradoxes of the agricultural New Deal.

47. Paul C. Mangelsdorf Oral History, November 1966, RG 13, RFA, RAC, 21.

48. Karin Matchett has done important work in drawing attention to Mangelsdorf's unconventional approach to corn breeding in Mexico, particularly in her dissertation and an article; see Karin Matchett, "At Odds over Inbreeding: An Abandoned Attempt at Mexico/ United States Collaboration to 'Improve' Mexican Corn, 1940–1950," *Journal of the History of Biology* 39, no. 2 (2006): 345–72; Karin Matchett, "Untold Innovation: Scientific Practice and Corn Improvement in Mexico, 1935–1965" (PhD diss., University of Minnesota, 2002). She does not, however, emphasize the role of US regionalism in honing Mangelsdorf's social philosophy of technology, nor the importance of his transregional comparisons in shaping the early MAP.

49. Fitzgerald, *The Business of Breeding*, 189–97.

50. Merle Jenkins, "Report of the First Southern Corn Improvement Conference," November 24, 1939, publisher unknown, Washington, DC, 33.

51. Paul C. Mangelsdorf to Merle Jenkins, May 12, 1943, folder titled "Jenkins, Merle T.," box 5, Mangelsdorf Papers.

52. Merle Jenkins to Paul C. Mangelsdorf, May 27, 1943, folder titled "Jenkins, Merle T.," box 5, Mangelsdorf Papers.

53. Paul C. Mangelsdorf to Richard Bradfield and Elvin C. Stakman, August 30, 1944, folder titled "Bradfield, Richard," box 2, Mangelsdorf Papers.

54. On Limón and his León breeding work, see Matchett, "At Odds over Inbreeding"; Cotter, *Troubled Harvest*, 151–52; "Informe de labores de la Secretaría de Agricultura y Fomento del primero de septiembre de 1942 al 31 de agosto de 1943," August 31, 1943, folder 606.3/97, box 999, Ávila Camacho Papers. On the MAP's early tensions with Limón, see Edwin Wellhausen Oral History, RG 13, RFA, RAC, 32–37.

55. Paul C. Mangelsdorf to Alfonso González Gallardo, December 10, 1943, folder 6, box 1, series 323, RG 1.1, RFA, RAC.

56. "Informe de labores de la Secretaría de Agricultura y Fomento del 1 de Sept. de 1943 al 31 de Ago. de 1944," August 31, 1944, folder 606.3/97, box 1001, Ávila Camacho Papers.

57. "Habla Agricultura sobre la polinización del maíz," *El Universal*, November 12, 1944, clipping from box 123, Fernández Papers.

58. "¿Qué es el maíz híbrido? Sus ventajas y limitaciones," *Tierra* 10 (July 1946), 579.

59. On the first distribution of synthetic seed to Mexican farmers, see "Semilla de maíz sintético para los agricultores," *Tierra* 2, no. 3 (March 1947): 158–69. On Wellhausen's embrace of open-pollinated synthetics over double-cross hybrids, see Edwin Wellhausen and Lewis Roberts, "Methods Used and Results Obtained in Corn Improvement in Mexico," *Iowa State College Agricultural Experiment Station Research Bulletin* 371 (December 1949), 527–28.

60. For evidence of other foundation leaders championing the emphasis on synthetic corn rather than double-cross hybrids, see Elvin C. Stakman, "Report on Agricultural Activities in Mexico," May 20, 1943, folder 60, box 10, series 323, RG 1.2, RFA, RAC; Jacob George Harrar, "Progress Report of RF Agricultural Program in Mexico," November 1, 1944, folder 3, box 6, series 323, RG 1.1, RFA, RAC; Elvin C. Stakman, "Report of Mexican Trip," September 20, 1945, folder 60, box 10, series 323, RG 1.2, RFA, RAC.

61. Carl O. Sauer to Joseph Willits, February 12, 1945, folder 4636, box 391, series 200, RG 1.1, RFA, RAC.

62. The primary exception was its wheat program, which will be discussed in detail in the following section.

63. "Report of the Oficina de Estudios Especiales," June 1, 1945, folder 1, box 6, series 323, RG 1.1, RFA, RAC. On the prioritization of cultural and nonchemical practices over commercial fertilizer, see "Activities of RF-SAF Cooperative Agricultural Program," December 31, 1944, folder 521, box 45, series 1.1, RG 6.13, RFA, RAC.

64. Richard Bradfield to Paul C. Mangelsdorf, July 23, 1946, folder 57, box 9, series 323, RG 1.1, RFA, RAC. For evidence of Mann's leadership of the extension program, see "Annual Meeting of the Advisory Committee," October 17, 1946, folder 67, box 10, series 323, RG 1.1, RFA, RAC.

65. Albert Mann to Henry A. Wallace, August 28, 1946, folder 12, box 2, series 323, RG 1.1, RFA, RAC.

66. Lázaro Cárdenas, *Obras—I: Apuntes 1941–1956* (Mexico City: Universidad Nacional Autónoma de México, 1973), 2:218.

67. "Sin agricultura, sería un fracaso la industrialización, opina Wallace," *Excélsior*, September 8, 1946, clipping from Cartas, 1946, S-Z, Gómez Papers; Henry A. Wallace, *The Reminiscences of Henry A. Wallace* (1951), Columbia University Oral History Research Office Collection, Rare Book and Manuscript Library, Columbia University, New York, 4942. For additional evidence that it was synthetic, open pollinated maize that the group was shown, see "Henry A. Wallace habla para *Tierra*," *Tierra* 12 (September 1946): 660–63.

68. Warren Weaver, *The Reminiscences of Warren Weaver* (1961), Columbia University Oral History Research Office Collection, Rare Book and Manuscript Library, Columbia University, New York, 655. On his career, see Warren Weaver, *Scene of Change: A Lifetime in American Science* (New York: Scribner's, 1970).

69. Stephen R. Niblo, *Mexico in the 1940s: Modernity, Politics, and Corruption* (Wilmington, DE: Scholarly Resources Books, 1999), 183.

70. "Cómo entiende el Lic. Miguel Alemán el problema agrario," *Siembra* 2, no. 28 (July 15, 1945), 2.

71. On Alemán's agrarian agenda, see Tzvi Medin, *El sexenio alemanista: Ideología y praxis política de Miguel Alemán* (Mexico City: Ediciones Era, 1990), chap. 5; Niblo, *Mexico in the 1940s*, 183–88; Ryan M. Alexander, "Fortunate Sons of the Mexican Revolution: Miguel Alemán and His Generation, 1920–1952" (PhD diss., University of Arizona, 2011), 200–208.

72. On the details of the agency's creation, see "Más técnica en nuestra agricultura," *Excélsior*, January 17, 1947, clipping from file P12675, Archivos Económicos, BMLT. On the Corn Commission, see Adolfo Olea-Franco, "La introducción del maíz híbrido en la agricultura mexicana: Una historia de equívocos científicos, intereses comerciales y conflictos sociales," in *Ciencia en los márgines: Ensayos de historia de las ciencias en México*, ed. Mechthild Rutsch and Carlos Serrano Sánchez (Mexico City: Instituto de Investigaciones Antropológicas, 1997); Adolfo Olea-Franco, "One Century of Higher Agricultural Education and Research in Mexico (1850s–1960s), with a Preliminary Survey on the Same Subjects in the United States" (PhD diss., Harvard University, 2001), 644–49; Ochoa, *Feeding Mexico*, 100–102; Cotter, *Troubled Harvest*, 194.

73. "Integró formalmente Comisión del Maíz," *Novedades*, October 19, 1946, clipping from folder 13, box 2, series 323, RG 1.1, RFA, RAC (translation is my own, not the foundation's).

74. Elvin C. Stakman, "Latin-American Agricultural Institutions," July 14, 1947, folder 37, box 6, series 300, RG 1.1, RFA, RAC; Paul C. Mangelsdorf to Elvin C. Stakman, August 9, 1948, folder 59, box 9, series 323, RG 1.1, RFA, RAC.

75. Edwin Wellhausen Oral History, June 1966, RG 13, RFA, RAC, 101–2, 104.

76. Norberto Aguirre to Miguel Alemán, February 27, 1952, folder 312/5160, box 947, Miguel Alemán Valdés Papers, Archivo General de la Nación, Mexico City. On patronage and clientelism in modern Mexico, see S. Kaufmann Purcell, "Mexico: Clientelism, Corporatism and Political Stability," in *Political Clientelism, Patronage, and Development*, ed. S. N. Eisenstadt and René Lemarchand (Beverly Hills, CA: Sage Publications, 1981); Kevin Middlebrook, *The Paradox of Revolution: Labor, the State, and Authoritarianism in Mexico* (Baltimore: Johns Hopkins University Press, 1995).

77. G. W. Gray interview with Edwin Wellhausen, August 15, 1952, folder 25, box 4, series 323, RG 1.1, RFA, RAC.

78. Wellhausen and Roberts, "Methods Used and Results Obtained in Corn Improvement in Mexico," 532.

79. On maize versus wheat in Mexico's agricultural history, see Jeffrey M. Pilcher, *¡Que Vivan los Tamales! Food and the Making of Mexican Identity* (Albuquerque: University of New Mexico Press, 1998), chaps. 1–2; Wright, *The Death of Ramón González*; John H. Perkins, *Geopolitics and the Green Revolution: Wheat, Genes, and the Cold War* (New York: Oxford University Press, 1997), especially chap. 5.

80. Elvin C. Stakman, Paul C. Mangelsdorf, and Richard Bradfield, "Agricultural Conditions and Problems in Mexico: Report of the Survey Commission of the Rockefeller Foundation," August–September 1941, folder 2, box 1, series 323, RG 1.1, RFA, RAC.

81. Elvin C. Stakman, "Report on Agricultural Activities in Mexico," May 20, 1943, folder 60, box 10, series 323, RG 1.2, RFA, RAC. On the first meeting and Gómez's insistence on wheat as priority, see Jacob George Harrar Diary, February 8–9, 1943, Officer Diaries microfilm (accessed digitally on CD), RFA, RAC.

82. See Pilcher, *¡Que Vivan los Tamales!* chap. 4.

83. Marte R. Gómez to Henry A. Wallace, February 21, 1941, Cartas, 1941, Q-Z, Gómez Papers.

84. Elvin C. Stakman, "Report on Agricultural Activities in Mexico," May 20, 1943, folder 60, box 10, series 323, RG 1.2, RFA, RAC. On the final agreement and balancing of corn and wheat, see "Proposals for a Memorandum of Understanding between the Secretaría de Agricultura and the Rockefeller Foundation," February 20, 1943, III–646–7, Archivo Histórico de la Secretaría de Relaciones Exteriores, Tlatelolco, Mexico City.

85. "The Rockefeller Foundation Oral History of Norman E. Borlaug," 1967 interview, CIMMYT Records [050], CIMMYT Records Textual 01, Norman E. Borlaug Digital Archive, College of Agriculture and Life Sciences, Texas A&M University, College Station, accessed November 5, 2016, borlaugarchives.tamu.edu (hereafter Borlaug Oral History), 72, 74.

86. On the early blueprint of the MAP wheat program under Borlaug, see "Report of the Oficina de Estudios Especiales," June 1, 1945, and "Report of the Oficina de Estudios Especiales," June 1, 1946, both in folder 1, box 6, series 323, RG 1.1, RFA, RAC.

87. Carl O. Sauer to Joseph Willits, February 12, 1945, folder 4636, box 391, series 200, RG 1.1, RFA, RAC.

88. Leon Hesser, *The Man Who Fed the World: Nobel Peace Prize Laureate Norman Borlaug and His Battle to End World Hunger* (Dallas: Durban House Publishing Company, 2006), 51; Norman E. Borlaug's undated, unpublished autobiography transcribed by Noel Vietmayer, 003 Early Draft of NEB's Biography, 001 Early Draft of NEB's Biography by Noel Viefmyer [*sic*], CIMMYT records [042], CIMMYT Records Textual 2, Norman E. Borlaug Digital Archive, College of Agriculture and Life Sciences, Texas A&M University, College Station, accessed

November 5, 2016, borlaugarchives.tamu.edu, 140. For a discussion of the confrontation, see Noel Vietmeyer, *Borlaug: Wheat Whisperer, 1944–1959* (Lorton, VA: Bracing Books, 2009), 67. Though Hesser and Vietmayer's books are uncritical hagiographies backed by minimal documentation, both are based on extensive interviews with Borlaug and were ultimately authorized by the wheat breeder himself. That Borlaug would have fabricated such an interaction—which is rather damning of him, at least in the eyes of critics of the green revolution's social prejudices—is highly unlikely. For further evidence of the tension between Borlaug and Harrar over wheat breeding outside central Mexico, see Borlaug Oral History, 165–66.

89. On the southward turn of the Cold War, see Odd Arne Westad, *The Global Cold War: Third World Interventions and the Making of Our Times* (New York: Cambridge University Press, 2005). On the invention of the Third World, see Vijay Prashad, *The Darker Nations: A People's History of the Third World* (New York: New Press, 2007).

90. Amanda McVety, *Enlightened Aid: U.S. Development as Foreign Policy in Ethiopia* (New York: Oxford University Press, 2012), 1. In the past generation there has been an outpouring of scholarship on the social, intellectual, and geopolitical history of "development" in the early Cold War; see, in particular, Escobar, *Encountering Development*; Gilbert Rist, *The History of Development: From Western Origins to Global Faith* (London: Zed Books, 2002); Michael Latham, *Modernization as Ideology: American Social Science and "Nation Building" in the Kennedy Era* (Chapel Hill: University of North Carolina Press, 2000); Nils Gilman, *Mandarins of the Future: Modernization Theory in Cold War America* (Baltimore: Johns Hopkins University Press, 2003); Stephen J. Macekura, *Of Limits and Growth: The Rise of Global Sustainable Development in the Twentieth Century* (New York: Cambridge University Press, 2015); David C. Engerman, Nils Gilman, Mark Haefele, and Michael E. Latham, eds., *Staging Growth: Modernization, Development, and the Global Cold War* (Amherst: University of Massachusetts Press, 2003); Amy L. Staples, *The Birth of Development: How the World Bank, Food and Agriculture Organization, and World Health Organization Changed the World, 1945–1965* (Kent, OH: Kent State University Press, 2006); David Ekbladh, *The Great American Mission: Modernization and the Construction of an American World Order* (Princeton, NJ: Princeton University Press, 2010); McVety, *Enlightened Aid*; Daniel Immerwahr, *Thinking Small: The United States and the Lure of Community Development* (Cambridge, MA: Harvard University Press, 2015).

91. On the centrality of food and agriculture to the origins and outcome of World War II, see Lizzie Collingham, *The Taste of War: World War II and the Battle for Food* (New York: Penguin, 2012). On the impact of neo-Malthusian thinking on the environmental movement and the Cold War, see Thomas Robertson, *The Malthusian Moment: Global Population Growth and the Birth of American Environmentalism* (New Brunswick, NJ: Rutgers University Press, 2012); Derek S. Hoff, *The State and the Stork: The Population Debate and Policy Making in US History* (Chicago: University of Chicago Press, 2012).

92. Warren Weaver to Jacob George Harrar, October 4, 1948, folder 16, box 3, series 323, RG 1.1, RFA, RAC.

93. Paul C. Mangelsdorf and Richard Bradfield, "Report on Trip to Colombia and Other South and Central American Countries," July 8, 1948, folder 360, box 32, series 1.1, RG 6.13, RFA, RAC.

94. Stakman, Mangelsdorf, and Bradfield, "Agricultural Conditions and Problems in Mexico." The word "hunger" appears but twice in this founding document, and only once—as late as page 48 of 60—to actually describe a scarcity of food.

95. "Agenda for the Annual Meeting of the Advisory Committee for Agricultural Activities of the Rockefeller Foundation," October 26, 1950, folder 67, box 10, series 323, RG 1.1, RFA, RAC.

96. "Annual Meeting of the Advisory Committee, Mexican Agricultural Program," October 30, 1947, folder 67, box 10, series 323, RG 1.1, RFA, RAC.

97. Borlaug's fight with Harrar is curiously absent from the Rockefeller Foundation archives, but is described in detail in Borlaug's two authorized biographies: Hesser, *The Man Who Fed the World*, 52–53; Vietmayer, *Borlaug*, 2:104–7 (although Vietmayer incorrectly deems the conflict to have happened in 1947). See also the undated interview Vietmayer conducted with Borlaug: [002] Establishment of the RF Office of Special Studies in Mexico, [006] Biography, CIMMYT records [041], CIMMYT Records Textual [2], Norman E. Borlaug Digital Archive, College of Agriculture and Life Sciences, Texas A&M University, College Station, accessed November 5, 2016, borlaugarchives.tamu.edu, 53–65. Borlaug likewise acknowledges the incident—in an offhanded manner; see Borlaug Oral History, 165–66. That the incident occurred in 1948 rather than 1947 is evidenced in Jacob George Harrar to Warren Weaver, December 20, 1948, and Jacob George Harrar to Warren Weaver, December 23, 1948, both in folder 64, box 11, series 323, RG 1.2, RFA, RAC, which make it clear that the tension was recent, but carefully sidestep the personal conflict between the two men.

98. On Borlaug's partnership with Rodolfo Elías Calles, see Borlaug Oral History, 169. On the junior Calles and his place in the Mexican Revolution, see Mary Kay Vaughan, *Cultural Politics in Revolution: Teachers, Peasants, and Schools in Mexico, 1930–1940* (Tucson: University of Arizona Press, 1997), 56–57.

99. On Spurlock's hacienda and his close bond to the Rockefeller Foundation, see Vietmayer, 003 Early Draft of NEB's Biography, 133–34; G. W. Gray interview with Edwin Wellhausen, August 15, 1952, folder 25, box 4, series 323, RG 1.1, RFA, RAC.

100. "Annual Report of the Director for the Mexican Agricultural Program," December 1, 1951, folder 1, box 6, series 323, RG 1.1, RFA, RAC; Norman E. Borlaug and J. A. Rupert, "Cómo aumentar la producción de trigo en México," *Tierra* 4, no. 7 (July 1949): 401–28.

101. Elvin C. Stakman, "Proposals for an Expanded Agricultural Program," 1951, folder titled "RF Report to C. I. Bernard '51," box 1, Mangelsdorf Papers.

102. "Entrevistas de *Tierra*: Vuelve a hablarnos el Doctor Harrar de los trabajos de la Oficina de Estudios Especiales y de los resultados obtenidos a la fecha," *Tierra* 4, no. 12 (December 1949): 736–40.

103. Edwin Wellhausen to Jacob George Harrar, March 2, 1956, folder 3, box 1, series 323, RG 1.2, RFA, RAC.

104. "How Rocamex Hybrids Reach the Farmers of Mexico," October 28, 1954, folder 62, box 10, series 323, RG 1.2, RFA, RAC. The report's chart (ibid., 10) clearly demonstrates the rapid decline in synthetic varieties after 1948.

105. William I. Myers to Chester Barnard, October 3, 1951, folder 20, box 3, series 915, RG 3.1, RFA, RAC. Myers was a conservative agricultural economist then recently added to the Advisory Committee; he would play a crucial role in dictating foundation policy during the 1950s. On his career in agriculture, see Douglas Slaybaugh, *William I. Myers and the Modernization of American Agriculture* (Ames: Iowa State University Press, 1996).

106. John S. Dickey to Warren Weaver, October 20, 1949, folder 19, box 3, series 323, RG 1.1, RFA, RAC.

107. Warren Weaver to John S. Dickey, William Myers, and Thomas Parran, November 21, 1949, folder 19, box 3, series 323, RG 1.1, RFA, RAC.

108. On general accounts of the green revolution in Asia during the 1950s and 1960s, see Cullather, *The Hungry World*; Perkins, *Geopolitics and the Green Revolution*, chaps. 7–8. On India and wheat, see Gupta, *Postcolonial Developments*; Prakash Kumar, *Development, American Aid, and Postcolonial Agriculture in India* (forthcoming). On rice and the Philippines in particular, see James Lang, *Feeding a Hungry Planet: Rice, Research, and Development in Asia and Latin America* (Chapel Hill: University of North Carolina Press, 1996); Elta Smith, "Imaginaries of Development: The Rockefeller Foundation and Rice Research," *Science as Culture* 18, no. 4 (2009): 461–82; Edmund K. Oasa, "The International Rice Research Institute and the Green Revolution" (PhD diss., University of Hawaii, 1981). On the foundation's Colombian program, see Rebecca Tally, "At the Mercy of the Millers: Empire, Science, and Import Substitution in Colombia, 1930–1966" (PhD diss., Cornell University, 2012); Timothy Lorek, "Developing Paradise: Agricultural Science in Colombia's Cauca Valley, 1920–1980" (PhD diss., Yale University, forthcoming).

109. James Sumberg, Dennis Keeney, and Benedict Dempsey, "Public Agronomy: Norman Borlaug as 'Brand Hero' for the Green Revolution," *Journal of Development Studies* 48, no. 11 (2012): 1592. On Borlaug's career as booster of the green revolution, see ibid., 1587–600; Cullather, *The Hungry World*, 244–48.

110. Elvin C. Stakman to George Harrar, August 21, 1953, folder 27, box 4, series 323, RG 1.1, RFA, RAC.

111. On the agricultural policy of the Alemán years and the greater Mexican Miracle, see Cynthia Hewitt de Alcántara, *Modernizing Mexican Agriculture: Socioeconomic Implications of Technological Change, 1940–1970* (Geneva: UN Research Institute for Social Development, 1976), chaps. 2–3; Steven E. Sanderson, *The Transformation of Mexican Agriculture: International Structure and the Politics of Rural Change* (Princeton, NJ: Princeton University Press, 1986); Wright, *The Death of Ramón González*, chap. 6. On the government's minting of a commemorative coin, see "Mabbot—Educator and Numismatist," *New York Times*, October 19, 1969, D41.

112. Paul C. Mangelsdorf Oral History, RG 13, November 1966, RFA, RAC, 110.

Chapter Six: Transplanting "El Tenesí"

1. "Aleman Says Mexicans Will Copy TVA, Build Dams on the Papaloapan," *Chattanooga Times*, May 7, 1947, clipping from folder titled "Pres. Aleman's Visit to TVA and US," Tennessee Valley Authority Corporate Library, Knoxville (hereafter TVA Library). The Hispanicization of "Tennessee" was fairly common in describing the state and river in Mexico. For an example, see David F. McMahon, *Antropología de una presa: los mazatecos y el proyecto del Papaloapan* (Mexico City: Instituto Nacional Indigenista, 1973), 51. Alemán's predecessor, Manuel Ávila Camacho, had formally broken the long hiatus in state visits between the two neighbors with a brief and secretive 1943 conference with Franklin Roosevelt in Corpus Christi, Texas, but it hardly matched the symbolic importance of Alemán's later visit. On the 1947 trip, see Miguel Alemán Valdés, *Remembranzas y testimonios* (Mexico City: Editorial Grijalbo, 1987), 268–72; Stephen R. Niblo, *Mexico in the 1940s: Modernity, Politics, and Corruption* (Wilmington, DE: Scholarly Resources Books, 1999), 175–77.

2. I am not the first to acknowledge the significance of historical comparisons between the TVA and the Mexican river valley commissions of the 1940s and 1950s. In previous scholarship, however, this transnational exchange is treated peripherally or in passing, and no other work has grappled seriously with both national historiographies or consulted archival collections in both countries. See Diana Schwartz, "Transforming the Tropics: Development, Displacement, and Anthropology in the Papaloapan, Mexico, 1940s–1970s" (PhD diss., University of Chicago, 2016); Patrick H. Cosby, "Leviathan in the Tropics: A Postcolonial Environmental History of the Papaloapan Development Projects in Mexico" (PhD diss., University of Florida, 2011); Roberto Melville, "Antropólogos mexicanos en el Valle del Tennessee," *Umbral XXI* 5 (1991): 21–28; Roberto Melville, "TVA y la Comisión del Tepalcatepec: Una comparación tentativa," *Sistemas hidráulicos, agricultura, y migración* (1994): 270–95; Marco A. Cálderon Mólgora, "Desarrollo integral en las cuencas del Tepalcatepec y del Balsas," in *La transformación de los paisajes culturales en la cuenca del Tepalcatepec*, ed. Juan Ortiz Escamilla (Zamora, Mexico: El Colegio del Michoacán, 2011); Niklas Robinson, "Revolutionizing the River: The Politics of Water Management in Southeastern Mexico, 1951–1974" (PhD diss., Tulane University, 2007); William E. Cole, Steven M. Neuse, and Richard Sanders, "TVA: An International Administrative Example," *Public Administration Quarterly* 8, no. 2 (1984): 166–83. For the two best studies of TVA's global career, although neither discusses Latin America in general or Mexico specifically, see David Ekbladh, *The Great American Mission: Modernization and the Construction of an American World Order* (Princeton, NJ: Princeton University Press, 2010); Daniel Klingensmith, *"One Valley and a Thousand": Dams, Nationalism, and Development* (New Delhi: Oxford University Press, 2007).

3. Albert O. Hirschman, *Development Projects Observed* (Washington, DC: Brookings Institution Press, 1967), 21–22.

4. On the natural history of the Tennessee River, see Kim Trevathan, *Paddling the Tennessee River: A Voyage on Easy Water* (Knoxville: University of Tennessee Press, 2001).

5. For the racial demographics, see Nancy Grant, *TVA and Black Americans: Planning for the Status Quo* (Philadelphia: Temple University Press, 1990), xxvii. The tenancy statistic describes the western counties of Alabama's Tennessee Valley; see Matthew L. Downs, *Transforming the South: Federal Development in the Tennessee Valley, 1915–1960* (Baton Rouge: Louisiana State University Press, 2014), 18 (table 1). On the valley's pre-TVA social history, see Downs, *Transforming the South*, 17–21.

6. On the history of river valley development in the early twentieth-century South, see Christopher J. Manganiello, *Southern Water, Southern Power: How the Politics of Cheap Energy and Water Scarcity Shaped a Region* (Chapel Hill: University of North Carolina Press, 2015), chaps. 1–2. On Muscle Shoals and Wilson Dam, see Downs, *Transforming the South*, chaps. 1–2; Timothy Johnson, "Nitrogen Nation: The Legacy of World War I and the Politics of Chemical Agriculture in America, 1916–1933," *Agricultural History* 90, no. 2 (2016): 209–29.

7. Philip Selznick, *TVA and the Grass Roots: A Study in the Sociology of Formal Organization* (Berkeley: University of California Press, 1949), 5. On the intellectual roots of the agency and the early negotiation to create it, see Sarah T. Phillips, *This Land, This Nation: Conservation, Rural America, and the New Deal* (New York: Cambridge University Press, 2007), 83–88; Paul Conkin, "Intellectual and Political Roots," in *TVA: Fifty Years of Grass-Roots Bureaucracy*, ed. Erwin C. Hargrove and Paul Conkin (Urbana: University of Illinois Press, 1983); Downs, *Transforming the South*, 60–67.

8. On the three board members' contrasting political visions, see Klingensmith, *One Valley and a Thousand*, chap. 1; Phillips, *This Land, This Nation*, 89–92; Erwin C. Hargrove, *Prisoners of*

Myth: The Leadership of the Tennessee Valley Authority, 1933–1990 (Princeton, NJ: Princeton University Press, 1994), 24–30; Aaron D. Purcell, *Arthur Morgan: A Progressive Vision for American Reform* (Knoxville: University of Tennessee Press, 2014); Roy Talbert, *FDR's Utopian: Arthur Morgan of the TVA* (Jackson: University Press of Mississippi, 1987); Arthur E. Morgan, *The Small Community: Foundation of Democratic Life* (New York: Harper and Brothers, 1942); Steven M. Neuse, *David E. Lilienthal: The Journey of an American Liberal* (Knoxville: University of Tennessee Press, 1996); James C. Scott, "High Modernist Social Engineering: The Case of the Tennessee Valley Authority," in *Experiencing the State*, ed. Lloyd I. Rudolph and John Kurt Jacobsen (New Delhi: Oxford University Press, 2006), 21–26; Downs, *Transforming the South*, 73–78.

9. On the first decade of the TVA's operation, see Phillips, *This Land, This Nation*, 93–107; Richard Lowitt, "The TVA, 1933–1945," in *TVA: Fifty Years of Grass-Roots Bureaucracy*, ed. Erwin C. Hargrove and Paul Conkin (Urbana: University of Illinois Press, 1983); Hargrove, *Prisoners of Myth*, chap. 5; David Lilienthal, *TVA: Democracy on the March: Twentieth Anniversary Edition* (New York: Harper and Brothers, 1953), chap. 1.

10. On the struggle between Morgan and Lilienthal as well as their competing visions, see Neuse, *David E. Lilienthal*, chap. 5; Purcell, *Arthur Morgan*, chap. 6; Lowitt, "The TVA," 44–46; Thomas K. McGraw, *Morgan vs. Lilienthal: The Feud within the TVA* (Chicago: Loyola University Press, 1970).

11. David Lilienthal, *TVA: Democracy on the March* (New York: Harper and Brothers, 1944), 215, xi, 179, 180, 8. On the book's sales and translations, see Neuse, *David E. Lilienthal*, 134–35.

12. For the best extensive critique of *TVA: Democracy on the March*, see Klingensmith, *One Valley and a Thousand*, 53–64. On the slow progress of the TVA during the 1930s, see Bruce Schulman, *From Cotton Belt to Sunbelt: Federal Policy, Economic Development, and the Transformation of the South, 1938–1980* (New York: Oxford University Press, 1991), 35–38. For a biting critique of the long-term failure of the TVA to raise incomes and living standards, see William U. Chandler, *The Myth of the TVA: Conservation and Development in the Tennessee Valley, 1933–1983* (Cambridge, MA: Ballinger Publishing Co., 1984), especially chap. 4. On the difficulties of dislocation and resettlement, see Michael McDonald, *TVA and the Dispossessed: The Resettlement of Population in the Norris Dam Area* (Knoxville: University of Tennessee Press, 1982). On the TVA's failures for black southerners, see Grant, *TVA and Black Americans*.

13. Lilienthal, *TVA: Democracy on the March*, chap. 19.

14. Schulman, *From Cotton Belt to Sun Belt*, 184. In the last decade there have been several major studies of the TVA's global career during the Cold War. See, in particular, Ekbladh, *The Great American Mission*; Phillips, *This Land, This Nation*, 252–54; Klingensmith, *One Valley and a Thousand*; Daniel Immerwahr, *Thinking Small: The United States and the Lure of Community Development* (Cambridge, MA: Harvard University Press, 2015); Nick Cullather, *The Hungry World: America's Cold War Battle against Poverty in Asia* (Cambridge, MA: Harvard University Press, 2010), especially chap. 4; Amy C. Offner, "Anti-Poverty Programs, Social Conflict, and Economic Thought in the United States and Colombia, 1948–1980" (PhD diss., Columbia University, 2012).

15. On the history of water and dams in Porfirian Mexico, see Luis Aboites Aguilar, *El agua de la nación: Una historia política de México, 1888–1946* (Mexico City: CIESAS, 1998); Martín Sánchez Rodríguez, "Del antiguo régimen a la revolución: Notas sobre proyectos de irrigación en México antes y después de 1910," in *Mexico in Transition: New Perspectives on Mexican Agrarian History, Nineteenth and Twentieth Centuries*, ed. Antonio Escobar Ohmstede and Matthew

Butler (Mexico City: CIESAS, 2013); Clifton B. Kroeber, *Man, Land, and Water: Mexico's Farmlands Irrigation Policies, 1885–1911* (Berkeley: University of California Press, 1983).

16. On the changing political meaning of dams in revolutionary Mexico, see Mikael Wolfe, "Water and Revolution: The Politics, Ecology, and Technology of Agrarian Reform in 'La Laguna,' Mexico" (PhD diss., University of Chicago, 2009), especially chaps. 4–6; Aboites Aguilar, *El agua de la nación*, chaps. 4–5; Sánchez Rodríguez, "Del antiguo régimen a la revolución."

17. Wolfe, "Water and Revolution," 230, chap. 5. See also Sterling Evans, "La angustia de La Angostura: Consecuencias socioambientales por la construcción de presas en Sonora," *Signos Históricos* 16 (2006): 46–79; Sterling Evans, "Yaquis vs. Yanquis: An Environmental and Historical Comparison of Coping with Aridity in Southern Sonora," *Journal of the Southwest* 40, no. 3 (1998): 363–96; Sterling Evans, *Damming Sonora: Water, Agriculture, and Environmental Change in Northwest Mexico* (Tucson: University of Arizona Press, forthcoming).

18. On the contradiction of nationalist dams built with transnational expertise, see Luis Aboites Aguilar, "The Transnational Dimensions of Mexican Irrigation, 1900–1950," *Journal of Political Ecology* 19 (2012): 70–80; Mikael Wolfe, "Bringing the Revolution to the Dam Site: How Technology, Labor, and Nature Converged in the Microcosm of a Northern Mexican Company Town, 1936–1946," *Journal of the Southwest* 53, no. 1 (2011): 1–31; Mikael Wolfe, "Yankee Technology and Nationalist Sensibilities: La Comisión Nacional de Irrigación in 1920s and 30s Mexico" (paper presented at the Latin American Studies Association Annual Meeting, Montreal, 2007).

19. Pedro de Alba, "Tierras inundadas y tierras sedientes," *El Nacional*, April 8, 1938, clipping from box 63, Ramón Fernández y Fernández Papers, Biblioteca Luis González, Colegio de Michoacán, Zamora, Michoacán, Mexico.

20. J.A.T., "La gran obra del gobierno Roosevelt: Una lección de socialismo—La Autoridad del Valle Tennessee," *Nuevo Orden* 3 (November 1940): 20–22.

21. "Los planeamientos económicos en el mundo y sus resultados," July 26, 1938, folder 545.3/220, box 895, Lázaro Cárdenas del Río Papers, Archivo General de la Nación, Mexico City.

22. Frank Tannenbaum to Sumner Welles, July 31, 1942, folder 3, box 4113, 812.001 Cardenas, Lazaro/259 1/2, record group (hereafter RG) 59: Records of the State Department, US National Archives and Records Administration II, College Park, Maryland (hereafter NA); Frank Tannenbaum to Lázaro Cárdenas, August 24, 1942, folder titled "Lázaro Cárdenas," box 1, Frank Tannenbaum Papers, Columbia University, New York. These two letters describe a US trip that Tannenbaum planned for Cárdenas in the early 1940s to see projects that had long interested the president, including the TVA.

23. On TVA visits by respective Mexican government representatives in the Cárdenas years, see Francisco Gómez-Pérez to Arthur E. Morgan, May 7, 1936, folder titled "184c (Mexico)," box 15, Information Office Correspondence, Records of the General Manager, RG 142: Records of the Tennessee Valley Authority, US National Archives and Records Administration Southeast Division, Atlanta, Georgia (hereafter NASE); Héctor Martínez d'Meza to Josephus Daniels, October 7, 1939, folder 12, box 51, 033.1211/168, RG 59, NA; "Visit of Mexicans," October 4, 1940, folder titled "184c (Mexico)," box 15, Information Office Correspondence, Records of the General Manager, RG 142, NASE.

24. Sanford Mosk, *Industrial Revolution in Mexico* (Berkeley: University of California Press, 1950), 220. On Ávila Camacho's "march to the sea," see Luis Aboites Aguilar, "Optimismo nacional: Geografía, ingeniería hidráulica y política en México (1926–1976)," in *Identidades, estado*

nacional y globalidad: México, siglos XIX y XX, ed. Brígida von Mentz (Mexico City: CIESAS, 2000), 124–32; Christopher Boyer, *Political Landscapes: Forests, Conservation, and Community in Mexico* (Durham, NC: Duke University Press, 2015), 171–72; Guillermo de la Peña, "Rural Mobilizations in Latin America since c. 1920," in *The Cambridge History of Latin America*, ed. Leslie Bethell (Cambridge: Cambridge University Press, 1994), 6:411–12, pt. 2.

25. For the announcement of the TVA study, see Francisco Castillo Nájera to Ezequiel Padilla, November 12, 1941, III–147–1, Archivo Histórico de la Secretaría de Relaciones Exteriores, Tlatelolco, Mexico City (hereafter AHSRE).

26. For a tally of Mexican visitors to the TVA in the Ávila Camacho years, see "Mexican Visitors," undated, folder titled "030-Mexico," box 20, General Correspondence, David Lilienthal Administrative Files, RG 142, NASE.

27. Francisco Castillo Nájera to David Lilienthal, July 29, 1941, III–146–1, AHSRE.

28. Francisco Castillo Nájera to Ezequiel Padilla, August 8, 1941, III–601–24, AHSRE.

29. Adolfo Orive Alba to Ezequiel Padilla, December 23, 1942, III–601–24, AHSRE.

30. On the initial meeting between Lilienthal and the six engineers, and for accompanying quotations, see David Lilienthal, *The Journals of David Lilienthal, Volume I: The TVA Years, 1939–1945* (New York: Harper and Row, 1964), 492.

31. "Proposed Training Program for Six Mexican Engineers," April 10, 1942, folder titled "184C (Mexico)," box 15, Information Office Correspondence, Records of the General Manager, RG 142, NASE.

32. "Orientation Program for Mexican Engineers," May 5, 1942, folder titled "091 Mexico thru 1942," box 347, Administrative Files, 1933–57, Records of the General Manager's Office, RG 142, NASE.

33. "Transmittal of Reports Made by Latin-American Engineers," September 7, 1942, folder titled "091 Mexico Thru 1942," box 347, Administrative Files, 1933–57, Records of the General Manager's Office, RG 142, NASE.

34. On reference to the engineers as "boys," see Ralph McDade to Lester Schlup, August 15, 1942, and Ralph McDade to R. M. Reeves, August 27, 1942, both in folder titled "425 Mexico," box 195, Correspondence and Reports 1933–48, Agricultural Development and Agricultural Relations, Records of the Correlating Committee, RG 142, NASE. On the racial politics of the TVA, see Robert Rook, "Race, Water, and Foreign Policy: The Tennessee Valley Authority's Global Agenda Meets Jim Crow," *Diplomatic History* 28, no. 1 (2004): 55–81. On the ambiguous racial status of Mexicans in the US South, see Julie M. Weise, *Corazón de Dixie: Mexicanos in the U.S. South since 1910* (Chapel Hill: University of North Carolina Press, 2015).

35. On the geography of the Papaloapan, see Thomas T. Poleman, *The Papaloapan Project: Agricultural Development in the Mexican Tropics* (Stanford, CA: Stanford University Press, 1964), chap. 3. On its 1944 flood, see Adolfo Orive Alba, *La política de irrigación en México* (Mexico City: Fondo de Cultura Económica, 1960), 90–91; Cosby, "Leviathan in the Tropics," 82–85.

36. Poleman, *The Papaloapan Project*, 46–47. On regional variation along with the Papaloapan basin's agrarian and agricultural history, see Gabriela Soto Laveaga, *Jungle Laboratories: Mexican Peasants, National Projects, and the Making of the Pill* (Durham, NC: Duke University Press, 2009), 27–37; Heather Fowler Salamini, *Agrarian Radicalism in Veracruz, 1920–1938* (Lincoln: University of Nebraska Press, 1978); Alfred H. Siemens, *Between the Summit and the Sea: Central Veracruz in the Nineteenth Century* (Vancouver: University of British Columbia Press, 1990); William W. Winnie, "The Papaloapan Project: An Experiment in Tropical Development," *Economic Geography* 34, no. 3 (1958): 227–48.

37. Manuel Ávila Camacho, "Acuerdo que declara de utilidad pública el estudio y construcción de las obras del río Papaloapan," *Diario Oficial*, December 9, 1944, 1–3.

38. On Alemán's life and evolving political ideology, see Ryan M. Alexander, *Sons of the Mexican Revolution: Miguel Alemán and His Generation* (Albuquerque: University of New Mexico Press, 2016); Jorge Basurto, *Del avilacamachismo al alemanismo, 1940–1952* (Mexico City: Siglo Veintiuno Editores, 1984); María Antonia Martínez, *El despegue constructivo de la revolución: Sociedad y política en el alemanismo* (Mexico City: CIESAS, 2004).

39. Miguel Alemán Valdés, "Síntesis del Programa de Gobierno," September 30, 1945, quoted in Hugo Rangel Couto, *El sistema del Valle del Tennessee: El desarrollo regional integral en la síntesis del programa de gobierno de Sr. Lic. Miguel Alemán* (Mexico City: unknown publisher, 1946), 7.

40. Lilienthal, *TVA: Democracy on the March: Twentieth Anniversary Edition*, 213.

41. "From *Ultimas Noticias*," January 8, 1946, translated clipping in folder titled "030 Mexico," box 20, General Correspondence, David Lilienthal Administrative Files, RG 142, NASE.

42. Marte R. Gómez to Herbert Bursley, May 28, 1945, Cartas, 1945, A-Ch, Marte R. Gómez Papers, Archivo Marte R. Gómez, Lomas de Chapultepec, Mexico City (hereafter Gómez Papers).

43. "Visit of the Honorable Marte R. Gómez, Minister of Agriculture of Mexico, and Party," April 17, 1946, Secretaría de Agricultura, 1946, Gómez Papers.

44. For Gómez's speech, delivered in English, see "Discurso con motivo de la visita a las obras de la T.V.A.," April 1946, Secretaría de Agricultura, 1946, Gómez Papers.

45. On the political transformations of the Alemán years, see Luis Medina, *Historia de la revolución mexicana, periodo 1940–1952: Civilismo y modernización del autoritarismo* (Mexico City: El Colegio de México, 1979); Alexander, *Sons of the Mexican Revolution*; Tzvi Medin, *El sexenio alemanista* (Mexico City: Ediciones Era, 1990).

46. "Discurso del Lic. Miguel Alemán Valdez [*sic*], al protestar como Presidente de la República, ante el Congreso de la Unión," December 1, 1946, published in *Los presidentes de México ante la nación: Informes, manifiestos y documentos de 1821 a 1966* (Mexico City: Imprenta de la Cámara de Diputados, 1966), 4:355–59.

47. On the bureaucratic politics of the transition from the National Irrigation Commission to the Secretariat of Hydraulic Resources, see Martin H. Greenberg, *Bureaucracy and Development: A Mexican Case Study* (Lexington, MA: D. C. Heath, 1970), chap. 3.

48. "Acuerdo que crea un organismo técnico y administrativo dependiente de la Secretaría de Recursos Hidráulicos, para planear, diseñar, y construir las obras que se requieren en la cuenca del río Papaloapan," *Diario Oficial*, April 24, 1947, 2–3.

49. "Esquema general del gigantesco proyecto del Papaloapan," *El Nacional*, March 15, 1947, clipping from file N28072, Archivos Económicos, Biblioteca Miguel Lerdo de Tejada, Mexico City (hereafter BMLT).

50. "Harnessing of Mexican River thru 'TVA' Aim," *Florence Times*, May 5, 1947, clipping from folder titled "Pres. Aleman's Visit to TVA and US," TVA Library.

51. "Office Memorandum regarding Visit of President Aleman of Mexico," April 25, 1947, folder titled "Aleman, Miguel," box 4, Administrative Files, 1933–57, Records of the General Manager's Office, RG 142, NASE.

52. "Aleman Views TVA Achievements at Chickamauga Dam, Muscle Shoals," *Chattanooga News–Free Press*, May 6, 1947, clipping from folder titled "Pres. Aleman's Visit to TVA and US," TVA Library.

53. "Alemán, en las magnas obras del Tennessee," *La Prensa*, May 7, 1947, 34.

54. "Enthusiastic Aleman Views TVA Projects," *Nashville Tennessean*, May 7, 1947, clipping from folder titled "Pres. Aleman's Visit to TVA and US," TVA Library. On the details of his visit to Muscle Shoals, see "Aleman Says Mexicans Will Copy TVA, Build Dams on Papaloapan," *Chattanooga Times*, May 7, 1947, clipping from folder titled "Pres. Aleman's Visit to TVA and US," TVA Library.

55. "Aleman's Visit," *Huntsville Times*, May 6, 1947, clipping from folder titled "Pres. Aleman's Visit to TVA and US," TVA Library.

56. "The Far-Sighted Aleman," *Birmingham News*, May 8, 1947, clipping from folder titled "Pres. Aleman's Visit to TVA and US," TVA Library.

57. "La maravilla del Tennessee que verá hoy el Presidente," *El Universal*, May 6, 1947, 1; "Alemán observó ayer en Tennessee lo que proyecta hacer en México," *El Universal*, May 7, 1947, 1.

58. "Se le hizo invitación para que envíe técnicos," *El Universal*, May 7, 1947, 1.

59. "Alemán hará, del Papaloapan, una réplica del Valle de Tennessee," *Excélsior*, May 13, 1947, clipping from file N28074, Archivos Económicos, BMLT.

60. "El Tennessee empezará en breve a tener su réplica en el Papaloapan," *El Universal*, May 9, 1947, clipping from file N28074, Archivos Económicos, BMLT.

61. "Del Papaloapan surgirá un nivel de vida más elevado," *El Universal*, May 7, 1947, 7.

62. "El Tennessee empezará en breve a tener su réplica en el Papaloapan," *El Universal*, May 9, 1947, clipping from file N28074, Archivos Económicos, BMLT.

63. "El Tennessee y el Presidente Alemán frente al Papaloapan," part I, *El Nacional*, June 19, 1947, clipping from file N28080, Archivos Económicos, BMLT; "El Tennessee y el Presidente Alemán frente al Papaloapan," part III, *El Nacional*, June 21, 1947, clipping from file N28080, Archivos Económicos, BMLT.

64. "El Tennessee y el Presidente Alemán frente al Papaloapan," part III, *El Nacional*, June 21, 1947, clipping from file N28080, Archivos Económicos, BMLT; "Plan armónico de Alemán en torno del Papaloapan," *El Universal*, June 20, 1947, clipping from file N28074, Archivos Económicos, BMLT, which despite its different title was also a reprinting of Orive Alba's June speech.

65. "El Tennessee y el Presidente Alemán frente al Papaloapan," part I, *El Nacional*, June 19, 1947, clipping from file N28080, Archivos Económicos, BMLT.

66. For an example of press comparisons of the Papaloapan and Tennessee Valleys after Orive Alba's declarations, see "La hora del Papaloapan," *El Universal*, July 23, 1947, clipping from file N28074, Archivos Ecónomicos, BMLT.

67. Adolfo Orive Alba to David Lilienthal, December 10, 1946, and Adolfo Orive Alba to David Lilienthal, January 16, 1947, both in folder titled "Alba, Adolfo Orive," box 3, Administrative Files, 1933–57, Records of the General Manager's Office, RG 142, NASE.

68. "Se le hizo invitación para que envíe técnicos," *El Universal*, May 7, 1947, 1.

69. Jack Lockhart and Herbert Wiggins to Miguel Alemán, August 5, 1948, 606.3/185, Miguel Alemán Valdés Papers, Archivo General de la Nación, Mexico City (hereafter Alemán Papers).

70. George Allen to Gordon Clapp, August 18, 1948, folder titled "MON-MONY," box 40, Records of the Chairman and the Members of the Board of Directors, 1945–57 (Clapp/Vogel), RG 142, NASE; Berlen O. Moneymaker, "Limestone Solution in the Papaloapan Basin, Mexico," 1948, TVA Library.

71. Andrew Weiss to Gerard H. Matthes, December 5, 1947, folder 40, box 30, Gerard H. Matthes Papers, Cornell University Rare and Manuscript Collections, Ithaca, New York (hereafter Matthes Papers). Andrew Weiss was another US national employed by the Secretariat of Hydraulic Resources, though his background was with the Bureau of Reclamation rather than the TVA.

72. For examples of Matthes's frequent comparisons between the river valleys of southern Mexico and the US South, see "Diary of Mexican Trip, January 1948," box 26, Matthes Papers; Gerard H. Matthes to Adolfo Orive Alba, October 26, 1948, folder 38, box 30, Matthes Papers; "Informe sobre el estudio de la rectificación del río Papaloapan y recomendación de que se apruebe," January 29, 1948, folder 39, box 30, Matthes Papers.

73. Roland Wank to W. L. Sturdevant, December 14, 1951, folder titled "WAN-WAS," box 62, Records of the Chairman and the Members of the Board of Directors, 1945–57 (Clapp/Vogel), RG 142, NASE.

74. Earl D. Hale to A. D. Rieger, March 19, 1952, folder titled "Mexico," box 81, Records of the Chairman and the Members of the Board of Directors, 1945–57 (Clapp/Vogel), RG 142, NASE.

75. On the resettlement of indigenous populations by the Papaloapan Commission, see Schwartz, "Transforming the Tropics." On the Miguel Alemán Dam and the flood control accomplishments of the commission, see Poleman, *The Papaloapan Project*, chap. 6; Orive Alba, *La política de irrigación en México*, chap. 12; Winnie, "The Papaloapan Project"; Reynaldo Schega, "Rectification of the Papaloapan River in Mexico," *Proceedings of the American Society of Civil Engineers* 71 (May 1951): 507–27.

76. On the successes and failures of the Papaloapan Commission's colonization programs, see Poleman, *The Papaloapan Project*, chaps. 6–7; David Barkin and Timothy King, *Regional Economic Development: The River Basin Approach in Mexico* (New York: Cambridge University Press, 1970), chap. 4.

77. On the agrarian economic transformations wrought by the Papaloapan project, see Peter T. Ewell and Thomas T. Poleman, *Uxpanapa: Agricultural Development in the Mexican Tropics* (New York: Pergamon Press, 1980); Sara J. Scherr, *Development and Equity in Tropical Mexico: Thirty Years of the Papaloapan Project* (Ithaca, NY: Cornell University Department of Agricultural Economics, 1983). On the differences between the TVA's "grassroots" approach and the Papaloapan project, see Cole, Neuse, and Sanders, "TVA: An International Administrative Example."

78. Cole, Neuse, and Sanders, "TVA: An International Administrative Example," 179.

79. Scott, "High Modernist Social Engineering," 28.

80. On Cárdenas's postpresidential career, see Marcela Mijares Lara, "Cárdenas después de Cárdenas: Una historia política del México Contemporáneo, 1940–1970" (PhD diss., El Colegio de México, forthcoming); Fernando Benitez, *Lázaro Cárdenas y la Revolución Mexicana* (Mexico City: Fondo de Cultura Económica, 1978), 3:215–52; Roberto Blanco Moheno, *Tata Lázaro: Vida, obra, y muerte de Cárdenas, Múgica, y Carrillo Puerto* (Mexico City: Editorial Diana, 1972), 391–32; Amelia Kiddle and Joseph U. Lenti, "Co-opting Cardenismo: Luis Echeverría and the Funeral of Lázaro Cárdenas," in *Populism in Twentieth-Century Mexico: The Presidencies of Lázaro Cárdenas and Luis Echeverría*, ed. Amelia Kiddle and María L.O. Muñoz (Tucson: University of Arizona Press, 2010); Amelia Kiddle, "Lázaro Cárdenas (1895–1970)," in *Iconic Mexico: An Encyclopedia from Acapulco to Zócalo*, ed. Eric Zolov (Santa Barbara, CA: ABC-CLIO, 2015).

81. Lázaro Cárdenas to Miguel Alemán, April 21, 1947, 508.1/168, Alemán Papers. Cárdenas also met with Alemán in Mexico City on the same day to discuss the proposal; see Lázaro Cárdenas, *Obras I—Apuntes* (Mexico City: Universidad Nacional Autónoma de México, 1973), 2:238–39.

82. On the geography and history of the Tepalcatepec basin, see Marco A. Cálderon Mólgora, "Lázaro Cárdenas del Río en la Cuenca Tepalcatepec-Balsas," in *La tierra caliente de Michoacán*, ed. José Eduardo Zárate Hernández (Zamora, Mexico: Colegio de Michoacán, 2001); Susana Glanz, *El ejido colectivo de Nueva Italia* (Mexico City: SEP-INAH, 1974); Christopher Boyer, *Becoming Campesinos: Politics, Identity, and Agrarian Struggle in Postrevolutionary Michoacán, 1920–1935* (Stanford, CA: Stanford University Press, 2003), 56–61; Jennie Purnell, *Popular Movements and State Formation in Revolutionary Mexico: The Agraristas and Cristeros of Michoacán* (Durham, NC: Duke University Press, 1999), 46; Barkin and King, *Regional Economic Development*; Elinore Magee Barrett, "Land Tenure and Settlement in the Tepalcatepec Lowland, Michoacán, Mexico" (PhD diss., University of California at Berkeley, 1970).

83. Lázaro Cárdenas to Miguel Alemán, April 21, 1947, 508.1/168, Alemán Papers.

84. Miguel Alemán to Lázaro Cárdenas, May 24, 1947, 508.1/168, Alemán Papers.

85. Marte R. Gómez to Lázaro Cárdenas, January 21, 1946, Cartas, 1946, C-D, Gómez Papers.

86. Interview with Cuauhtémoc Cárdenas, June 3, 2016 (transcript in possession of author).

87. Lázaro Cárdenas to David Lilienthal, February 3, 1946, folder titled "CAA-CAR," box 2, General Correspondence, David Lilienthal Administrative Files, RG 142, NASE.

88. "El régimen y el caciquismo del brazo," *El Universal*, June 9, 1947, clipping from file N28080, Archivos Económicos, BMLT.

89. "Por acuerdo del C. Presidente de la República … ," May 15, 1947, 508.1/168, Alemán Papers.

90. Miguel Alemán to Lázaro Cárdenas, June 1, 1947, 508.1/168, Alemán Papers.

91. Rafael Zubarán Capmany, "El régimen y el caciquismo del brazo," June 9, 1947, *El Universal*, clipping from file N28080, Archivos Económicos, BMLT.

92. For irrigation and roadway construction statistics, see Cálderon Mólgora, "Lázaro Cárdenas del Río en la cuenca Tepalcatepec-Balsas," 248–50. Cárdenas quoted in Henrik Infield and Koka Freier, *People in Ejidos: A Visit to the Cooperative Farms of Mexico* (New York: Frederick A. Praeger, 1954), 149. On the program and accomplishments of the Tepalcatepec Commission, see Cálderon Mólgora, "Desarrollo integral en las cuencas del Tepalcatepec y del Balsas"; Stephanie Baker Opperman, "Modernization and Rural Health in Mexico: The Case of the Tepalcatepec Commission," *Endeavour* 37, no. 1 (2013): 47–55; Barrett, "Land Tenure and Settlement in the Tepalcatepec Lowland"; Melville, "TVA y la Comisión del Tepalcatepec," though Melville's essay emphasizes comparison over transnational entanglement.

93. Guillermo Arizcorreta to Raymond Paty, January 18, 1954, folder titled "CAR-CARF," box 39, Administrative Files, 1933–57, Records of the General Manager's Office, RG 142, NASE.

94. Cárdenas, *Obras I—Apuntes*, 2:619.

95. Eduardo Chavez to Raymond Paty, July 11, 1957, folder titled "091 Mexico 1946–1957," box 347, Administrative Files, 1933–57, Records of the General Manager's Office, RG 142, NASE.

96. Cuauhtémoc Cárdenas to Herbert Vogel, September 25, 1957, folder titled "Mexico," box 81, Records of the Chairman and the Members of the Board of Directors, 1945–57 (Clapp/Vogel), RG 142, NASE.

97. Interview with Cuauhtémoc Cárdenas, June 3, 2016 (transcript in possession of author).

98. "Schedule for Visit: General Lázaro Cárdenas, Mexico, and Party," February 2, 1959, folder titled "184 C Foreign (Mexico)," box 26, Records of the Board of Directors, 1957–72 (Smith/Wagner/Hays/Welch), RG 142, NASE.

99. Herbert Vogel to Lázaro Cárdenas, February 18, 1959, folder titled "184 C Foreign (Mexico)," box 26, Records of the Board of Directors, 1957–72 (Smith/Wagner/Hays/Welch), RG 142, NASE.

100. A. R. Jones to Milton Eisenhower, February 12, 1959, folder titled "184 C Foreign (Mexico)," box 26, Records of the Board of Directors, 1957–72 (Smith/Wagner/Hays/Welch), RG 142, NASE.

101. Lázaro Cárdenas, *Obras I—Apuntes, 1957–1966* (Mexico City: Universidad Nacional Autónoma de México, 1973), 3:86–87.

102. Lázaro Cárdenas to Herbert Vogel, August 13, 1962, folder titled "184 C Foreign (Mexico)," box 26, Records of the Board of Directors, 1957–72 (Smith/Wagner/Hays/Welch), RG 142, NASE. On the history and accomplishments of the Balsas Commission, see Cálderon Mólgora, "Lázaro Cárdenas del Río en la cuenca Tepalcatepec-Balsas"; Boyer, *Political Landscapes*, 172–73.

103. On the social, economic, and agricultural transformations born from the Tepalcatepec and Balsas Commissions, see Barrett, "Land Tenure and Settlement in the Tepalcatepec Lowland," chap. 8; Barkin and King, *Regional Economic Development*, 197–200; Melville, "TVA y la Comisión del Tepalcatepec."

104. On the common patterns of proyectismo, see Poleman, *The Papaloapan Project*, 9. The TVA itself was hardly innocent of such impulses.

Epilogue

1. Tanalís Padilla, *Rural Resistance in the Land of Zapata: The Jaramillista Movement and the Myth of the Pax Priísta, 1940–1962* (Durham, NC: Duke University Press, 2008), 114; Theodore Rosengarten, *All God's Dangers: The Life of Nate Shaw* (Chicago: University of Chicago Press, 1974), 466. Nate Shaw was Rosengarten's pseudonym for Cobb. On Jaramillo's career, see also Gladys McCormick, *The Logic of Compromise in Mexico: How the Countryside was Key to the Emergence of Authoritarianism* (Chapel Hill: University of North Carolina Press, 2016), chap. 2.

2. Little scholarship has considered the converging fates of the US South and Latin American nations during recent decades; for an important exception, see Richard Tardanico and Mark B. Rosenberg, eds., *Poverty or Development: Global Restructuring and Regional Transformations in the U.S. South and the Mexican South* (New York: Routledge, 2000).

3. On southern political transformations after World War II, see John Egerton, *Speak Now against the Day: The Generation before the Civil Rights Movement in the South* (New York: Alfred A. Knopf, 1994), 398–416; Bruce Schulman, *From Cotton Belt to Sunbelt: Federal Policy, Economic Development, and the Transformation of the South, 1938–1980* (New York: Oxford University Press, 1991), chap. 5.

4. "Jamie Whitten, Who Served 53 Years in House, Dies at 85," *New York Times*, September 10, 1995, D13. I borrow the place over people binary from Schulman, *From Cotton Belt to Sunbelt*, chap. 11. On the ideological renovation of the USDA in the late war years and beyond, see Jess Gilbert, *Planning Democracy: Agrarian Intellectuals and the Intended New Deal* (New Haven, CT: Yale University Press, 2015), chap. 10; Richard S. Kirkendall, *Social Scientists and Farm Politics in the Age of Roosevelt* (Columbia: University of Missouri Press, 1966), chaps. 11–13. On the

262 • Notes to Pages 194–195

contrast between Whitten and his predecessors, see Mary Summers, "The New Deal Farm Programs: Looking for Reconstruction in American Agriculture," *Agricultural History* 74, no. 2 (2000): 241–57; Jess Gilbert, "Agrarian Intellectuals in a Democratizing State: A Collective Biography of USDA Leaders in the Intended New Deal," in *The Countryside in the Age of the Modern State: Political Histories of Rural America*, ed. Catherine M. Stock and Robert D. Johnston (Ithaca, NY: Cornell University Press, 2001).

5. On the transitions in Mexican agrarian and agricultural policy during the 1940s, see Stephen R. Niblo, *Mexico in the 1940s: Modernity, Politics, and Corruption* (Wilmington, DE: Scholarly Resources Books, 1999), chap. 4; Padilla, *Rural Resistance in the Land of Zapata*, chap. 4; McCormick, *The Logic of Compromise in Mexico*, chap. 3; Enrique C. Ochoa, *Feeding Mexico: The Political Uses of Food since 1910* (Wilmington, DE: Scholarly Resources Books, 2000), chaps. 4–5. On the pivotal role played by the war itself in reorienting Mexican politics, see Halbert Jones, *The War Has Brought Peace to Mexico: World War II and the Consolidation of the Post-Revolutionary State* (Albuquerque: University of New Mexico Press, 2014).

6. For the irrigation statistic, see Cynthia Hewitt de Alcantara, *Modernizing Mexican Agriculture: Socioeconomic Implications of Technological Change, 1940–1970* (Geneva: UN Research Institute for Social Development, 1976), 18. On the impact of Mexico's green revolution on smallholders, see Laura González Martínez, *Respuesta campesina a la revolución verde en el Bajío* (Mexico City: Universidad Iberoamericana, 1992). On the geopolitics of federal investment in Mexican agriculture after 1940, see Sterling Evans, *Damming Sonora: Water, Agriculture, and Environmental Change in Northwest Mexico* (Tucson: University of Arizona Press, forthcoming); Angus Wright, *The Death of Ramón González: The Modern Agricultural Dilemma* (Austin: University of Texas Press, 1990); Steven E. Sanderson, *The Transformation of Mexican Agriculture: International Structure and the Politics of Rural Change* (Princeton, NJ: Princeton University Press, 1986); Arturo Carrillo Rojas and Mario Cerutti, eds., *Agricultura comercial, empresa y desarrollo regional en el noroeste de Mexico* (Culiacán, Mexico: Universidad Autónoma de Sinaloa, 2006). Ironically, by the 1970s many northwestern farmers abandoned staple grain crops in favor of the more lucrative export vegetable market for US consumers, forcing Mexico to once again import basic grains. On the northwest's later transition toward export crops, see Wright, *The Death of Ramón González*; Gustavo Esteva, *The Struggle for Rural Mexico* (South Hadley, MA: Bergin and Garvey Publishers, 1983); Billie DeWalt, "Mexico's Second Green Revolution: Food for Feed," *Mexican Studies / Estudios Mexicanos* 1, no. 1 (1985): 29–60.

7. On the economic neglect of the land reform sector, see Laura Randall, ed., *Reforming Mexico's Agrarian Reform* (Armonk, NY: M. E. Sharpe, 1996); Hewitt de Alcantara, *Modernizing Mexican Agriculture*.

8. On postwar politics in the USDA, see Shane Hamilton, *Trucking Country: The Road to America's Wal-Mart Economy* (Princeton, NJ: Princeton University Press, 2008), chap. 3. On the Agricultural Adjustment Administration and the Agricultural Stabilization and Conservation Service's role in the demise of sharecropping, see Pete Daniel, *Breaking the Land: The Transformation of Cotton, Tobacco, and Rice Cultures since 1880* (Urbana: University of Illinois Press, 1985), chap. 8; Pete Daniel, *Lost Revolutions: The South in the 1950s* (Chapel Hill: University of North Carolina Press, 2000), chap. 3; Gavin Wright, *Old South, New South: Revolutions in the Southern Economy since the Civil War* (Baton Rouge: Louisiana State University Press, 1986), chap. 8.

9. On the dehumanization of southern cotton culture, see Charles S. Aiken, *The Cotton Plantation South since the Civil War* (Baltimore: Johns Hopkins University Press, 1998), chap. 4;

Pete Daniel, *Dispossession: Discrimination against African American Farmers in the Age of Civil Rights* (Chapel Hill: University of North Carolina Press, 2013); Clyde Woods, *Development Arrested: The Blues and Plantation Power in the Mississippi Delta* (New York: Verso, 1998), chaps. 6 and 7; Greta de Jong, *You Can't Eat Freedom: Southerners and Social Justice after the Civil Rights Movement* (Chapel Hill: University of North Carolina Press, 2016). On the "neoplantation," see Merle Prunty Jr., "The Renaissance of the Southern Plantation," *Geographical Review* 45 (October 1955): 459–91.

10. On the social politics of federal investment in Mexican agriculture, see Padilla, *Rural Resistance in the Land of Zapata*; McCormick, *The Logic of Compromise in Mexico*. On the US South, see, in particular, Daniel, *Dispossession*.

11. Daniel, *Lost Revolutions*, 54–55. On the legal battle against USDA racial segregation, see Daniel, *Dispossession*. On the Henriquista challenge of 1952, see Padilla, *Rural Resistance in the Land of Zapata*, chap. 4. On agrarian revolt and state repression in the Cold War era, see Alexander Aviña, *Specters of Revolution: Peasant Guerrillas in the Cold War Mexican Countryside* (New York: Oxford University Press, 2014); Renata Keller, *Mexico's Cold War: Cuba, the United States, and the Legacy of the Mexican Revolution* (New York: Cambridge University Press, 2015); McCormick, *The Logic of Compromise in Mexico*.

12. Mike Davis, *Planet of Slums* (New York: Verso, 2006), 4; James N. Gregory, *The Southern Diaspora: How the Great Migrations of Black and White Southerners Transformed America* (Chapel Hill: University of North Carolina Press, 2005), 15; Daniel, *Dispossession*, 6. On rural-rural migration to Mexico's northwest, see, in particular, Wright, *The Death of Ramón González*.

13. Gregory, *The Southern Diaspora*; Isabel Wilkerson, *The Warmth of Other Suns: The Epic Story of America's Great Migration* (New York: Random House, 2010). While both Gregory and Wilkerson's books are important reinterpretations, neither does a good job in linking out-migration with the agricultural transformations of the postwar era; the word "agriculture" appears in the index of neither book. On the conservative politics of the "urban crisis," see Thomas J. Sugrue, *The Origins of the Urban Crisis: Race and Inequality in Postwar Detroit* (Princeton, NJ: Princeton University Press, 1996); Kevin M. Kruse, *White Flight: Atlanta and the Making of Modern Conservatism* (Princeton, NJ: Princeton University Press, 2005). On cultural exchanges born from the diaspora, see John Egerton, *The Americanization of Dixie: The Southernization of America* (New York: Harper's Press, 1974).

14. Paz quoted in Diane E. Davis, *Urban Leviathan: Mexico City in the Twentieth Century* (Philadelphia: Temple University Press, 1994), 2. On the transformation of Mexico City in the post-1940 period, see Judith Adler Hellman, *Mexican Lives* (New York: New Press, 1994); Jonathan Kandell, *La Capital: The Biography of Mexico City* (New York: Random House, 1988). On the cultural manifestations of rural-urban migration, see Jeffrey Pilcher, *Cantinflas and the Chaos of Mexican Modernity* (Wilmington, DE: Scholarly Resources Books, 2001); Anne Rubenstein, "Bodies, Cities, Cinema: Pedro Infante's Death as Political Spectacle," in *Fragments of a Golden Age: The Politics of Culture in Mexico since 1940*, ed. Gilbert Joseph and Anne Rubenstein (Durham, NC: Duke University Press, 2001).

15. On the bracero program and the migration of agricultural labor, see Deborah Cohen, *Braceros: Migrant Citizens and Transnational Subjects in the Postwar United States and Mexico* (Chapel Hill: University of North Carolina Press, 2011); Michael Snodgrass, "Patronage and Progress: The Bracero Program from the Perspective of Mexico," in *Workers across the Americas: The Transnational Turn in Labor History*, ed. Leon Fink (New York: Oxford University Press,

2011). On northern maquiladora zones, see Jefferson Cowie, *Capital Moves: RCA's Seventy-Year Quest for Cheap Labor* (Ithaca, NY: Cornell University Press, 1999); Melissa Wright, *Disposable Women and Other Myths of Global Capitalism* (New York: Routledge, 2006).

16. Davis, *Planet of Slums*, 1; J. R. McNeill and Peter Engelke, "Into the Anthropocene: People and their Planet," in *Global Interdependence: The World after 1945*, ed. Akira Iriye (Cambridge, MA: Belknap Press of Harvard University Press, 2014), 456.

ARCHIVES AND MANUSCRIPT COLLECTIONS CONSULTED

Mexico

Archivo General de la Nación, Mexico City

    Fondo de Presidentes
        Lázaro Cárdenas del Río Papers
        Manuel Ávila Camacho Papers
        Miguel Alemán Valdés Papers

    Records of the Secretaría de Agricultura y Recursos Hidráulicos (Group 215)

Archivo Histórico de la Secretaría de Relaciones Exteriores, Tlatelolco, Mexico City

    Francisco Castillo Nájera Papers

Archivo Marte R. Gómez, Lomas de Chapultepec, Mexico City

    Marte R. Gómez Papers

Biblioteca Luis González, Colegio de Michoacán, Zamora, Michoacán

    Ramón Fernández y Fernández Papers

Biblioteca Miguel Lerdo de Tejada, Mexico City

    Archivos Económicos

Hemeroteca Nacional, Universidad Nacional Autónoma de México, Mexico City

UNITED STATES

Bancroft Library, University of California, Berkeley

Walter E. Packard Papers

College of Agriculture and Life Sciences, Texas A&M University, College Station

Norman E. Borlaug Digital Archive

Columbia University Rare Book and Manuscript Library, New York

Columbia University Oral History Research Office Collection

Frank Tannenbaum Papers

Cornell University Rare and Manuscript Collections, Ithaca, New York

Gerard H. Matthes Papers

Duke University Rare Book, Manuscript, and Special Collections Library, Durham, North Carolina

Josephus Daniels Papers

Fisk University Libraries, Nashville, Tennessee

Julius Rosenwald Fund Papers

Franklin Delano Roosevelt Presidential Library, Hyde Park, New York

Claude Wickard Papers

President's Official File

President's Personal File

President's Secretary's File

Sumner Welles Papers

Harvard University Archives, Cambridge, Massachusetts

Paul C. Mangelsdorf Papers

Library of Congress, Manuscript Division, Washington, DC

George Foster Peabody Papers

Henry A. Wallace Papers

Josephus Daniels Papers

Rockefeller Archive Center, Tarrytown, New York

Frederick T. Gates Papers

General Education Board Papers

John D. Rockefeller Papers

Rockefeller Family Papers

Rockefeller Foundation Archives

Southern Historical Collection at the Louis Round Wilson Library,
University of North Carolina at Chapel Hill

Josephus Daniels Papers

Southern Tenant Farmers' Union Papers (microfilm)

Southwestern Collections and Special Collections Library, Texas Tech University, Lubbock

Seaman A. Knapp Papers

Special Collections Research Center, University of Chicago, Chicago, Illinois

Julius Rosenwald Papers

Tennessee Valley Authority Corporate Library, Knoxville

Newspaper Clippings

US National Archives and Records Administration, Southeast Division, Atlanta, Georgia

Record Group 142: Records of the Tennessee Valley Authority

US National Archives and Records Administration II, College Park, Maryland

Record Group 16: Records of the Office of the Secretary of Agriculture

Record Group 33: Records of the Extension Service

Record Group 54: Records of the Bureau of Plant Industry, Soils, and

Agricultural Engineering

Record Group 59: Records of the State Department

Record Group 83: Records of the Bureau of Agricultural Economics

Record Group 96: Records of the Farmers Home Administration and Its Predecessors

INDEX

Page numbers in *italics* refer to illustrations.

abolitionism, 42, 103

Afghanistan, 166

Africa, 6, 7, 72, 101, 112, 113, 129, 152, 166, 198

African Americans, 16, 17, 20, 35, 38, 57, 88, 162, 170, 193, 195, 196; in Mexico, 59–60, 61; northbound migrations of, 45, 197; northern philanthropy and, 35, 46, 47, 102, 103–4, 107, 108–9, 117, 118; role of in Populist revolt, 25, 28; as tenants and sharecroppers, 44; the USDA and, 56, 57, 108, 118, 196

Agrarian Code, 38

agrarismo, 26, 131, 146, 191, 193; Cárdenas influenced by, 38–39, 183; decline of, 81, 83, 135, 194, 195; FSA influenced by, 44–58, 71, 96; internationalism of, 86, 94; New Deal influence on, 76–86; among professional class, 32–33; renaissance of, 71; US sympathy for, 42, 44, 49, 57, 71, 75, 76, 79–80, 93, 95–97, 115, 127; Zapatistas' commitment to, 28–29, 31, 36, 134

agribusiness, 11, 66, 151, 181, 194–95, 198

Agricultural Adjustment Administration (AAA), 43, 56, 76, 195, 201n7, 246n46; conflicts within, 66; damage done by, 52; southern planters' influence on, 45–46

agricultural extension, 10, 34, 83, 109, 110, 196

Agricultural Stabilization and Conservation Service, 195

Agrónomos Regionales, 136

agronomy, 32, 33, 82, 83–84, 100, 134. *See also* green revolution

Aguanaval River, 59

Alabama, 11, 38, 60, 101, 112, 170, 175–76

Alba, Pedro de, 76

Alcocer, Ignacio, 170

Alemán, Miguel, *148*, 149, 188, 189, 193, 196; conservatism of, 72, 146, 147, 172–73; food production stressed by, 146, 147, 157; Tennessee Valley Authority (TVA) replicated by, 11, 158–61, 172–84

Alexander, Will, 46–47, 48–49, 51–55

Almazán, Juan Andreu, 67

American Cyanamid Corporation, 154

American Farm Bureau Federation, 196

American Federation of Labor, 51

anarchists, 42

Anderson, Edgar, 140

antitrust laws, 33

Appleby, Paul H., 50–51, 70

Arkansas, 2, 38, 58, 61, 77, 81, 82, 118

Army Corps of Engineers, 180

Arnall, Ellis, 193

Asia, 6, 7, 72, 101, 104, 111, 112, 113, 117, 119, 152, 155, 156, 158, 166, 198

Atlantic Crossings (Rodgers), 5

Ávila Camacho, Manuel, 75, 126, 133, 144; as centrist, 67, 131, 135–36, 147, 193; grain shortages battled by, 136, 138; Mexican Agricultural Program (MAP) founded by, 99, 132; presidency assumed by, 67–68, 120, 132; US war effort aided by, 136–37; water resource policies of, 169–73

Babícora (Hearst estate), 18

Bailey, Liberty Hyde, 118

Baja California, 1, 196

Baldwin, C. B., 56, 57

bananas, 172

Bankhead, John H., Jr., 51, 53

Bankhead Bill (Farm Tenant Act; 1937), 51–53, 55, 56, 59, 64, 68; Daniels's backing of, 93; Mexican interest in, 77

beans, 7, 99, 122, 125, 139, 172

Bellamy, Edward, 163

Benedict, Ruth, 75

Bennett, Hugh H., 70, 83

Berle, Adolf, 62

Betton, Farish, 61, 62

Bloque de Agrónomos Revolucionarios, 134

Boas, Franz, 75

boll weevil, 104–6, 127

Borlaug, Norman E., 151–54, 156, 158, 194

braceros, 198

Bradfield, Richard, 98, 124–25, 126, 139, 140, 144–45, 153

Brain Trust, 62–63

Bravo, Armando, 170, *171*

Brazil, 5, 14
British Guiana, 112
Brookings Institution, 48, 50
Bureau of Agricultural Economics (BAE), 43, 76, 77, 96
Butler, J. R., 60
Buttrick, Wallace, 103–4, 107, 111, 116, 127

Cabañas, Lucio, 196
cactus, 24
California, 198
Calles, Plutarco Elías, 30, 32, 37, 39, 83, 90, 94, 135, 167
Calles, Rodolfo Elías, 154
Campaigns against Hunger (Bradfield, Stakman, and Mangelsdorf), 126
Campbell, Thomas, 108
campesinos, 37, 83, 131, 157, 175, 191, 193; Cárdenas's backing of, 161, 182, 183; Daniels's sympathy for, 76, 89, 90–91, 94; decline of, 11, 196, 197; farms abandoned by, 156; government neglect of, 160, 183, 196; hybrid corn and, 148–51; land redistribution backed by, 32–33; Rockefeller Foundation and, 131–36, 157; sharecroppers and, 39, 40–72, 96, 127; water rights demanded by, 168; Zapata's leadership of, 26
"Canción del ejido, El" (Escobedo), 68
Cárdenas, Cuauhtémoc, 95, 183–84, 185, *186*, 187
Cárdenas, Lázaro, 2, 3, 61, 76, 77, 117, 160, *186*, *187*, 191, 194; Chapingo visited by, 145–46; Daniels cultivated by, 94–95, 97; early years of, 38–39; energetic leadership of, 53–54; foreign landlords targeted by, 87, 94; as governor, 38; land reforms of, 4, 10, 31, 40–41, 44, 56, 59, 60, 64, 69, 72, 74–75, 78, 79, 80, 94, 95, 100, 122, 131, 133, 136, 151, 183; Michoacán project led by, 189–90; moderating views of, 66–67, 193; as nationalist, 74; New Deal influence on, 169; post-presidency of, 182–90; presidency assumed by, 40; presidency relinquished by, 132; Roosevelt likened to, 73, 94; State Department skepticism toward, 65, 94; water resource policies of, 168, 169
Carnegie, Andrew, 103
Carranza, Venustiano, 28, 29, 30, 32
Carver, George Washington, 35, 108
Cash, W. J., 170

Castillo Nájera, Francisco, 56, 63, 77, 170
Castro, Fidel, 82
Catholic Church, 29, 32
Cedillo, Saturnino, 63
chahuixtle, 151
Chapingo, 80, 82, 139–40, 143–46, 151–52, 155
Chavez, Eduardo, 175
Chickamauga Dam, 159, 175, *176*
Chihuahua, 18, 26
Chile, 155
China, 104, 119, 166
Civilian Conservation Corps (CCC), 4
climate change, 199
Coahuila, 2, 59, 78, 167
coal, 18
Cobb, Ned, 191–92
Cold War, 3, 6–7, 10, 72, 132, 192, 193, 194; globalization of, 152–56, 158; green revolution and, 99–100, 110; Mexican Agricultural Program (MAP) and, 146–47, 153, 155; Tennessee Valley Authority (TVA) and, 166, 189
Collapse of Cotton Tenancy, The (Johnson, Embree, and Alexander), 52, 55
Collier, John, 70
Colombia, 7, 99, 155, 156, 166
Colorado Fuel and Iron Company, 110
Colored Farmers' Alliance, 25, 27
Colwell, William, 140, 144–45, 151
Comisión del Balsas, 186, 187–88
Comisión del Maíz, 147–49, 154
Comisión del Papaloapan, 161, 175, 179, 181–82, 184
Comisión del Tepalcatepec, 161, 184, 187–88
Comisión Nacional Agraria, 33
Comisión Nacional de Irrigación, 167, 168, 169, 170
Commission on Interracial Cooperation, 46
Communism, 6, 38, 99, 157
Confederación Nacional Campesina, 77
Cooperative Extension Service, 34, 83, 109, 110, 196
corn, 7, 8, 99, 106, 108, 125, 132, 172; double-cross hybrid, 141–44, 148, 149, 154, 157; Mexican Agricultural Program (MAP) and, 143–44, 147, 148–50, 153–54, 157; open-pollinated, 142, 143, 148–49, 154; price of, 137; shortages of, 136–138; Wallace's interest in, 66, 122
Cosamaloapan, 171

cotton, 8, 18, 58, 62; cooperative farming of, 78–79; fluctuating price of, 31, 35, 44, 109; mechanized cultivation of, 195; monoculture of, 47, 99, 103, 105, 109, 127, 128, 162, 179; shift away from, 105–6, 108, 176; slavery linked to, 19

Coughlin, Charles, 54

Country Life movement, 33, 27, 102–3

credit, 32, 82, 89, 157, 162, 193, 194; from banks, 60, 61, 183; cooperative, 24, 74, 78; for ejidatarios, 30, 77, 78, 133, 135, 188; from Farm Security Administration (FSA), 56, 57, 70, 79, 81; Populist demands for, 28. *See also* debt

crop diseases, 7, 125

Cuba, 5, 82, 112

Cullather, Nick, 110

Cusi family, 173

dams, 3, 164; Cárdenas's support for, 168; drawbacks of, 62; in La Laguna, 80; in Mexico, 156, 167, 168, 172, 173, 179–81, 184, 187; residents displaced by, 166, 180–81; in Tennessee Valley, 159, 163, 164, *171, 173, 175, 176,* 177, 180, 185, *187. See also* irrigation; waterpower

Daniels, Addie, *92, 121*

Daniels, Josephus, 63, 68, 73, 75–76, 78–79, 86, 87–97; Mexican agricultural program backed by, 113, 115–17, 120–22, 124, 127–28, 130; moderating views of, 89, 91–93, 96, 97, 101–2; as white supremacist, 75, 88; Wallace and, 120

Darker Phases of the South (Tannenbaum), 47

Davis, Chester C., 50–51

Davis, Mike, 198

debt: in central-southern Mexico, 19–20, 21; commodity prices and, 37; Populist war on, 33; in US South, 8, 16, 21, 35, 44, 106, 109. *See also* credit

Democracy Comes to a Cotton Kingdom (Senior), 62, 122

Democratic Party (US), 16, 18, 28, 57, 192–93

Denegri, Carlos, 131

development, 6–9, 65, 72, 99, 101, 110, 126, 131, 152, 158, 160, 164, 174, 188

Dewey, John, 75

Díaz, Porfirio, 15–19, 20, 24, 74, 90; capitalists allied with, 44; Eurocentrism of, 83; expulsion of, 36, 38, 48, 86, 167; natural resources exploited by, 167; reelection sought by, 25–26

Dickey, John S., 155

disfranchisement, 26, 34, 35, 37, 88–89, 111

DuPont de Nemours Company, E. I., 151

Durán, Antonio, 134

Durango, 2, 59, 78

Dwyer, John, 95

Eastland, James, 193

Egypt, 112

ejidos, 24, 131, 147, 174, 196, 197; agrarista commitment to, 134–38; Cardenista policy toward, 53–54, 69, 96, 133, 146, 168, 183, 184, 187, 193; corn production in, 150; Gómez's policy toward, 134–36, 138; illegal rental of, 188; in political crossfire, 17, 96, 132–34; reinvention of, 29–30, 49; skepticism toward, 32, 71, 94, 151–57, 194; US interest in, 56–57, 61, 64, 68, 69, 90, 91, 98, 120, 124, 127, 130, 138, 144–45; Zapatistas' defense of, 27

El Mante (collective), 68

Embree, Edwin, 46–52, 54, 55

Escobedo, Tomás, 68

Evans, Rosalie, 18

Ezekiel, Mordecai, 70, 79, 81

Farmers' Alliance, 12, 24–25, 27, 102; class hierarchy threatened by, 30; declining membership of, 28; political avenues stressed by, 36

Farmers Home Administration, 72

Farmers' Union, 34

Farm Security Administration (FSA), 2–3, 41, 43–44, 61, 66, 76, 80, 93, 118; agrarismo's influence on, 44–58, 71, 96; criticisms of, 57, 81–82; Ferrell inspired by, 122–23; gutting of, 72, 82; Mexican interest in, 77, 96

Farm Tenant Act (Bankhead Bill; 1937), 51–53, 55, 56, 59, 64, 68; Daniels's backing of, 93; Mexican interest in, 77

fencing laws, 17

Fernández y Fernández, Ramón, 2–3, 5, 80–82

Ferrell, John A., 113–17, 121–24, 127–28, 130

fertilizer, 7, 99, 100, 130, 151, 156, 164, 175–76

flood control, 180

Flores Muñoz, Gilberto, 77–78

Foglio Miramontes, Fernando, 77
Food and Agriculture Organization, 72
Ford Foundation, 155
Foreman, Clark, 46
Fosdick, Raymond B., 119, 138; Daniels's
    overtures to, 116–17; Mann recruited
    by, 140; Mexican agricultural program
    considered by, 122–23, 125–27; New
    Southern Program launched by, 118
France, 14–15
Frente Revolucionario de Agrónomos
    Mexicanos, 134

Gates, Bill, 130
Gates, Frederick T., 103–4, 106, 108, 111, 127
Gaud, William, 7, 99
General Education Board (GEB): black
    education backed by, 104; black farmers
    neglected by, 127, 128; establishment of, 8,
    100, 103; higher education funded by, 111,
    117; Mexican activities of, 111, 116, 117,
    123, 126–28; USDA partnership with,
    106–11, 126, 127; US South targeted by,
    100, 101, 104, 106, 111, 116, 118, 123, 125,
    138, 140
Georgia, 2, 25, 39, 47, 56, 81, 112, 118, 162
Germany, 4
Gilbert, Jess, 55, 56, 65
globalization, 19
Goldman, Emma, 47
Gómez, Marte R., 82, 85, 139, 183; during
    agricultural crisis, 137–38; Chapingo
    visited by, 145–46; extension service dis-
    banded by, 136; Fosdick's overtures to,
    126; as governor, 131, 135; hybrid corn
    viewed by, 144; in Tennessee, 173–74; as
    Wallace's guide, 68, 135; wheat production
    stressed by, 150–51; as Zapatista, 131, 134
González Gallardo, Alfonso, 143
Good Neighbor policy, 42, 86, 89
Grady, Henry, 20
Grandes problemas nacionales, Los (Enríquez),
    24
Grange, 102
Great Britain, 4
Great Depression, 4, 9, 42, 86, 124, 126, 163,
    188–89; cultural exchange during, 71;
    Rockefeller philanthropy during, 100,
    117–18, 119; rural poor besieged by,
    37–38, 117, 127; US southern reformism
    during, 46, 119

Great Migration, 45, 197
Great Society, 57
green revolution, 7, 10, 97, 109, 111, 119,
    129–58, 167, 198, 199; as Cold War
    weapon, 99–100, 110; Daniels's backing of,
    113, 115, 120–21; failures of, 129–30, 156;
    Ferrell's backing of, 121–22; urbanization
    and, 192, 197; US roots of, 8, 83, 100, 101,
    102, 103, 126, 128
Gunn, Selskar M., 115, 239n65

haciendas, 17; attacks on, 27, 70, 83, 115, 134;
    breakup of, 60, 69, 78, 91, 93; exploitation
    by, 19–20; growth of, 9, 24, 36; US
    analogues to, 159; US-owned, 172
Haiti, 5, 14
Hale, Earl D., 180
Hampton Institute, 47
Hanson, Frank B., 126, 139, 140
Harrar, Jacob George, 126, 138–39, 150–51,
    152, 153–54
Harwood, Jonathan, 243n7
Hearst, William Randolph, 18, 94
Henríquez Guzmán, Miguel, 196
herbicides, 195
Hi-Bred Corn Company, 66, 141
Hill, Lister, 193
Hirschman, Albert O., 160
Hitler, Adolf, 119
hookworm, 112–15
Hoover, Herbert, 41, 87
Hopkins, Harry, 62
How the Other Half Is Housed (Vance), 54
Huerta, Victoriano, 87
Hull, Cordell, 70, 95
hydraulic engineering, 33, 163, 167, 168, 169,
    172, 173, 174, 179, 184, 186, 189, 194

Ickes, Harold, 62
illiteracy, 19–20
income tax, 33–34
India, 7, 65, 99, 104, 112, 155, 156, 166
indigenismo, 42, 75
Infante, Pedro, 197
Institute for Research in Social Science, 118
Instituto Mexicano de Estudios Agrícolas,
    77
integrated development, 160, 164, 174, 179,
    184, 185
Inter-American Conference on Agriculture,
    64

intermarriage, 20, 88
International Health Board (IHB), 112, 113
International Rice Research Institute, 155
Iowa, 66, 101, 105, 129, 130, 143
irrigation, 32, 59, 132, 194; as Cardenista
  policy, 74, 77, 78, 133, 184, 193; of ejidos,
  49, 62, 78, 80, 133; excessive, 62, 130; in
  Papaloapan basin, 172–75, 181; political
  attractiveness of, 167; of wheat farms, 150,
  151, 152, 156. *See also* dams
Italy, 5

Japan, 104, 119
Jaramillo, Rubén, 191–92, 196
Jenkins, Merle T., 142, 143
Johnson, Charles S., 46, 51, 52, 54, 55
Johnson, Lyndon B., 57
Johnston, Oscar, 57
Jones, J. Marvin, 53, 68
Juárez, Benito, 15, 20
Julius Rosenwald Fund, 46

Kester, Howard, 58
Knapp, Seaman A., 104–9, 110, 111, 119, 122,
  126, 127
Knight, Alan, 74
Kramer, Paul, 131
Kuhn, Clifford, 56
Ku Klux Klan, 28, 47

La Laguna, 2, 11, 44, 59–62, 78–79, 85, 168
land grant colleges, 33
land privatization, 17–18, 19
Land Utilization Program, 80
latifundia, 3–4, 13, 20, 31, 199
Lázaro Cárdenas Dam, 168
League of Nations, 116
Lerdo de Tejada, Sebastián, 15
life expectancy, 21
Liga de Agrónomos Socialistas, 2, 80, 134
Liga Nacional Campesina, 76
Lilienthal, David, 164, 165–66, 170, 173, 179,
  181, 184, 189
Limón García, Eduardo, 83–84, 143
literacy tests, 31
Littell, Norman, 70
logging, 18
Lombardía, 183
Long, Huey, 54
López Mateos, Adolfo, 186–87
Lorentz, Pare, 168

Louisiana, 5, 104
lynching, 35, 46, 51

Madero, Francisco, 25–26, 28, 32, 167
maguey cactus, 24
maize, 7, 8, 99, 106, 108, 125, 132, 172;
  double-cross hybrid, 141–44, 148, 149,
  154, 157; Mexican Agricultural Program
  (MAP) and, 143–44, 147, 148–50, 153–54,
  157; open-pollinated, 142, 143, 148–49,
  154; price of, 137; shortages of, 136–138;
  Wallace's interest in, 66, 122
malaria, 112, 164, 184
Malthus, Thomas, 153
Mangelsdorf, Paul C., 98, 124–25, 126, 151,
  156–57, 158; food scarcity foreseen by,
  153; Mexican Agricultural Program
  (MAP) guided by, 139, 140–44, 148;
  synthetic corn favored by, 142, 143, 149
Mann, Albert R., 118–19, 123, 124, 125, 127,
  140, 145, 147, 158, 239n65
maquiladoras, 198
Martino, César, 84–85
Marxism, 74
Matthes, Gerard H., 179, 180
Mazatecs, 172
mechanization, 62, 82, 109, 133, 194, 195,
  196–97
Mencken, H. L., 101
Mérigo Jané, Salvador, 170
Messersmith, George, 137
Mexican Agrarian Revolution, The (Tannenbaum), 48, 90
Mexican Agricultural Program (MAP): Cold
  War politics and, 146–47, 153, 155; demonstration and extension programs of, 145;
  launch of, 10, 99, 101, 128, 132; as model
  program, 7, 155–56, 157; organizational
  structure of, 139–40; orthodoxy shunned
  by, 10, 132, 144, 157; synthetic maize
  program of, 143–44, 147, 148–50, 153–54,
  157; US antecedents of, 8, 10, 100, 155;
  wheat program of, 150–54, 158
Mexican Constitution (1917), 33, 36, 38, 53;
  land tenure provisions of, 29–30, 49, 51, 55
Mexican Revolution, 3, 9, 13, 32, 44, 49, 167,
  187; agronomy spurred by, 82–83;
  historiography of, 24, 48; land reform
  linked to, 74; US radicals inspired by, 42,
  71
Michoacán, 162, 182, 183, 184, 187, 188, 190

Miguel Alemán Dam, 180–81
Miller, Harry "Dusty," 242n102
Mind of the South, The (Cash), 170
minifundia, 198
mining, 18
Miramontes, Fernando Foglio, 85
Mississippi, 2, 5, 34, 106, 107, 112, 193
Mississippi Delta, 49, 81, 105
Mississippi River Commission, 180
Mitchell, H. L., 2, 3, 4, 5, 11, 58–59, 60–61, 62
Mixtecs, 172
Molina Enríquez, Andrés, 24, 25, 29–30
Moneymaker, Berlen O., 179
Montenegro, Roberto, 84, 85
Morelos, 13, 19, 26, 29, 32, 35–36, 191
Moreno, Mario, 197
Morgan, Arthur E., 163–66, 179, 181, 190
Morgan, Harcourt A., 164, 165
Morrow, Dwight, 87
Múgica, Francisco, 67
muralists, 71, 139
Mussolini, Benito, 5
Myers, William I., 251n105

Nacional Reguladora y Distribuidora, 138
National Autonomous University of Mexico
    (UNAM), 33, 80, 185
National Bank of Agricultural Credit, 82
National Bank of Ejidal Credit, 60, 61, 82,
    183
National Confederation of Peasants, 136
National Cotton Council, 57
National Recovery Administration (NRA),
    4–5
National School of Agriculture, 33, 124, 139
Native Americans, 42
Navarro Novelo, Manuel, 170
Nazas River, 59, 168
Nazism, 4
New Deal, 2, 3, 39; agrarian, 9–10, 41, 43, 45,
    50, 54, 73, 75, 81, 96, 100, 125, 127; agri-
    cultural, 43, 45, 246n46; contradictions of,
    43; intellectual architects of, 62; Mexican
    inspiration for, 4, 70, 74, 96; Mexico
    inspired by, 55–56, 63, 74, 77–78, 81, 86,
    96, 169; reorientation of, 54; right-wing
    opposition to, 193; rural South targeted
    by, 42. *See also* Agricultural Adjustment
    Administration (AAA); Farm Security
    Administration (FSA); Tennessee Valley
    Authority (TVA)

New Deal and the Six-Year Plan, The (Flores
    Muñoz), 77–78
"New South" era, 13, 15, 16, 18, 20, 24, 88,
    102
New Southern Program, 118–19, 123, 125,
    140
North Carolina, 83, 87, 88–89, 90, 91, 93, 113,
    121
Nueva Italia, 183

Oaxaca, 19, 162, 171, 172, 180, 182
Obregón, Álvaro, 28, 30, 32
Ocala Demands, 13, 14, 27–28
Odum, Howard W., 46, 54, 118, 170
Office of Inter-American Affairs, 120
Oficina de Estudios Especiales, 139
Ogden, Robert C., 102, 103
oil industry, 18, 103, 117, 123, 127
oilseed, 136–37
Orive Alba, Adolfo, 168, 170, 173, 175,
    177–79, 180, 181, 182
Oropeza Mendoza, Gabriel, 170
Orozco, José Clemente, 71
Orozco, Pascual, 26
Ortiz, Pablo Campos, 40
Osborn, Fairfield, 153
Osterhammel, Jürgen, 205n3
Our Plundered Planet (Osborn), 153

Packard, Walter E., 79–80
Pakistan, 65, 99
Papaloapan River basin, 161–62, 171–84,
    188–90
Parrés, José, 64
Partido Nacional Revolucionario (PNR), 32,
    40, 61, 63, 64
Partido Revolucionario Institucional (PRI),
    193–94, 198
Paz, Octavio, 197
Peabody, George Foster, 47, 48, 89, 90
peaches, 109
peanuts, 109
peones acasillados, 60
People's Party, 28
Pepper, Claude, 193
Perkins, Frances, 62
pest control, 6, 7, 11, 99, 100, 125, 156
Philippines, 7, 99, 104, 112
Pilcher, Jeffrey, 150
Pioneer Hi-Bred, 66, 141
Plan de Ayala, 13, 14, 26–27

Plan de Movilización Agrícola, 136
Plan Sexenal, 3, 39, 40, 41, 63, 70, 76, 94
plant breeding, 6, 7, 82, 123, 129, 132, 146, 149, 154, 155, 158
poll taxes, 31
population growth, 7, 198
populists, 9, 13, 22, 27, 28; electoral defeat of, 31, 33; enduring influence of, 30, 33–34; in North Carolina, 88; political avenues stressed by, 36
Porfiriato. *See* Díaz, Porfirio
Portes Gil, Emilio, 63
Preface to Peasantry (Raper), 54
President's Committee on Farm Tenancy, 54–55
price controls, 43
Progressives, 33, 34, 37, 102, 111
Public Works Administration, 4
Puerto Rico, 64, 126

railroads, 9, 12, 18–19, 24, 30, 33
Raleigh News and Observer, 87, 88, 93
Raper, Arthur F., 54, 81
Reconstruction, 4, 5, 14, 15, 16, 20
Redfield, Robert, 75
Renda, Mary, 131
Republican Party (US), 16, 37, 86
Resettlement Administration (RA), 43, 52, 53, 54, 55, 56, 63, 79, 80, 96
rice, 155
River, The (film), 168–69
Rivera, Diego, 71, 80, 139
Road to Survival, The (Vogt), 154
Roberts, Lewis M., 140
Rockefeller, John D., 8, 34, 47, 103
Rockefeller, John D., Jr., 103, 104
Rockefeller, Nelson, 119–20
Rockefeller Foundation, 97, 98, 115, 127, 129–31; demonstration programs funded by, 70; divisions within, 124, 156; founding of, 112; Mexican activities of, *see* Mexican Agricultural Program (MAP); Rosenwald programs funded by, 46; US South activities of, *see* General Education Board (GEB); worldwide reach of, 112–13, 117, 119
Rockefeller Sanitary Commission for the Eradication of Hookworm Disease, 112, 113
Rodgers, Daniel, 5
Rodríguez, Abelardo, 94

Roosevelt, Eleanor, 52
Roosevelt, Franklin D., 2, 3, 10, 31, 46; agrarian reforms of, 41, 72; aristocratic background of, 38–39; Cárdenas likened to, 73, 94; cautiousness of, 39, 45, 52, 53; Daniels appointed by, 88, 89, 115; election of (1932), 86, 87; Good Neighbor policy of, 42, 86, 89; as governor, 38; Mexican praise for, 76; as polio sufferer, 39, 47; reelection of (1936), 54, 58; reelection of (1940), 67; tenant farmers and, 39, 54–55; Tennessee Valley Authority (TVA) launched by, 163–64. *See also* New Deal
Rose, Wickliffe, 116
Rosenwald, Julius, 34, 46
Rostow, Walt, 6
rubber, 136–37
Ruiz Cortines, Adolfo, 73, 181

salinization, 62
San Pedro Coxtocán, 18
Sauer, Carl O., 129, 130, 140, 144, 151–52
Schega, Reynaldo, 175
Schultes, Richard, 98, 124
Scott, James C., 129, 181–82
Sears, Roebuck and Company, 34
segregation, 31, 34, 46, 88, 102, 131, 185, 192–93
Senior, Clarence, 58–59, 60–62, 122
Shadow of the Plantation (Johnson), 54
sharecroppers, 2, 9, 11, 12, 20, 26, 88, 105, 131, 192, 195–96; advocacy for, 39, 46–47, 71, 79, 103, 108; campesinos and, 40–72, 96, 127; government disregard of, 39, 193; growing number of, 109; informal assistance for, 44–45; powerlessness of, 19, 34, 142; in Texas, 141; white, 51, 119
Share Croppers' Union, 38, 191
Shiva, Vandana, 129
silver, 28
Sinaloa, 167, 194, 196
Six-Year Plan, 3, 39, 40, 41, 63, 70, 76, 94
Slater, John Fox, 102
slaves, 5, 14, 19, 42
Smith-Lever Act (1914), 109, 110, 111
Sociedad Agronómica Mexicana (SAM), 83, 84
Soil Conservation Service, 83–84
soil erosion, 37, 103, 104, 109, 162, 170
Sonora, 95, 152–54, 156, 167
Sonoran Dynasty, 32, 36

South Carolina, 34, 47, 118
Southeast Asia, 155
Southern Regions of the United States (Odum), 54, 118
Southern Tenant Farmers' Union (STFU), 2, 38, 54, 96; conflicts within, 58; cosmopolitanism of, 44; decline of, 61, 71; in La Laguna, 58–62; radicalism of, 45, 46
Soviet Union, 6, 42, 157
Spurlock, Richard, 154
Stages of Economic Growth, The (Rostow), 6
Stakman, Elvin C., 124–25, 126, 139, 140, 147, 150, 151, 153–54, 156
Standard Fruit Company, 172
Standard Oil Company, 103, 127
stock laws, 17
stock market crash (1929), 30, 37, 41
strikes, 2, 58, 59
Suárez, Eduardo, 78–79
Subsistence Homesteads Division, 43, 64
sugar, 19, 26, 172

tamales, 150
Tamaulipas, 112
Tannenbaum, Frank, 43, 183; at Brookings Institution, 48; Cárdenas and, 65, 68; Cotton Belt visited by, 35–36, 47, 49, 58, 109; cotton monoculture decried by, 109; Daniels mentored by, 89–90, 91; at Lake George conference, 47, 48–49; land tenure reforms proposed by, 50–53, 54, 55, 57, 93; Mexican reforms admired by, 49–50, 53, 58–59, 89–90; political skills of, 51, 52; Wilson allied with, 64
Taylor, Carl, 81
tenant farmers, 12, 19, 31, 35, 44, 51, 109, 111; evictions of, 57; informal assistance for, 44–45; Roosevelt's attention to, 39, 54–55
Tennessee, 11, 118, 162, 170, 175
Tennessee River, 162–63
Tennessee Valley Authority (TVA), 4, 10, 11, 43, 158–90; launch of, 163–64; rural development and, 162–67
Tepalcatepec valley, 162, 182–88
Texas, 24, 25, 104, 105, 124, 141, 198
Thomas, Norman, 58
Thorne, Henry, 168
Thurmond, Strom, 193
tiendas de raya, 19–20

Tillman, Ben, 34
Tlahualilo Land Company, 78
tobacco, 19
tortillas, 150
tourism, 42
Truman, Harry, 6, 145, 146, 152
tuberculosis, 112, 184
Tugwell, Rexford, 44, 52–53, 54, 56, 62–64, 66, 70, 80, 96
Turner, John Kenneth, 21
Tuskegee Institute, 35, 47, 108
Tuxtepec, 171
TVA: Democracy on the March (Lilienthal), 165–66, 181
2,4-D (herbicide), 195

United Fruit Company, 172
United Nations, 72, 159
University of North Carolina, 54, 113
urbanization, 7, 99, 131, 160, 164, 189, 192, 197, 198, 199
US Agency for International Development, 72
US Civil War, 8, 15, 17, 18, 19, 47, 88, 102, 115, 116, 122, 162
US Department of Agriculture, (USDA), 2, 4, 10, 41, 50, 51, 54; agrarian liberals in, 71; black hiring eschewed by, 109; Cooperative Extension Service of, 34, 83, 109, 110, 196; farm demonstration program of, 104–11, 119, 126, 127; La Laguna experiment and, 78–79, 85; Mexican links with, 64–65, 80; "modernized" agriculture backed by, 75; postwar reorientation of, 193; social planning by, 62–63, 73, 83. *See also* Farm Security Administration (FSA)

Valle Nacional, 19
Valley of the Tennessee, The (film), 185
Vance, Rupert B., 54, 170
Vanderbilt, Cornelius, 103
vanilla, 17
Vardaman, James, 34
Veracruz, 17–18, 86, 87, 112, 162, 171, 172, 182, 183
Vietnam, 99, 155, 166
vigilantes, 44
Villa, Francisco "Pancho," 28–29, 87, 182
Vogel, Herbert, 185, *186*
Vogt, William, 153

Wagner Act (1935), 53
Wallace, Henry A., 44, 50, 52, 64, *69*, 77, 81, *84*, *85*, *121*, 130, *145*; agricultural innovations of, 66; Bankhead Bill backed by, 51; Chapingo visited by, 145–46; Gómez's entreaties to, 138; La Laguna experiment and, 78–79, 85; Mexican admiration for, 84–85; Mexican agricultural program backed by, 121, 122–23; in Mexico, 65, 66, 67–70, 97, 120, 121, 135, 136, 145; radicalization of, 66, 70; as social planner, 62–63; USDA shift announced by, 54
Wallace, Henry C., 66
Wallace, Ilo, *121*
Wank, Roland, 180
Washington, Booker T., 35
waterpower, 3, 11, 160, 164. *See also* dams
Watson, Thomas E., 21–23, 25, 28
Weaver, Warren, 147, 153, 155
Weiss, Andrew, 259n71
Wellhausen, Edwin, 149–50, 151, 153, 158; Corn Commission resented by, 148–49; maize breeding overseen by, 144, 154; as

Mexican Agricultural Program (MAP) recruit, 139–40
wheat, 18, 24, 99, 124, 150–54, 156, 158, 194
Whitten, Jamie, 193
Wickard, Claude, 70
Wilson, M. L., 44, 62, 64–65, 70, 77, 81, 96
Wilson, Woodrow, 87, 88, 89, 102, 116
Wilson Dam, 163, *175*
Wolf, Eric, 131
Wolfe, Mikael, 62
Woodward, C. Vann, 9

Yaqui Valley, 95
yellow fever, 112
Yépez, José, 170, *171*
Yucatán, 16, 19, 26, 36, 64

Zapata, Emiliano, 13, 21–23, 36, 134, 136, 182, 194; assassination of, 29, 31, 32, 136; land redistribution backed by, 28, 168; Morelos revolt led by, 26–27
Zimmerman, Andrew, 131
Zubarán Capmany, Rafael, 184

Also in the series

David Ekbladh, *The Great American Mission: Modernization and the Construction of an American World Order*

Martin Klimke, *The Other Alliance: Student Protest in West Germany and the United States in the Global Sixties*

Andrew Zimmerman, *Alabama in Africa: Booker T. Washington, the German Empire, and the Globalization of the New South*

Ian Tyrrell, *Reforming the World: The Creation of America's Moral Empire*

Rachel St. John, *Line in the Sand: A History of the Western U.S.-Mexico Border*

Thomas Borstelmann, *The 1970s: A New Global History from Civil Rights to Economic Inequality*

Donna R. Gabaccia, *Foreign Relations: American Immigration in Global Perspective*

Jürgen Osterhammel, *The Transformation of the World: A Global History of the Nineteenth Century*

Jeffrey A. Engel, Mark Atwood Lawrence, and Andrew Preston, eds., *America in the World: A History in Documents from the War with Spain to the War on Terror*

Adam Ewing, *The Age of Garvey: Global Black Politics in the Interwar Era*

Kiran Klaus Patel, *The New Deal: A Global History*